U0846525

《中国经济学》编辑委员会

主　任：

张曙光　（北京天则经济研究所）

本年度执行主编：

陈志武　（耶鲁大学管理学院）

委　员：（按汉语拼音顺序）

陈志武　（耶鲁大学管理学院）

樊　纲　（中国国民经济研究所）

李稻葵　（清华大学经济管理学院）

李　实　（北京师范大学经济学院）

林毅夫　（北京大学中国经济研究中心）

卢　锋　（北京大学中国经济研究中心）

茅于轼　（北京天则经济研究所）

盛　洪　（北京天则经济研究所）

唐寿宁　（中国社会科学院经济研究所）

汪丁丁　（北京大学中国经济研究中心）

余永定　（中国社会科学院世界经济与政治研究所）

张曙光　（北京天则经济研究所）

张维迎　（北京大学光华管理学院）

周其仁　（北京大学中国经济研究中心）

周业安　（中国人民大学经济学院）

北京天则经济研究所编

中国经济学

2007

执行主编

陈志武

格致出版社 上海人民出版社

Foreword

Chen Zhiwu

Since the Reform and Open-Door Policies started in 1978, economics research in China has advanced into a new stage. Early on, China had an economy but no real economics as an academic research field. But, since then, a research profession in economics has gradually emerged. Consequently, there are not only economic policy professionals, but also academic economists in China.

In the past thirty years, the Chinese economy and society have experienced three types of transformation: that from an agrarian society into an industrial society, that from a planned economy to a market-oriented economy, and that from a closed society to an open society. Each one of these transformations alone can disrupt a society and cause dislocations in both societal structure and social culture, let alone all three transformations happening at the same time. And the social and economic phenomena which these three transformations have brought about to the Chinese society provide rich and unique data for not only economic research, but also social sciences in general. Studying economic facts and problems that arise in the complex transition process will contribute to human acknowledge about the depth and extent of social changes that economic development brings to a society, and this will enrich our understanding of human societies. In this sense, we are living in a golden time full of new research opportunities in economics and other social sciences.

With the increasing depth of Chinese economic research and the expanding international academic exchange, scholars in China have gradually started to apply the neoclassic analytical framework and research methodology to probe economic issues arising from the economic and social transition process. The neoclassic principle of economic analysis and research methodology, which have no geographical limits, can be applied to address economic issues in any economic environment and under any institutional arrangements.

There are 15 papers selected in this book, "Economics in China—2007", which provides a snapshot of Chinese economic scholars' work in 2007. The following considerations are applied in the selection process: the research methodology must be internally consistent and formal; data must be used if it is an empirical study; analysis must be supported by a formal analytical framework; the research topic must be one of general interest in modern economics, or related to a real economic issue if it is a China-specific topic; exceptions are given to papers on economic history and economic methodology review. But, the selecting process cannot be perfect as it is bound to be subjective. For this reason, some high-quality papers published in 2007 may have been excluded from this collection. We have selected these 15 papers only to provide an overview of economic research done in China in 2007.

The selected papers are mostly focused on ages-long agenda and topics in economics. But, some of the papers attempt to apply the modern economic analytical framework to interpret patterns and phenomena that have emerged out of China's economic transition process.

Economic methodology

"The Status, Roles and Limitations of Econometrics", written by Hong Yongmiao, illuminates the basic thoughts and methodologies of econometrics and its status, roles and limitations in modern economics, and discusses its difference from mathematical economics, mathematical statistics, and economic statistics. A variety of economic and financial examples illustrate how econometrics can be used in empirical studies.

Its substance not only considers econometrics as technical tools for the empirical studies, but also emphasizes the essence of econometrics as economic methodology. The author aims to understand the roles and limitations of econometrics from the basic methodological perspective, not limit with the technical level. This contributes to evaluate and acknowledge the roles of econometrics in economic theory system objectively and rationally.

In the past several years, some oversea Chinese economists have produced a series of papers on the economic methodology to address themselves' insights on economic educations and researches from the different perspectives, such as "Explicating the current economics in China—how do economics and media interact and co-involve?" by Chen Zhiwu, "Basic analytical frameworks and research methods in the modern economics" by Tian Guoqiang, "Understanding the modern economics" by Qian Yingyi, "Economics, economists and economic educations" by Xu Chenggang and so on. These articles represent the vital importance of combining the normative analy sis of economic research with the Chinese styled facts based on the core and extent of modern economic research method and framework, specially focus on conflicts and harmonies between the instrumental rationality and valuable judgement in the academic research.

Research on Chinese regional economy and market integration

"Civil trade and regional border effect", written by Zhao Yongliang and Xu Yong, introduces the two-region trade gravity model and the governmental expenditure preference and study inter-provincial bilateral trade relations and the degree of market separation. The paper uses the three industries' data from 28 provinces and for 1997, 2002, 2005 to analysis the border effect and market integration such as public spending ratio, the ratio of SOE, financial independence, import ratio, employment ratio. Their conclusions represent the barrier in the western China is higher than eastern China, the barrier of industrial commodity is lower than agricultural goods, partly verify local governments are apt to protect their materials, state the enhancement of financial independence of local governments and control over economy are factors to produce the inter-provincial trade barriers and market separation. And they consider the increase of the non state-owned economy will reduce the border effect of trade, undermine the trade barriers, enhance the market mechanism, improve the market integration.

Several comments about this topic follow:

1. Between economic developed provinces and economic developing provinces there are one-to-one supportive relations. Under this condition, the data which are generated in the trade stream between the marched provinces may be nonsingular. So how to control the inter-provincial support in the model?

2. The behavior of the central state-owned firms is differ-

ent from the one of the local state-owned firms. Since the provincial state-owned firms are largely influenced by the provincial governments, the inter-provincial economic activity of the central state-owned enterprises increases the volume of trade. Though the decrease of the scale of state-owned economy can increase the degree of market-oriented reform, but following the logics of the paper, we don't get the conclusion that the high ratio of state-owned firms which include the central and local ones will produce the decrease of inter-provincial trade and the increase of border effect. In the other words, using the whole state-owned firms' data does not reflect the topic of this paper.

3. The acknowledge concerning about the barrier of industrial commodity is lower than agricultural goods is problematic. In fact, the statement that the "Jiandaocha" price between industrial and agricultural commodity still exist is better than the one that local government prefers the protection of agricultural goods. From the perspective of term of trade, the TOT of industrial commodity is better than the one of agricultural goods. So this does not verify and illustrate the provincial market separation, but the separation between industrial and agricultural sector.

"Regional integration, economic growth and political improvement", written by Xu Xianxiang et. al. , studies a topic in new political economy—how does the motivation of political improvement of local governmental officers influence the regional integration and economic growth. They build the game model of political improvement of local governmental officers and do empirical analysis. In addition, through controlling the several conditions, they try to explain the different behaviors of local governmental officers in the different areas under the unified logics which is internal consistent. Meanwhile, the findings of this paper: the one is the central government use the index of economic performance to evaluate local offers that induces them to work hard. The other is when the condition is sufficient the rational local government will spontaneously choose regional integration and almost lead to a unified market in the whole China.

We can think about this theme further: it involves with the incentive compatibility in the local governmental offers political improvement model. If the index of administrative performance is only the economic growth rate, the main officers in the local government will behave based on the increase of the economic growth rate. If the regional integration can contribute to the local economic growth, the choice is incentive compatible. But we should introduce the occupation duration into this analysis, they does not do it.

Furthermore, the behavioral choice of local governmental officers is dependent with the economic environment. This should be the one of the sufficient conditions which is referred to. The developed provinces in the eastern China relatively gain more in the regional integration while they have more incentive to do it.

Foreign direct investment and economic development in China

"Foreign investment in Modern China: Scale and effect analysis" by Yang Decai studies the scale and return of foreign investment in China and its impact on the development of local enterprises and the economy. He considers that the positive effect of the FDI is significant and it is not the barrier of local enterprise development, but induces the growth and development of them. As the indirect investment, though the industrial loan such as railway loan has a certain negative effect, it improves the infrastructure in China and indirectly contributes to the economic growth. So the effect is similar to that of FDI. Note that the choice between the shareholders' rights and creditors' rights as an implement of foreign investment is the problem of contract design. Like the other scholars, it only focuses on the two kinds of rights from the China's side and ignores the foreign investor's perspective. Under the economic environment which is ruled by person and anti-foreigns, the arrangement of creditor's rights maybe safer to the foreign investors than the other arrangements. About that, Oliver Hart, Robert Townsend and so on have written several seminal papers such as about the optimal capital structure in corporation and optimal security design. Though their analyses base on firm, it helps us to understand the capital arrangement of foreign investment from the late Qing. Generally speaking, from the investor's perspective, when rights of contracts, investor's property and legal environment is far away from perfection, creditor's rights of the fixed income are better than the shareholder's rights.

"The spillover effect analysis of foreign direct investment on Chinese enterprise" by Ping Xinqiao et. al. studies the relation between FDI and the development of Chinese manufacturing industry, specially probes the technical spillover effect of FDI with the Chinese first nation economical general survey data of December 31, 2004. The findings of this paper are: FDI is significantly related with the total productivity of Chinese manufacturing industry positively, but this coefficient overestimates the degree of the technical spillover effect of FDI, the relation between the ratio of foreign capital within industry and the total productivity of domestic firms is not obvious. Only the ratio of the capital from Hongkong, Macao, Taiwan is significantly related with the total productivity of Chinese manufacturing industry positively. The foreign capital enters can hinder that the domestic capital enterprise improves themselves R&D in order to catch up to the international advanced level and, but the Hong-Kong, Macao and Taiwan capital enters can obviously reduce the gap between them and the domestic capital enterprise in the technical level.

"SOE Reform as Signaling and Credible Commitment" by Zhu Linke and Wang Zheng states how the FDI facilitate the SOE reform from signaling and credible commitment hypotheses. The logics of this paper are: under asymmetrical information, SOE reform may act as a signal for market-oriented reform of the local government. In order to convince the foreign investors that is open, the local government has motivation to enforce more SOE reforms. Meanwhile, the SOE reform decreases the incentive of the local government to intervene at the market, which would make it credible commitment to maintaining fair competition, hence attract more FDI. In the empirical analysis part they use the panel data of 28 provinces from 1991 to 2002. The signaling hypotheses turned out to be consistent with the case of the eastern China during the period from 1991 to 1996.

First, like the article mentioned above, the reform of state-owned firms and FDI may be specified by the same other factors. Without the estimation of simultaneous equations, the coefficients will be misled. Furthermore, the number of the sample data is less than the level which assures the credibility of regression results.

Secondly, the paper tries to verify the lemmas that FDI improves the reform of state-owned firms through competition pressure and through providing the fund, and the lemma that the reform of state-owned firms providing the fund for the infrastructure improves FDI. The first lemma is not be supported by empirical data. And the later two are consistent with empirical analysis. The confusion is: have the two propositions in this paper more explaining power and theoretic robustness than the three lemmas in the large literature. But the paper only expresses the signaling hypotheses match the fact of Eastern before the mid of 1990s.

Thirdly, how should we understand the possible causality relation in the interactive mechanism between the reform of state-owned firms and FDI? Or what specifies them? How are they specified?

The three papers analyze the influence of FDI on the development of China's economy and domestic capital from the foreign perspective. They have also formed certain historical span. This enlightenment which studies to us is, all should place in a more long-time historical sight to any economic problem analysis to carry on. About the modern China economy, the mainstream opinion is the China is varying, but it is pushed by the external shocks, such as "shock—response" theory which is stated by John King Fairbank. And whether does the resource of economic development in China from the external shock, or from the internal force's self-filling? The three papers also explain this issue from FDI perspective. From the analyses mentioned above we can see that in spite of negative effect, the positive effect of FDI finally will finally contribute to the stable development of economy through the absorption of internal mechanism and well-functioned institutions.

Research on Chinese dual economic society and the Sannong problem

"China's Lesser Know Migrants" by Deng Quheng and Bjorn Gustafsson focuses on permanent migration from rural to urban areas. Using large sample survey for 2002, they study the scale of permanent migrants and destination. They find that the probability of becoming a permanent migrant is positively related to parental education, belonging to the ethnic majority and the parent's membership in the Communist Party. Then they analyze the employment probability of permanent migrants and factors which influence the wage level and verify the relations between independent variable and dependent variables such as the gender, education level, marriage, age etc.. Finally, permanent migrants' income relates to the way which do they gain the Hukou(professional way and non-professional way).

"The department choice and gender difference in the Chinese rural labor force migrating process", written by Yi Junjian and Di Longbow, empirically analyzes the departmental choice in Chinese rural labor force migrating process. They study the gender discrimination between employment departments of rural migrating labor force. They consider the employment search way and the education level significantly influence the department choice in Chinese rural labor force migrating process, but the characteristics of family and former residential place have little effects. Meanwhile, though there is gender discrimination in department choice of Chinese rural labor force migrating process.

These two papers analyze the micro-behavioral mechanism of rural labor force migration from different perspectives which contribute to understand migration in urbanization process under dual economy. The internal mechanism of migration is complicated including economic, social, cultural factors. And in the transition of economy and society in China the psychological mechanism is more complicated. The two papers study the cause of the migration from rural to urban and consequent effects based on the analyzing the individual's characteristic variables and other economic variables.

About migration and mobility, we can consider the questions as follows: who want to migrate? Why do they migrate? Where do they come from? Where do they want to move to? What will be produced after their migration? The research on migration and mobility has several theoretic perspectives such as dual economy theory, human capital theory, supply-demand theory, push and pull theory, assimilation theory and so on. Among them, dual economy theory and push and pull theory are more popular. The two papers combine the three theories-dual economy theory, push and pull theory and human capital theory.

"Specialization and evolutionary of agricultural organization: based on the analysis of indirect pricing theory model" is written by Xiang Guocheng and Han Shaofeng which extend the indirect pricing theory of Yang Xiaokai and Yew-Kwang Ng in order to explain evolutionary path of agricultural organization uniformly and analyze effects of the specialization evolutionary, transaction efficiency, production and transaction risks and so on.

From the research method, the paper applies the infra-marginal analysis to evolutionary path of agricultural organization from collective economy, family economy to agriculture commercialization, agriculture industrialization and peasants' team. They introduce the specialization economy, transaction risk and cost into the framework to analyze the evolutionary path of economic organization structure from autarky to commercialization. They try to extend this research method to analyze more problems. But the infra-marginal analysis has great power in the organization substitution and choice, does not cover the research on internal marginal change of single economic organization, such as the specification of organization scale, the factors which affect the border of organization and so on. The lack of this research context will negatively influence the study on the change direction and process of agricultural organization in some degree. In addition, we should study the possibility and condition of internal solution existing, while focusing on the corner equilibrium.

Research on Chinese economic history

How should we use the modern economic theory to rethink and research the Chinese history specially Chinese economic history? After Daron Acemoglu, Simon Johnson, James Robinson and Andrea Shleifer etc. have applied the modern econometric methods to research the rise of western world which significantly influences the researches on the relation between progress and development of human society and institutional factors, the historical scholars gradually renew their insights. At the London School of Economics and Political Science, Ma Debin and his partners have followed this method to study the economic development history of China empirically comparing with the Japan and Western European. Unfortunately the research of this field in China does not progress well. Definitely from these researches that we should emphasize we can understand Chinese history better than that from traditional local research frameworks.

In "China's Macro-economy in the Great Depression", Guan Hanhui introduces the Chinese macroeconomic phenomena in the Great Depression and analyze it academically. The findings of this paper as follows: two factors played important role in China's economy of depression, one is Silver Standard, and the other is competitive bank system. Silver Standard caused China's economy being different from those Gold Standard countries. Unlike Western countries lived through the Great Depression by adopting active finance policy, China's money supply had not decreased in depression owing to competitive bank system, so bank crises did not swept China, which was an important reason why Chinese economy suffered little in Great Depression.

In fact, in 1930s the Great Depression provides the historic experiencing facts to economists for understanding the run of macro-economy more comprehensively. This paper tries to explicate the cause that China's economy is better than the other countries during those times from the monetary institution perspective.

The paper compares the economic growth rate of China with that of main Western counties from 1932 to 1936. The conclusions of data analysis reflect during that period the

China's economy is better than France's and America's, almost same to Germany's and UK's, worse than Japan's. From the logics, if we want to state the positive effect of the special monetary institution in China on the macro economy, we should control the other factors. That is to say we will study the cause why the economic growth rates of Germany, England and Japan were larger and get the common factors which will be controlled in analysis of China's economy. From this point, this paper is not strict to verify the hypotheses empirically.

In the section "China's banking system and money supply in 1930s", the author refers to private-owned banks, Qianzhuang(money shops) and foreign banks. Specially to the foreign banks, the paper states that they did not obey Chinese domestic laws under the extraterritoriality, but does not deeply analyze the role of foreign banks on the development of the private-owned banks and Qianzhuang and competitions. During those times, there were different foreign courts in Shanghai Concession which led to competition of the legal judgement. So the author does not refer to that what the competition influenced on the competition and efficiency of the whole banking system.

Economic growth and macro-economic policies in China

"Re-discussion on the quarrels of growth mode in Eastern Asia" by Li Yifu and Ren Nuoen studies the theoretic basis and development of the TFP method and addresses the pros and cons of the Asian economic growth model.

In light of the debate on the Asian economic growth, they claim that the TFP analysis by Paul Krugman of the East Asian economic growth experience is wrong to some degree. And they do not agree with the research findings by many Chinese scholars following this framework to study the source of China's economic growth in order to judge the sustainability of the economic growth model.

Firstly, they do not agree with Krugman on non-technical progress of Asian economic growth. But it is problematic that the disagreement on conclusion leads to reject the TFP method. Anyway, whether the conclusion in Krugman's paper is right or not, it is wrong to judge the analytical method from the conclusion because that different production functions, parameter choices, sources of data will lead to the different conclusions under the same analytical method.

Secondly, when we study the source of economic growth, we should consider the labor, capital, technology and institutions. The economic growth from the inputs of labor and capital is not sustainable. China has undergone the stage of the big population bonus (abundant labor force resource), so objectively it tries to do stable economic growth from technology and institution innovation.

Thirdly, the advantage of backwardness may be change into disadvantage of backwardness from technology and institution innovation. The globalization of economy produces the good environment which contributes to introduce the advanced technology. The transferability and replicability of technology make Chinese technical level catch up with the advanced ones through the introduction of technology. The advantage of backwardness has manifested significantly in the twenties or thirties years from the Reform and Openness. But if we consider the institutional aspect, the finding is the advantage of backwardness in technology may be change into disadvantage of backwardness in the whole development. From this perspective, it is too soon to conclude the Eastern Asian mode or Chinese mode because of the lack of observable samples and time points.

In the paper "the welfare loss of governmental debts in production-type public expenditure economy", Lin Xixi and Gong Liutang build the production-type close endogenous model influenced by governmental public expenditure, and study the optimal debt scale from the data simulation and sample, consider the welfare lose of the change of debts. They consider the effect of governmental macro-economic policy on the economic growth and source allocations, and the welfare consequence.

The papers focus on the welfare loss of production-type public expenditure of governmental financing behavior in economics. If we understand from the opposite side, we can get the conclusion that social welfare will increase when the economic resource is transferred from the government to consumer. The research topic in fact is concerning about the problem of optimal governmental scale from the alternative perspective. What the government scale reaches while the social welfare is most?

In the model, we assume the governments have no economic considerations, the objection of government and the consumer's objection are compatible. The behavior of the government heads for the maximization of the life-time utility of consumer. This assumption does not match the economic environment, the conclusion can be weaken in the analysis, because the government is not abstractive without the principal-agent relation and concrete benefit. In fact, Once the government's power is not constrained, even with constrain the governor will embrace the self-interest, "government" becomes the interest group beyond the individual's welfare, so the government has the pressure on the economic growth, and the internal incentives of enlarging the scale of economic resource control. So, how we introduce the desirable government' utility function into the analytical framework is the further research path.

Research on the efficiency of economic policy under the hierarchical government's games

In the paper "'former expropriation, later tax-return'", Wu Liansheng & Li Chen study that the local government establishes and enforces the grace policy "former expropriation, later tax-return" of firm income tax, and the central government cancels this grace policy. And they study the efficiency of central governmental tax policy through using data of the public corporations.

In the process of China's transition from the Planed economy to the market economy, the central government has gave a certain relatively independent interest and autonomy of economic administration to the local governments which has made this local government have an adequate bargaining power. In the other side, because of the differences of goal between local and central government the local governments do not execute the policies of the central government effectively.

The finding of the paper is that the grace policy "former expropriation, later tax-return" in income tax of local government reduces the income tax burden of the firms which do not get the grace income tax policy from the central government and makes them indifferent with the firms which get the grace income tax policy from the central government. It reveals that the grace policy "former expropriation, later tax-return" in income tax of local government influences the rules of the central government's policies and significantly increase the income tax burden of the firms that should get the grace policy from the central government then make their income tax significantly higher than the firms' burden which get the grace policy. So though the cancellation of this policy from the central government would affect the interest of local governments negatively, the effects of the taxation policies from the central government could recover through the cancellation is enforced by the local governments.

The paper studies the efficiency of the special policy enforcement in the China's transition period. The authors focus on the conflict and coordination of the interests between the central government and the local governments in the consideration of the policy "former expropriation, later tax-return" and effects of them on policy enforcement. In the empirical part, they control the effects of corporation scale, the financial leverage, capital structure, the opportunity of investment, beneficial ability and the ratio of state-owned shares on the taxation rate of the corporation. They are very meaningful from the empirical research method.

The possible improved aspects are: is there the combination of control variables which contribute to be analyzed and match the economic environment better? We should check the problem the multi-collinearity of the control variables chose by the authors. In addition, the author refer to that the income tax of firms is the important sources of the public financial income of local governments. Changing the expropriating part of the income tax of firms will change the behavior of local government. Of course, the policy coordination is an important cause. And note that the consequence of game between the central and local government are policy compromise.

Empirical methodology and new political economy

In the paper "industrial crop, food available rights and famine: verification on Sen's theory", Fan Ziying and Meng Lingjie state that the main cause of the differences of rural death rate in the China's famine period is institutional and match the analytical logics of Sen's FAR theory from the theoretical perspective.

The article firstly introduces the condition of famine and the background of research, secondly briefly introduces the theories of Sen's food available rights and the food available decrease. In the empirical analysis part, they use the data from 1959 to 1961 in the famine period to verify the institutional distortion "state monopoly for purchase and marketing" empirically, they conclude the institutional factor significantly affects the differences of rural death rate in the China's famine period in food-lacking areas. The significance of this difference reveals at the main areas of industrial crop earlier than the Old food-lacking area in the food-lacking area. And the total effect of the former is stronger than the later. So the specification of the main area of industrial crop constraint the FDR in this area, and the FDR decide the death rate in the famine period.

This article follows the research in the paper of Lin Yifu and Yang Tao(2000) in order to resolve the explanation problems: the change of administration area and the huge difference of the rural death rate.

The statement of the food availability decrease and the Sen's FDR in this paper indicates that the latter's theoretic extent covers the former, and the latter's explanation power is better that the former. So the two theories are not in the same level. Based on these, the conclusion is obvious that which is better to explain involving problems in the China's famine in the two theories.

In addition, the empirical analysis focus on the institution of purchase and marketing, not on the explaining variables such as public eatery, the quantity of right party and so on in the involving literature about China's famine. Under this condition of non-controlling the other variables(most of them are institutional factors) and only analyzing the institution of "state monopoly for purchase and marketing", the study can lead the variable through the significance test easily. So in order to make the conclusion more reasonable, we should pick up the main factors and control the other factors then reveal the effect of the institution "state monopoly for purchase and marketing" on the famine.

Inter-disciplinary research in economics

In the paper "centralization and decentralization: the unified research of new economic geographical model and the structure of the urban internal space and the effect of external scale economics", Chen Liangwen and Yang Kaizhong combine the structure of the urban internal space and the effect of external scale economics in the new economic geographical model. Through analyzing the centralization and decentralization factors influenced by the urban scale, the finding is the urban internal transportation cost as the decentralization factor and the effect of external scale economics as the centralization will affect the centralization degree of economic activity from the opposition directions.

This paper focus on the theoretical analysis with scale return of centralization and the transaction cost. The model makes clear that after the introduction of the effect of external scale economics the centralization of the economic activity in some area may be a stable equilibrium since the transportation cost is zero through data simulation. So that is to say the degree of effect of external scale economics is bigger than that of transaction costs (the direction is opposition). But the question is that when some preconditions or parameters changed, does there exist the status "after the introduction of transportation, since the effect of external scale economics is sufficiently large the unlimited decentralization of the economic activity in some area may be a stable equilibrium"? in other words, since the paper does the data simulation analysis about one possible alternative, the authors should make clear that the condition the degree of effect of external scale economics is bigger(smaller) than that of transaction costs.

The analytical method of this paper has some important value and revelation on the researches of regional economics and urbanization. The transaction cost analysis indicates its role in centralization of economic activity and urban scale. The research of centralization and decentralization stands on the main factor analysis. Of course, the main factors are one similar to the ones in this paper—the effect of external scale economics and transportation costs. We should combine this analytical method with the local economic problems.

Concluding Remarks

In China, economic research is catching up with the international economist community. Before this change in recent years, economics and other social sciences in China had mostly followed the non-quantitative framework prior to World War Ⅰ, and the difference between top academic journals and the mass media was minor, implying the lack of professionalization in academic economics. The economics discipline did not develop much into an independent profession. But, recent years has witnessed a change and an economics research profession has emerged. We hope that the 15 selected papers in this book will serve to encourage more scholars to work and contribute to human knowledge about economics.

目 录

Contents

前　言

陈志武
（耶鲁大学管理学院教授）
孙涛
（山东大学经济系助理教授）

自1978年改革开放至今，伴随经济增长和结构转型，经济学研究或对中国经济的研究也进入一个全新的发展阶段，中国从只有经济但没有“经济学”转变到既有经济也开始有经济学的状态。相应地，中国不只是有“经济师”，而且开始有“经济学家”。

过去30年，中国经济和社会的转型主要包括三个方面：其一是从农业社会转向工业社会；其二是从计划经济转向市场经济；其三是从封闭经济走向开放经济。其中任何一方面的变革都会给一个社会结构和文化传统带来深刻的影响——解构和重构，而三个方面的转型同时进行所引出的各种经济和社会现象，当然为经济学研究提供了极大丰富的、弥足珍贵的素材。对这些复杂的转型进程中所显现的经济事实和问题进行研究，将有助于深化和拓展人类对经济发展和社会变迁过程的认识，同时也将丰富经济学的理论知识体系。这即是中国特定时期所带来的特殊研究机会、发现学问的立足点。

随着中国经济学研究的深入和国际学术交流的增加，国内的经济学研究者越来越多地习惯于运用现代主流经济学的分析框架和研究方法，探讨经济和社会转型过程中所产生的经济现象和问题。现代主流经济学的基本分析原理和研究方法是没有地域界限的，作为分析平台和基准可以用来研究任何经济环境和经济制度安排下的各种经济问题。一般意义上说，从现代主流经济学分析框架和研究方法的角度来看，并不存在独立于历史和他国的经济分析框架和研究方法，尽管其中某些具体的研究方法和分析框架只可用来研究特定地区在特定时间内的经济行为和现象。事实上，这正体现了现代主流经济学分析框架的稳健性：它的精髓在于表明经济学的研究必须界定清楚某时某地具体的经济、政治和社会环境等先决条件。既然经济理论是包括逻辑自洽的假设、推理和结论三个构件，那么我们就不能不同时关注实际研究问题的局限条件与理论的假设相吻合。如果局限条件与假设吻合，经验事实又与理论的结论相一致，我们就认为理论经受了经验的检验，就证实这个理论是正确的。

《中国经济学——2007》选编了 15 篇论文，这是 2007 年经济学学者们研究成果的一个影像，具有一定的代表性。在遴选的过程中，主要考虑以下几点原则：研究方法是规范的，做实证分析时有数据支持，或者具有较为严整的理论分析框架或模型支持；研究内容上要么紧扣现代经济学的研究主题，要么关注中国现实经济问题，针对性较强；最后就是有些论文涉及经济史议题，或者是综述性论文、经济学方法论文章。不过，遴选的工作本身就是挂一漏万的，不可能包括所有高水平的论文。另外，值得说明的是，论文的入选并不意味着编选者认同论文中作者的观点、主张或者结论。作为一项社会科学，经济学的研究成果应放在时间跨度更长的经济和社会变迁历史进程中检视。在这一认识下，对发表时间间隔如此相近的论文进行摘选，更多是对2007年度经济学研究论文一个介绍和说明。

入选论文的研究主题反映了现代经济学一直在研究的议题和试图回答的一些问题，而且，中国的基本经济情境使得经济学者们面临的问题集中在如何解释和解决经济制度转型过程中所产生的各种现象及问题。

经济学方法论

洪永淼的《计量经济学的地位、作用和局限》一文阐述计量经济学的基本思想和方法论，其在经济学研究中的地位、作用和局限性，以及与数理经济学、数理统计学及经济统计学之间的差异，并且运用大量经济学和金融学中的事例说明计量经济学的应用。文章的主旨在于不仅仅是把计量经济学作为实证研究的技术分析工具，而侧重强调计量经济学作为经济学基本方法论的重要性。作者的用意在于从基本方法论的层次上理解计量经济学的作用和局限性，而不只限于工具层面。这无疑有助于理性客观地评价和认识计量经济学在整个经济学大厦中的地位。

近些年来，一些海外华人经济学家们发表一系列关于经济学研究范式和方法的文章，从不同角度对经济学的教育和研究提出了自己的见解，如笔者的《解读经济学在中国的现状——经济学与媒体是如何互动发展的?》、田国强的《现代经济学的基本分析框架和研究方法》、钱颖一的《理解现代经济学》、许成钢的《经济学、经济学家和经济学教育》等。这一系列文章都在说明现代经济学研究方法和框架的内核与外延的基础上，强调经济学研究的规范分析和中国经济特征经验事实相结合的重要意义，特别关注了学术研究过程中的工具理性和价值判断之间可能的冲突和协调。

中国区域经济与市场一体化的研究

赵永亮和徐勇的论文《国内贸易与区际边界效应——保护与偏好》，论文基于两地区贸易引力模型，引入政府支出偏好，考察中国省际双边贸易的关系和市场分割程度。论文采用 1997 年、2002 年、2005 年 28 个省份的三次产业数据分析影响边检效应和市场一体化的因素，如公共支出比率、国有企业比重、财政自主变量、进口率、就业率等。分析结论表明中国中西部区域壁垒高于东部区域；工业品贸易壁垒低于农业品贸易壁垒，部分验证我国地方政府对原料品更具有地方保护偏好；地方政府对财税自主权的增强以及对经济控制力的加强，都是导致省际贸易壁垒（或市场分割）的因素。并且认为非国有经济比例的提高能够减少边界效应，弱化贸易壁垒，强化市场运行机制，促进市场的一体化程度。

对论文分析及论证的有关商榷意见如下：

1. 在经济发达省份和中西部经济欠发达省份之间存在配对帮扶（搭对子）的情形，在这种情况下，某两个配对省的贸易流产生的数据可能是奇异的。所以，如何在模型中控制省际扶持？

2. 中央属国有企业和地方属国有企业的行为方式有很大区别。如果说省级地方政府的保护主义显著影响地方国有企业，那么，央属国有企业跨省的经济活动可能主要是增加省际贸易量。尽管国有经济规模的减少会提高市场化程度，但是，按该论文的逻辑，并不一定得到国有企业（包括央属和地方属）的比例高导致省际贸易减少，增加边界效应。换而言之，运用笼统的国有企业经济数据或许不能反映所论证的主题。

3. 关于工业品贸易壁垒低于农业品贸易壁垒观点的认识，其实，与其说是地方政府对农产品更具保护偏好，还不如说在工农业产品价格的“剪刀差”问题仍然显著存在的情况下，从贸易条件（Term of Trade）的优劣来看，对外贸易工业品要优于贸易农产品。所以说，这并不能检验和说明省际的市场分割，而或许能说明了工农业间的市场分割。

徐现祥等人的论文《区域一体化、经济增长与政治晋升》研究了一个新政治经济学范畴的论题——地方官员的政治晋升激励对区域一体化以及经济增长的影响，建立了地方官员晋升博弈模型，并作实证分析。另外，通过控制不同的条件，力图对不同地区政府官员的迥异行为给出内在逻辑一致性的解释。同时，文章也给出了另外两个结论，一个是表明了中央基于经济绩效晋升地方政府官员能够有效地激励地方官员努力工作；另一个是当条件成熟时，理性的地方政府会自发地选择区域一体化，而且最终几乎可以实现全国统一开放的大市场。

关于这篇论文可以有如下思考：在地方政府官员晋升最大化的模型中涉及激励相容问题。如果政绩评价的指标是单一的经济增长率，那么地方政府主要官员的行为必然围绕着增加经济增长率。如果区域一体化有利于当地经济增长指标的提高，那么区域一体化的选择是激励相容的，不过，这一分析还应加入任期年限的影响，模型中没有能体现这一点。

另外，地方政府官员的行为选择还依赖于外部的经济环境，这理应是文章所指条件成熟与否的一方面，比如临近东部沿海的经济发达省份相对有条件进行区域一体化的尝试，也是指这些省份更有机会在区域经济融合中获得更大的发展空间。

外国直接投资和中国经济发展的议题

杨德才的《近代外国在华投资：规模与效应分析》一文考察近代外国在华投资的规模和盈利状况，对中国本土企业的成长与发展以及对中国经济的发展产生的影响。作者认为近代外国在华直接投资的正效应是非常明显的，不仅没有成为中资企业发展的阻碍，而且还刺激并促进了中资企业的成长与发展。以铁路借款等“实业借款”形式出现的间接投资，虽然也具有一定的负面效应，但由于这些间接投资对近代中国基础设施的改善和供给、对中国实业的发展有一定的促进作用，所以，将其连同国外直接投资效应相联系。要指出的是，外国投资到底该以股权还是以债权的形式进入，这是一个契约设计问题，本文和以往的学者一样，只是从中国方面来回答股权投资更好还是债权形式更好的问题，却忽视了外方投资者的视角，亦即在当时的人治以及总体排外的环境下，债权安排可能更能让境外投资者感到安全。关于这方面，Oliver Hart，Robert Townsend 等学者有过“企业最优资本结构问题”、“证券最优设计”的经典论文，虽然他们的论文以企业作为基点，但对于理解晚清以及以后的外资进入中国的形式选择，会有很关键的帮助。一般而言，从投资者角度讲，当契约权益、投资者产权、法治环境都不可靠时，固定收益型债权安排会优于股权类安排。

平新乔等人的分析报告《外国直接投资对中国企业的溢出效应分析》用 2004 年 12 月 31 日中国第一次全国经济普查数

据，研究外国直接投资与中国制造业发展的关系，重点考察外国直接投资的技术溢出效应。本文的研究结论认为，外国直接投资显著地与中国制造业的总生产率正相关。但是这种正相关系数会过高地估算国外直接投资对中国的技术溢出程度；产业内的外资份额已与内资企业的总生产率不显著相关了，只有港澳台资份额仍与内资企业的总生产率显著正相关；外资进入会妨碍内资企业通过研发自主创新而缩小与国际先进水平之间距离，而港澳台资进入会显著地缩小内资企业与港澳台资企业在技术水平上的差距。

朱可林和王争的论文《作为信号发送和可置信承诺的国企改革》从信号发送假说和可置信承诺假说两个角度，说明外国直接投资如何促进国企改革。文章的理论逻辑为，在信息不对称下，国企改革可以成为地方政府市场化努力的信号，为了发送信号吸引外国直接投资，地方政府有激励进行更多的国企改革。同时，国企改革减少了地方政府干预市场的程度和能力，从而使得维护市场竞争的承诺变得可信，因此能吸引更多的外国直接投资。实证分析部分采用从 1991 年到 2002 年 28 个省市的面板数据，结果显示，信号发送假说较好地吻合了 1991—1996 年期间中国东部沿海地区的情况。

首先，正如文章所提到的那样，国企改革和国外直接投资可能存在同步被其他因素决定的情况，在没有采取联立方程估计的条件下，可能造成估计结果的偏误。此外，分时段分地区分析的模型由于样本数据点比较少，这也可能影响回归结果的可信程度。

其次，论文还检验了外国直接投资通过竞争压力而促进国企改革的命题；通过提供资金支持来促进国企改革的命题；以及国企改革通过为基础设施建设提供收入来源而促进外国直接投资增加的命题。前一个命题没有得到实证结果的支持，而后两个命题则与实证结果一致。问题在于，对本文所强调的两个假说和以往文献涉及较多的三个命题检验中，是不是存在着两个假说比以往三个命题更强的解释力和理论的稳健性？然而，论文只是表明了信号发送假说较好地吻合了90年代中前期东部地区的情况。

再次，研究国企改革与外国直接投资的相互作用机制过程中怎样理解它们之间可能的因果关系，或者被哪些因素同步决定，怎样被决定。

这三篇论文从外国直接投资（或外国投资）的角度，分析这一外部经济力量对中国经济整体运行以及内资经济发展的影响，从时间上看，这三篇论文的研究也形成了一定的历史跨度。这对我们研究的启示是，对任一经济问题的分析都应该放在一个更为长久的历史视域中进行。对近代中国经济状况的认识，西方学术界的主流看法是，中国是有变化的；但是它是在外力的影响下发生的，例如费正清所提出的“冲击—回应”论。而中国经济发展的来源究竟是外部的冲击，还是来自内部的自我实现力量？这三篇论文也是通过外国直接投资这一具体的视角说明这一问题，我们可以在上述具体分析中看到，即使抛开负面效应，外国直接投资所带来的正面效应最终也还是要通过内在机制的吸收和制度配套，才能对经济有持久和稳定的积极影响。

中国二元经济社会以及“三农”问题的研究

在《中国的永久移民》一文中，邓曲恒和古斯塔夫森将研究的对象集中于中国农村到城市的永久移民这一群体，数据来自中国社会科学院经济研究所2002年居民收入分配调查，考察了永久移民的规模和迁移目的地。他们发现，永久迁移的概率跟年龄、民族、父母教育水平和父母党员身份相关。然后，他们对永久移民的就业概率和工资收入的因素进行分析，验证了被解释变量与性别、教育水平、党员身份、婚姻状况、年龄等特征变量的关系。最后分析了永久移民的收入与他们获取户口的方式（职业途径和非职业途径）有关。

易君健和狄龙波的论文《中国农村劳动力迁移过程中的部门选择与性别差异》，对农村劳动力迁移就业过程中的部门选择行为展开经验分析，并在此基础上研究农村迁移劳动力就业部门之间的性别歧视。本文认为，就业搜寻渠道和个人教育水平对迁移劳动力的部门选择存在显著的影响；而家庭和迁出地等特征变量对其部门选择的影响较小；同时，虽然农村迁移劳动力在部门选择过程中存在显著的性别差异，但是其性别差异主要是来自个体特征变量之间的差异，纯粹性别歧视并不显著。

这两篇文章从不同的角度分析中国农村人口向城市迁移的微观行为机制，有助于理解二元经济背景下城市化进程中人口迁移的问题。人口迁移行为的内在机制是复杂的，有经济的、社会的、文化的等方面影响因素，而在中国经济转轨和社会转型的过程中，这一行为的心理机制尤为复杂，这两篇论文在分析个体特征变量和相关经济变量的基础上，研究了中国农村人口向城市迁移的原因和影响后果。

关于人口的迁移和流动，可以从如下的问题中进行考虑：谁要迁移（主体）？为什么他们要迁移（动机）？他们来自哪里（迁出地）？他们要移到哪里（迁入地）？他们到那里后会造成什么冲击（外部性后果）？城乡人口迁移和流动的研究有如下的理论角度：比如二元经济理论、人力资本理论、供需理论（supply demand theory）、推拉理论、同化理论（assimilationism）等。其中最有影响力的是二元经济理论和推拉理论。这两篇文章综合运用了二元经济理论、推拉理论和人力资本理论。

在《分工与农业组织化演进：基于间接定价理论模型的分析》中，向国成和韩绍凤在扩展杨小凯和黄有光的间接定价理论的基础上，力图对中国改革开放以来农业组织化的演进路线进行统一的理论解释，分析了其中分工演化、交易效率、生产和交易风险等因素的综合影响。

从研究方法的角度，文章将超边际分析运用于农业组织由集体经济、家庭经营、农业商业化、农业产业化、农民团队化的演进路线。把专业化经济、交易风险和交易费用纳入分析框架，探讨人类经济组织结构从自给自足向商业化与企业化演进的路线。就这一研究方法，作者进行拓展应用的尝试。不过，超边际分析在组织替代和转换的问题上有较强的分析力，但并不能很好地涵盖研究单一经济组织内部的边际变化，比如说组织规模大小的界定，影响组织边界的因素等，这些研究内容的缺乏在一定程度上会影响对农业组织的变迁方向和进程的分析。另外，关注角点均衡的同时，也应该考查内点解存在的可能性和条件。

中国经济史中有关问题的研究

如何用现代经济理论来重新梳理、研究中国的历史特别是经济史呢？在 Daron Acemoglu、Simon Johnson、James Robinson and Andrea Shleifer 等学者用现代计量经济学方法对西方的崛起进行一系列研究后，史学界耳目一新，他们的研究对人类社会的进步发展跟制度等因素的关系有了非常突出的影响。在伦敦经济学院，马德斌教授与他的合作研究者近几年在按照同一思路对中国相对于日本、西欧的近代经济发展史进行全方面的系统量化研究。相比之下，国内这方面的研究进展有限，自然这些研究应该重视，而且也可以为我们认识中国自己的历史带来新视角，这至少比传统国学研究范式更有希望。

在《20 世纪 30 年代大萧条中的中国宏观经济》中，管汉晖主要针对当时世界范围内经济大萧条中的中国宏观经济表现进行历史回顾和经济理论分析。他论述了货币制度和银行体系是中国经济表现较好的重要原因。文章认为银本位使中国经济萧条过程中的货币本位锚定机制迥然不同与西方金本位制国家，而不同的地方主要表现在财政政策干预上。中国由于当时特殊的银行体系，货币供给没有急剧减少，银行危机也没有普遍发生。

事实上，20 世纪 30 年代的世界经济大萧条为经济学家提供了更全面理解宏观经济运行的历史经验事实。管汉晖力图从金融和货币制度的角度揭示中国经济比世界绝大多数国家表现更好的原因。

文章比较了 1932 年到 1936 年间中国与西方主要国家的经济增长率。数据表明，那时期，中国的经济增长要好于法国和美国，与德国和英国大致相当，而低于日本。从逻辑角度讲，如果要说明中国独特的金融货币制度对宏观经济的良好作用，应该剔除其他因素。也就是说，要适当分析德国、英国及日本经济增长率较高的原因，把共同因素抽取出来，在对中国经济分析中作剔除。从这个意义讲，本文的分析不是严格的对假设进行实证。

在"20 世纪 30 年代的中国银行体系和货币供给"一节，作者谈及私营银行和钱庄，以及外资银行。特别是外资银行，文章论述了它们在治外法权之下并不遵守中国的规章法令，但是没有深入分析外资银行对中国私营银行和钱庄的发展以及竞争程度方面所起的作用。在那时期，上海租界有多国法院，也有民国政府法院，它们的同时存在必然引出法制间的竞争。那么，这种法制竞争对当时整个银行业的竞争与效率带来过什么影响？这些是作者没有涉及的。

中国经济增长和宏观经济政策议题

《东亚经济增长模式相关争论的再探讨》一文中，林毅夫和任若恩通过对东亚经济增长模式相关争论的回顾，以及对一些国家和地区经济增长经验的研究，对全要素生产率方法发展和理论基础进行分析，从而讨论东亚经济增长模式争论对中国未来经济发展的启示。

基于东亚经济增长模式的学术争论为论述起点，论文认为克鲁格曼依据全要素生产率分析东亚经济增长所得出的结论是不成立的，进而对国内许多沿用这一研究路线分析我国经济增长的源泉，并以此判断我国现有经济增长模式的可持续性这一逻辑思路的不认同。

首先，该文不认可克鲁格曼对东亚经济增长没有技术进步成分的结论。不过，因为不认同结论，进而否定全要素生产率这一分析方法，是值得商榷的。姑且不论，克鲁格曼分析结论正确与否。就分析方法的争论而言，在同一分析方法下，不同的生产函数形式、参数的选择、数据的来源等都会造成结论的迥异。因而，根据分析结论否定分析方法并不适当。

其次，在分析经济增长的来源时，我们必然要考虑劳动、资本、技术和制度等因素，劳动和资本投入的增长所带来的经济增长不具备持续性，中国经历了高人口红利（丰富的劳动力资源）的发展阶段，客观上也需要在技术和制度创新上寻求经济的稳定持续增长。

再次，技术和制度创新方面的"后发优势"抑或成为"后发劣势"。经济的全球化给先进技术的引进创造了良好的环境，技术的可移植性和可复制性使得中国可以在短时期内通过引进发达国家的技术和发明达到一定的生产技术水平。技术方面的"后发优势"在改革开放以来二三十年体现得非常明显。但是考虑到制度方面的问题，我们就会发现技术上的"后发优势"很容易就可能转变为整体发展的"后发劣势"。从这个意义上讲，对东亚模式或说中国模式的结论还为时过早，因为所能观察到的统计样本和时间长度还远远不够。

在《生产性公共开支经济中政府债务的福利损失》一文中，林细细和龚六堂构建政府公共开支影响生产的封闭内生经济分析模型，研究最优债务规模，从数值模拟和现实样本，考虑公债变化带来的福利损失问题。考察政府宏观经济政策对经济增长和资源配置的影响，及其产生的福利后果的问题。

论文的视角是在生产性公共开支的经济中政府融资行为所带来的福利损失问题，文章的结论从相反的方向理解，同样在生产性公共开支的经济中政府经济资源向消费者转移会带来社会福利的提高。这个研究主题实际上也是从一个角度探讨政府的最优经济规模问题，政府多大时社会福利最高？

在论文的模型分析中，假定政府没有任何私人目的，政府的目标和消费者的总体目标相一致，政府的作为是最大化消费者的一生总效用。这一假定并不符合经济情境，在分析中可能会使结论弱化，因为实际的政府不是脱离了委托代理关系、具体当权人利益的抽象政府。实际上，一旦政府权力不受制约，甚至是即使受到制约也还是隐藏着权力者私利的，那么，"政府"就成了超出社会公民效用总和的利益团体，于是，政府就有自己的经济增长目标压力，也有扩大经济资源控制范围的内在冲动，所以，怎样在分析框架加入合理的政府效用函数是有意义的进一步研究的方向。

层级政府博弈条件下经济政策的有效性研究

吴联生和李辰《"先征后返"、公司税负与税收政策的有效性》研究地方政府自行制定并实施的企业所得税"先征后返"优惠政策，以及中央政府取消该项优惠政策的经验事实。运用上市公司的数据，从企业所得税负担的角度研究中央政府税收政策的有效性。

在中国由计划经济体制向市场经济体制转轨的过程中，中央政府赋予了地方政府一定的相对独立的利益和经济管理自主权，使地方政府具备了相当的谈判力量。另外一个方面，由于地方政府与中央政府的目标差异，可能导致中央政府的政策并不能得到地方政府的有效执行。

研究的结果表明，地方政府的"先征后返"所得税优惠政策，降低了不享受中央政府认可的所得税优惠政策的公司的所得税负担，从而使它们与享受中央所得税优惠政策的公司的所得税负担没有显著差异。这表明地方政府的"先征后返"所得税优惠政策，影响了中央政府税收优惠政策的规定，显著提高了原来享受该优惠政策的公司的所得税负担，并最终使他们的所得税负担显著高于享受中央政府认可的所得税优惠政策的公司。这表明中央政府取消“先征后返”优惠政策的规定，虽然会影响地方政府的利益，但是的确在一定程度上得到地方政府的执行，并最终使中央政府税收政策的有效性得到了恢复。

论文研究中国在经济体制转型时期较为特殊的政策实施有效性的问题，将观察的视角放在公司税负“先征后返”这一问题中地方政府和中央政府利益的冲突与协调，进而对政策实施效果的影响。在实证分析部分，控制了公司规模、财务杠杆、资产结构、投资机会和获利能力、国有股比例等其他相关因素对公司实际税率的影响。从选题和实证研究方法上，这些都很有意思。

文章可能改进之处在于，是否有更利于分析和符合现实经济状况的控制变量组合？在本文所选择的控制变量中要检验一下可能的多重共线性问题。另外，在结论部分，作者提到了企业所得税是地方政府财政收入的重要来源，改变企业所得税归属可以改变地方政府的行为。当然，这样的政策协调是一个重要的原因，不过，还应该注意的是，中央政府和地方政府的博弈还可能是[illegible]另外一些政策优惠或妥协换取某一政策的实施效果。

实证分析方法与新政治经济学

范子英和孟令杰的论文《经济作物、食物获取权与饥荒：对森的理论的检验》的实证研究指出，中国三年自然灾害时期农村死亡率的差异主要是因为制度性因素，从而在理论上契合了森对食物获取权的分析逻辑。

文章首先介绍了饥荒时期的状况和研究的背景，接着对森的食物获取权和食物供给量下降两种饥荒理论，并对研究中国饥荒的文献作简单介绍。在实证分析部分，采用 1959—1961 年饥荒发生年份的数据，对统购统销这一制度性扭曲进行了经验上的验证，得出缺粮区中制度对饥荒年份农村死亡率的差异影响显著。缺粮区中的经济作物主产区在饥荒的早期就非常显著，而传统缺粮区只是在饥荒末期才起作用；并且前者在饥荒年份对死亡率的总影响要比后者强得多。所以对经济作物主产区的划分限制了该地区的食物获取权利，而食物获取权利在饥荒年份对死亡率起到决定作用。

文章是在林毅夫和杨涛 2000 年论文基础上的进一步研究，力图解决行政区划的变动以及解释农村地区人口死亡率的巨大差异这两个问题。

论文在表述传统的解释饥荒的食物供给量下降理论（FAD）和森的食物获取权理论时，实际上表明了后者的理论外延几乎完全涵盖了前者，那么后者的解释力必然比前者要好，所以这两种理论并不是一个同等层次的论述，进而在这基础上验证这两种理论对中国饥荒的解释力优劣，结论是显见的。

另外，论文的实证分析集中于征购制度，而不在体现于有关中国大饥荒相关文献中所关注的影响变量，如公共食堂、右派数量等。这样的情况下，没有控制其他因素（大多数也是制度性因素），较为单一地分析统购统销的制度，容易使该因素通过显著性检验。所以，如何提取主要影响因素，并且在实证分析中加以控制，进而揭示具体的统购统销制度对大饥荒的影响才能使结论更加趋于合理。

经济学边缘科学和交叉科学的研究

陈良文和杨开忠的论文《集聚与分散:新经济地理学模型与城市内部空间结构、外部规模经济效应的整合研究》,在新经济地理学的研究框架中融合了城市内部空间结构和外部规模效应。论文通过对城市规模影响的集聚与分散因素分析得出结论,作为重要分散因素的城市内部通勤成本和作为重要集聚因素的外部规模经济效应从相反的方向对经济活动的集聚程度产生影响。

文章的研究视角是集聚的规模收益和交易成本之间的理论分析,论文对模型的数值模拟结果表明,在引入外部规模经济效应后,即使运输成本为零,经济活动完全集聚在某一地区也可能是稳定均衡的。这似乎表明,外部规模经济效应在影响的程度上占优交易成本(影响的方向相反)。问题在于,某些前提条件或模拟参数发生变化时,会不会产生"在引入运输成本后,即使规模经济效应无限大,经济活动无限分散也可能是稳定均衡"的情形? 也就是说,既然论文对其中的一种可能做了数值模拟分析,那似乎也就应该表明外部规模经济效应在影响的程度上占优于(或被占优于)交易成本的条件。

该论文的分析方法和思路对区域经济学和城市化的研究有十分重要的价值与启示,交易成本分析的具体化明确指出其在经济活动聚集或城市规模中的影响,集聚和分散的力量立足于主因素分析,当然,所分析的主因素并不是必须同本论文抽象出的一样——外部规模经济效应和通勤成本。宜将这一研究方法和思路与中国本土化的问题相结合作具体的案例分析。

结　束　语

在中国，经济学研究正在走上轨道。直到近几年发生变化之前，在中国，经济学和其他社会科学领域还基本停留在1900年之前的范式和框架上，在一级学术刊物和大众媒体之间的距离很短，甚至不存在，这说明这些表面上的专业学科实际上没有专业也没有学科上的深化。不过，跟改革开放的经济发展过程一道，经济学也在快速地把失去的课程补回来。只是由于意识形态的壁垒，经济学研究的追赶速度远比实体经济增长的速度慢许多拍。在这些补课和追赶的过程中，进步显然很快，也走在社会科学同行中的前面，但在中国的经济学界找到自己的定位点之前，更多的摸索是必要的。

本集收集的15篇论文基本反映了2007年发表的学术论文状况，以供有兴趣的同行和业余爱好者参考。也希望借此鼓励我们都去努力，共同增加人类关于我们生活中的经济和社会的知识。

收入的15篇论文分别来自，《经济研究》4篇，《经济学（季刊）》5篇，《管理世界》2篇，《中国社会科学》1篇，《世界经济》1篇，《南方经济》1篇，《世界经济文汇》1篇。编者对所有参与推荐的机构和个人，对15篇文章原发表刊物的支持和帮助表示感谢。

20世纪30年代大萧条中的中国宏观经济*

管汉晖

（清华大学经济管理学院）

一、引　言

现代宏观经济学起源于20世纪30年代世界经济大萧条，一方面，这是由于大萧条改变了人们对于市场经济可以良好运行的信念，另一方面，20世纪30年代世界经济的经历深深地影响着经济学家们的观念以及政策建议。正如Bernanke(1995)所言，对今天的经济学家来说，20世纪30年代世界经济崩溃的解释仍然是魅力无穷的智力挑战，经济学家们仍然没有了解大萧条的全部，大萧条也仍然是宏观经济学的一个主要研究领域。

根据现有的数据，中国1932年到1936年的经济增长率分别为3.68%、−0.72%、−8.64%、8.30%、5.87%，年均经济增长率为1.7%。这些数字高于法国和美国在整个大萧条时期的增长率(0.6%和0.5%)，与德国和英国大致相当(1.7%和1.8%)，只是低于日本(3.7%)。①如果考虑到1929年到1932年的情况，那么中国的经济增长率还要高得多②，因此，在整个

① 中国的数据来自Yeh, K.C.(1977)，其他国家来自麦迪逊(1997)。

② 如后文所述，1929年至1932年当世界经济陷入严重萧条时，中国经济却处于繁荣之中。

大萧条期间，说中国经济比世界上绝大多数国家表现要好是不为过的。

对大萧条的最新研究发现，大萧条之所以从一国开始，进而演变成为一场世界性的经济危机，金本位制起到了重要作用，这种作用无论是在世界性的价格水平和产出下降，还是在这些国家最后的经济恢复中都得到体现（Temin，1993；Bernanke，1995）。有两个方面的证据可以支持这个结论，第一，使得萧条发生的货币冲击正是通过金本位在不同国家之间传导的，其具体的传导机制是由通货紧缩导致的金融危机（Romer，1993）；第二，历史统计显示，西方国家离开金本位的时间对于其经济恢复起到了重要作用，那些很早就脱离金本位的国家可以再膨胀它们的货币供给和价格水平，经济衰退因而程度较浅，经济恢复也比其余国家早，而那些始终留在金本位的国家，则陷入了通货紧缩的恶性循环，在萧条中越陷越深（Eichengreen and Sachs，1985）。

大萧条期间，当主要西方国家纷纷恢复在第一次大战时期放弃的金本位时[①]，中国是世界上唯一实行银本位的大国。另一方面，中国自鸦片战争后就开始逐渐融入世界经济体系，到20世纪30年代时中国的经济开放度已经非常高。在如此高的经济开放度下，中国经济怎样度过20世纪30年代那场世界性的经济大萧条，就是一个值得研究的重要问题。到目前为止，国际经济学界对这段时期中国宏观经济中的一部分现象做过研究，例如Friedman（1992）与Brandt和Sargent（1989）关于美国白银收购政策对中国经济的影响进行过争论，但还未对大萧条中的中国宏观经济进行系统研究。本文用经济学方法回顾这段

① 英国于1925年、法国于1928年恢复金本位，到1929年，几乎所有的市场经济国家都加入了金本位集团，只有一些拉美和亚洲国家还实行银本位。

历史，力图还原历史本来的面貌，并对中国经济的表现与主要的金本位国家进行对比。

本文第二部分回顾中国宏观经济在世界性大萧条中的表现，阐述银本位的作用；第三部分探讨中国经济在大萧条时期表现较好的一个重要因素，即 20 世纪 30 年代的银行体系；第四部分在 Bernanke(1995)研究的基础上，在世界性经济危机的背景下来观察中国，比较中国经济与金本位国家的差异；最后是总结性评论。

二、1929—1937 年的中国宏观经济走势

1929 年，从美国开始的经济萧条通过金本位的传导，逐渐蔓延到其他主要西方国家，演变成一场世界性的经济危机（见表 1）。从 1929 年开始，以美英法为代表的金本位国家物价都急剧并且持续下跌。但是自 1929 年至 1931 年，中国上海、天津和广州三个代表性城市的批发物价却都呈上升趋势，总体来看，中国的平均物价上升了 25%左右，显示出这几年出现了轻微的通货膨胀。

大萧条初期中国经济与西方国家表现存在如此巨大的差异，其根源在于中国是当时世界上唯一采用银本位的大国，使得自己一定程度上隔离于世界经济的萧条之外，并且出现了短暂的繁荣。由于银在金本位国家只是一种普通的商品，因此总体物价的下跌也包括银在内，表 2 的数据显示，银价在 1929 年开始连续四年下跌，其价值几乎跌去了一半（从 85.4 跌到 45.2）。银价的跌落从两个方面对中国经济产生影响，第一是贸易条件的改善，第二是信用的扩张。

表1　1929—1937年中美英法四国批发物价指数

年份	上海	天津	广州	美国	英国	法国
1929	104.5	111.1	96.7	137	135.3	627
1930	114.8	115.9	101.4	124	114.1	554
1931	126.7	122.6	112.6	105	97.6	502
1932	112.4	112.9	113.8	93	94.1	427
1933	103.8	101.0	104.5	95	93.7	398
1934	97.1	92.3	94.3	107	96.4	376
1935	96.4	95.5	84.6	114	99.5	338
1936	108.5	110.6	105.4	115	106	410
1937	123.8	130.0	118.6			

资料来源：中国的批发物价数据来自杨格(1981)，基年为1926年；美英法的数据来自刘佛丁等(1996)，基年为1913年。

首先来看贸易，由于中国是银本位国家，银价相对于金价的下降，其作用相当于中国货币的汇率相对于金本位国家的一次贬值，按照金价衡量的中国产品价格比从前更加便宜。银价下跌，主要是相对于黄金而言，而不是相对于一般货物，银价的跌落大致与按照金价计算的物价跌落相伴随。①汇率的贬值有利于中国产品的出口，使进口减少，促进了国内的生产。从理论上说，有两种相反的力量对中国的出口贸易产生影响，一种是由于银价相对于金价降低，中国产品在世界市场上的竞争力更强；另一种是由于金本位国家发生经济萧条，其购买力降低，导致对中

① 例如，1929年在外汇市场上，1中国元等于36美分，在接下来的两年里，银的金价下降了40%，于是1中国元只相当于21美分，因为其他国家的物价下降，中国可以按照自己的货币对出口要求更高的价格，尽管按照金价来说，它们的价格更低了。

国产品的需求下降。对于进口来说，汇率下跌起了与保护关税相同的作用，使得进口价格上升。从现实数据来看，中国的出口物价指数虽然从1929年的105上升到1931年的107，但比较起来，进口物价上升得更多，从107上升到了150。虽然表2的数据显示出口的绝对值在这几年是下降的，但下降的幅度比世界出口要小得多。从1929年到1931年，反映在黄金和白银的净进口中，中国有国际收支盈余。

表2　中国1929—1936年与贸易相关的数据

年份	物价指数		外汇指数	银价指数	白银的净出口或净进口	以国币计值的贸易额(100万元)	
	出口	进口	1926年＝100	1926年＝100	(1 000关两)	进口	出口
1929	105.2	107.7	85.9	85.4	＋105 826	1 620	1 070
1930	108.3	126.7	59.5	61.7	＋67 006	1 723	944
1931	107.5	150.2	45	46.5	＋45 445H	2002	915
1932	90.4	140.2	55.8	45.2	－6 672	1 524	569
1933	82.0	132.3	62.7	56.1	－9 257	1 345	612
1934	71.7	132.1	73.5	77.4	－164 780	1 030	535
1935	77.6	128.4	82	103.5	－38 124	919	576
1936	96.1	141.7	65	72.8	－160 220	941	706

资料来源：进出口物价指数来自杨格(1981)，外汇指数、银价指数以及白银的进出口来自郑友揆(1984)，(＋)表示净进口，(－)表示净出口，外汇指数是根据中国对外贸易中四个主要国家(日、美、英、德)的汇率，以及他们的贸易值为权数计算的平均指数，进出口额来自杨格(1981)。

银价下跌导致白银的进口，增加了银行的储备和货币供应数量，也使一般物价水平升高，白银流入还增加了信贷的供应。货币供应量的增加促使商业活跃，而且各种外币成本价格升高，使那些喜欢向国外投资的人改向国内寻求投资出路，银根充足，信贷宽裕，地产和建筑业也在上海等大城市开始繁荣起来。在这几年里，白银价格下降在很大程度上刺激了中国国内的生产，1929—1931 年间白银存量大大增加，特别是后两年进口约 5.2 亿元，三年之内仅上海一地的存银就增加了一半以上，5.2 亿元的净进口中约有 4/5 分散到其他通商口岸和内地（杨格，1981），货币供应的充足促进了工业发展，全国工业生产总值从 1929 年的 7 700 多亿元增加到 1932 年的 9 200 多亿元（见表 3）。

表 1 和表 2 的数据显示出，中国从 1929—1931 年的世界银价下跌中受益，但 1929—1931 年银本位给中国经济带来的短暂繁荣在 1931 年秋天逆转，这一年的 9 月英镑脱离金本位，1932 年日元脱离金本位，接着是日本和一些国家的货币相继贬值，特别是日元贬值了 40%，其结果是中国对外贸易中占半数以上国家的汇率急剧上涨①，表 2 显示的外汇指数在 1931 年以后有一个大的攀升，银价在 1932 年以后也从下降的趋势转为上升，汇率升值的结果是出口贸易 1931 年后急剧下降，从 9 亿多元猛降到 5.69 亿元（表 2 最后一列）。

1933 年，美国脱离金本位，使中国的汇率上升更加严峻，美联储放弃金本位后，将货币准备金改为“金三银一”的比例，为了达到这一比例，美国开始在国际市场上收购白银，使得白银价格大幅度上升，中国白银开始流失，这一措施对于大萧条期间的中国经济产生了重要影响。美国白银收购政策的初衷是罗斯福政府屈服于国内利益集团的压力，这些利益集团认为美国应该改变其货币基础，促成国内价格的上涨，同时银价的上升也可以增强中国等用银国家的购买力，推动美国的出口，以此来使美国摆

---

① 1932 年，在中国的对外贸易构成中，英国占 26.2%，美国占 18.7%，日本占 17.9%，见杨格（1981）。

脱萧条。英、日、美等国脱离金本位使萧条开始波及中国，美国的白银收购使得萧条变得更加严重，从1932年开始，白银由净进口变为净出口，说明了中国对外贸易变为逆差。美国收购白银的政策使得白银价格暴涨，银价从1932—1933年的低水平涨到1935年中期的最高峰，上升了两倍半左右（表2第4列），汇率上升的后果主要表现在两个方面，第一是贸易，第二是农业。

1933年当美国脱离金本位后，中国的货币不断升值，从1932年底的19美分，上升到1933年底的33美分（Friedman，1992），几乎又回到了1929年的水平，白银购买政策使升值的压力继续加大，中国的出口急剧下降，1933年相比于1930年下降了30%。另外，银价的升高减少了侨汇，这进一步恶化了中国的国际收支。比贸易恶化更严重的是，白银流失造成通货紧缩，进而造成了农业萧条。白银从内地各处注入上海，再从上海流失到海外，资金由于买卖政府公债可获巨大利润而被吸引到上海，银价高涨也使得内地商人收罗白银运向海外出售，成为有利可图的生意，内地的债权人和银钱兑换商纷纷收回借款，并把白银送往通商口岸。

银价和汇率上涨使得中国的经济萧条加深了，上海和广州批发物价的低点，出现在1935年夏天，天津的批发物价指数于1934年降到最低点（见表1），农业地区的物价更为糟糕。注入上海的白银造成农村地区的经济衰退，农民出售产品价格持续下跌，他们买进货物时所付出的价格却在步步上升，农村送到城镇市场上出卖的东西减少，而送到城市购买货物的白银却增多。农民付出的价格一般都降低了，在某些地区下降了1/3以上，在价格下降的同时，产出也持续下降（见表3）。

表3 中国1931—1936年农业价格指数和农业产值

年份	农业价格指数(1931年=100)	农业产值(10亿中国银元)
1931	100	24.4
1932	72	19.2
1933	61	15.4
1934	56	13.1
1935	57	14.7
1936	60	15.6

资料来源:杨格(1981)。

面对持续的白银外流和汇率上涨,1934年10月,中国政府采取措施,宣布开征白银出口税10%,同时规定,如果伦敦银价折合上海汇兑的比价,与中国中央银行当天市价核定的汇价之间出现差额,则按照这一差额的数目,同时加征白银平衡税。这些措施的实施,目的是保护白银储备,同时制止汇率的继续上升,也切断了汇率与国外银价的关系。

对白银开征机动的出口税与缓和汇率上涨,初步收到了防止通货紧缩恶化的效果。1935年中国进一步改革,废除了银本位,实行法币本位,规定所有白银均应按照时价交售给政府,不得增值。但是因为实施改革之际,国外银价比国内高出2/3,允许各商业银行向中央银行缴存60%的白银和40%的政府债券(按照市场牌价的80%计算),以领取钞票,这一权利自缴存白银起享受两年,这一措施带有通货膨胀性质,因为它促使货币的流通量扩大。

对白银征收出口税以及随后的法币改革使中国经济最终摆脱了通货紧缩,并走出了大萧条。改革的成果是显著的,1936年主要谷物收成的价值达法币56亿元,比1933年至1935年的平均产值高出 17 亿元，几乎增加了 45%。1935 年后汇率又开始下降，扭转了 1933 年后持续升值的趋势（表 2 第 3 列），外汇价格水平有利的体现是大大促进了出口，改革之后的头几个月内中国出现了几十年来从未有过的贸易顺差，出口超过了进口，国外对中国出口货物的需求增加，特别增强了农业生产者的购买力。而且，进口贸易虽然受到汇率水平低的影响，但是不久随即重见起色，1937 年上半年，进口比上年同期增加了 40%（杨格，1981）。货币供应量的加大，适应了币制改革之后出现的经济复苏和对货币需求增加的局面，也刺激了物价的上涨（见表 1）。

本节回顾了中国经济在大萧条中的表现，总的说来，中国经济在整个萧条期间的表现与西方大多数国家绝然不同，当世界性的经济危机于 1929 年开始蔓延时，中国在 1929—1931 年却由于实行银本位制而有短暂的经济繁荣，但是从 1932 年开始，大多数西方国家先后放弃金本位，摆脱了固定汇率的束缚，并进而采取扩张性的货币政策，逐渐走出了萧条并开始经济复苏，中国经济却于 1932 年开始进入萧条，其原因开始主要是因为西方国家放弃金本位使得中国的货币升值，此后由于美国实行白银收购政策使得中国白银外流，造成严重的通货紧缩，恶化了中国的贸易条件，并造成严重的农业危机。1934 年对白银征收出口税和 1935 年实行的货币改革，使中国得以采取扩张性的货币政策，并最终走出了经济危机。

但是一个值得注意的现象是，如表 4 所示，在整个大萧条期间，无论汇率贬值还是升值，外贸情况如何改变，中国的工业生产基本上处于不断上升之中，并没有受到萧条的严重冲击，这是与其他西方国家完全不同的经济现象。①而且对于经济周期高

① 西方国家在大萧条中的工业衰退，见 Temin（1993）和 Romer（1993）。

度敏感的建筑业在整个萧条期间也处于不断发展之中，资本形成除了1934年有过短暂的下挫，也是不断上升的，为什么会出现这种现象，工业生产没有受到萧条的冲击，还是另有其他原因？要回答这一问题，还需要仔细考察中国在萧条期间的货币供给。

表4　中国1929—1936年的工业生产(按1933年国币计算)

单位：国币10亿元

年份	产品总值	净增价值	建筑业	国内资本形成
1929	773.8	278.2		
1930	821.1	296.4		
1931	886.9	320.0	0.4	1.27
1932	921.5	334.1	0.41	1.49
1933	1 006.3	369.7	0.44	1.5
1934	1 042.6	395.0	0.44	1.12
1935	1 104.1	441.8	0.46	1.6
1936	1 227.4	499.1	0.49	1.95

资料来源：Yeh, K. C. (1977)。

三、20世纪30年代的中国银行体系和货币供给

不同于世界上很多国家通过积极的财政政策走出经济萧条，在整个20世纪30年代，中国的财政政策基本上无所作为。虽然也实行了赤字财政，但中国政府能够调动的财源不多。关税是政府收入的主要来源，大约占到总数的一半，盐税占1/4左右，财政开支主要用于军事，1928—1929年占84%，在1929年至1937年也从未降至2/3以下。军事上的巨大开支阻碍了政

府把更多的资金投入到经济发展之中，当时已经有人批评说政府财政上的决策几乎完全是以非经济因素为基础的。财政中用于教育、文化和经济建设的数目，从 1934 年至 1937 年财政年度的报表中能够查到的数字列举如下（见表 5）。

表 5　1929—1937 年国民政府的收入、支出和赤字

单位：100 万元

年份	支出	收入	赤字	占支出的比例	教育与文化	经济建设
1929	434.0	334.0	100	23		
1930	585.0	484.0	101	17.3		
1931	775.0	558.0	217	28		
1932	749.0	619.0	130	17.4		
1933	699.0	614.0	86	12.3		
1934	836.0	689.0	147	17.6	13	7
1935	941.0	745.0	196	20.8	32	26
1936	1 073.0	817.0	256	23.8	37	88
1937	1 167.0	870.0	297	25.4	42	54

资料来源：杨格（1981）。

表 5 的数据说明，政府用于经济建设的资金和其总的支出相比基本上是微不足道的，虽然德国和日本通过扩充军备，进而刺激生产来走出经济危机，但是中国工业远远没有德、日那样的发展水平，因此巨大的军事开支并不能够起到促进经济扩张的作用。既然财政政策没有作为，使得中国经济走出萧条的重担就落在了货币政策身上。表 6 显示了中国 1930—1936 年期间货币供给的情况。

表 6 的数据显示了中国 1930—1936 年货币的供给及其组

成部分，由此可见，在1930—1932年间，银币是处于增长之中的，如前文所述，这是白银相对于黄金贬值后白银从国外流入的结果，1932年以后的银币则完全相反，其不断减少的存量说明了西方国家脱离金本位和汇率贬值以及美国的白银收购造成中国的白银外流。铜币的趋势也是不断减少的，但在整个大萧条期间总的幅度并不大。在总货币的构成中，与前面两项不同的是，在整个大萧条期间，纸币和银行存款则处于不断上升之中，这使得中国的货币供给不断增长，这才是导致工业生产始终没有下降的原因。而货币供给的增长，其根源又在于中国竞争性的银行体系。这个体系包括政府银行、私营银行和钱庄，还有外国银行，它类似于美国历史上曾经出现过的自由银行制度(Rolnick and Weber, 1983; Brandt and Sargent, 1989)，正是这个银行体系在大萧条期间的存款和发放纸币使得总的货币供给不断增长，以下分别予以分析。

表6　中国1930—1936年的货币供给(年终总量)

单位：100万元

年份	银币	铜币	纸币	银行存款	总货币
1930	2 200	287.7	956.3	3 392.1	6 836.1
1931	2 271	281.4	896.9	3 591.5	7 040.8
1932	2 289	275.1	924.4	3 880.8	7 369.3
1933	2 275	268.8	978.8	4 290.6	7 813.2
1934	1 995	262.5	1 108.9	4 620.9	7 987.3
1935	1 703	256.2	1 413.5	5 460.1	8 832.8
1936	1 391	250	2 438.6	6 394.2	10 473.8

资料来源：Rawski(1989)，这里采用其低值。

(1) 政府银行，包括中央银行和其他政府银行。中央银行成立于1928年10月,政府授予中央银行以发行钞票、铸造和流通货币、经营外汇、掌管公债的发行等权利,它所发钞票的准备金,60%为金银条块或其铸币,40%为政府债务和商业证券。在1935年之前,中央银行在地位上和其他政府银行几乎是等同的,并不具备"银行之银行"的职能,既不能使用贴现政策,也不能进行公开市场购买,在业务上它与其他政府银行是处于竞争地位的。中央银行是当时仅有的完全属于政府的银行,其他的三家政府银行中国银行、交通银行、中国农业银行,政府只是占有一定的股权或者一定程度上被政府所控制,它们都有独立发行钞票的权利。省立和地方设立的银行之中也有许多发行钞票,虽然相对于中央政府银行,其所发钞票的数量不大。

(2) 私营银行和钱庄。现代式私营银行在1928年至1937年间发展十分迅速,共新设124家,到1937年已经有164家,在全国各地共设有1 597处分支机构,这些分支行向各地的生产和贸易或其他经济活动提供各种贷款,在这段时间内,总资本增长了一倍以上,从1.17亿元增加到2.8亿元,它们发行钞票的速度远比政府银行为快。老式钱庄在现代式银行发展起来之前,承担着为全国办理财政金融业务的职责,收受存款并放贷资金,钱庄一般都在中国或外国银行里存放贷款,并从它们那里获得信贷,这些钱庄是中国分散经营银行制度的重要组成部分,它们分布各地,对当地的信用状况非常熟悉。

(3) 外资银行。在20世纪30年代,外资银行的总数约有25家,它们分属于美、英、荷、法、德、意、日,它们在治外法权之下受本国法律的管辖,不遵守中国的规章法令,它们经营与国际贸易和国际收支有关的业务,也办理外国在中国的投资和借款,以及买卖外汇。此外,它们直接或者间接地投资于中国铁路的建设,扶植轻工业的发展,还经营中国各大城市的房地产。

20世纪30年代中期，中国各银行发行自己的钞票和接受存款，各种政策和规定都有利于货币的扩张，这与金本位国家在大萧条中由于银行倒闭导致的货币紧缩形成鲜明的对照。在1935年货币改革之前，银行发行纸币被要求有100%的储备，其中的60%要以白银、黄金和外汇的形式持有，剩下的40%以证券的形式持有，对于存款没有储备要求。在1931—1935年间，银行储备对纸币的比例大约是35%，这个比例主要由银行持有政府债券来保持(Brandt and Sargent，1989)，华资各银行活期存款的现金准备率从20世纪20年代早期的11%—18%减少至30年代的6%—8%，以上这些规定都放大了货币乘数，使得中国的货币乘数没有出现金本位国家那样显著下降的情况。货币乘数是现金—存款比率和储备金—存款比率的递减函数，前者是由公众决定的，后者是由商业银行决定的。在不发达国家，公众偏好用现金交易，所以货币乘数相对较小；相反，在银行体系发达的国家里，货币乘数较大。在大萧条中，由于银行恐慌导致公众现金—存款比率以及商业银行储备金—存款比率的上升，从而导致货币乘数的急剧下降，这是大萧条期间各国货币供给下降的一个主要原因，但是这一情况在中国没有出现。

1933年白银外流导致通货紧缩时，中国也曾经发生一次挤兑风潮，但中央银行毫不迟疑地付给现银，这使得货币危机没有如西方国家那样传染开来。各政府银行1928—1935年币制改革期间增发的钞票，都得到很好的流通，现代华资私营银行所发钞票数额也迅速增加，1935年币制改革之后的20个月中，钞票的流通总额增加了一倍以上，自7.65亿元增加到19.12亿元。①促成钞票增加的主要因素是用钞票代理已经收归国有的

① 1937年中期数据，见杨格(1981)。

银币，金陵大学1935年8月27日所做的一次抽样测验表明：1930年银币占通货总额的68%，而纸币只占32%，到1935年比例变为纸币占55%，银币减至45%。[①]币制改革之后，信贷也被有意识地扩大，这一政策带有通货膨胀性质，它使价格大致恢复到1931年的水平，造成扩大的一个重要因素是各银行能够以向中央银行缴存六成白银和四成证券的办法领取钞票，通货数量也由于有资金回流而增加，原先为了投机或者转移资本买进的大量外汇也纷纷脱售以换取本国纸币。1935年币制改革时政府曾声明，中央银行将逐步收回所有其他银行发出的钞票，并在两年以后享有独家发行钞票的权利。但在币制改革之后，朝向中央银行独家发钞目标取得的进展很小，各私营银行所发钞票虽然从流通中迅速退出，但是中国银行和交通银行两家在发钞总数中所占份额都没有减少，中国农业银行由于在1937年初以前一直不受中央控制，发钞数目竟然增长了7倍，各省银行所发钞票也在增多，自1935年11月3日到1937年中期，中央银行所发钞票，在钞票总额中所占比例只从18%增加到20%。

表7 1929—1936年中美英法货币比较(以本国单位计算)

单位：100万元

年份	中国		法国		英国		美国	
	M1	增长率	M1	增长率	M1	增长率	M1	增长率
1929			101 562	0.100	1 328	0.025	26 434	−0.057
1930	6 836.1	0.030	111 720	0.099	1 361	−0.097	24 922	−0.121
1931	7 040.8	0.047	122 748	−0.010	1 229	0.108	21 894	−0.071
1932	7 369.3	0.060	121 519	−0.059	1 362	0.034	20 341	−0.029

① 1937年中期数据，见杨格(1981)。

（续表）

年份	中国		法国		英国		美国	
1933	7 813.2	0.022	114 386	−0.008	1 408	0.029	19 759	0.153
1934	7 986.5	0.106	113 451	−0.048	1 449	0.080	22 774	0.187
1935	8 832.8	0.186	108 009	0.086	1 565	0.121	27 032	0.141
1936	10 473.7		117 297		1 755		30 852	

资料来源：中国的数据来源同表6，美英法的数据来自Bernanke(1995)。

由以上分析可见，无论是1935年前的银行体系，还是1935年货币改革后的银行体系，从体系本身到各种政策措施都是有利于货币扩张的，1932年后银本位给中国造成的通货紧缩效应远远不能抵消中国竞争性银行体系带来的货币扩张，大萧条带来的紧缩主要局限在中国农村，农村经济凋敝以后，内地的资金往城市集中，反而促进了银行存款的增加(吴承禧，1934)。货币扩张既促进了交通运输和建筑业的发展，也促进了资本形成，这些都使1929—1936年期间中国的工业生产处于不断增长之中。表7比较了大萧条期间中、美、英、法四国货币发行情况，中国在整个期间M1货币一直是处于增长的，其他国家则都有下降的年份。具体说来，下降的时间与其脱离金本位的时间是一致的，英国于1931年脱离金本位，美国于1933年脱离金本位，它们的货币供给都在这一年转为正的增长，法国一直到1936年才离开金本位。因此，在整个萧条期间，其货币始终是紧缩的，这是法国经济在萧条中衰退最严重的主要原因。

四、中国与金本位国家的国际比较

表8的数据是1931—1935年中国与金本位国家主要宏观

经济变量的比较，表中的数据均为变化率，为了更好地说明中国与金本位国家的差别，中国的数据向前延伸一年，26 个金本位国家①的数据来自 Bernanke(1995)，根据每年脱离金本位还是留在金本位对两组数据取平均值。对于所有的金本位国家来说，共同的特点是货币收缩是经济衰退的重要原因，但是在 1932 年前后，那些留在金本位的国家和脱离金本位的国家的数据呈现出很大的差异，差异的原因在于那些脱离金本位的国家有更大的政策自由来实行扩张性的货币政策。对于每一组数据来说，都显示出了中国在大萧条时期的主要宏观经济变量呈现出与金本位国家不同的轨迹。

对于货币供给来说，所有的金本位国家内部货币存量在 1931 年都有急剧的收缩，但是到了 1932 年，那些离开金本位的国家货币供给转为正的增长，其他金本位国家的收缩则持续到 1935 年，而且收缩的程度不断加深。中国的货币供给在这些年份则基本处于不断增长的上升通道之中，除了 1933 年与 1932 年相比有所下降，这正是那些离开金本位的国家货币贬值导致中国白银外流的转折年份。更进一步说，这种收缩的大部分可以归结于 M1 对通货比例的下降，这背后的机制又是银行倒闭导致的货币乘数变小(银行危机主要发生在 1931 年)，主要是由于公众现金—存款比例和商业银行储备金—存款比例的上升。在 1933 年到 1935 年，那些留在金本位国家的货币继续紧缩，而那些离开金本位国家的货币则转而扩张。和货币供给一样，中国的 M1 对通货比例也基本处于持续上升之中，这说明中国的货币乘数没有变小，没有大规模的银行倒闭事件发生。

---

① 这些国家是：澳大利亚，阿根廷，奥地利，比利时，加拿大，丹麦，芬兰，法国，德国，希腊，匈牙利，意大利，日本，拉脱维亚，荷兰，挪威，新西兰，波兰，罗马尼亚，瑞典，西班牙，瑞士，英国，美国，爱沙尼亚，捷克斯洛伐克。

价格水平的变化和货币存量密切相关，虽然在1931年所有的金本位国家价格水平都有急剧的下降，但是在那些离开金本位的国家，批发物价指数在1932—1933年得以稳定，在1934年转而上升，而那些留在金本位的国家批发物价则一直持续下降到1935年。在金本位国家中，由于不同国家经历国际收支的赤字和盈余之间存在着对称性，赤字国家必然出口黄金，而盈余国家必然进口黄金，而金本位使得各国的汇率都固定在一个水平，因此，如果一个国家存在着贸易赤字，那么其调整机制必然是紧缩而不是贬值。换句话说，就是国内价格的调整而不是汇率的调整，因为更低的价格从而更低的国内产出可以减少进口和增加出口，从而改善贸易条件并且吸引到黄金和外汇储备。这是金本位国家在萧条期间价格运行的内在机制，中国因为是银本位国家，其价格变化与这种机制迥然不同，中国批发物价在1930年和1931年上升，说明汇率贬值、白银内流后带来通货膨胀，1932年转入下降；1933年和1934年下降幅度增大，说明金本位国家贬值和美国白银收购政策使得中国汇率升值和经济严重萧条；1935年物价指数虽然为负，但已经显著减轻；1936年终于转为正值，说明政府对白银征收出口税和实行货币改革以及扩大货币供应收到了效果。

产出的下降同样和货币以及价格水平的下降高度相关，金本位国家的制造业生产在1930—1931年开始下降，留在金本位的国家和脱离金本位的国家之间呈现出显著的差异，那些处于金本位的发展中国家更是无法摆脱大萧条的冲击，因为工业化国家对于他们产品的需求下降，他们的价格水平下降了，还有一些国家则主动让其价格水平下降，其目的是为了保持他们的货币价值，无论是哪一种情形，当总需求曲线沿着向上倾斜的总供给曲线向下移动时，萧条一定会伴随着紧缩而来。中国的制造业产出只是在 1933 年出现过短暂的下降，其余年份基本上都是上升的，这说明由于货币供应充足，中国的工业生产并没有像其他的金本位发展中国家一样受到萧条的严重冲击。

再来看实际工资的情况，许多国家之所以在大萧条中越陷越深，一个重要因素是名义工资相对于价格水平的变化不能灵活调整，使得实际工资一直高出于市场出清水平，这造成了大量的失业。这一点在表 8 的金本位国家体现得更明显，这些国家的实际工资在整个萧条期间一直是正增长的。相反，脱离金本位的国家由于可以扩张货币，价格水平上升，其实际工资一直处于负增长。中国由于不存在严重的货币紧缩，因此，实际工资的发展趋势和那些脱离金本位的国家一样，实际工资的负增长说明工资弹性较大，失业不会成为一个严重的问题。

实际出口和实际进口的趋势不像前面几项那么显著，由于脱离金本位后可以扩张货币，由此造成的贬值起到了促进出口的作用，因此，脱离金本位国家的出口相对于那些还留在金本位国家明显要好，中国的情况则介于两者之间，金本位国家和非金本位国家的进口增长率之间没有显著的差异。这可能说明金本位集团下降的国内收入水平和改善的贸易条件之间具有互相抵消的作用，中国的进口增长率从 1930 年以后一直是负增长，这一方面是因为萧条使得中国的购买力下降，另一方面也是由于这段时间中国取得关税自主权后提高关税率的作用。

表 8 显示的中国和主要金本位国家宏观变量的变化与货币冲击具有真实效应的理论高度一致，它说明 20 世纪 30 年代货币供给的下降对实体经济带来了严重的负面影响，而不是货币紧缩是产出下降的被动反映，货币紧缩在所有国家里都是导致大萧条的一个重要因素。表 8 的数据显示，那些在 20 世纪 30 年代初期就迅速放弃金本位的国家，由于可以增加货币供给，使

表 8　中国与金本位国家主要宏观变量比较

年　　份	1930	1931	1932	1933	1934	1935	1936
制造业生产							
平均	−0.066	−0.116	−0.09	0.076	0.1	0.074	0.072
留在金本位的国家		−0.117	−0.173	0.086	0.025	−0.001	
脱离金本位的国家		−0.113	−0.057	0.078	0.12	0.008	
中国		0.000	0.003	−0.044	0.039	0.078	
批发物价							
平均	−0.116	−0.122	−0.045	−0.017	0.018	0.024	0.048
留在金本位的国家		−0.14	−0.133	−0.065	−0.037	−0.038	
脱离金本位的国家		−0.084	−0.011	−0.002	0.033	0.036	
中国	0.063	0.090	−0.063	−0.088	−0.083	−0.025	0.174
M1 货币供给							
平均	0.016	−0.088	−0.068	−0.006	0.019	0.027	0.074
留在金本位的国家		−0.142	−0.052	−0.009	−0.016	−0.037	
脱离金本位的国家		−0.102	0.014	−0.03	0.002	−0.006	
中国	0.030	0.047	0.060	0.022	0.106	0.186	
M1 对通货比例							
平均	0.030	−0.129	−0.006	−0.024	−0.002	−0.011	−0.011
留在金本位的国家		−0.142	−0.052	−0.009	−0.016	−0.037	
脱离金本位的国家		−0.102	0.014	−0.03	0.002	−0.006	
中国	0.028	0.035	0.050	0.070	0.104	−0.015	

（续表）

年　　份	1930	1931	1932	1933	1934	1935	1936
实际工资							
平均	0.122	0.094	0.007	−0.009	−0.023	−0.022	−0.018
留在金本位的国家		0.11	0.064	0.032	0.006	0.016	
脱离金本位的国家		0.059	−0.02	−0.025	−0.032	−0.031	
中国	−0.035	−0.007	0.004	−0.042	−0.018	−0.020	
实际出口							
平均	−0.073	−0.179	−0.222	0.014	0.056	0.021	0.072
留在金本位的国家		−0.193	−0.292	−0.008	0.015	−0.024	
脱离金本位的国家		−0.146	−0.192	0.021	0.067	0.03	
中国	−0.007	−0.261	0.240	−0.049	0.088	−0.028	
实际进口							
平均	−0.071	−0.211	−0.264	0.004	0.038	0.02	0.049
留在金本位的国家		−0.159	−0.25	−0.006	−0.067	−0.012	
脱离金本位的国家		−0.315	−0.271	0.008	0.07	0.027	
中国	0.052	−0.185	−0.082	−0.127	−0.019	−0.072	

资料来源：表中的数据均为变化率，金本位国家的数据来自 Bernanke(1995)，中国的制造业数据来自 Yeh, K. C. (1977)，批发物价数据根据杨格(1981)加总后取平均值，M1 和通货的数据均来自 Rawski(1989)，此处取其低估计值，实际工资取自 Rawski(1993)，名义出口和进口值取自杨格，再根据刘佛丁、王玉茹(1996)的出口和进口物价指数调整。

价格水平回升，可以较快地从萧条中恢复，而那些仍然留在金本位的国家则在萧条中越陷越深。中国经济之所以在大萧条期间表现较好，就是因为相对于金本位国家，货币始终没有出现严重的紧缩，因而批发物价的下降和实际工资的上升没有金本位国家那么剧烈。

五、结　语

本文回顾了中国宏观经济在大萧条时期的表现，阐述了其背后的机制，并进而将中国与其他主要的金本位国家进行了比较。本文的结论主要有以下几点：

第一，中国经济在世界经济大萧条时期的表现再一次证实了国际经济学界对于萧条的基本结论，即大萧条中的货币冲击具有真实效应。关于货币冲击导致大萧条加深的观点在国际学术界曾经引起了广泛的争论，这一观点遭到了一些经济学家的反对，他们认为萧条中的货币收缩只是货币对产出的一种被动反应，经济危机的实际原因在于经济的真实面，例如美国 1929 年消费水平的突然下降(Temin，1993；Romer，1993)。更多的经济学家则认为萧条之所以变得越来越大，由金本位引起的货币危机在国家之间的传染对于实体经济起到了收缩作用，大萧条的一个最主要教训就是政府没有努力消除货币供给的减少，特别是采取有力的措施来防止银行倒闭。本文的研究说明，中国在大萧条中的经历支持主流的观点，1929 年后的白银内流、货币贬值和 1932 年后的白银外流、货币升值对于中国的实体经济确实有着重要的影响。

第二，有两个因素在大萧条时期的中国经济中起到了重要作用，一个是银本位，一个是竞争性的银行体系。银本位使中国经济萧条的进程迥然不同于西方金本位国家，不同于西方国家主要通过财政政策度过大萧条，中国由于特殊的银行体系，货币供给始终没有减少，银行危机也没有普遍发生，这是中国经济在整个大萧条时期表现较好的一个重要原因。

第三，本文的研究发现，中国经济在这场世界性的经济危机中的表现比世界上大多数国家要好①，但是如果进一步分析这种良好表现的原因，与其说是政府政策的成功，还不如说是市场机制的成功。正如 Rawski(1993)批评 Friedman(1992)论述美国的白银收购政策对中国经济产生的影响时所说的那样，20 世纪 30 年代的中国经济，体现了一种没有管制的市场体系良好运转的典范，家庭和企业都可以进行真正的"自由选择"。只是这样的自由选择，是在当时的中国中央政府还不能够行使全部主权的历史背景下进行，例如直到 1933 年 5 月，中国才首次有机会实施自主关税，外资银行在华经营的许多业务都得到治外法权的保障，因此，这样的自由选择打上了半殖民地的烙印。

参考文献

阿瑟·杨格:《一九二七至一九三七年中国财政经济状况》，中国社会科学出版社 1981 年版。

陈争平:《1895—1936 年中国国际收支研究》，中国社会科学出版社 1996 年版。

孔敏:《南开经济指数资料汇编》，中国社会科学出版社 1988 年版。

刘佛丁、王利华、王玉茹:《二十世纪三十年代前期的中国经济——评美国学者近年来关于美国白银政策对中国经济影响的讨论》，《南开经济

① 那些在大萧条中表现较好的国家，都是非金本位国家或者很早就脱离金本位然后大幅度贬值其货币的国家，例如西班牙因为政治上的原因，佛朗哥政权没有加入金本位，从而没有经历任何萧条，日本则是在 1932 年脱离金本位并且将其货币贬值 40%。

研究》1995 年第 2 期。

刘佛丁、王玉茹:《中国近代的市场发育与经济增长》,高等教育出版社 1996 年版。

麦迪逊:《世界经济二百年回顾》,改革出版社 1997 年版。

王业键:《中国近代货币与银行的演进:1644—1937》,台北中央研究院经济研究所 1981 年。

吴承禧:《中国的银行》,上海商务印书馆 1934 年版。

巫宝三:《中国国民所得:一九三三年》,上海中华书局 1947 年版。

约翰·梅纳德·凯恩斯:《就业、利息和货币通论》,商务印书馆 1999 年版。

郑友揆:《中国的对外贸易和工业发展(1840—1948 年)——史实的综合分析》,上海社会科学出版社 1984 年版。

钟思远、刘基荣:《民国私营银行史》,四川大学出版社 1999 年版。

Arthur J. Rolnick and Warren E. Weber, 1983, "New Evidence on the Free Banking Era", *American Economic Review*, Vol. 73, No. 5.

Barry Eichengreen and Jeffery Sachs, 1985, "Exchange Rates and Economic Recovery in the 1930s", *Journal of Economic History*, Vol. 45, No. 4.

Ben S. Bernanke, 1995, "The Macroeconomics of the Great Depression: A Comparative Approach", *Journal of Money, Credit and Banking*, Vol. 27, No. 1.

Christina D. Romer, 1993, "The Nation in Depression", *Journal of Economic Perspectives*, Vol. 7, No. 2.

Hou, Chi-ming, 1963, "Economic Dualism: The Case of China 1840—1937", *Journal of Economic History*, Vol. 23, No. 3.

Loren Brandt and Thomas J. Sargent, 1989, "Interpreting New Evidence About China and U. S Silver Purchases", *Journal of Monetary Economics*, Vol. 23, No. 1.

Milton, Friedman, 1992, "Franklin D. Roosevelt, Silver, and China", *Journal of Political Economy*, Vol. 100, No. 1.

Milton Friedman and Anna Schwartz, 1963, *A Monetary History of the United States*, 1867—1960, Princeton: Princeton University Press for NBER.

Obstfeld Maurice and Rogoff Kenneth, 1996, Foundations of International Macroeconomics, MIT Press.

Peter. Temin, 1993, "Transmission of the Great Depression", *Journal of Economic Perspectives*, Vol. 7, No. 2.

Thomas G. Rawski, 1989, *Economic Growth in Pre-war China*, Berkeley: University of California Press.

Thomas G. Rawski, 1993, "Milton Friedman, Silver, and China", *Journal of Political Economy*, Vol. 101, No. 4.

Yeh, K. C., 1977, "China's National Income, 1931—1936", in "Modern Chinese Economic History", The Institute of Economics, Academia Sinica.

(原载《经济研究》2007 年第 2 期)

中国的永久移民

邓曲恒

（中国社会科学院经济研究所）

古斯塔夫森

（瑞典哥德堡大学社会工作系）

一、引　　言

中国在20世纪50年代逐渐建立了户口制度。户口制度限制了居民从农村到城市的迁移，也在很大程度上造成了城市居民和农村居民之间生活水平的巨大差异（Chan，1994；Knight and Song，1999；Zhao，2000；Liu，2005）。改革开放后，中国经济迅速增长，而居住在城市的人口也越来越多。一些农村居民没有城市户口，作为短期流动人口进入城市。短期流动人口中大部分是年轻的体力劳动者，从事工资报酬较低的工作。与城市居民相比，短期流动人口在住房、劳动保护、社会福利方面享受不到同等待遇（Zhao，2000；Meng and Zhang，2001；蔡昉等，2001）。

与短期流动人口不同，永久移民持有城市户口，尽管两者都来自农村。永久移民可以通过接受较好的教育、提干或参军等职业途径获得城市户口。除此之外，还存在其他获得户口的方式，如家庭团聚、土地被政府征用、或者在某些城市购买住房。[1]户口甚至在一些地方可以直接购得(陆益龙,2002; Wong and Wai-Po, 1998;陈金永,2004)。

与学术界对短期流动人口的浓厚兴趣相比,农村到城市的永久移民这一群体还没有得到深入研究。本文则试图从多个角度研究永久移民。我们想知道,永久移民的规模有多大?他们有什么特征?他们迁移到了何种城市?他们具有何种家庭背景?同是出身农村,永久移民的生活处境是不是要比农民好?进一步地,永久移民的收入要高出农民多少?而永久移民在迁移目的地的适应状况也是一个饶有兴味的研究论题。相比于通过职业途径获得户口的永久移民,通过其他途径获得户口的移民在城市劳动力市场上的表现又是如何?

根据国际移民的相关文献,我们估计永久移民在城市中的处境较佳,尽管他们在到达城市初期可能处于不利地位。永久移民是一个自我选择的群体,许多永久移民受过较长时间的教育。甚至有理由认为,在同等条件下,永久移民与城市原住民相比反而要处于优势地位。既然永久移民能够成功地从不利环境中挣脱出来,他们也应该能够比城市原住民更好地捕捉和把握机会。然而,与城市原住民相比,永久移民也可能处于劣势。众所周知,社会关系在中国有着十分重要的作用。永久移民在城市建立社会网络的时间较短,因而他们在寻找工作以及在工作中获得提升方面就处于劣势。因而,我们现在还不能断言永久移民比城市原住民过得好还是差。

---

① 如无特别说明,本文所论及的户口都是指城市户口。

二、户口制度①

新中国成立初期，人口流动并没有受到限制。出于对农村人口大量涌入城市的担忧，中国在20世纪50年代中期逐渐建立了户口制度。根据户口制度的规定，所有居民都必须在当地登记，户口登记状况不能随意变更，而农业户口向城镇户口的转变更是难上加难。这样中国的城市居民和农村居民就成为两个分割的群体，而政策制定从此也是城乡有别。

户口制度的引入是实行计划经济的需要，同时它的效力也仰仗着计划经济的力量。城镇户口是获得城市正式工作的必要条件。城市正式工作不仅意味着稳定的收入流，而且意味着工作单位所提供的住房、廉价食品、医疗保障和养老保障等福利。如果没有城市户口，就无法获得城市工作，也就很难在城市生存下去。只有因组织需要而调动工作时，城市居民才能进行迁移。在农村地区，所有的成年人都必须参加集体农作以获得工分，并凭借工分来获得食物配给。公社向上级政府上交农作物，以此为城市的工业化作贡献。

农村居民可以通过几种途径获得城市户口而成为永久移民。我们首先来看职业途径。其中一种途径便是教育，大中专毕业生通常都被给予城市户口，而这些教育机会的获得在原则上都是基于学业成绩的。通过这种途径获得户口的永久移民通常都接受了较长时间的教育，他们的户口通常在参加工作时得到正式变更。农村党员并不自动获得城市户口，但党员身份有助于城市户口的获得。农村党员往往有机会担任

① 本节的写作基于张庆五(1983)、Cheng 和 Selden(1994)、Chan 和 Zhang(1999)、陈金永(2004)、陆益龙(2002)、Wang(2004)、Wu 和 Treiman(2004)。

农村干部(村支书、村主任等)。一些农村干部得到提升,因而可能获得城市户口。还有一个途径就是参军,军官在退役后可以获得城市户口和城市工作。除了这三种与职业相关的途径以外,一部分农村居民基于两地分居等家庭方面的原因而获得户口。而农民的土地被政府征用后,也可以获得城市户口(Wong and Wai-Po, 1998)。某些城市规定,在该城市购买商品房可以申请当地城市户口。也有一些地方政府直接出售城镇户口,以增加财政收入。与户口制度建立初期时的情形相比,现行的户口制度处于一个大为不同的外部环境之中,户口制度正在逐渐放松。[①]

三、数据介绍

本文所使用的数据来自中国社会科学院经济研究所2002年中国居民收入分配调查。[②]基于研究需要,本文使用了城市住户调查、农村住户调查和暂住户调查三套数据。城市样本覆盖12个省份的6 835户居民,它被用来识别永久移民,也成为第六节和第七节分析永久移民在城市劳动力市场上的表现的数据基础。城市样本还被用来估计永久移民的规模和分析永久移民的迁移目的地。暂住户调查覆盖了12省的农村到城市的短期流动人口。第五节利用了这2 000户流动人口来估计农村到城市的短期流动所带来的经济收益。农村住户调查包括了22个省份的9 200户农村居民。第五节使用了这部分数据来分析影响永久迁移的因素,并估计农村居民的永久迁移和短期流动的经济收益。

① 一些城市实行了蓝印户口。而户籍制度改革也在一些小城镇进行试点。

② 关于本文所用数据的详细说明,请参见Li等(2007)。

四、永久移民的规模以及迁移目的地

我们根据城市居民获得城镇户口的时间来鉴别他们是否是永久移民。在 20 082 个具有城镇户口的样本居民中，4 069 人是在出生一段时间以后才获得城市户口的，后者构成了城市样本的 20.3%。[①]而根据最新统计，2004 年中国城镇总人口为 5.4 亿。这样我们可以估计出永久移民的数量大致为 1.1 亿，这可能是对永久移民规模的首次估计。而根据国务院研究室的最新报告，2004 年进城务工的农民有 1.2 亿（国务院研究室，2006）。因此，当年居留在城市的人口中就有 35% 具有农村出身的背景。

表 1 提供了按性别和年龄分组的永久移民的数量和比例。可以看到，男性在永久移民中的比重要高于其在城市原住民中的比重。很明显，青少年在永久移民中的比重较低。可以看出，在各个年龄组中，31—35 岁年龄组永久移民在全部城市居民中的比例最高，达到了 32%。这一年龄组出生于 1967—1971 年之间，当他们成年时，正处于改革开放后高等教育发展较快、户籍制度也有所松动的时期。而对早他们一个时代出生的人们（cohort）而言，情况则完全不同。41—45 岁年龄组在“文革”期间成年，这一年龄组中只有 17% 是永久移民。

---

① 样本中的永久移民为通过接受教育、提干、参军、土地被征用、购买城市商品房、直接购买户口等方式获得城市户口的原农村居民。第七节将根据获取城市户口的途径对永久移民进行分类考察。

表 1　按性别和年龄组分类的城市原住民和永久移民

	城市原住民		永久移民	
	%	观测值	%	观测值
性别				
男性	48.94	7 836	52.35	2 130
女性	51.06	8 177	47.65	1 939
年龄组				
<16	16.82	2 694	5.58	227
16—20	7.94	1 271	3.10	126
21—25	5.96	954	3.51	143
26—30	4.71	755	6.51	265
31—35	7.10	1 137	13.05	531
36—40	10.74	1 719	13.86	564
41—45	10.79	1 728	8.90	362
46—50	13.17	2 109	12.36	503
51—55	8.92	1 429	10.74	437
56—60	4.38	701	7.54	307
60＋	9.47	1 516	14.84	604
观测值		16 013		4 069

资料来源：中国社会科学院经济研究所收入分配课题组 2002 年住户调查数据。下同。

表 2　移民密度的决定因素

解释变量		解释变量	
就业率	0.468** (0.197)	西部	−0.056 (0.039)
中小城市	—	人均收入	−0.008 (0.006)
大城市	−0.067* (0.039)	常数项	0.010 (0.140)
东　部	−0.080* (0.043)	Adjusted R^2	0.2135
中　部	—	观测值	77

注:(1) 括号内是标准误。***,**,*分别表示在 0.01、0.05 和 0.1 的水平上显著。下同。

(2) 因变量是城市中永久移民占全部城市居民的比重。

我们接下来探究永久移民倾向于迁移到何种性质的城市。我们计算了每个城市中永久移民占全部城市居民的比重,也即移民密度,其均值为 0.224。中小城市的移民密度为 0.254,而大城市的移民密度则为 0.136。这也是合乎常识的,大城市住房比较紧张,生活成本较高,对移民的限制也要比中小城市严格。我们还可以发现,移民密度在中部地区(0.284)要高于东部(0.163)和西部(0.231)。从人均收入和就业率等城市特征来看,低收入城市以及就业率较高的城市中永久移民的比重较高。然而,低收入城市往往也是小城市,因此对移民密度进行回归分析可能更有说服力。表 2 的分析结果表明,当其他城市特征得以控制以后,城市人均收入和移民密度之间的关系就不再是显著的了。然而,城市的就业率仍然具有显著的正向作用,城市规模和区域虚拟变量也是显著的。从移民密度的回归方程,我们可以估计出,北京的移民密度为0.112。而对于中部地区的小城市来说,如果将城市人均收入设定在它们的样本均值,随着城市就业率的变化(0.505—0.834),移民密度在0.192—0.346之间变动。

五、永久移民:以迁出地为视角

本节我们从迁出地的角度来分析永久移民。基于这一目的,我们将永久移民和农村样本合并。这里我们假定农村样本中没有人拥有城市户口。当估计永久移民在农村出身的人口中的比重时,我们也考虑到了农村样本和城市样本的代表性问题,并对此做了相应调整。①

表3 永久移民、农民、农村出身人口的描述性统计量(%)

个人特征	永久移民	农民	农村出身人口(永久移民+农民)	永久移民占农村出身人口的比例
男性	52.10	52.02	52.06	11.52
女性	47.90	47.98	47.94	11.49
少数民族	3.75	13.96	8.86	3.37
汉族	96.25	86.04	91.15	12.70
党员	32.85	5.67	19.26	42.98
其他	67.15	94.33	80.74	8.47

① 2002年城市人口和农村人口在全国人口中的比例分别为39.09%和60.91%(国家统计局,2005)。而当我们将农村样本和城市样本进行合并后,农村样本量占全部样本量的64.79%,因而我们通过随机抽样增加了城市样本量。而永久移民在全部城市居民中的比例则保持不变。

（续表）

个人特征	永久移民	农民	农村出身人口（永久移民＋农民）	永久移民占农村出身人口的比例
小学及以下	14.47	43.38	28.93	4.26
初　　中	25.77	42.02	33.90	7.55
高　　中	19.49	9.90	14.70	20.77
中　　专	12.49	3.22	7.86	34.08
大专及以上	27.78	1.49	14.64	71.31
年龄均值(岁)	43.45	33.04	34.24	
观测值	4 937	37 969	42 096	11.51

注：样本进行了调整，永久移民的人数从调整前的 4 069 人增加到调整后的 4 937人。

表 3 提供了永久移民、农村居民、所有农村出身的人口的描述性统计量。可以看到，11.5％的农村出身人口为永久移民。除了性别构成比较接近以外，永久移民和留在农村的农民在其他特征上存在着很大的差异。永久移民要比农村居民平均年长 10 岁。永久移民中少数民族的比例较低，只有 3％的农村少数民族成为永久移民，而汉族中的这一比例为 13％。这一较大差异的出现，是因为中国的少数民族大多居住在偏远地区，种种条件的限制在很大程度上降低了他们成为永久移民的可能性。考虑到获得城市户口的一个途径是成为干部，很容易理解党员中的永久移民比例要大大高于非党员。而教育也可以增加获得户口的可能性，28％的永久移民有大学学历，而农民中的这一比例小于 2％。我们的计算表明，71％的具有大学学历的农村出身人口获得了城市户口。

我们通过估计迁移概率模型来分析永久迁移的影响因素。

既然存在多种获得户口的途径，就有可能存在诸多影响因素，而且这些因素可能随着时间地点而改变。然而，我们受到数据的制约。例如，调查数据没有提供被调查者在何处长大成人的信息，我们只知道他们是出身于农村的。因而，我们只能依赖父母亲的有关信息以及相对稳定的个人信息来分析农村居民永久迁移的概率。

我们根据出生时间将样本分为三个子样本。从表 4 的回归结果我们可以看到，在各个子样本中自变量的影响大体是一致的。民族和父母教育水平对成为永久移民的可能性都有很强的影响。父母的党员身份也影响成为永久移民的概率，但是没有教育水平和民族的影响大。性别的系数在多数情况下都不显著。

利用表 4 的回归结果，我们根据一些特征估计了永久迁移的概率。①从估计结果来看，年龄越大，成为永久移民的概率也就越高。概率最低的情形出现在少数民族、出身于低教育水平和非党员父母的家庭。对 1951 年以前和 1972 年以后出生的农村出身人口而言，成为永久移民的概率分别只有 4%和 0.5%。另外一个极端是父母是党员而且受过小学或初中教育的汉族农民。这一情形中，1951 年以前出生的农村出身人口成为永久移民的概率是 69%。

我们现在来比较永久移民和农民在 2002 年的收入状况，以估计迁移到城市所带来的经济收益。农村出身人口除了通过永久迁移来享受城市化的好处之外，也可以选择成为短期流动人口。这两种情况我们都进行了考虑，其中短期流动人口的样本来自第三节提到的暂住户调查。通过对永久移民、短期流动人

---

① 由于篇幅限制，我们没有报告具体的模拟结果。有兴趣的读者请参考 Deng 和 Gustafsson(2006)中表 6。

口以及农民的人均收入的比较①，我们发现，短期流动人口的人均收入通常要高出农民两倍，而永久移民的人均收入则是农民的三倍之多。少数民族农民的收入要低于汉族 34%。然而，收

表 4 永久迁移的概率：logit 模型

出生年份	1972 年以后		1952—1971 年		1951 年以前	
	模型 1	模型 2	模型 1	模型 2	模型 1	模型 2
男性=1，其他=0	−0.175 (0.183)	−0.224 (0.186)	0.062 (0.055)	0.056 (0.055)	−0.061 (0.070)	−0.171** (0.072)
少数民族=1，其他=0	−1.977*** (0.474)	−1.922*** (0.476)	−0.982*** (0.126)	−0.979*** (0.126)	−1.434*** (0.186)	−1.483*** (0.188)
父母是党员=1，其他=0	0.443** (0.213)	0.429** (0.215)	0.702*** (0.063)	0.715*** (0.063)	0.602*** (0.117)	0.790*** (0.121)
父母文化在小学及初中=1，其他=0	2.424*** (0.298)	2.437*** (0.300)	1.811*** (0.058)	1.865*** (0.059)	1.665*** (0.073)	1.730*** (0.076)
父母文化在高中及以上=1，其他=0	6.659*** (1.153)	6.904*** (1.162)	4.195*** (0.349)	4.250*** (0.350)	2.783*** (0.707)	2.732*** (0.749)
自身年龄		1.687 (1.316)		−0.201*** (0.077)		0.188** (0.080)
自身年龄平方		−0.027 (0.024)		0.003*** (0.001)		−0.001 (0.001)
常数项	−3.336*** (0.290)	−29.036 (18.049)	−2.706*** (0.055)	0.861 (1.542)	−1.667*** (0.059)	−9.747*** (2.459)
Pseudo R-squared	0.208 9	0.225 3	0.158 5	0.160 9	0.117 7	0.156 5
观测值	1 100	1 100	11 709	11 709	5 612	5 612

① 收入包括现金收入和实物收入、农业收入（农村）、转移收入等。我们没有列出详细的描述性信息，有兴趣的读者请参考 Deng 和 Gustafsson(2006)中表 7。

入的民族差异在永久移民和短期流动人口之间要小得多。这说明,尽管少数民族身份影响着成为永久移民的可能性,然而,一旦少数民族成为永久移民,他们与汉族永久移民相比,并没有很大的劣势。党员的收入要高于非党员,这一差异在农民和永久移民中比较明显,而在短期流动人口中则不太明显。

在三个群体中,教育与收入都有着或大或小的正向联系。在成年永久移民中,人均收入随着年龄的提高而增加,并在46—50岁达到高峰。在这之后,年龄组之间的收入差异比较小。对短期流动人口和农民而言,年龄组之间收入的差异较为不明显。这说明农民和两类外流者的收入差异跟年龄有很大的相关性。两类外流者和农民的不同特征也可能导致了他们之间的收入差异。

为了测度个人特征对收入差距的贡献,我们做了如下的实验:首先,我们根据年龄组定义了10个子样本。在第一个方程里,我们将人均收入对永久移民和短期流动人口这两个虚拟变量做了回归。这样常数项就代表了不同年龄组农民的收入。在第二个方程里,我们加入一些解释变量,如受教育年限、党员身份。图1给出了永久移民和短期流动人口两个虚拟变量的系数估计值,并显示了农民和两类外流者在调整后的收入差距。①

首先,我们可以发现永久移民较长的教育年限以及更高的政治地位,确实影响着永久移民和农民之间的收入差距。然而,这些差异只能解释一小部分的收入差距。第二,给定教育和党员身份,永久移民和短期流动人口都有较强的经济激励流出农村,因为他们的收入比留在农村高。第三,对于短期流动人口来

① 由于篇幅限制,我们没有报告相应的回归结果。感兴趣的读者请参考Deng和Gustafsson(2006)中表A1。

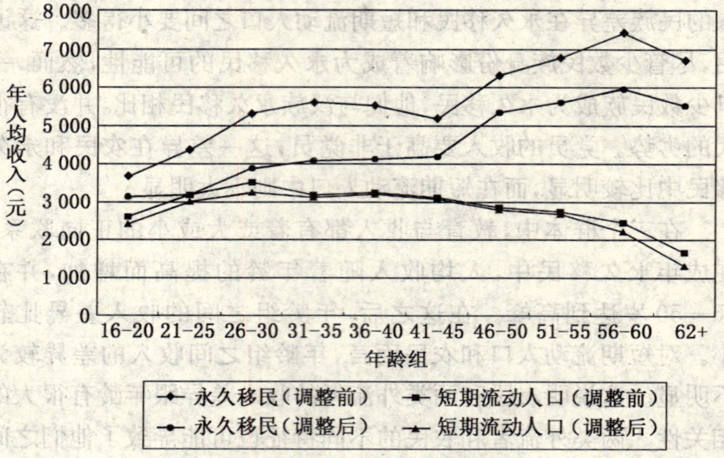

注:根据受教育年限和党员身份进行了调整

图 1　永久移民和短期流动人口与农民的收入差距

说,他们有激励去争取城市户口。这可以从经调整后的永久移民的收入曲线比短期流动人口高得知。短期流动人口与农民的收入差异则在调整后和未经调整时差不多。这说明,农民和短期流动人口在教育和党员身份这些特征上相差无几。我们可以将获得城市户口的经济收益,视为永久移民和短期流动人口在30—60 岁期间(假设趋势不变)的收入差异。经过计算可得出,这一收入差异的总和(假定年贴现率为 5%)是 79 982 元。①当然,户口的全部经济收益还包括更好的社会福利以及退休后所享受到的养老金。

我们可以将这一结果与农民购买户口的现实价格做一个对比。陈金永(2004)给出了 20 世纪 90 年代早期的一些数字。

① 对比 2002 年城市职工的平均工资收入(12 422 元),人们或许能对户口的经济价值有更直观的了解。

1990 年上海市区户口的价格是 81 457 元(2002 年价格),而郊区和郊县的价格分别是 40 729 元和 20 364 元。而在河南省,1992 年户口的价格在 11 249 元和 56 247 元之间变动(2002 年价格)。户口的价格普遍低于农民获得户口的经济收益,因此城市化的收益被地方政府与农民所分享了。

六、迁移目的地:永久移民和城市原住民的就业概率和工资收入差异

在本节和下一节中,我们转而研究永久移民在城市劳动力市场上的表现,并主要关注经济活动人口(16—60 岁)的收入。我们首先来比较永久移民和城市原住民的个人特征。①尽管永久移民和城市原住民的平均教育年限都为 11 年,然而永久移民教育水平的分布更为不均。相比于他们父母亲的教育水平,年轻一代的教育水平提高得非常快。城市原住民和永久移民的民族构成基本一样。永久移民总体上比原住民年长两岁。部分地基于这一原因,永久移民中已婚者的比例也较高。既然党员身份对于获得城市户口有正向影响,也就很容易理解永久移民中党员的比例要高于原住民这一现象。65%的原住民处于就业状态,而永久移民的这一比例是 73%,两者相差 8 个百分点。我们接下来分析,永久移民和城市原住民在就业概率上的差异是否是由个人特征的差异以及地区差异导致的。

我们通过 logit 模型来估计所有城市居民的就业概率。自变量包括受教育年限、婚姻状况、政治面貌、民族、年龄以及是否是永久移民这一虚拟变量。回归方程还包括了城市虚拟变量。

① 由于篇幅限制,我们没有报告具体的描述性统计量。感兴趣的读者请参考 Deng 和 Gustafsson(2006)中表 8。

同时我们也分性别估计了方程。正如所预期的，估计结果显示(见表5)，就业概率与教育水平、党员身份正相关。对于男性而言，已婚对工作有正向的作用；但对于女性而言其作用却是负的。民族变量的系数估计值的t值较低。可以看到，是否是永久移民虚拟变量的估计值在所有方程都是正的，而且在统计上高度显著。图2给出了具有典型特征的男性和女性的就业概率，并在永久移民和城市原住民之间进行了区分。永久移民的就业概率在各个年龄组都要高于城市原住民，男性的就业概率也要高于女性。男女性之间在就业概率上的差异随着年龄的增大而缩小，到临近退休时又开始扩大。永久移民和城市原住民在就业概率上的差异也经历了一个先缩小后扩大的变动过程。

表5 就业率的logit模型估计

	男女性混合样本	男性子样本	女性子样本
男性＝1，其他＝0	1.198*** (0.048)		
受教育年限	0.205*** (0.009)	0.146*** (0.014)	0.235*** (0.013)
已婚＝1，其他＝0	0.329*** (0.093)	0.632*** (0.157)	−0.338*** (0.126)
党员＝1，其他＝0	0.648*** (0.065)	0.454*** (0.094)	0.763*** (0.095)
汉族＝1，其他＝0	−0.047 (0.126)	0.011 (0.192)	−0.061 (0.172)
年龄	0.788*** (0.019)	0.776*** (0.027)	0.919*** (0.029)

（续表）

	男女性混合样本	男性子样本	女性子样本
年龄平方	−0.010*** (0.000 2)	−0.010*** (0.000 3)	−0.012*** (0.000 4)
永久移民＝1，其他＝0	0.346*** (0.062)	0.447*** (0.101)	0.293*** (0.083)
常数项	−15.604*** (0.435)	−14.515*** (0.643)	−16.882*** (0.628)
Pseudo R^2	0.340 1	0.370 3	0.336 5
Log Likelihood	−6 282.62	−2 595.55	−3 423.05
预测准确率(%)	80.78	85.01	78.71
观测值	14 972	7 370	7 602

注：城市虚拟变量估计结果未列出。括号内是标准误。以下表6同。

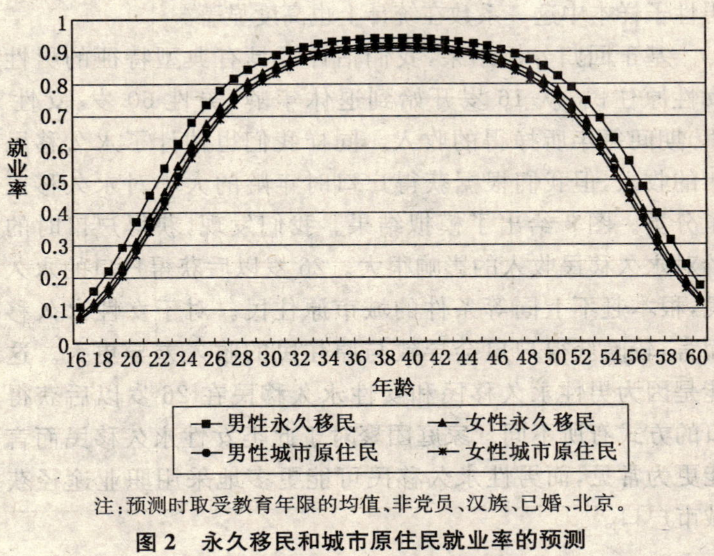

注：预测时取受教育年限的均值、非党员、汉族、已婚、北京。

图2　永久移民和城市原住民就业率的预测

接下来，我们采用不同的模型设定形式对对数小时工资进行回归。表 6 报告了回归结果。女性的教育收益率要高于男性，而永久移民和原住民之间的教育收益率没有什么差异。男性的教育收益率为 7%，而女性的教育收益率为 9%。与先前研究的较低估计相比，这一结果显示了中国城镇地区的教育收益率正在逐渐攀升(Zhang et al.，2005)。正如以前的研究所表明的，党员身份对于收入的影响是正的，尽管党员身份影响收入的机制并不十分显而易见。男性对收入也有正的影响。从我们的估计结果来看，民族身份在城市对收入没有影响。

如果将永久移民和原住民混合成一个样本，我们发现永久移民这一虚拟变量对收入有正的影响(8%)，而且是统计上高度显著的。然而，这一作用在女性样本中则不明显。对于男性和女性而言，获城市户口后的年数，对收入都有显著的正向作用。获城市户口后的年数的平方项的系数估计值则是负的，而且在男性子样本中这一系数在统计上也高度显著。

基于回归分析结果，我们估计了具有典型特征的男性和女性原住民，从 16 岁开始到退休年龄(男性 60 岁、女性 55 岁)期间每年所挣得的收入。同样我们也估计了永久移民每年的收入，但我们根据获得户口时年龄的大小对永久移民做了分类。图 3 给出了模拟结果。我们发现，获得户口时的年龄对永久移民收入的影响很大。26 岁以后获得户口的永久移民，根本赶不上同等条件的城市原住民。对于女性永久移民而言，较晚获得户口会导致与原住民的收入差异更大。这可能是因为男性永久移民和女性永久移民在 26 岁以后获得户口的方式有所不同。家庭团聚对于此类女性永久移民而言可能更为常见，而男性永久移民可能更多地采用职业途径获得城市户口。

表 6　对数小时工资的估计结果

	城市居民混合样本			城市原住民	永久移民	永久移民		
	男性和女性	男性	女性			男性和女性	男性	女性
男性=1,其他=0	0.131*** (0.012)			0.129*** (0.014)	0.134*** (0.026)	0.116*** (0.026)		
受教育年限	0.078*** (0.002)	0.070*** (0.003)	0.090*** (0.004)	0.079*** (0.003)	0.076*** (0.004)	0.074*** (0.004)	0.064*** (0.005)	0.085*** (0.008)
已婚=1,其他=0	0.104*** (0.025)	0.129*** (0.035)	0.080** (0.036)	0.105*** (0.028)	0.139** (0.055)	0.165*** (0.055)	0.235*** (0.081)	0.103 (0.081)
党员=1,其他=0	0.165*** (0.015)	0.181*** (0.018)	0.141*** (0.025)	0.146*** (0.017)	0.201*** (0.029)	0.194*** (0.029)	0.226*** (0.034)	0.148*** (0.053)
汉族=1,其他=0	0.001 (0.033)	−0.003 (0.042)	0.030 (0.054)	0.028 (0.038)	−0.102 (0.070)	−0.094 (0.070)	−0.049 (0.092)	−0.080 (0.112)
年　龄	0.045*** (0.005)	0.049*** (0.007)	0.042*** (0.009)	0.042*** (0.006)	0.048*** (0.011)	0.036*** (0.012)	0.031** (0.016)	0.057*** (0.021)
年龄平方	−0.000 4*** (0.000 1)	−0.000 5*** (0.000 1)	−0.000 4*** (0.000 1)	−0.000 4*** (0.000 1)	−0.000 5*** (0.000 1)	−0.000 4** (0.000 1)	−0.000 3 (0.000 2)	−0.001** (0.000 3)

（续表）

	城市居民混合样本			城市原住民	永久移民	永久移民		
	男性和女性	男性	女性			男性和女性	男性	女性
永久移民=1，其他=0	0.058*** (0.015)	0.080*** (0.020)	0.037 (0.024)					
获城市户口后的年数						0.018*** (0.005)	0.014** (0.007)	0.018** (0.007)
获城市户口后的年数的平方项						−0.000 3*** (0.000 1)	−0.000 2* (0.000 1)	−0.000 2 (0.000 1)
常数项	−0.259** (0.127)	−0.136 (0.169)	−0.336* (0.201)	−0.257* (0.143)	0.068 (0.338)	0.135 (0.341)	0.209 (0.504)	−0.233 (0.520)
Adjusted R^2	0.327 1	0.322 6	0.314 7	0.321 3	0.351 9	0.357 4	0.351 3	0.322
观测值	9 845	5 493	4 352	7 501	2 344	2 344	1 381	963

注：因变量是对数小时工资。

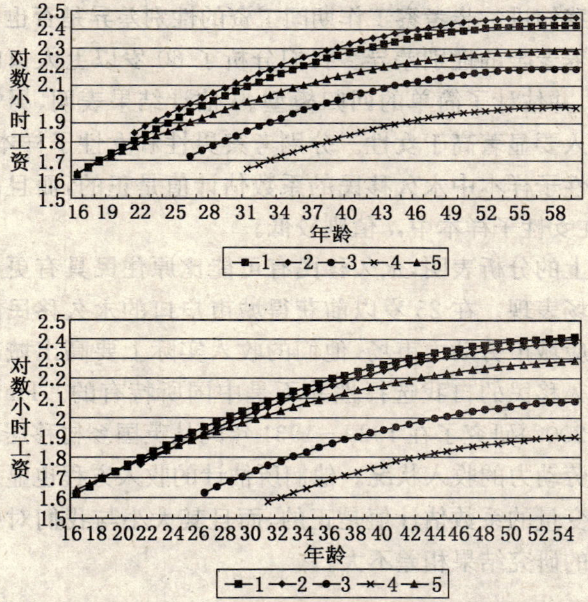

图 3　城市原住民和永久移民的年龄—对数小时工资曲线

注：预测变量取值为受教育年限的均值、汉族、党员、已婚、北京。(1)20 岁以前获得户口的永久移民；(2)21—25 岁之间获得户口的永久移民；(3)26—30 岁之间获得户口的永久移民；(4)31 岁之后获得户口的永久移民；(5)城市原住民。

与此相反，在较年轻时获得户口的永久移民的收入要高于城市原住民。例如，在 21 岁到 25 岁之间获得户口的女性移民在 40 岁时的收入要高出同等年龄的原住民 7%。而在 25 岁之前获得户口的男性移民与城市原住民之间的收入差异更大。例如，在 21 岁和 25 岁之间获得户口的男性移民在 40 岁时的收入要高出同等年龄的原住民 16%。

我们发现获得户口时的年龄对永久移民在城市劳动力市场上的表现有重要影响，这与 Liu(2005)利用本课题组 1995 年调查数据所得到的分析结论是一致的。我们还发现了性别差异的存在。我们进一步考察工作期间工资的性别差异是否也意味着退休后养老金的性别差异。我们分析了 60 岁以上人口的养老金收入，并估计了简单的回归模型。①估计结果表明，男性的养老金收入要显著高于女性。分别考察男性和女性子样本，我们发现男性子样本中永久移民的系数估计值是正的，而且高度显著，但在女性子样本中，t 值则较低。

以上的分析表明，永久移民有可能比原住民具有更好的劳动力市场表现。在 25 岁以前获得城市户口的永久移民能够很好地适应城市劳动力市场，他们的收入实际上要高出城市原住民。永久移民的自我选择性并不是中国所特有的。Hatton 和 Bailey(2002)研究了在 1929—1931 年间从英国乡村移居到伦敦的男性劳动力的收入状况。他们所估计的收入方程也显示了移民虚拟变量的系数估计值是正的，而且其大小与我们对中国永久移民的研究结果相差不大。②

七、获取户口的不同途径与劳动力市场表现

本节我们将区分通过不同途径获得户口的永久移民，并考察他们在城市劳动力市场上的不同表现。我们将获得城市户口的途径区分为职业途径以及非职业途径。前者包括接受良好教育、提干、参军等，后者则包括土地征用、购买城市商品房、直接

① 为了节约篇幅，这里没有报告估计结果。感兴趣的读者请参考 Deng 和 Gustafsson(2006)中表 A2。

② 另外一个有意思的对比是，内地移民在香港劳动力市场上的表现。Liu 等(2004)发现内地移民的收入要比香港居民低很多，尤其是对那些刚移居香港的内地劳动力而言。然而，随着在香港居住时间的延长，内地移民和香港居民之间的收入差异逐渐变小。而对那些较年轻时移居香港的内地移民而言，他们与香港居民的收入差异微乎其微。

购买户口等。职业途径通常意味着永久移民在劳动力市场的状况较好，能够成为白领，而对于那些通过非职业途径获得户口的永久移民而言，则不一定如此。

城镇住户调查询问了人们获取户口的途径。在16—60岁的永久移民中，1 117人通过职业途径获得户口，210人通过非职业途径获得户口。我们将机关、企事业单位负责人、专业技术人员、办事人员等工作视为白领工种。表7显示，通过职业途径获得户口的永久移民中，82%的人从事白领工作，而通过非职业途径获得户口的永久移民中，只有29%的人从事白领工作。

表7　通过职业途径和非职业途径取得户口的永久移民的特征

	通过职业途径获得户口			通过非职业途径获得户口		
	白领	蓝领	白领和蓝领	白领	蓝领	白领和蓝领
男性(%)	72.8	67.7	71.9	44.4	47.4	46.6
汉族(%)	94.0	96.5	94.4	100.00	98.7	99.1
党员(%)	62.1	32.8	56.9	25.4	7.1	12.3
已婚(%)	97.1	96.0	96.9	88.9	87.8	88.1
年龄	41.3	40.2	41.1	37.7	38.5	38.3
受教育年限	13.5	11.2	13.08	11.4	9.1	9.8
获城市户口后的年数	21.1	20.8	21.1	16.1	13.4	14.1
家庭规模	3.1	3.2	3.2	3.5	3.40	3.4
年工作小时	2 120	2 288	2 150	2 105	2 542	2 417
年工资收入	14 828	10 592	14 065	14 300	8 816	10 390
对数小时工资	1.8	1.4	1.8	1.8	1.0	1.2
观测值	916	201	1 117	63	156	219
样本构成	82.0%	18.0%	100%	28.8%	71.2%	100%

通过职业途径取得户口的永久移民大多是男性、党员、受到较好教育者。他们在城市生活的时间也比通过非职业途径取得户口的永久移民长。而通过非职业途径取得户口的永久移民的工资收入要比通过职业途径取得户口的永久移民低 26%。我们感兴趣的是，这一收入差异在多大程度上，可以解释为两类永久移民之间的工种分割。

利用 Brown 等(1980)的方法，我们可以将这两类移民之间的工资收入差异分解为可解释的工种内差异、不可解释的工种内差异、可解释的工种间差异、不可解释的工种间差异。因而，我们能够得知两类永久移民从事工种的不同，在多大程度上导致了两者之间的收入差异。而工种内差异则可以显示这两类永久移民在特定工种内部的工资收入差距。然而，囿于观测值较少，我们不得不将相关工种合并成白领和蓝领两大类。这有可能影响到我们的分析结果，也有可能使得很大一部分差异不能得到解释。

我们首先估计了一个 logit 模型，来分析两类移民工种选择的概率。我们也对从事不同工种的两类永久移民分别估计了工资收入方程。[①]回归结果表明，受教育年限和党员身份是工种选择的重要决定因素，这对两类移民都是如此。而年龄和年龄的平方项对工种选择的作用，只对通过职业途径获得户口的永久移民而言是显著的。

表 8 给出了分解结果，我们发现两类永久移民的收入差异的 40%可以被工种间的差异解释，而 60%则可以被工种内的差异解释。此外，一半的收入差异可以被特征的差异解释，而另一半则无法解释。不可解释部分中，工种内部分(35%)要高出工

---

① 由于篇幅限制，我们没有报告相应的回归结果。感兴趣的读者请参考 Deng 和 Gustafsson(2006)中表 A3。

种间部分(16%),这说明了,工种内的不平等对待比在获取工种方面的歧视更加严重。与此相对照的是,可解释部分中工种内和工种间的贡献相差不大。

表 8　对两类永久移民收入差距的 Brown 分解结果

	对数小时工资	比例(%)
全部收入差距	0.580 0	100
工种内差距	0.346 6	59.76
可解释部分	0.144 2	24.86
不可解释部分	0.202 4	34.90
工种间差距	0.234 4	40.24
可解释部分	0.139 6	24.07
不可解释部分	0.093 8	16.17
全部可解释部分	0.283 8	48.93
全部不可解释部分	0.296 2	51.37

本节的分析表明,永久移民的收入与他们获取户口的方式相关。通过职业途径获取户口的永久移民比通过非职业途径获得户口的永久移民的收入要高得多。收入差异的一半可以由特征的差异得到解释,而另一半则可以归因于他们在劳动力市场上所受到的不平等对待。工种间的差别存在,但是工种内的差别更大。

八、结　论

本文利用 2002 年的大样本住户调查数据,研究了出身农村但随后移居城市而且持有城市户口的永久移民。我们估计了永久移民的数量，并分析了他们的基本特征，同时我们对永久移民与留在农村的农民以及城市中的短期流动人口进行了比较。我们还分析了永久移民和城市原住民在城市劳动力市场上的表现。

根据我们的估计，永久移民大约有1亿人之多，占城市居民的20%。这意味着永久移民的规模与城市中的短期流动人口相差无几。但相比于永久移民，短期流动人口吸引了研究者更多的目光。按出生组区分，在成年于改革开放后的人群中，永久移民在城市居民中的比例最高。而在成年于“文革”期间的人群中，永久移民占城市居民的比例最低。大部分永久移民居住在小城市、就业率高的城市以及中部地区。

与农民相比，永久移民的收入要高得多。教育程度和党员身份能够解释两者之间的收入差异的一部分，但是大部分的收入差异不能得到解释。这说明人们有非常强的激励往城市迁移。我们还发现，没有城市户口的短期流动人口的收入也比农民高。然而，短期流动人口的收入要低于永久移民，这意味着他们也有很强的激励去争取城市户口。

永久移民的经济状况与城市原住民不相上下。实际上，永久移民的就业率还要高于城市原住民。在25岁以前得到城市户口的永久移民在劳动力市场的表现非常好，他们的收入反而还要高出城市原住民。而在退休后，男性永久移民的养老金也要高于城市原住民。但对于26岁以后获得城市户口的永久移民而言，他们的经济状况要差于城市原住民。

永久移民可以通过职业途径和非职业途径取得城市户口，我们可以据此对永久移民进行分类。职业途径包括接受较长时间的教育、提干、参军等，而非职业途径则包括土地征用、购买商品房、直接购买户口等。职业途径通常意味着永久移民在城市劳动力市场中处于一个比较有利的地位，他们的收入也比通过非职业途径取得户口的永久移民高。两类移民之间的收入差异部分地可以由他们之间的特征差异得以解释。然而，这两类移民在劳动力市场上也受到了不平等对待。这一不平等对待主要是来自工种内的差别，而工种之间的差别程度较低。

与西方发达国家一样，中国的城镇地区也面临着外来人口持续涌入的压力。然而，对西方发达国家而言，这些外来人口大都不是本国公民。而在中国的情形里，这些外来人口大都是本国公民，只不过他们持有不同类型的户口而已。如何处理外来人口的户口问题，是中国政府当前和今后所面临的挑战。如果不给予外来人口与城市人口相同的权利，可能会出现某种不和谐的社会音符。然而，如果过快放松对城市户口的控制或者简单地取消户口制度，那么外来人口会快速涌入城市，这反过来又极易导致社会冲突。

参考文献

蔡昉、都阳、王美艳：《户口制度和劳动力市场保护》，《经济研究》2001年第12期。

陈金永：《中国户籍制度改革和城乡人口迁移》，《中国劳动经济学》2004年第1期。

国家统计局：《中国统计年鉴2005》，中国统计出版社2005年版。

国务院研究室：《中国农民工调研报告》，中国言实出版社2006年版。

陆益龙：《1949年以后的中国户籍制度》，《北京大学学报》2002年第2期。

张庆五：《户口登记常识》，法律出版社1983年版。

Brown, Radall S., Moon, Marilyn, and Zoloth, Barbara S., 1980, "Incorporating Occupational Attainment in Studies of Male-Female Earnings Differentials", *Journal of Human Resources*, 15,1:3—28.

Chan, Kam King, 1994, *Cities with Invisible Walls*, Hong Kong: Oxford University Press.

Chan, Kam Wing and Li Zhang, 1999, "The Hukou System and Rural-Urban Migration in China: Processes and Changes", *China Quarterly*: 818—855.

Cheng, Tiejun and Selden, Mark, 1994, "The Origins and Social Conzequences of China's *Hukou System*", *China Quarterly*:644—668.

Deng, Quheng and Björn Gustafsson, 2006, "China's Lesser Known Migrants", IZA Discussion Paper No. 2152.

Hatton, Timothy, J. and Bailey, Roy, E. , 2002, "Natives and Migrants in the London Labour Market, 1929—1931", *Journal of Population Economics*, 15(1):59—81.

Knight, John and Song, Lina, 1999, *The Rural-Urban Divide*, *Economic Disparities and Ineractions in China*, Oxford: Oxford University Press.

Li, Shi, Luo Chuliang, Wei Zhong and Yue Ximing, 2007, "Appendix-The 1995 and 2002 Household Surveys: Sampling Methods and Data Description", in Gustafsson, Li and Sicular ed. , *Inequality and Public Policy*, Cambridge University Press, forthcoming.

Liu, Park-Wang, Zhang, Junsen, Chong, Shu-Chen, 2004, "Occupational Segregation and Wage Differentials between Natives and Immigrants: Evidence from Hong Kong", *Journal of Development Economics*, 73:395—413.

Liu, Zhiqiang, 2005, "Institution and Inequality: The *Hukou* System in China", *Journal of Comparative Economics*, 33:133—157.

Meng, Xin and Zhang, Junsen, 2001, "The Two-Tier Labour Market in Urban China. Occupational Segregation and Wage Differentials between Urban Residents and Rural Migrants in Shanghai", *Journal of Comparative Economics*, 29:485—504.

Wang Fei-Ling, 2004, "Reforming Migrant Control and New Targeted

People: China's Hukou System in the 2000s", *China Quarterly*: 115—132.

Wong, Linda and Huen Wai-Po, 1998, "Reforming the Household Registration System: A Preliminary Glimpse of the Blue Chop Household Registration System in Shanghai and Shenzhen", *International Migration Review*, Vol. 32, No. 4:974—994.

Wu, Xiaogang and Treiman, Donald, J., 2004, "The Household Registration System and Social Stratification in China: 1955—1996", *Demography*, 41(2):363—384.

Zhang, Junsen, Zhao, Yaohui, Park, Albert and Song, Xiaoqing, 2005, "Economic Returns to Schooling in Urbna China", *Journal of Comparative Economics*, 33:730—752.

Zhao, Yaohui, 2000, "Rural-to-Urban Labour Migration in China: The Past and the Present", in Loraine A. West and Yaohui Zhao ed., *Rural Labour Flows in China*, Institute of East Asian Studies, University of California, Berkeley.

(原载《经济研究》2007 年第 4 期)

计量经济学的地位、作用和局限*

洪永淼

（厦门大学王亚南经济研究院）

一、引　言

计量经济学已经成为现代经济学和管理学教育必不可少的一部分，它和微观经济学与宏观经济学一起构成了中国高校经济管理类本科生和研究生必修的三门经济学核心理论课程，并在中国经济学界受到越来越广泛的关注。然而，中国计量经济学的发展落后于微观经济学和宏观经济学。中国经济学界对计量经济学这一现代经济学核心课程存在着一些认识上的误区。比如，不少人认为计量经济学仅仅是经济学实证研究的技术分析工具，没有意识到计量经济学作为经济学研究基本方法论的重要性；很多人不了解计量经济学与数学、数理经济学、数理统

* 本文系根据作者在康奈尔大学经济学系、清华大学经济管理学院、上海交通大学安泰经济管理学院、山东大学经济研究中心以及厦门大学王亚南经济研究院讲授高级计量经济学课程的基础上总结而成的，并在教育部 2006 年“计量经济学与金融计量学暑期学校”和上海社会科学院学术研讨会上宣读过。本文得到了中国自然科学基金会海外杰出青年基金“新的金融计量模型及其应用研究”项目和厦门大学与教育部“长江学者奖励计划”的资助。作者感谢匿名审稿人以及蔡宗武、陈彬、段琳琳、郭晔、贾新明、李宝良、宋江红、王翼、许有淑、赵向琴和朱平芳等老师与同学的仔细阅读以及十分有益的建议。

计学以及经济统计学之间的区别，将计量经济学等同于应用数学或应用统计学，认为计量经济学只不过是一个经济数学模型加上一个随机扰动项而已。还有，实证研究中，经常不注意计量经济学方法与工具所适用的范围和前提条件，不恰当地将它们应用于其前提条件明显不成立的经济数据或经济问题，从而得出错误的结论。所有这些认识上的偏差，正妨碍着计量经济学的应用、推广和发展。本文的目的，是从方法论的角度出发，阐述计量经济学在经济学研究中的地位、作用以及局限性，从而使大家对计量经济学作为现代经济学研究基本方法论的重要性和局限性，有一个比较清晰的认识。

本文首先从现代经济学的数量分析特征出发，阐述计量经济学在现代经济学中的地位和作用；然后，通过比较计量经济学与数理经济学、数理统计学和经济统计学之间的差别，强调计量经济学作为经济学研究基本方法论的重要性；接着，通过经济学和金融学中具有代表性的重要实例，具体详细地说明计量经济学方法和工具的应用，以及在应用时需要注意的若干问题。这些例子包括消费函数和乘数效应，理性预期和资产定价，规模报酬不变，转型经济改革成效评估，有效市场假说，市场风险和波动聚集，以及劳动经济学和金融学的久期分析(duration analysis)，等等。这些实例说明了计量经济学如何用于经济结构分析和重要结构参数估计，如何用于检验经济理论和发展经济理论，如何进行经济行为分析和逻辑分析，从而采用正确的计量经济学方法并正确地陈述结论，以及如何针对经济数据的特点和具体问题的本质，选择合适的计量经济学模型和工具。同时，还强调了在使用计量经济学模型进行结构分析时正确设定理论模型的重要性，以及计量经济学在非传统领域也有广泛的应用。最后，本文将阐述由经济数据的非实验性和经济结构的时变性所导致的计量经济学分析的局限性。

二、计量经济学的地位

现代市场经济充满不确定性和风险，一个经济人做出一项决策后，其后果往往无法预知。现代经济学就是研究在充满不确定性因素的条件下如何公平而有效地配置有限资源。现代经济学可大致分为四个领域：宏观经济学、微观经济学、金融经济学和计量经济学。其中，宏观经济学、微观经济学和计量经济学已经成为中国高校经济类本科生和研究生必修的三门核心经济理论课程。同大多数的自然科学学科一样，现代经济学研究的一般方法可归纳为以下几个步骤：

第一，收集数据和总结经验特征事实（empirical stylized facts）。经验特征事实一般从观察到的经济数据中提炼出来。比如，微观经济学中著名的恩格尔曲线（Engel's curve）就是一个经验特征事实，它刻画家庭生活用品支出占总收入的比例随着家庭总收入的上升而递减；宏观经济学中一个著名的经验特征事实是菲利普斯曲线（Phillips curve），它描述一个经济的失业率和通货膨胀率之间的负相关关系（后来又出现了“高失业高通胀”和“低失业低通胀”的正相关现象）；还有，金融市场的波动常常会交替出现，大波动后通常会紧跟着另一个大波动，而小波动后会紧跟另一个小波动，这就是金融学中有名的经验特征事实——市场波动聚集（volatility clustering）。经验特征事实是经济学研究的出发点，比如，时间序列计量经济学中的单位根（unit root）和协整（cointegration）理论，就是基于 Nelson 和 Plossor（1982）在实证研究中发现大多数宏观经济时间序列都是单位根过程这一经验特征事实而发展起来的。

第二，建立经济理论或模型。找到经验特征事实以后，经济学家会建立经济理论或模型，以解释这些经验特征事实。这一阶段的关键是建立合适的经济数学模型。

第三，实证检验。这一步的工作需要把经济理论或模型转化为可用数据检验的计量经济模型。经济理论或模型通常只指出经济变量之间的因果关系和数量关系，没有给出确切的函数形式。从经济数学模型到计量经济模型的转化过程中，需要对函数形式做出假设，然后利用观测到的数据，估计未知参数值，并进一步验证计量经济模型的设定是否正确。

第四，应用。计量经济模型通过实证检验后，可用来检验经济理论或经济假说的正确性，预测未来经济的变动趋势以及提供政策建议。

可以看出，对经济理论进行数学建模和对经济现象进行实证分析已成为现代经济学的两个基本分析方法。事实上，这是几代经济学家努力使经济学成为像自然科学（如物理学）那样的一门科学的必然结果。在北美，经济学博士生教育非常注重包括数学建模和实证研究的数量分析训练。

数学建模在经济学中具有十分重要的作用。有很多方法，诸如图形描绘和文字论述等，都可用来描述经济理论。但是，任何经济理论如果可用数学工具来表述，就能够确保其逻辑的一致性和正确性。正如马克思所指出的，在一门学科中能够使用数学是该学科成熟的重要标志。

在经济学中使用数学已有很长一段历史。古诺（Cournot，1838）撰写的《财富论中的数学原理》被认为是最早在经济分析中使用数学的著作之一。“边际革命”（marginal revolution）是经济学发展的一个重要里程碑，尽管它当时没有使用数学工具，但后来经济学家发现，边际效应、边际产出和边际成本等概念，与微积分中的导数概念相对应。数理经济学家瓦尔拉斯(Walras, 1874)在提出一般均衡理论时,使用了大量的数学工具;冯·诺依曼和摩根斯坦恩(Von Neumann and Morgenstern, 1944)提出的博弈论,起源于数学的一个分支,博弈论现已成为微观经济学的重要基石。

在经济学研究中使用数学有几个重要作用:

第一,数学能精确简洁地刻画经济理论的最重要本质。例如,凯恩斯(Keynes, 1936)提出的宏观经济学理论,主要研究经济总量(比如国民生产总值、消费、失业、通货膨胀、利率、汇率等)之间的关系,这一理论可以简要地用如下两个等式来表述(封闭经济假设):

$$\begin{cases}\text{国民收入恒等式:} Y = C + I + G \\ \text{消费函数:} C = \alpha + \beta Y\end{cases}$$

其中,Y 表示收入,C 表示消费,I 表示私人投资,G 表示政府支出,参数 α 表示维持生存的最低消费,参数 β 表示边际消费倾向。若我们用国民收入恒等式减去消费函数,整理后求偏导,可以得到政府支出的乘数效应(即政府增加公共开支一元钱,最终可增加多少元 GDP):

$$\frac{\partial Y}{\partial G} = \frac{1}{1-\beta}$$

凯恩斯理论的基本思想可以用上述两个或三个数学等式来表述。

第二,经济学中复杂的逻辑分析可通过数学工具得到大大简化。经济学入门课程里,常常通过文字和图表描述的方式进行分析,既直观又浅显易懂。然而,文字或图表对复杂的经济分析往往无能为力。例如,在均衡分析中,局部均衡分析可用一个二维坐标系中两条曲线的交点来表示均衡点，这两条曲线分别是需求曲线和供给曲线。然而，在更为复杂的一般均衡分析中，图表显然无能为力，因为涉及很多商品。一般均衡理论是经济学中的一个基本理论，它研究在竞争性市场经济中，市场力量能否推动相互联系的诸多产品和服务市场同时达到均衡。具体地说，假设有 n 种商品，第 i 种商品的需求为 $D_i(P)$，供给为 $S_i(P)$，n 种商品的价格向量为 $P=(p_1, p_2, \cdots, p_n)$。一般均衡分析就是研究是否存在一个能使市场出清的价格向量 P^*，满足 $D_i(P^*)=S_i(P^*)$，$i=1, \cdots, n$。这个问题看似比较简单，却很难找到一个有效解，因为需求函数和供给函数一般不是线性的。瓦尔拉斯没能解决这一问题。许多年以后，阿罗(Arrow)和德布鲁(Debreu)应用数学的不动点定理(fixed point theorem)，严格证明了均衡价格向量的存在。可见，在一般均衡理论的发展过程中，数学起了至关重要的作用。

第三，数学建模是经济理论实证化的必经之路。我们生活在一个数字时代，许多经济和金融现象都体现为数据。我们只有把经济理论"数字化"，才能把理论和数据联系起来，才能验证经济理论能否解释经济现实。为此，需要把经济理论转化成可以检验的数学模型，进而用观察到的数据对该模型进行估计和检验，并以模型分析实际问题。

现代经济学的另一个主要特征是实证分析。在北美，绝大部分经济金融学术研究均是实证研究。为什么实证分析非常重要呢？一个重要原因是，使用数学尽管可确保理论本身的逻辑一致性和正确性，却不能保证经济学成为一门真正的科学。即使数学推导准确无误，如果经济理论的基本假设不正确，或不切合实际，那么它在实践上将毫无用处。这种情况并不少见。作为一门科学，经济理论必须与实践相结合并保持一致，也只有这样，经济理论才能够解释过去的经济事件，预测未来的经济发展趋势。

那么，如何验证经济理论是否可以解释现实呢？实际上，几乎不可能或很难用经济数据检验经济理论的前提假设是否正确。但是，我们可以通过考察经济理论的推论与观测到的数据之间是否一致来检验。在经济学发展的早期阶段，实证研究通常是使用案例分析或间接验证的方法。比如，亚当·斯密在《国富论》中就是用案例分析方法来解释专业化分工的优势所在。今天，简单的案例分析方法仍然有用，但只限于实证研究的辅助性探索性分析，因为其精确性常常受到质疑，特别是当经济现象比较复杂，而获得的数据又很有限的时候，严格的实证分析需要使用计量经济学方法。

计量经济学在过去的几十年中发展非常迅速，主要有以下几个原因。第一，如上所述，经济理论需要实证检验；第二，高质量经济数据的获得已逐渐变得相对容易；第三，计算技术的发展使得数据处理的成本越来越低，计算机升级的速度远远快于经济数据积累的速度。

尽管在绝大多数的计量经济学文献中没有明确论述，现代计量经济学实际上是建立在以下基本公理之上的：

公理1：任何经济系统都可以看作是服从一定概率分布的随机过程(stochastic process)。

公理2：任何经济现象(经济数据)都可以看作是这个随机数据生成过程(data generating process)的实现(realizations)。

我们无法验证这两个公理。它们是很大一部分计量经济学家和经济学家对经济学的基本观点和理念。并不是所有的经济学家，甚至不是所有的计量经济学家都同意这些看法。比如，有一些经济学家把经济系统看作是非随机的混沌过程(chaotic process),经济现象是由该混沌过程产生的一些拟随机数。然而,Granger 等(1993)和 Lucas(1977)等大多数经济学家和计量经济学家都认为经济系统中存在大量的不确定性,随机分析方法优于非随机分析方法。比如,萨缪尔森(Samuelson, 1939)提出了其著名的乘数—加速数模型,用一个非随机的二阶差分方程来刻画总产出。在一定的参数范围内,这个差分方程可以产生一定的周期,该周期为常周期,有固定的时长。毫无疑问,这个模型在描述宏观经济波动方面颇有建树。但是,随机结构更能真实地反映经济的周期行为,因为任何一个经济的经济周期都不会是均匀发生的。Frisch(1933)论证了存在一个能把互不相关的随机扰动变量合成随机的具有不均匀周期行为的结构传播机制(structural propagation mechanism)。尽管不是所有的不确定性都能用概率论很好地刻画,但概率论是描述不确定性最好的数量工具。随机经济系统的概率规律可以被看作为"经济运行规律"(law of economic motions)。计量经济学的主要任务就是,用观测到的经济数据,以经济理论为指导,使用计量经济学方法和工具,构建合适的计量经济模型,揭示经济运行规律,并用以验证经济理论或经济假说以及指导经济实践。

上述计量经济学公理表明,我们不可能精确地描述经济变量之间的数量关系。任何经济模型都不能囊括经济中各种各样的随机因素,任何点预测(point forecast)都不可能完全精确。因此,我们只能用观测到的数据推断经济系统中的概率规律,而不是去确定经济变量之间精确的函数关系。在进行计量经济建模时,经济理论起着非常重要的指导作用,特别是确定重要的经济变量及解释它们之间的因果关系。经济理论或经济假说常常可表述为对经济系统的概率规律的约束条件,通过检验这些约束条件的有效性，我们就可以验证经济理论或经济假说是否正确。但是，计量经济建模不能仅仅依靠经济理论的指导。数理统计知识、经济统计知识、经济数据特点、实证研究经验、研究目的等，也起着重要的作用，不可缺少。

三、计量经济学与数理经济学、数理统计学及经济统计学的区别

尽管计量经济学是经济学研究的一种基本数量分析方法，但它和数学、数理经济学、数理统计学以及经济统计学之间有本质区别。首先，在经济学研究中，计量经济学和数学的作用不同。数理经济学家的主要任务是用数学工具研究经济理论问题并将经济理论表述为严谨的数学模型形式，而不必考虑经济理论的实证问题。经济学家常常先有一些概念、直觉、想法，并通过简单逻辑分析得到一些初步结论，但是这些结论是否正确或者在什么条件下成立，需要用数学这一最严谨的逻辑工具来论证。数学的使用可排除一些似是而非的观点或结论。然而，数学的推导过程正确并不能保证经济理论可以解释经济现实。要检验经济理论是否可以解释经济现实，需计量经济学的方法和工具。同自然科学的发展一样，经济理论的发展经历了从推翻不能解释最新经验特征事实的现有经济理论，到提出能解释最新经验特征事实的新经济理论这样一个不断重复、不断上升、不断完善的创新过程。在这个过程中，计量经济学起到了关键的作用。不存在绝对正确和恒久有效的经济理论。任何经济理论都只是相对真理，只能在特定的历史阶段解释某些经济现实，在一定时期内与相应的历史数据相吻合。当人们利用现有的数据来检验时，一些经济理论可能不会被拒绝。若现有的数据十分

有限，有可能出现多个不同甚至是相互矛盾的经济理论或模型同时并存的情形。但随着新数据的产生，现有的理论，特别是与实际相去较远的理论往往将由于无法解释新的数据而首先被拒绝。在许多情况下，使用新的计量经济学方法或者新的经济数据可导致新的发现，从而催生新的经济理论。

尽管数理统计学为计量经济学提供了很多有用的理论、方法和工具，但计量经济学并不是其基本理论的应用。作为现代经济学的一个重要组成部分，计量经济学有自己的历史发展轨迹，有不少自身特有的方法和工具。例如，汉森(Hansen, 1982)提出广义矩估计(generalized method of moments estimation, 简称 GMM)，其背景是，由于经济变量的条件概率分布是未知的，经济结构参数值不能用统计学中经典的最大似然估计(maximum likelihood estimation，简称 MLE)方法来估计。为了估计理性预期模型(rational expectations models)，汉森提出了利用由欧拉方程组成的一些特定的矩条件进行参数估计。另外一个例子是作为时间序列计量经济学的核心内容的单位根和协整理论(Engle and Granger, 1987; Phillips, 1987)。Nelson 和 Plosser(1982)在实证研究中发现大多数的宏观经济数据都是单位根过程，标准的统计推断理论不能使用，由此催生了单位根和协整的时间序列计量经济学理论。再则，就是金融计量学的发展。金融时间序列通常有一些独特的特征，比如价格波动的聚集性、厚尾分布、价格变动的突然跳跃性、价格变动之间不相关但不独立，等等。对金融数据的这些特征以及诸如金融风险管理、套期保值和衍生产品定价等的实际需要，使得很多常规的时间序列分析方法(如 ARMA 建模)不再适用，因此需要发展新的金融计量分析方法，对诸如价格变动的方差或整个条件概率分布建模。最后，劳动经济学和计量经济学可谓互有裨益。

由于高质量微观经济数据的获得，如美国密歇根大学的 PSID (Panel Studies of Income Dynamics)、俄亥俄州立大学的 NLS (National Longitudinal Surveys) 及宾夕法尼亚大学的 Penn-World Tables 等，使得劳动经济学在实证研究方面硕果累累，其理论在过去的几十年中得到了快速的发展；另一方面，由于大量微观经济数据有一些共同特征，比如，数据归并(censoring)和内生性(endogeneity)，需要发展适合这些微观数据特点的新的计量分析方法和工具。微观计量经济学和面板数据计量经济学因而得到了快速发展。

如前文所述，计量经济学的主要任务是通过对经济数据进行建模以揭示经济运行规律，但计量经济学不等同于经济统计学。经济统计学是对经济数据的统计分析，特别是经济数据调查、收集、整理并分析经济变量之间的数量关系及其统计显著程度。第二节中所提到的“恩格尔曲线”和“菲利普斯曲线”就是经济统计学所揭示的两个重要的经济特征事实，它们在微观经济学和宏观经济学的发展中起着非常重要的作用。计量经济学也是研究经济变量之间的数量关系，但更主要的是关注经济变量之间的因果关系，以揭示经济运行规律。不管是数理统计还是经济统计的方法与工具，均不能确认经济变量之间的数量关系是否为因果关系。因果关系的确认，必须借助于经济理论的指导。计量经济建模必须和经济理论有机结合起来，而且经济理论本身常常就是我们的研究对象。

计量经济学学会的创始人 Fisher(1933)在《计量经济学》期刊的创刊号中指出：“计量经济学学会的目标是促进各界实现对经济问题定性与定量研究和实证与定量研究的统一，促使计量经济学能像自然科学那样，使用严谨的思考方式从事研究。但是，经济学的定量研究方法多种多样，每种方法单独使用都有缺陷，需要与计量经济学相结合。因此，计量经济学绝不是经济统计学，也不能等同于一般的经济理论，尽管这些理论中有相当一部分具有数量特征；同时，计量经济学也不是数学在经济学中的应用。实践证明，统计学、经济理论、数学这三个要素是真正理解现代经济生活中数量关系的必要条件，而不是充分条件。只有三个要素互相融合，才能发挥各自的威力，才构成了计量经济学。”

四、计量经济学的应用

计量经济学在经济学研究中的作用，主要表现在以下几个方面：(1)验证经济理论或模型能否解释以往的经济数据（特别是重要的经验特征事实）；(2)检验经济理论和经济假说的正确性；(3)预测未来经济发展趋势，并提供政策建议。为了说明计量经济学在经济学研究中的作用，以及在应用计量经济学方法和工具时需要注意的问题，我们现在详细讨论一些在经济学和金融学中具有代表性的实例。

例 4.1：凯恩斯理论、乘数效应和政策建议。

首先，我们说明计量经济学如何应用于经济结构分析。前文提到，最简单的凯恩斯模型（Keynes model）可以通过如下的方程组来描述

$$\begin{cases} Y_t = C_t + I_t + G_t \\ C_t = \alpha + \beta Y_t + \varepsilon_t \end{cases}$$

这里，其他变量的含义不变，ε_t 表示消费的随机扰动项。参数 α 和 β 都有很好的经济学含义，α 表示最低消费水平，β 表示边际消费倾向。政府支出的收入乘数效应取决于边际消费倾向 β，即：

$$\frac{\partial Y_t}{\partial G_t}=\frac{1}{1-\beta}$$

为了考察公共财政政策的成效，需要知道政府支出对总收入的乘数效应。假如中国政府为了保持8%的年经济增长率，将采用积极的财政政策。如果政府的投入太少，将难以实现既定的经济增长目标，而过多的开支则可能造成政府赤字，因此政府需要知道每年发行多少国债最为合适，这就需要知道 β 值。然而，经济理论只阐述收入和消费之间存在正相关关系，但没有提及各个国家 β 值究竟是多少。毋庸置疑，民族历史文化会影响一国居民的消费习惯，即由于文化的差异，不同国家的 β 值必然不同。而且，同一个国家在不同经济发展阶段的 β 值也可能不同。计量经济学家已提出针对各种消费数据一致估计 β 这一重要结构参数值的计量方法。实际上，仅仅通过经济理论，我们甚至无法知道具体消费函数形式。设定消费函数为线性关系仅是为了理论上的方便。尽管消费函数形式未知，计量经济学家还是提出了用观测数据一致估计消费函数的可行方法，即非参数方法（Pagan and Ullah, 1999）。

例 4.2：理性预期和动态资产定价。

我们接着说明计量经济学是如何应用于检验经济理论和发展经济理论的。假设经济人具有不变的相对风险厌恶效用函数，其一生总效用为

$$U=\sum_{t=0}^{n}\beta^t u(C_t)=\sum_{t=0}^{n}\beta^t\frac{C_t^{\gamma}-1}{\gamma}$$

这里，$\beta>0$ 是经济人的时间贴现因子，$\gamma\geqslant 0$ 是风险厌恶参数，$u(\cdot)$ 是经济人在每个时期的效用函数，C_t 是第 t 期的消费，I_t 代表第 t 期经济人的信息集。令 $R_t=P_t/P_{t-1}$ 为从第 $t-1$ 期到第 t 期的资产收益率（P_t 是第 t 期的资产价格）。最优化问题

为经济人在预算约束为$C_t = P_t q_t \leqslant W_t + P_t q_{t-1}$的条件下，决定其各期消费$\{C_t\}$满足$\max\limits_{\{C_t\}} E(U)$。这里，$q_t$表示第$t$期购买的资产总量，$W_t$表示第$t$期经济人的收入。定义跨期边际替代率(marginal rate of intertemporal substitution)

$$MRS_{t+1}(\theta) = \frac{(\partial/\partial C_{t+1})U(C_{t+1})}{(\partial/\partial C_t)U(C_t)} = \left(\frac{C_{t+1}}{C_t}\right)^{\gamma-1}$$

其中，模型参数向量为$\theta = (\beta, \gamma)$。则经济人最优化问题的一阶条件为

$$E[\beta MRS_{t+1}(\theta)R_{t+1} \mid I_t] = 1$$

也就是说，跨期边际替代率对总收益率贴现后的条件期望值为1。这个一阶条件通常被称为经济系统的欧拉方程(Hansen and Singelton, 1982)。

那么，如何估计模型参数θ呢？如何检验理性预期模型的有效性呢？这里，我们不能使用传统的MLE，因为经济变量的条件概率分布是未知的。在这种情况下，计量经济学家提出了基于条件矩或欧拉方程的一致估计方法来估计θ值，这就是前文提到的GMM估计。

基于美国经济数据的实证研究表明，风险厌恶参数γ的实际估计值常常太小，不足以解释美国股票市场和债券市场收益率之间的差异(Mehra and Prescott, 1985)。这就是有名的风险溢价之谜(risk premium puzzle)。为解决这个难题，需要提出新的能够获得较大γ值的资产定价模型，以反映风险厌恶的可能时变性和经济人对高风险的厌恶。后来的Campbell和Cochrance(1999)提出的基于消费的资产定价模型就是这样一个理论。由这个例子可以看出，以计量经济学为基础的实证分析是如何推动经济理论向前发展的。

例 4.3:生产函数和规模报酬不变。

数理统计学中的很多方法和工具在实际中有广泛的应用。但是这些统计方法和工具不一定适用于分析经济数据和经济结构。我们现在用一个微观经济学的例子来讨论如何选择适合横截面经济数据特点的计量经济学方法来检验经济假说,以及说明在进行经济结构分析时,正确设定计量经济模型的重要性。

假设第 i 家企业有劳动 L_i 和资本存量 K_i 两种要素,产出为 Y_i,则其生产函数是投入(L_i, K_i)到产出(Y_i)的映射:

$$Y_i = \exp(\varepsilon_i)F(L_i, K_i)$$

其中,ε_i 是随机扰动项(若 Y_i 是农业产出的话,ε_i 表示天气条件等不确定性因素)。我们说生产技术具有规模报酬不变(constant return to scale,简称为 CRS)性质,如果对所有实数 $\lambda > 0$,有 $\lambda F(L_i, K_i) = F(\lambda L_i, \lambda K_i)$。CRS 是完全竞争市场经济存在长期均衡的必要条件。如果某一行业不满足 CRS,生产技术具有规模报酬递增(increasing return to scale)性质,则该行业将出现自然垄断。在这种情形下,为保护消费者利益,政府必须采取规制措施。因此,检验一个行业是否具有 CRS 性质具有重要的政策含义。

检验 CRS 的常用方法是假设生产函数为柯布—道格拉斯生产函数,即 $F(L_i, K_i) = AL_i^{\alpha}K_i^{\beta}$。这样,CRS 就变成关于参数 (α, β) 的约束条件 $H_0: \alpha + \beta = 1$。如果 $\alpha + \beta > 1$,则表明存在规模报酬递增。

在统计学上,常用的检验单维参数约束的方法是著名的 t-检验。遗憾的是,许多横截面经济数据具有条件异方差(conditional heteroskedasticity)特性(比如大企业的产出具有更大的波动性),这个 t-检验因为假设条件同方差(conditional homoskedasticity)而不合适。我们需要一个在存在异方差时仍适用的检验方法。怀特(White, 1980)提出一种在条件异方差情况下如何一致估计参数估计量的方差的重要方法,这种方差估计可用于构造合适的参数检验方法。

需要强调的是,CRS 与 $H_0:\alpha+\beta=1$ 等价是以真实生产函数为柯布—道格拉斯函数形式为前提的。该生产函数形式的设定是一个附加假设,并不属于 CRS 这一经济假说的一个组成部分。如果该附加假设不正确,那 CRS 与统计假说 $H_0:\alpha+\beta=1$ 就不等价。因此,生产函数模型设定正确是计量经济学推论正确的前提条件。

例 4.4:转型经济的改革效果检验。

在经济实证分析时,必须注意进行经济行为分析和逻辑分析,以采用正确的计量经济学分析方法,并且正确地陈述结论。为了说明这一点,我们考虑一个广义的柯布—道格拉斯生产函数(求对数后):

$$\ln Y_{it}=\ln A_{it}+\alpha\ln L_{it}+\beta\ln K_{it}+\gamma\ln BONUS_{it}+\delta CONTRACT_{it}+\varepsilon_{it}$$

这里 $i=1,\cdots,n$, $t=1,\cdots,T$, 其中下标 i 表示第 i 家企业,下标 t 表示第 t 期, $BONUS_{it}$ 是企业工资总支出中奖金的比例, $CONTRACT_{it}$ 表示企业职工中有固定期限(如三年)的合同工的比例。这是一个面板数据模型(Hsiao, 2003)。

在 20 世纪 80 年代,发放奖金和实行合同工制度是中国国有企业改革的两个主要激励措施。改革前,中国国有企业采取固定工资制和终身聘任制。经济理论告诉我们,引入奖金和合同工制度将激励工人努力工作,从而提高企业的劳动生产率(Groves, Hong, McMillan and Naughton, 1994)。

为了检验这两个改革措施的成效,我们考虑如下的原假设 $H_0:\delta=\gamma=0$。在这里,即使我们假定存在条件同方差,传统的 t

检验和 F 检验也不能使用。这是因为,Y_{it} 和 $BONUS_{it}$ 之间很可能存在某种因果关联,即生产率高的企业,无论工人是否努力工作,都会付给工人较高的奖金,这会导致扰动项 ε_{it} 与奖金 $BONUS_{it}$ 之间存在相关,因而 OLS 估计量不能一致估计真实参数值 γ, t 检验和 F 检验也因此不能使用。计量经济学家提出了一种重要的估计方法,可有效地过滤掉从产出到奖金的因果关系所产生的影响,从而获得参数 γ 值的一致估计,这就是计量经济学中著名的工具变量法(instrumental variables estimation,简记作 IV 估计)。我们因此可使用基于工具变量法的检验方法来评估改革成效。工具变量法可用于一致估计可能存在双向因果关系的经济结构模型。这一方法特别适合非实验性的数据分析,因而至今仍广泛使用于经济实证分析。

在评估经济改革成效时,如果统计假设 $H_0:\delta=\gamma=0$ 未被拒绝,我们并不能马上下结论说改革没有成效。这是因为上述加入改革变量的广义生产函数模型,仅是检验改革成效的方法之一。还存在很多其他可能性,比如改革可能影响劳动和资本的边际产出(即通过劳动和资本的系数表示),这些可能性并没有被检验。所以,如果统计假设 $H_0:\delta=\gamma=0$ 未被拒绝,我们只能说未找到证据推翻改革没有成效这一经济假说。

例 4.5:有效市场假说和金融市场收益率的不可预测性。

在实证分析中,必须注意计量经济学方法和工具所适用的范围和条件。如果前提条件明显不成立,相应的计量经济学方法和工具将不适用。在这种情况下,使用不适用的计量分析方法和工具将会导致错误结论。我们现在通过如何检验有效市场理论来说明这一点。

我们用 Y_t 表示第 t 期的股票收益,用 $I_{t-1}=\{Y_{t-1},Y_{t-2},\cdots\}$ 表示在第 $t-1$ 期所有股票收益的信息集合。弱式有效市场假说

(weak form of efficient market hypothesis，简记作 EMH)是指，股票收益的历史信息不可能预测未来的股票收益，即：

$$E(Y_t \mid I_{t-1}) = E(Y_t)$$

等式左边 $E(Y_t \mid I_{t-1})$是给定信息集 I_{t-1} 的 Y_t 的条件期望值，代表在 $t-1$ 期拥有已知信息 I_{t-1} 时能够实现的期望收益；等式右边 $E(Y_t)$则是 Y_t 的无条件均值，代表长期市场平均收益，是买入—持有投资策略(buy-and-hold trading strategy)的平均收益。如果 EMH 成立，那么过去的股票市场信息对预测未来的股票收益无任何帮助。EMH 的一个重要含义就是，当市场有效时，基金经理与普通投资者相比，并无任何取得长期更高投资收益的优势。

为检验 EMH，可考虑以下的 p 阶自回归模型(AR(p))：

$$Y_t = \alpha_0 + \sum_{j=1}^{p} \alpha_j Y_{t-j} + \varepsilon_t,\ t = 1, \cdots, T$$

其中，p 是事先选定的滞后阶数，ε_t 是随机扰动项满足 $E(\varepsilon \mid I_{t-1}) = 0$。EMH 意味着

$$H_0: \alpha_1 = \alpha_2 = \cdots = \alpha_p = 0$$

倘若存在任何非零自回归系数 α_j，$1 \leqslant j \leqslant p$，则 EMH 不成立。因此，EMH 的有效性可以通过检验所有 α_j 是否都为零来进行。如果存在条件同方差，即 $\mathrm{var}(\varepsilon_t \mid I_{t-1}) = \sigma^2$，线性回归模型中经典的 F 检验在大样本条件下仍可使用。然而，倘若存在波动聚集，$\mathrm{var}(\varepsilon_t \mid I_{t-1})$ 具有时变性，那么即使有很大样本，F 检验也不能用了。同样地，当存在波动聚集时，常用的 Box and Pierce 基于前 p 阶样本自相关系数平方之和的混合 Q 检验(Box and Pierce, 1970)也不能用，因为 Q 统计量在

存在波动聚集时不再服从 χ^2 的渐近分布。因此，我们必须找到一个在波动聚集条件下可适用的检验方法。波动聚集是国内外金融市场普遍存在的一个重要特征事实（陈灯塔和洪永淼，2003）。

需要指出的是，若我们拒绝了所有自回归系数 α_j，$1\leqslant j\leqslant p$，都为零的原假设，则 EMH 不成立，而且，线性 AR(p)模型对资产收益有预测能力。然而，若我们不能拒绝自回归系数 α_j 都为零的原假设，我们只能说没有证据推翻 EMH，而不能说 EMH 成立。这是因为，线性 AR(p)模型只是检验 EMH 的众多模型之一。

例 4.6：波动集聚（volatility clustering）和 ARCH 模型。

并非所有计量经济学模型均可用某一种估计方法来估计。在实证研究中，必须具体问题具体分析，针对实际问题的本质，正确选择合适的估计方法。为了说明这一点，我们考虑如何估计金融市场波动模型。自 20 世纪 70 年代起，石油危机、浮动汇率制度和美国高利率政策等重大经济事件加剧了世界经济的不确定性，人们在做经济决策时，不得不考虑这些不确定性因素，因此如何度量这些不确定性成了一个重要课题。在经济学中，波动性是度量不确定性和市场风险的一个主要计量工具，对研究波动溢出（volatility spillover）、金融危机传染病（financial contagion）、期权定价（options pricing）和计算风险值（value at risk）等，均十分重要。

波动性通常用在给定第 $t-1$ 期的信息集 I_{t-1} 时，资产收益 I_t 的条件方差 $\sigma_t^2=\text{var}(Y_t\mid I_{t-1})$ 来度量。条件方差建模的常见例子是 Engle（1982）提出的自回归条件异方差模型（autoregressive conditional heteroskedasticity model，简记作 ARCH 模型）。ARCH(q)模型假设

$$\begin{cases} Y_t = \mu_t + \varepsilon_t,\ \varepsilon_t = \sigma_t z_t,\ \{z_t\} \sim \text{i. i. d.}(0,\ 1) \\ \mu_t = E(Y_t \mid I_{t-1}),\ \sigma_t^2 = \alpha + \sum_{j=1}^{q} \beta_j \varepsilon_{t-j}^2, \\ \quad \alpha > 0,\ \beta_j > 0,\ 1 \leqslant j \leqslant q \end{cases}$$

此模型可以解释金融市场波动聚集这一经验特征事实，即一个大波动后常紧跟另一个大波动，而一个小波动后常紧跟另一个小波动。它还能解释金融收益的非正态厚尾分布特征。更为复杂的波动性模型，如 Bollerslev（1986）的 GARCH 模型（generalized ARCH model），也已被提出并广泛应用于金融市场波动实证研究。

在实际应用中，如何估计波动模型参数是一个很重要的问题。这里，假定条件均值模型 μ_t 和条件方差模型 σ_t^2 已正确设定，这意味着标准化的随机扰动项$\{z_t\}$必须满足 $E(z_t \mid I_{t-1}) = 0$ 和 $E(z_t^2 \mid I_{t-1}) = 1$。由于$\{z_t\}$的概率分布未知，$Y_t$ 的条件概率分布也未知。所以，常规的 MLE 不能使用。尽管如此，我们可假设$\{z_t\}\sim$i. i. d. N(0, 1)或其他的拟概率分布。这样，就可以得到给定信息集 I_{t-1}下的 Y_t 的条件概率分布，并用类似 MLE 的方法进行参数估计。虽然 z_t 可能不是 i. i. d. N(0, 1)且我们知道这一点，但计量经济学家证明，即使$\{Y_t\}$的条件概率分布模型设定错误，只要其条件均值模型 μ_t 和条件方差模型 σ_t^2 设定正确，仍可以通过这种方法得到条件均值模型和条件方差模型中的真实参数值的一致估计。当然，不知道 z_t 的真实概率分布的代价是，我们所得到的参数估计量的方差要比知道 z_t 的真实概率分布的参数估计量的方差要大。这种方法被称为拟最大似然估计方法（quasi-MLE，简记作 QMLE，见 White, 1994）。条件概率分布模型设定错误的 QMLE 估计量的渐近方差与条件概率分布模型设定正确的 MLE 估计量的渐近方差不同，这类似于条件异方差时 OLS 估计量的渐近方差和条件同方差时 OLS 估计量的渐近方差不同。由于 QMLE 估计量的方差与 MLE 估计量的方差不同，基于 MLE 的似然比检验（likelihood ratio test）在 Y_t 的条件概率分布模型设定错误情形下就不能再使用了。这是因为似然比检验的渐近 χ^2 分布是在条件概率分布模型设定正确的前提下得到的。在实际应用中，很多人在计算 QMLE 估计量的方差时，采用的是 MLE 估计量的方差公式，这是不正确的。对 QMLE 估计量的方差的错误计算，将导致错误的推论与结论（White，1994）。

例 4.7：经济事件久期分析。

作为实证研究的基本方法论，计量经济学在非传统领域也具有广泛的应用，下面的久期分析（duration analysis）充分显示这一点。人们常常对"一个工人失业了多长时间才能重新找到工作"、"两次交易或两次价格变动之间的时间间隔有多久"、"过多久会出现财务危机（比如违约风险）"，"一个家庭经过多久才会脱贫"等问题感兴趣，对这类问题的分析被称为久期分析。

在实践中，人们主要对某个还未结束的经济事件将持续多长时间比较感兴趣。假设 T_i 是一个经济事件（如某一工人失业）的持续时间，其概率密度函数为 $f(t)$，概率分布函数为 $F(t)$。在久期分析中，有两个基本概念，一个是生存函数（survival function）：

$$S(t)=P(T_i>t)=1-F(t)$$

另一个是危险率（hazard rate）：

$$\lambda(t)=\lim_{\delta\to 0^+}\frac{P(t<T_i\leqslant t+\delta\mid T_i>t)}{\delta}=\frac{f(t)}{S(t)}$$

危险率 $\lambda(t)$ 是指某事件持续了 t 期后结束的瞬时概率。它度量一个正在进行的事件立即结束的可能性，危险率可以被解释为经历一段时间后找到工作、开始交易或出现违约风险等的可能性。值得注意的是，$\lambda(t)$和概率密度 $f(t)$是等价的，给定其中的任何一个，即可以求出另一个。但是，$\lambda(t)$具有更丰富的经济含义，很多经济理论或经济结构模型直接对 $\lambda(t)$的设定给出约束。

不同个人的危险率可能不一样。为了体现个人之间的差异，我们可假设每个人的危险率取决于自身的一些特征因素 X_i，并具有如下的关系式：

$$\lambda_i(t) = \exp(X_i'\beta)\lambda(t)$$

这个模型被称为比例危险率模型（proportional hazard model），最初由 Cox（1972）提出。参数 $\beta = (\partial/\partial X_{it})/n\lambda_i(t)$ 表明个人特征变量 X_i 对久期的影响，可以被解释为个人 i 的因素 X_i 对危险率的边际影响。例如，假设 T_i 是第 i 个工人的失业持续时间，那么 β 值就表明，这个工人的年龄、教育程度、性别等特征变量对失业持续时间的影响，这种分析在劳动力市场有重要的政策含义。有关劳动经济学的久期分析，Kiefer（1988）和 Lancaster（1990）做了很好的综述与总结。

给定 X_i，可得到久期随机变量 T_i 的条件概率密度函数 $f_i(t) = \lambda_i(t)S_i(t)$。这里，生存函数为 $S_i(t) = \exp[-\int_0^t \lambda_i(s)\mathrm{d}s]$。由于知道 T_i 的条件概率分布，我们可以通过 MLE 估计真实 β 值。

以上的经济学和金融学代表性实例说明了如何用经济变量的概率规律的条件均值、条件方差乃至整个条件概率分布函数本身来研究经济金融问题，特别是分析经济结构，检验经济理论和经济假说，刻画市场风险和波动性，以及揭示经济事件久期规律，等等。这些例子表明，经济问题的实证研究可以用经济系统的概率规律来分析，但对每一个具体的问题，到底是应该对条件期望、条件方差或对整个条件概率分布建模，则取决于所研究问题的本质。同时，必须注意经济数据的特点以及各种计量经济学方法与工具的适用范围和条件，注意经济结构的因果关系和逻辑关系，以选择正确的计量模型、方法与工具，并对统计推断结论给予正确的经济学解释。

五、计量经济学分析的局限性

尽管经济学和金融学研究的一般方法论与自然科学研究的方法论非常相似，都是从观察、抽象、检验到应用这些步骤，但是经济学和金融学还远未达到自然科学(比如物理学)那样成熟的境界。特别是经济学和金融学的分析与预测没能像自然科学那么准确[参考 Granger(2001)对宏观经济预测实践的评价]。同其他的统计分析一样，计量经济学是对大量经济数据或对大量有着相同或相似特征的随机经济事件的平均行为的分析。然而，经济数据不能由大量的重复随机实验产生，因为经济系统不是一个可以控制的实验过程，而且不能重复。绝大多数的经济数据在本质上都不是实验数据，这导致了计量经济学分析的若干局限性。

首先，经济理论或模型作为对复杂现实经济的简化抽象，只能刻画主要的或重要的经济因素。而实际观测到的数据却是由许多因素共同作用的结果，其中，有些因素是未知的或不可观测的，没有包括在经济模型中，因此反映不出它们的影响。这点与自然科学不同，自然科学研究可以通过可控实验过滤或消除次要因素的影响。在经济学领域，经济学家通常是被动的观测者，大多数收集到的经济数据都是非实验性的。因此无法从观测到的经济数据过滤出经济模型以外的因素所产生的那一部分影响，这便造成经济实证研究的困难。

计量经济学家发明了不少计量经济学方法，在无法过滤出模型以外因素的影响的情况下，仍可一致估计模型因素的影响。例如，考虑一个简单线性回归模型

$$Y_i = X_i'\beta + \varepsilon_i,\ i = 1,\ \cdots,\ n$$

这里 Y_i 是收入，X_i 包含教育程度（如在校上学时间）等可观测的解释变量。这一模型可用来研究教育回报率。但是，教育程度 X_i 是内生性变量，因为它可能取决于经济人的能力（用 α_i 表示）。换句话说，一个人的收入 Y_i 取决于其教育程度 X_i 和能力 α_i，而能力 α_i 可能与 X_i 相关。由于能力 α_i 是不可观测的，在上述模型设定中，能力 α_i 对收入 Y_i 的贡献就被包含在随机扰动项 ε_i 中，因此 ε_i 和 X_i 相关。在这种情况下，OLS 估计方法不能一致估计出真实 β 值，即教育回报率。然而，使用计量经济学家所发明的工具变量法可以一致地估计 β 值，虽然我们无法从收入 Y_i 中过滤出能力 α_i 的贡献部分。

然而，并不是所有经济问题都有类似工具变量法的方法可以用来一致估计模型因素的影响，例如 Lo 和 Mackinlay(1988)在使用方差比检验（variance ratio test）研究美国股市有效性时，发现美国股市价格指数收益率存在序列正相关（serial correlation）。但是这一序列正相关不能马上被解释为美国股市有效性不成立，这是因为股市价格指数是由很多公司股票价格加权平均而得的。当有消息进入股市时，大公司常常先获知消息（即所谓的 informed 交易者）而先行交易，因此其价格先变动；小公司通常信息滞后（所谓的 uninformed 交易者），其交易和股价随后变化。这一不同步交易的现象即使在市场有效性成立时也会导致股票价格指数收益率存在序列正相关。目前没有计量

经济学的方法可以过滤掉由不同步交易而产生的股指收益率那一部分的正相关。Lo 和 Mackinlay(1988)采用一个市场微观结构行为模型，假设美国股市存在一定比例的 informed 交易者和 uninformed 交易者，这一模型只能解释他们所发现的股指收益率序列正相关系数的一小部分，因此他们认为美国股市有效性不成立。但是这一结论取决于他们提出来的交易行为模型的现实合理性，而这一点并没能得到数据验证。

最近出现的实验经济学，在可控的实验条件下研究经济人的行为(Samuelson, 2005)，因而能够控制数据生成过程，使产生的数据仅受人们感兴趣的模型因素影响。然而，实验经济学的触角是有限的，我们难以想象如何在一个有 13 亿人口的巨大经济体中进行大规模的实验，比如，为了研究经济转型，我们能让中国与前东欧的社会主义国家重复多次的经济改革吗？事实上，即使人数不是很大，用实验方法来研究某些经济问题也是不现实的。例如，为了研究税率对某一群体消费行为的影响，人们可以通过实验方法来研究，即随机选择对一部分人实行较低的税率，而对另一部分人实行较高的税率。很显然，这样的实验方案对实行较高税率的人们是不公平的。

其次，经济发展是一个不可逆或不可重复的过程。这导致每一个经济变量常常只有一个观测值。举例说明，中国过去十年的 GDP 年增长率$\{Y_t\}$为：

Y_{1997}	Y_{1998}	Y_{1999}	Y_{2000}	Y_{2001}
9.3%	7.8%	7.6%	8.4%	8.3%
Y_{2002}	Y_{2003}	Y_{2004}	Y_{2005}	Y_{2006}
9.1%	10.0%	10.1%	9.9%	10.7%

不同年份的 GDP 增长率应被看成不同的随机变量，且每个随机变量 Y_t 只有一个观测值。如果一个随机变量只有一个观测值，

就无法做统计分析。如前文所述,统计分析是研究大样本的“平均”行为,且这些样本是从同一个数据生成过程中产生的。为了对经济数据进行统计分析,经济学家和计量经济学家常常要假设一个经济系统的运行规律具有不随时间和个体改变的某些特征,比如经济系统具有时间“平稳性”(stationarity)或不同经济人的数据生成过程具有“同质性”(homogeneity)。所谓“平稳性”就是指经济关系和经济结构不随时间变化,或者说经济系统的概率分布(至少是概率分布的一些重要方面)不随时间变化。在平稳性假设条件下,不同年份的 GDP$\{Y_t\}$可视为具有同样的概率分布,且它们之间的“关系”不随时间变化。因此我们就可以将不同 GDP 变量$\{Y_t\}$的观测值看作是从同一个概率分布产生出来的随机数,因而可以进行统计分析。所谓“同质性”,是指不同的个体(如消费者、企业等)拥有同样的概率分布,或者至少他们的概率分布具有某些重要的共同特征。这样,不同个体的经济变量的观测值就可以看作是由同一个或类似的概率分布产生出来的随机数。

现实中,很多经济变量并不满足“平稳性”或“同质性”假设。对此,计量经济学家找到不少有用方法。时间序列计量经济学家常常通过一定的变换,将不平稳的时间序列经济变量变成一个平稳的时间序列。例如:可以通过差分法,将一个差分平稳过程(difference-stationary process)变成一个平稳时间序列,或者通过除趋势法走势(detrending),将一个趋势平稳过程(trend-stationary process)变成一个平稳时间序列。同样地,横截面经济数据常存在个体差别,即“异质性”(heterogeneity)。对此,计量经济学家常常用一些重要的个体特征变量(可以包含不可观测的特征变量)来刻画这些异质性。通过这些个体特征变量控制后的经济变量的概率分布可以看作具有“同质性”。例如在失业久期分析中，劳动经济学家常假设失业工人重新就业的概率与工人的特征变量 X_i（如文化程度，年龄，性别等）有关，他们使用 Cox(1972)的比例危险率模型 $\lambda_i(t)=\exp(X_i'\beta)\lambda(t)$，这里 $\lambda_i(t)$ 为失业工人 i 的“危险率”函数，即该工人失业持续时间为 t 后重新就业的概率，$\lambda(t)$ 为对每个工人都一样的“基准危险率”函数。这个比例危险率模型假设每个失业工人的“异质性”可以由他的特征变量 X_i 来刻画。由控制变量 X_i 解释后的失业持续时间的概率分布就具有“同质性”了。很显然，计量经济学分析是否有效取决于变量变换和特征变量控制是否能够将原始数据变成具有“平稳性”或“同质性”的数据，这样，才可以将它们看作是来自同一个概率分布或有着类似特征的概率分布，才能使用不同经济变量的时间序列数据或截面数据来进行统计分析。计量经济学分析需要这样一些前提条件，而这些条件在实践中是很难检验的。很显然，如果这些假设不成立，统计推断当然不可能准确。

第三，经济关系常常具有时变性。自然科学中很多学科，如物理学，能够精确地把握物体运动规律和预测物体运动变化，一个重要原因是所研究的物理系统在相当长的一段时间内不具有时变性。经济系统则有很大不同，常常有结构性变化。比如，技术变革、人口结构变化、金融危机会导致体制演变和结构调整。这些变动将引起经济人行为的变化，从而造成经济关系和经济结构具有时变性。若经济关系不稳定，就很难有准确的样本外推预测(out-of-sample forecasts)，也很难制定有效的经济政策。当经济结构发生改变时，即使能很好地解释过去历史的经济模型，也不一定能对未来做出较准确的预测。

具有结构时变性的经济系统是一个非平稳过程，但这种非平稳过程一般不能通过变换(如差分)变成平稳时间序列。由于经济结构的时变性，经济运行规律随时间改变，不同时期的经济运行规律有不同的特征和表现形式。在这种情况下，时间序列数据不能简单“汇总”在一起进行统计分析。

经济结构时变性有两种基本表现形式：一种是突变式结构变化(abrupt structural breaks)，另一种是渐进式结构变化(evolutionary structural changes)。突变式结构变化通常由突如其来的重大事件引起，如战争、政策变动、金融危机等。如果我们知道经济结构突变的时间点，而且这种变化已发生过一段时间(因此有足够的突变后样本数据)，那么针对这种情形计量经济学已有一套比较完整的理论和方法来解决经济结构时变化引起的困难。一个例子就是著名的邹式检验(Chow, 1960)。如果我们不知道突变式结构变化的时间点，甚至不知道有多少次突变性结构变化，这种情况目前计量经济学尚未发展出一套比较满意的理论和方法来分析经济结构，虽然在这方面已取得不少重要进展。

渐进式结构变化是假设经济结构和经济关系有时变性，但是这种时变性不是突如其来的，而是缓慢地演变，具有连续性特点。渐进式结构变化相对突变式结构变化更有现实可能性。这是因为即使客观环境在短期内有剧烈变动，人们的经济行为也有可能需要一段时间逐步调整与适应。此外，即使个人的行为有突变式特征，由求和加总而得到的宏观经济变量亦有可能会显示出渐进式变化的特点。

渐进式结构变化可造成经济实证研究的很大困难。比如，一个时间序列若包含一个随时间缓慢变化的截距项，那么这一非平稳过程将显示出与一个平稳“长记忆”(long memory)过程相似的特征，因此有可能被误认为长记忆过程，从而导致错误结论。总的说来，计量经济学尚未有一套理论和方法来克服渐进式结构改变所产生的困难和问题。

另一方面，经济系统在一定时期内有可能是平稳但非线性的过程。在这种情况下，使用线性计量模型分析时间序列数据时很可能会表现出结构时变性。如何区分结构非线性和结构时变性一直是宏观经济学家和计量经济学家的一个难题。

第四，数据质量。任何计量经济学研究的成功都离不开大量高质量的数据。随着计算技术的进步以及统计抽样理论与实践的发展，经济数据的质量越来越高。比如，超级市场通过大量使用条码扫描系统可获得每一笔的精确交易数据，证券市场能同步记录每笔高频金融交易数据。然而，经济数据可能存在各种缺陷。例如，经济数据可能存在测量误差，可能存在样本的选择偏差(selection bias)，数据与经济模型中的变量的定义可能不相符，一些经济变量数据缺失，甚至在本质上是不可观测的(如幸福指数或痛苦指数)，等等。这些数据缺陷所造成的困难有些是可以克服的。比如，当数据存在测量误差时，如果测量误差是随机性的，其造成的困难可以用适当的计量经济学方法来克服。以估计线性回归模型为例，当自变量存在测量误差时，OLS 估计可能会出现偏差，但这可以通过使用工具变量法来消除。

然而，有一些数据缺陷所造成的困难是不可能或很难克服的。一个例子是测量误差存在系统性偏差。例如当调查个人灰色收入时，人们因为担心需要上缴收入税而倾向于低报其收入。同样的，中国过去一段时期以 GDP 为主要业绩考核指标的官员考核制度，造成地方政府官员倾向于多报 GDP 总量或 GDP 增长率。

另一方面，宏观经济数据大都由微观数据加总而成。这种“加总”(aggregation)有可能会改变经济变量之间的关系。以消费函数为例，假设 X_{it} 和 Y_{it} 分别是第 i 个家庭在第 t 期的收入和消费，这个家庭的消费函数为

$$Y_{it}=\alpha_i+\beta_i X_{it}+\varepsilon_{it},\ i=1,\cdots,n,\ t=1,\cdots,T$$

这里 β_i 是第 i 个家庭的边际消费倾向。现在令 $X_t=\sum_{i=1}^{n}X_{it}$ 和 $Y_t=\sum_{i=1}^{n}Y_{it}$ 代表整个经济在第 t 期的总收入和总消费，那么我们有

$$Y_t=\alpha+\beta_t X_t+\varepsilon_t,\ t=1,\cdots,T$$

这里的斜率参数

$$\beta_t=\sum_{i=1}^{n}\beta_i X_{it}\Big/\sum_{i=1}^{n}X_{it}$$

是整个经济在第 t 期的边际消费倾向。除非所有家庭的收入在每个时期均同步增长，否则整个经济的边际消费倾向参数 β_t 将不是一个常数，而且具有时变性。换言之，"加总"导致整个经济的消费函数不再是线性关系。

经济数据和经济系统的上述特征，不可避免地造成了计量经济学实证研究的局限性，使之难以达到与一些自然科学学科那样的成熟程度，这是我们应用计量经济学工具与方法时需要时常记住的。同时，必须强调，计量经济学所面临的局限性不是计量经济学本身所特有的，而是整个经济学科所面临的局限性。事实上，正是由于经济系统的非实验性、不可逆性和时变性，以及经济数据的种种缺陷，计量经济学理论本身的发展已相对成熟和全面。但是这种实证研究方法论的先进，仍无法代替或克服由经济系统和经济数据特点所造成的局限性，而使得经济学的分析与预测远没有像很多自然科学学科那样精确。这是经济

学和自然科学一个最大的区别。

参考文献

陈灯塔、洪永淼:《中国股市是弱式有效的吗？——基于一种新方法的实证研究》,《经济学(季刊)》2003 年第 3 卷第 1 期。

Bollerslev, T. , 1986, "Generalized Autoregressive Conditional Heteroskedastcity", *Journal of Econometrics* 31:307—327.

Box, G. E. P. and D. A. Pierce, 1970, "Distribution of Residual Autorelations in Autoregressive Moving Average Time Series Models", *Journal of American Statistical Association* 65:1509—1526.

Campbell, J. Y. and J. Cochrance, 1999, "By Force of Habit: A Consumption-Based Explanation of Aggregate Stock Market Behavior", *Journal of Political Economy* 107:205—251.

Chow, G. C. , 1960, "Tests of Equality between Sets of Coefficients in Two Linear Regressions", *Econometrica* 28:591—605.

Cournot, A. , 1838, Researches into the Mathematical Properties of the Theory of Wealth, trans. by Nathaniel T. Bacon, with an essay and an biography by Irving Fisher, McMillan: New York, 2nd edition, 1927.

Cox, D. R. , 1972, "Regression Models and Life Tables(with Discussion)", *Journal of Royal Statistical Society*, *Series B*, 34:187—220.

Engle, R. , 1982, "Autoregressive Conditional Hetersokedasticity with Estimates of the Variance of United Kingdom Inflation", *Econometrica* 50:987—2008.

Engle, R. and C. W. J. Granger, 1987, "Cointegration and Error-Corretion Representation, Estimation and Testing", *Econometrica* 55:251—276.

Fisher, I. , 1933, "Report of the Meeting", *Econometrica* 1:92—93.

Frisch, R. , 1933, "Propagation Problems and Impulse Problems in Dynamic Economics", in Economic Essays in Honour of Gustab Cassel, London: Allen and Unwin.

Granger, C. J. W., 2001, "Overview of Nonlinear Macroeconometric Empirical Models", *Journal of Macroeconomic Dynamics* 5:466—481.

Granger, C. J. W. and T. Terasvirta, 1993, *Modeling Nonlinear Economic Relationships*, Oxford University Press: Oxford.

Groves, T., Hong, Y., McMillan, J. and B. Naughton, 1994, "Incentives in Chinese State-owned Enterprises", *Quarterly Journal of Economics CIX*: 183—209.

Gujarati, D. N., 2006, *Essentials of Econometrics*, 3rd Edition, McGraw-Hill: Boston.

Hansen, L. P., 1982, "Large Sample Properties of Generalized Method of Moments Estimators", *Econometrica* 50:1029—1054.

Hansen, L. P. and K. Singleton, 1982, "Generalized Instrumental Variables Estimation of Nonlinear Rational Expectations Models", *Econometrica* 50:1269—1286.

Hsiao, C., 2003, *Panel Data Analysis*, 2nd Edition, Cambridge University Press: Cambridge.

Keynes, J. M., 1936, *General Theory of Employment, Interest and Money*, McMillan Cambridge University Press: Cambridge, U. K.

Kiefer, N., 1988, "Economic Duration Data and Hazard Functions", *Journal of Economic Literature* 26:646—679.

Lancaster, T., 1990, *Econometric Analysis of Transition Data*, Cambridge University Press: Cambridge, U. K.

Lo, A. and A. C. Mackinlay, 1988, "Stock Prices do not follow Random Walks: Evidence from a Simple Specification Test", *Review of Financial Studies* 1:41—66.

Lucas, R., 1977, "Understanding Business Cycles", in Stabilization of the Domestic and International Economy, Karl Brunner and Allan Meltzer, eds., *Carnegie-Rochester Conference Series on Public Policy*, Vol. 5. North-Holland: Amsterdam.

Mehra, R. and E. Prescott, 1985, "The Equity Premium: A Puzzle",

Journal of Monetary Economics 15:145—161.

Nelson, C. R. and C. I. Plosser, 1982, "Trends and Random Walks in Macroeconomic Time Series: Some Evidence and Implications", *Journal of Monetary Economics* 10:139—162.

Pagan, A. and A. Ullah, 1999, *Nonparametric Econometrics*, Cambridge University Press: Cambridge.

Phillips, P. C., 1987, "Time Seres Regression with a Unit Root", *Econometrica* 55:277—301.

Samuelson, L., 2005, "Economic Theory and Experimental Economics", *Journal of Economic Literature XLIII*:65—107.

Samuelson, P., 1939, "Interactions between the Multiplier Analysis and the Principle of Acceleration", *Review of Economic Studies* 21: 75—78.

Von Neumann, J. and O. Morgenstern, 1944, *Theory of Games and Economic Behavior*, Princeton University Press: Princeton.

Walras, L., 1874, Elements of Pure Economics, or, Theory of Social Wealth, translated by William Jaffe. Fairfield, PA; Kelley, 1977.

White, H., 1980, "A Heteroskedasticity-Consistent Covariance matrix Estimator and a Direct Test for Heterokedasticity", *Econometrica* 48: 817—838.

White, H., 1994, *Estimation, Inference and Specification Analysis*, Cambridge University Press: Cambridge.

(原载《经济研究》2007 年第 5 期)

东亚经济增长模式相关争论的再探讨*

林毅夫
（北京大学中国经济研究中心）
任若恩
（北京航空航天大学经济管理学院）

关于我国的经济增长模式是近年来国内经济学界争论的热点问题之一。很多研究尝试用全要素生产率（TFP）的方法分析我国经济增长的来源，以此判断我国现有经济增长模式的可持续性，并据此提出未来经济增长模式的改革建议。这个问题之所以引起人们关注，原因之一是关于东亚经济增长模式的争论。

著名经济学家保罗·克鲁格曼（Paul Krugman）依据其他一些人对亚洲四小龙经济增长的经验研究，于 1994 年在国际甚有影响的《外交》杂志上撰文指出，东亚的经济增长完全可以用要素投入的增加来解释，全要素生产率没有贡献，因此，他推断在东亚经济的增长中没有技术进步的成分，不存在所谓的"东亚奇迹"，并认为东亚经济的增长不可持续。克鲁格曼的观点提出

* 林毅夫感谢北京大学中国经济研究中心"十五"211 工程项目"WTO 之后的中国经济"对本文研究的支持。任若恩感谢国家自然科学基金面上项目（项目编号 70173029）、重点项目（项目编号 70531010）、创新研究群体科学基金（项目编号 70521001）对本研究的支持。

后马上在国际学术界引起一场争论，但是，1997 年东亚金融危机爆发后，许多人认为克鲁格曼对东亚经济增长模式的批评预见了后来的危机，因而成为国际舆论界的主流观点。

国内经济学界对于我国经济增长模式的争论深受克鲁格曼的影响，争论中许多学者依据克鲁格曼的观点来评论我国经济增长模式的可持续性，并提出放弃以要素投入为主的增长模式，改为以全要素生产率增长为主的增长方式。

本文将澄清克鲁格曼论断的假设，指出他关于东亚经济增长与技术进步无关的观点的缺失，并讨论东亚经济增长模式对我国未来经济发展的启示。在本文的第一节中，我们将首先对东亚经济增长模式的争论做一简单的历史回顾；第二节中，我们则将根据学术界在全要素生产率和世界经济史等方面的研究成果来分析、评价克鲁格曼的观点，并说明克鲁格曼的观点实际上是难以成立的；第三节主要讨论东亚经济增长模式争论对中国未来经济发展的启示。

一、东亚经济增长模式争论的由来

（一）世界银行报告的基本结论

克鲁格曼对于东亚经济增长模式的批判，源于世界银行 1993 年出版的一本著名报告《东亚的奇迹：经济增长和公共政策》（*The East Asian Miracle*: *Economic Growth and Public Policy*，World Bank Policy Research Reports，1993）。世界银行的这本报告试图分析并总结东亚 4 个新兴工业化经济体（韩国、新加坡、中国台湾和中国香港）经济增长的经验，并希望通过总结这些经验为其他发展中国家的经济发展指出道路。

世界银行报告的主要结论如下：

(1) 坚持宏观管理的重要性，包括稳定的商业环境，低通货膨胀，有利于鼓励固定资产投资；谨慎的财政措施，辅之以其他措施保证经济增长中的公平共享与高经济增长的成果；有利于出口竞争性的汇率政策；金融发展和逐步的自由化保证国内储蓄的最大化，推进资源的有效分配，以及与全球金融系统的融合；尽可能减少价格扭曲；采取措施推进初等教育，创立不同技能的劳动力结构，以利于外向经济的发展。

(2) 需要一个强有力的政府管理体系，保证长期发展意愿的实现，追求产出与就业的快速增长；政府与工商业之间的互动，同时政府要在工商业者之间创造竞争的环境。

(3) 政府需要采取积极的政策加快工业化的步伐，增加出口中的工业产品份额；外向发展政策加上汇率政策，就成为达到外部平衡，产生加速 GDP 增长的需求，促使生产吸收技术，保持国际竞争力的手段。在工业化的过程中，东亚政府有选择地选取了关税保护和鼓励出口的政策，其中不乏道义规劝、补贴和金融手段，使得实业界可以获得低成本的融资。

(4) 政府清楚地表明了可以获得政府支持的条件，方法是实用的，手段可以灵活使用，在目标不能完成的时候将废止使用。

(二) 克鲁格曼的批评

按照哥伦比亚大学著名国际经济学教授 Bhagwati(1996) 在 Cornell 大学的一个演讲的回顾，在克鲁格曼之前耶鲁大学的 T. N. Srinivasan 教授就对世界银行的研究加以批评，他的理由和克鲁格曼的批评一致，认为在四小龙的经济快速增长中没有全要素生产率的贡献，因此也就没有技术进步的作用或效率的改善。东亚经济的重要推动力是资本的积累，资本投入可以解释经济增长的 80%，因此没有所谓的东亚经济奇迹。

引起国际舆论界高度关注的则是克鲁格曼 1994 年在《外交》杂志(Foreign Affairs, 1994)上发表的一篇题为《亚洲奇迹的神话》(Myth of Asia's Miracle)的文章。克鲁格曼对东亚增长模式的批评主要依靠了 Kim 和 Lau 的研究(1994)及 Young(1992, 1994)的实证研究,因此,我们称之为 Krugman-Kim-Lau-Young 批评。

克鲁格曼认为,美国经济的增长主要来源于全要素生产率,苏联的经济增长则主要靠要素投入的增加,苏联的增长方式不能持久,导致最后的崩溃;而东亚经济的增长基本上也是靠要素投入的增加。因此,他认为东亚经济的增长也是不能持续的,是纸老虎。后来东亚金融危机的出现,使他的观点大为盛行。

(三)一些经济学家对克鲁格曼批评的批评

其实克鲁格曼的批评并没有得到国际学术界的普遍接受,他的文章发表后,国际学术界就有一些系统的批判,但未为国内学术界和媒体所关注。下面主要介绍 3 篇对克鲁格曼文章的系统批评。

第一篇文章是前面提到的哥伦比亚大学的 Bhagwati,他 1996 年 5 月 3 日在 Cornell 大学的一个讲座中全面批评了克鲁格曼的观点,其主要结论如下:

(1) 首先东亚经济奇迹是现实的存在,而不是如克鲁格曼所说的神话,东亚奇迹的主要表现就是私营部门投资增长得如此之快,这是其他国家历史上难以比拟的;

(2) 这样一种基本面的突出特征产生的重要原因是这些国家所采用的出口导向的发展战略;

(3) 大量出口收入的增长可以有能力大量进口含有新技术的资本设备,这样在快速增长的投资中能够含有越来越多的技术进步的成分。这一结果导致了双重的收益,一方面是出口推动的投资的快速增长，另一方面是进口中所包含的技术进步所产生的收益；

(4) 由于东亚这些国家或地区的较高程度的识字率和教育水平，新一代资本品的社会贡献大大高于相应的国际成本，因此进一步强化了进口中所包含的技术进步产生的收益；

(5) 外商直接投资(FDI)与贸易一样具有较高的生产率，反映了出口导向发展战略的成功，而进口替代战略的不成功则是由于既不能吸引较多的外商直接投资，也不能从这些投资中获得较高的回报；

(6)人们所关注的“产业政策”与东亚经济的增长关系并不大，甚至有负面的影响；

(7) 东亚经济增长模式已经在一些其他国家得到应用并且获得了很好的后果；

(8) 他特别指出克鲁格曼把苏联与东亚相比较是错误的，苏联的增长依靠公共储蓄与投资，而东亚依靠的是私人储蓄和投资，在吸收外国技术方面也不同，因此亚洲经济的增长与苏联不同，是可以持久的。

第二篇文章由现任中国香港岭南大学校长陈坤耀(Edward K. Y. Chen，1997)写的。陈坤耀原任中国香港大学教授，是国际学术界最早研究东亚新兴工业化经济的学者，他对克鲁格曼文章的批评更多集中于克鲁格曼的文章对全要素生产率的误解，陈坤耀的文章包括了一些偏重技术层面的分析，也更多触及了克鲁格曼的文章在经济学理论方法方面的缺陷。陈坤耀对克鲁格曼文章的主要批评可以概括如下：

(1) 在经济增长的核算中，作为技术进步代表变量的全要素生产率是核算中的残差，因此，很大程度上决定于投入要素的数据是如何测定的；

(2) 关于东亚经济奇迹的争论，与所用的数据有关，也与相应的定义和概念有关，他认为克鲁格曼、Young 和许多参与这场争论的人并没有很好地了解全要素生产率研究的理论与实证的发展，在一些基本概念上出现了错误；

(3) 陈坤耀论文的最重要贡献是清楚地区分了技术进步与全要素生产率增长的区别。他指出：在实证研究中，一些人习惯用全要素生产率代表技术进步，这实际上是一个误解。所谓技术进步包括与资本融合在一起的(embodied)和不包括资本投入的(disembodied)两类。而全要素生产率增长所测定的仅是不包括资本投入的技术进步。因此，如果全要素生产率的增长比较低，只说明不包括资本投入的技术进步比较低，而与资本融合在一起的技术进步仍然是存在的。更准确的表述是，全要素生产率所体现的技术进步是不包括资本投入的(disembodied)、Hicks 中性的(Hicks-neutral)技术进步。而在一般场合人们所谈论的技术进步的范围要大得多。在这个意义上，全要素生产率的增长不等于技术进步，而且，取得不包括资本投入的技术进步并非没有成本。基于这些，他认为克鲁格曼对东亚经济增长模式的批评是一个误导。

第三篇文章是亚洲开发银行的研究报告(Felipe, 1997)，在这篇研究报告中，作者对亚洲地区有关全要素生产率的实证研究做了系统、深入的评述和分析。作者在分析方法层面的讨论是比较深入的，所指出的许多问题与上面所介绍的陈坤耀的论文的分析比较接近，在此不再赘述。但 Felipe 的分析走得更远，他几乎怀疑在目前这样的全要素生产率的分析框架内能够正确地理解亚洲经济发展过程的实际意义。

在此特别需要提到中国内地学者郑玉歆的文章(1998)，这篇文章发表的时间比较早，但对克鲁格曼文章的主要问题都涉及了，例如文章正确地指出了由于方法不同、数据不同而可能导致全要素生产率的不同估计，因此直接在国家之间比较全要素生产率增长率所可能产生的误差。该文章还指出了在分析中生产函数设定不同的重要性，以及对技术进步和全要素生产率的概念上已经出现的混乱。郑玉歆的文章对克鲁格曼的文章及相关文章中在有关全要素生产率的计量方法中所存在的问题做了十分深入的分析和批评。该文章还正确地指出了“要素投入作为增长来源的相对重要性是随时间变化的，是和经济发展阶段以及和要素的性质密切相关的”。十分可惜这样一篇指出克鲁格曼的文章中的基本问题，并加以深入分析的论文没有得到足够的重视，也没有能够阻碍一些人继续宣传与此有关的一些似是而非的观点。

（四）国际学术界对这场争论的回顾与重新检讨

在21世纪的开始，经济学家们对东亚奇迹的争论重新产生了兴趣，并从一个新的历史角度对当年的东亚奇迹的争论再次做了回顾与审视。2001年世界银行出版了一本新书《从奇迹到危机再到复苏：东亚四十年的经验教训》（*From Miracle to Crisis to Recovery: Lesson from Four Decades of East Asian Experience*），这本由Stiglitz和Yusuf主编的论文集从历史的角度对有关东亚经济奇迹的争论做了深入的分析，实际上对这场争论做了总结。其中Stiglitz所撰写的第13章“重新考虑东亚奇迹”（Rethinking The East Asian Miracie）对上述克鲁格曼的批评做了回应，他对生产率计算结果的稳健性一直存在怀疑，并提出以下观点：

（1）曾经有研究证明，只要将人力资本的计量方法稍加改变，就会大大改变全要素生产率的计算结果，因此全要素生产率计算的结果与所采用的方法和数据关系很大。由于结果的变异

较大,因此展开立论就比较缺乏基础;

(2) 如何将资本加以汇总的理论与方法上的困难更是尽人皆知,这一问题在最新研究中虽然有比较大的进展,但仍然可能有较大的不确定性;

(3) 计算全要素生产率的方法是标准的 Solow 残差法,这个方法的假设是生产要素的报酬等于其边际产出,这只有在完全竞争的市场中才可能,而亚洲国家的市场显然不是完全竞争的市场。因此,Stiglitz 教授对上述 Krugman-Kim-Lau-Young 批评中所涉及的全要素生产率计算提出了质疑,同时对这些论文中对全要素生产率计算结果的解释也提出了质疑。他认为某种意义上,关于全要素生产率的争论实际是无事忙。

在同一文集中的另一篇文章(Pack, 2001)也从技术进步和经济增长的角度分析了关于东亚经济奇迹的争论。该研究认为在过去的几十年,亚洲新兴工业化经济积累了大量的资本和技术劳动力,并且十分有效地在生产活动中使用这些资本和劳动。许多研究都证明,这些经济体中的大量企业十分成功地吸收了国际上的技术和知识,这些技术和知识可能体现在设备中,也可能体现在中间投入中,也可能是一种不包括资本投入(disembodied)的技术和知识。而在这些经济体中都存在一些强大的工业基地,在这些基地中,有现代化的设备,良好的组织,强大的营销能力,大量的高效率的工人和灵活应付外部冲击的能力。

而在亚洲金融危机期间,以上这些成就都被人们所忘记,流行的观点是衰退不可避免,而政府和企业都不再具有竞争力。但亚洲金融危机之后这些经济体经济的迅速复苏,再次证明上述所获得的成就还是存在的,并在继续发生作用。包括在最近的有关全球经济不平衡的讨论中,曾有人指出过去几年,一个重要的调整已经发生,即一些发展中国家和新兴工业化经济(大多数在亚洲)都积累了大量的外汇,已经从国际资本市场上的债务国(地区)变成了债权国(地区)。这些现象的出现未尝不表明当年对一些东亚经济的悲观论断是站不住脚的。

梁启源教授最近也根据他本人参与的“亚洲太平洋多个经济体生产率国际比较项目”(KLEMS)中有关中国台湾地区全要素生产率的研究对 Krugman-Kim-Lau-Young 的批评重新作了考察(Lian, 2002)。他讨论了 Young 的研究在方法论上存在的问题,并加以改进,结果发现认为中国台湾地区的经济增长不存在技术进步的批评是不成立的。

二、我们对克鲁格曼批评的分析与评价

在这一节我们力图全面讨论克鲁格曼批评,有些评论与前面提到的学者的批评相似,为了相对完整,我们也再次做了阐述。

(一) 关于全要素生产率计算方法的发展历史及其意义

全要素生产率测量是近 50 年来经济理论和实证研究的一个焦点领域,研究目的是想在数量上确定不同投入因素对经济增长的贡献。单要素生产率如劳动生产率和资本生产率只考虑一种要素的投入,而全要素生产率考虑的是所有的投入要素(劳动、资本等),因此在分析上要优于单要素生产率。在经济增长核算理论中全要素生产率是一个“残差”,等于产出增长率与各个被计算到的投入要素增长率加权和之差。

为了解释我们的观点,需要回顾一下全要素生产率计算方法的历史,该历史可以分成三个时期:第一个时期为 Solow 以前时期,最早提到生产率概念的是 Copeland(1937),以及 Copeland 和 Martin(1938)。最早实际估计这个变量的是 Stigler(1947),

Stigler在其1947年的研究中已独立地提出了全要素生产率的概念与分析方法。最早将生产函数方法与生产率联系在一起的是Tinbergen(1942)。总量生产函数的起源是所谓Cobb-Douglas生产函数,这一模型最初的目的是揭示生产中的规律并希望利用经济数据来验证这些生产中的理论模型。Tinbergen首先把这一生产函数用于研究经济增长问题,他在模型中增添了一个时间趋势,并用这一项来表示效率,也就是生产率的概念。

第二个时期为Solow 1957年文章到Jorgenson和Griliches 1967年文章之间。首先将生产函数与指数方法的理论联系表述出来的是Solow(1957)。Solow在1957年那篇文章,提出了一个计算全要素生产率的方法,但认为美国的经济增长80%来自全要素增长率,也就是技术进步的实证结论并没有得到后人的赞同。现在讨论美国经济的全要素增长率问题,通常强调的是Solow的理论贡献,很少提他的经验结论。在此期间,研究美国经济的全要素生产率以Kendrick和Denison为代表。这些人的实证分析结论,跟Solow当年是不一样的。

第三个时期为Jorgenson和Griliches 1967年文章之后。该文章批评了Denison等人的工作,认为他们在投入的计量上存在误差,因而高估了经济增长中全要素生产率的贡献。他们的论文认为从理论上分析,所谓的全要素生产率实际上是一种计算上的误差,这个误差来自对投入要素衡量的不准确或是某些对生产有贡献的要素没有被包括在生产函数中所致,如果把各种投入要素都包括在内并准确衡量,则这个误差不存在,全要素生产率就为零。因此,当发现一个国家的全要素生产率高,很可能只代表对这个国家的投入要素的衡量不准确或是某些投入要素未被包括在内。同时,也意味着全要素生产率的研究必须对投入要素有准确的衡量,并且,跨国的研究应该采用一致的测算方法才有可比性。

目前国际学术界的大量研究所依据的全要素生产率的计算方法是根据以上所提到的建立在第三时期所发展的方法。这一点的最重要的标志就是OECD所出版的关于资本估计的手册(OECD, 1999)和关于生产率估计的手册(OECD, 2001)。该方法仍然保留着完全竞争市场和规模收益不变的假设。对于该核算方法的上述基本假设可能不满足的问题也早已被人们所认识,之所以没有发展出新的核算方法,就在于在如此复杂、成熟的体系中改变一些基本假设并不是很容易,需要考虑太多因素,同时还需要满足已有体系的许多要求,这方面的努力一直还没有获得成果。

而对于全要素生产率核算的基础理论——生产者行为理论的挑战,特别是对于生产者理论中的利润最大化目标函数的假设的研究也很多,如销售最大化(Baumol, 1967),还有管理效用最大化(Williamson, 1964)和利润满意(Simon, 1959)等。但是,微观经济学的厂商理论是一个完整的体系,试图按照其他的目标函数来建立系统的厂商理论的研究,并对微观经济学的厂商理论给出完整的替代体系似乎还没有真正成熟。

目前通用的估计全要素生产率的方法有两种:一种是增长核算方法,其理论模型简洁,来自新古典增长理论,是一种非参数的实证估计方法,计算方法主要依靠统计性质与经济学性质很好的一些指数公式。另一种是经济计量学方法,一般将总产出或增加值作为因变量,将不同的投入变量作为自变量,通过参数估计的方法来研究。经济计量学方法测算全要素生产率虽然可以放松增长核算方法中完全竞争市场和规模收益不变等假设,但必须对估计的参数给出先验假设,并且受样本观察值数量的限制,容易出现参数估计不稳定等统计上的问题。而非参数方法将指数方法与生产函数相联系，更适合于定期的生产率统计研究。OECD(2001)生产率手册推荐使用增长核算的方法来估计全要素生产率，这也是目前采用最广泛的测量全要素生产率的方法。美国劳工统计局(BLS)从1983年开始公布的美国全要素生产率，就是用增长核算方法来估计的。

现在有些全要素生产率的研究直接应用回归分析方法(例如最小二乘方法)来估计一个带时间趋势项的生产函数，这种研究在方法论上是有问题的。原因是：以经济计量方法来估计全要素生产率的基础是生产函数的经济计量估计，而生产函数的计量估计并不是一个单方程的简单回归分析的问题，而是包括生产要素需求的联立方程体系的估计问题，这一点在国内许多关于生产函数估计和全要素生产率估计的研究中都没有得到正确的理解和运用。即使是C-D生产函数的估计也不是简单的回归分析，至少有4种以上基于联立方程体系估计的估计方法。关于生产函数的经济计量估计可以参考李子奈的《计量经济学——方法和应用》和任若恩的《计量经济方法论——关于在中国应用的研究》。而在英文的文献中，则有大量的研究，如最早的经典文献Marschak和Andrews(1944)，Nerlove 1965年的专著，Intriligator 1978年的教科书，Jorgenson 1986年的综述等；关于估计全要素生产率的经济计量方法，可见Nadiri和Prucha 2001年论文中的介绍。

目前全要素生产率国际比较研究以KLEMS项目最有影响。KLEMS项目是最近几年由哈佛大学的Jorgenson教授和日本庆应大学的黑田教授等人共同倡议的国际间的全要素比较项目，K是资本(capital)，L是劳动(labor)，E是能源(energy)，M是物质生产部门产生的中间投入要素(intermediate-input)，S是服务生产部门产生的中间投入要素，即左边是产出，右边是生产总产值中的五个组成部分。这个等式中特别把能源提出来，就是为了将来好研究环境问题。KLEMS研究方法的基础是双国生产函数模型，并在这一模型框架下估计两国之间的全要素生产率的差距。这一方法最初由Jorgenson与西水(Jorgenson and Nishimizu, 1978)提出并用于日本和美国的经济增长因素的比较研究，并通过计算两国的全要素生产率的差距，来解释国家之间在增长因素方面的不同。计算的理论基础是微观经济学中的生产者理论和对偶理论。由于生产函数采用超越对数函数形式，对生产技术的描述可以限制在假设尽可能少的框架中(Christensen, Jorgenson, Lau, 1971, 1973)。这一方法可以利用指数的形式计算，也可以利用经济计量学的方法计算(Jorgenson and Kuroda, 1988; Jorgenson et al., 1988)。这一分析框架已用在双国与多国之间的比较，以及宏观和产业部门之间的比较(Christensen, Cummings Jorgenson, 1980, 1981; Jorgenson and Kuroda, 1992; Conrad, 1992)。在最初的研究中，生产函数是由增加值和资本、劳动等变量构成。在随后的发展中，增加值改为总产值，在解释变量中又包括了中间投入。

KLEMS项目目前已经形成了一个多机构参加的组合(Consortium Project Institutions)，其中包括美国的4个机构(The Conference Board, Harvard University, Brookings Institute, Federal Reserve Bank of New York)和荷兰、意大利、英国、德国、法国、西班牙、芬兰、丹麦、加拿大、日本等国家的一些机构(Timmer, 2000)。在亚洲区域，与此相似的项目ICPA(International Comparison of the Productivity among Pan-Pacific Counties)也已接近完成，该项目包括日本、韩国、中国等国家和地区。KLEMS项目研究的目的是：投入要素的变化对经济增长、生产率和国际竞争力的影响，国家间增长的基本要素的区别，劳动力的质量与构成的变化和差异对国际竞争力的作用，国家之间高技术产业的生产率和国际竞争力的差异。

克鲁格曼的批评其实有一个非常致命的错误。他引用 Solow 1957 年所做的分析，认为在美国经济增长当中，有 80% 以上是通过技术进步取得的，是全要素生产率的贡献。但是，Jorgenson 等人 1987 年出版的书是根据 Jorgenson 和 Griliches 1967 年文章之后研究方法进行研究的典范，该研究认为，美国从 1948 年到 1979 年的经济增长因素分析中，资本是最重要的，劳动的贡献是第二重要的，而全要素生产率的贡献排在第三位。克鲁格曼不可能不知道 Jorgenson 和 Griliches 1967 年文章之后对全要素生产率研究的新发展，和 Jorgenson 等人 1987 年这本书的新结论，但是他仍然用了 Solow 1957 年的结论。

（二）经济发展史研究的发现

在前面讨论陈坤耀对克鲁格曼批评的批评中提到技术进步包括与资本融合在一起的（embodied）和不包括资本投入的（disembodied）两类。不同发展程度的国家取得技术进步的方式可能不同，发达国家所使用的技术处于国际技术的最前沿，发达国家的企业要取得技术创新，必须自己进行新技术的研发，而研发的投入在目前通用的生产率的研究中并不包括在投入要素内，依靠这种方式取得的技术进步属于不包括资本投入的技术进步。与此相反，发展中国家可以利用和发达国家的技术差距以引进技术的方式取得技术创新，发展中国家引进的技术通常包括在新的机器设备里，属于包括资本的技术进步。因此，以同样的方式来研究一个国家不同的发展阶段，那么，发展早期的全要素生产率将会较低，而达到发展阶段后，全要素生产率将会较大，这个理论推断在对美国和日本的经济史研究中得到证实。

Hayami 在其新著《发展经济学：从贫穷到富裕》（*Develop-*

ment Economics:*From Poverty to the Wealth of Nations*)的第5章主要讨论了“经济发展中的资本积累”的问题。该章介绍了Abramovitz(1993)的有关经济史的研究,根据他的估算,对美国来说,在1800—1855年和1855—1890年间,全要素生产率对劳动生产率增长的贡献要大大小于资本—劳动比例增长的贡献,这说明在此期间,资本产出比例在增加。这一研究也大致证明了,在通常人们认为美国工业革命开始(19世纪40年代和50年代)后的初期阶段,资本积累是经济增长的主要推动力。对日本来说,经济史的研究也揭示了大致相似的增长类型。按照Hayami和Ogasahara(1995)的研究,如果假定日本的工业革命开始于19世纪和20世纪之交的年代,在其后的工业革命的第一阶段和第二阶段也出现了资本—劳动比率的增长率超过劳动生产率的增长率,因此也同样表明资本—产出比率的增长和提高。全要素生产率的增长只能解释劳动生产率增长的10%,其余是投入要素的贡献。

日本的研究和美国的研究结果都表明,在随后的工业发展的高级阶段,全要素生产率对经济增长的贡献逐步提高,资本的份额在达到一个高点后开始下降。前面已经谈过,克鲁格曼对东亚经济的分析所依据的实证研究之一就是Kim和Lau(刘遵义,1994)。而按照Hayami书中的分析,Kim和Lau(刘遵义,1994)的研究恰恰证明了东亚的4个新兴工业化经济体的发展经历显示了与美国和日本早期发展相类似的增长模式。

三、小结:东亚经济奇迹争论对中国的意义

从克鲁格曼挑起的这场“东亚经济奇迹”争论的回顾中,我们可以得到几点对我国未来发展有意义的结论:

第一，全要素生产率的计算和经济增长因素的分析具有一个严谨的理论体系和分析框架，如何从概念上正确把握特别重要。克鲁格曼对东亚经济奇迹的批评主要是对全要素生产率的经济意义没有正确把握，以及对不同发展程度的国家或地区在全要素生产率上的不同表现缺乏了解造成的。因此，我们不要简单地根据克鲁格曼对“东亚经济奇迹”的批评来评论我国的经济发展经验，并作为讨论我国未来经济发展模式的依据。

第二，对于一个国家经济的长期可持续发展来说，重要的是技术的不断创新，而不在于全要素生产率的高低。从美国和日本等国家在未成为最发达国家之前，全要素生产率低，只有到了发达阶段时全要素生产率才高的事实可以看出：这些国家在还处于发展中阶段时，技术创新主要是靠从发达国家引进技术设备，只有到了发达阶段各个产业的技术大多已经处于世界的最前沿时才转而以不表现为资本的研发来取得技术创新。目前，我国还处于发展中阶段，和发达国家还有很大的技术差距，要善于利用这个差距，在尽可能的范围内引进合适的先进机器设备，这样全要素生产率的水平虽然会较低，但是，技术创新和经济发展的速度反而会较快。

第三，我国虽然应该多利用引进技术来取得技术创新，但是，并不是就不用进行自主研发。首先，发达国家劳动力昂贵，发达国家的技术通常尽量自动化以减少劳动力的使用。我国劳动力相对便宜，从发达国家引进技术时，通常需要进行一些流程的研发创新，在不影响产品质量的前提下，应该尽量以劳动力来替代昂贵的自动化设备，这样可以降低成本，增加效益。其次，有些产业我国有比较优势，但是没有比我国更发达的国家还留在这个产业里，因而也无法从其他国家引进时，或是，在这个产业里我国和发达国家的差距只是最后一两个关键的技术而难于从发达国家引进时，我国就需要在这样的产业自己进行新产品和新技术的研发。秉持这两个原则，随着我国经济的发展，产业水平的提高，需要自主研发的领域将会越来越多，全要素生产率的水平也就会越来越高。

参考文献

郑玉歆：《全要素生产率的测算及其增长的规律——由东亚增长模式的争论谈起》，《数量经济技术经济研究》1998年第10期。

李子奈：《计量经济学——方法和应用》，清华大学出版社1992年版。

任若恩：《计量经济学方法论——关于在中国应用的研究》，中国人民大学出版社1992年版。

Abramovitz, M., 1993, "The Search for the Sources of Growth: Area of Ignorance, Old and New", *Journal of Economic History*, 53(June): 217—243.

Bhagwati, J., 1996, The Miracle That Did Happen: Understanding East Asia in Comparative Perspective, Keynote Speech Delivered at Cornell University on the Occasion of Conference on "Government and Market: The Relevance of the Taiwanese Performance to Development Theory and Policy in honor of Professor Liu and Tsiang.

Baumol, W. J., 1967, *Business Behavior, Value and Growth*, Rev. Ed. New York: Harcourt Brace Jovanovich.

Caves, D. W., L. R. Christensen, and E. W. Diewert, 1982a, "Multilateral Comparison of Output, Input and Productivity Using Superlative Index Numbers", *Economic Journal* 92, No. 365(March): 73—86.

Caves, D. W., L. R. Christensen and E. W. Diewert, 1982b, "The Economic Theory of Index Numbers and the Measurement of Output, Input and Productivity", *Econometrica* 50, No. 6(November): 1393—1414.

Chen, E. K. Y., 1997, "The Total Factor Productivity Debate: Determinants of Economic Growth in East Asia", *Asian-Pacific Economic*

Literature, 11(1):18—38, 54—70.

Christensen, L., D. Cummings and D. W. Jorgenson, 1980, "Economic Growth, 1947—1973: An International Comparison", in J. W. Kendrick and B. Vaccara eds., *New Development in Productivity Measurement*, New York: Columbia University Press: 595—698.

Copeland, M. A., 1937, "Concepts of National Income, Studies in Income and Wealth", Vol. 1 NewYork, NBER:3—61.

Copeland, M. A. and E. M. Martin, 1938, "The Correction of Wealth and Income Estimates for Price Changes, Studies in Income and Wealth", Vol. 2 New York, NBER:85—135.

Conrad, K., 1992, "Inter-country Changes in Productivity in the Manufacturing Sector of Five OECD Countries, 1963—86", in: B. G. Hickman(eds.), *International Productivity and Competitiveness*, Oxford University Press, New York.

Denison, E. F., 1962, "The Sources of Economic Growth in the United States and the Alternatives Before US", New York, Committee for Economic Development.

Diewert, W. E. "Duality Approaches to Microeconomic Theory", in Handbook of Mathematical Economics, Vol. 2, edited by K. J. Arrow & M. D. Intriligator.

Diewert, I. and A. Nakamura, 1998, A Survey of Empirical Methods of Productivity Measurement, In *Handbook of Econometrics*, Vol. 5.

Felipe, J, 1997, "Total Factor Productivity Growth in East Asia: A Critical Survey", Economics and Development Center Report Series No. 65, Asian Development Bank, Manina.

Griliches, Z., 1995, "The Discovery of the Residual: An Historical Note", NBER Working Paper 5348.

Hayami Y., and Ogasahara, J., 1995, "The Kuznets versus the Marx Pattern in Modern Economic Growth: A Perspective from the Japanese Experience", Department of Agricultural, Resource and Management Economics

Working Paper, No. WP 95—13 (Ithaca, NY: ARME, Cornell University).

Hulten, Charles R., 2000, "Total Factor Productivity: A Short Biography", NBER Working Paper 7471.

Intriligator, M. D., 1978, *Econometrics Model, Techniques and Application*, Prentice-Hall, Inc. Englewood Cliff, N. J.

Jorgenson, D. W., 1986, "Econometric Methods for Modeling Producer Behavior", in *Handbook of Econometrics*, Vol. Ⅲ, edited by Z. Griliches and M. Intriligator.

Jorgenson, D. W. and Z. Griliches, 1967, "The Explanation of Productivity Change", *Review of Economic Studies*, Vol. 34, No. 3, July: 249—283.

Jorgenson, D. W. and M. Nishimizu, 1978, "U. S. and Japanese Economic Growth, 1952—1974: An International Comparison", *Economic Journal* 88, no. 352: 707—726.

Jorgenson, D. W., F. M. Collop and B. M. Fraumeni, 1987, *Productivity and U. S. Economic Growth*, Cambridge, MA: Harvard University Press.

Jorgenson, D. W. and Z. Grilliches, 1972, "Issues in Growth Accounting: A Reply to E. F. Denison", *Survey of Current Business* 52, No. 5. pt. 2(May): 65—94.

Jorgenson, D. W. and M. Kuroda and M. Nishimizu, 1987, "Japan-U. S. Industry-Level Comparisons, 1960—1979", *Journal of Japanese and International Economies* 1(March): 1—30.

Jorgenson, D. W. and M. Kuroda, 1992, "Productivity and International Competitiveness in Japan and the United States, 1960—1985", in: B. G. Hickman (eds.), *International Productivity and Competitiveness*, Oxford University Press, New York.

Jorgenson, D. W. and K. Stiroh, 2000, "Raising the Speed Limit: US Economic Growth in the Information Age", Paper for Seminar at the Brookings Institute.

Jorgenson, D. W. and L. Frank, 2001, "Industry-level Productivity and International Competitiveness between Canada and the United States", Industry Canada Research Monograph.

Kendrick, J. , 1961, *Productivity Trends in the United States*, New York: NBER.

Kim, Jong-Ⅱ, and Lawrence Lau, 1994, "The Sources of Economic Growth of the East Asian Newly Industrialized Countries", *Journal of Japanese and International Economies* 8(3): 235—271.

Krugman, P. , 1994, "Myth of Asia's Miracle", *Foreign Affairs*.

Lian, Chi-Yuan, 2002, "Industrial Structure Changes and the Measurement of Total Factor Productivity Growth: The Krugman-Kim-Lau-Young Hypothesis Revisited", Paper for Third ICPA workshop in Tokyo.

Marschak, J. and W. Andrews, 1944, "Random simultaneous Equations and the Theory of Production", *Econometrica*, Vol. 12, No. 3 & 4.

Nerlove, M. , 1965, Estimation and Identification of Cobb-Douglas Production Functions, Rand McNally & Company.

Nadiri, M. I. , 1980, "Producers Theory", in *Handbook of Mathematical Economics*, Vol. 2, edited by K. J. Arrow & M. D. Intriligator.

Nadiri, M. and I. Prucha, 2001, "Dynamic Factor Demand Models and Productivity Analysis", in Hulton, Dean and Harper eds. *New Development in Productivity Analysis*, University of Chicago Press.

OECD, 2001, Productivity Manual A Guide to the Measurement of Industry-level and Aggregate Productivity Growth, Paris.

Pack H. , 2001, "Technological Change and Growth in East Asia: Macro versus Micro Perspectives", in J. Stiglitz and S. Yusuf (editors), *Rethinking the East Asian Miracle*, Oxford, Oxford University Press for the World Bank.

Simon, H. , 1959, "Theories of Decision-Making in Economics and Behavioral Science", *American Economic Review*, 59:253—283.

Solow, R. K. , 1957, "Technical Change and the Aggregate Production Function", *Review of Economics and Statistics*, 39:312—320.

Stigler, G. J., 1947, *Trends in Output and Employment*, New York, NBER.

Stiglitz, J. E., 2003, "From Miracle to Crisis to Recovery: Lesson from Four Decades of East Asian Experience", Chapter 13 in *Rethinking The East Asian Miracle*.

Tinbergen, J., 1942, "Zur Theorie Der Langristigen Wirtschaftsentwicklung", Weltwirtschaftiches Archiv, Band 55: 511—549, English translation, "On the theory of Trend Movements", In Jan Tinbergen, Selected Papers, eds., L. H. Klassen, L. M. Koyck and H. J. Witteveen, Amsterdam: North Holland, 1959.

Williamson, O. E., 1964, *The Economics of Discretionary Behavior: Managerial Objectives in a Theory of the Firm*, Englewood Cliffs, N. J.: Prentice-Hall., Inc.

Young, Alwyn, 1992, "A Tale of Two Cities: Factor Accumulation and Technological Change in Hong Kong and Singapore", *National Bureau of Economic Research Macroeconomics Annual* 1992.

Young, Alwyn, 1994, "Lessons from the East Asian NICs: A Contrarian View", *European Economic Review* 38: 964—973.

(原载《经济研究》2007 年第 8 期)

经济作物、食物获取权与饥荒：对森的理论的检验*

范子英　孟令杰

（南京农业大学经济管理学院）

一、引　言

虽然农业技术一直进步，世界粮食产出也呈现上升趋势，但是随着粮食产出总量增加的是粮食生产波动性的加剧（Sen，1981），并由此增加饥荒发生的可能性，比如1943年孟加拉国发生的大饥荒以及1972—1974年发生在埃塞俄比亚的大饥荒。中国自1949年以来以7%的耕地养活了占世界21%的人口，粮食生产取得了巨大的进步，但是在进步的同时，一部分人却由于得不到足够的食物挨饿甚至死亡。因此在农业技术高度发展的今天，对于饥荒的研究不管是从世界范围还是中国都有积极的意义，同时对于不平等和贫困的研究也有一定的启发。

新中国成立不久就经历了一场大的自然灾害，传统称为“三

---

* 作者对北京大学CCER林毅夫、南京农业大学钟甫宁、复旦大学陆铭提出的宝贵修改意见表示感谢，另外感谢同济大学黎德福、合肥工业大学李静、南京农业大学胡冰川和石慧在本文撰写过程中提供的帮助，感谢匿名评审人提出的详细的修改意见。本项目得到南京农业大学经济管理学院项目资助。

年自然灾害”时期或“三年困难时期”。由于这三年我国的粮食产量下降显著，人均粮食特别是农村人口的人均粮食急剧减少，并由此造成了人口的非正常死亡，因此国外一些文献也称其为“灾荒”时期（范子英、孟令杰，2005）。

建国初期的国民经济非常落后，当时衡量一国综合国力的是钢产量，为了尽快摆脱落后的局面，中国从1952年开始逐渐采取当时的苏联模式，实行重工业优先发展的战略，但是50年代的中国经济基础薄弱，城市资源根本无法支持该战略的有效实行，为了有效快速地增加积累，政府有意压缩各种要素的投入成本，降低城镇居民的工资水平，同时为了保障城镇居民的生活资料有效供给，政府从农村抽调了大量资源并且压缩农产品的价格，这样整个重工业化进程的负担几乎全部转移到农民身上。为了有效地组织资源的调拨，政府在1953年实行了粮、油、棉的计划收购和征购，即农户在完成国家派购的任务后才可以进行农产品的自由交易（赵德馨，1988），然而实际上政府已经最大限度地征购了农产品，农民基本上没有剩余产品可以拿来交换了，农产品自由市场基本上不存在（Walker，1984）。随着重工业化进程的加快，城市从农村抽调了越来越多的资源，动员大量农村劳动力进城从事工业生产，这加剧了城市生活物资的供应，同时削弱了农业生产。①城市的粮食供给一度出现紧张的状况，使得政府不得不加大对农产品的征购来保障城镇居民的基本生活资料供给，所以1955年3月又制定了对粮食的定产、定购、定销的“三定”政策，该政策相对于之前的政策更加严格，规定凡完成派

① 比如1957年全国农村劳动力为1.931亿人，由于当时农业生产基本上还处于相当落后的状态，所以农村中并不存在普遍的劳动力过剩，1958年，国家职工增加了2 000万人，总数达到了4 532万人，农业和工业劳动者的比例由上年的13.8∶1下降到3.5∶1（柳随年、吴群，1984）。

购任务后还有余粮的农户为余粮户，国家对该余粮户的余粮进行统购(焦贵玺等，1991)，这样就完全取消了农产品自由市场，统购统销制度也最终确立。

对农产品的统购使得政府完全控制了粮食的供给，由于禁止和排挤了私商的活动，政府成为价格的唯一制定者，但由于不存在自由市场，该价格并不能反映产品的供给和需求状况，只是作为当时政府分配物资的一个辅助手段。当粮食收获之后，各地将征购的粮食上交国家，国家再统一分配，由于政府制定对粮食的统购统销政策的初衷是为了保障城镇的食物供给，城镇居民成为粮食分配最先考虑的对象，同时为了有效地控制需求，并把资源分配给特定的人群，实行了严格的户籍制度来控制目标人群的数量，1954 年又开始启用粮票制度，后来逐渐发展到对相应的工业品也需要相应的票证，如布票等。而广大的农村地区基本上被排除在这种统销政策范围之外，特别是粮食主产区，在完成国家统购任务之后的粮食才能由农民自由支配，并且统购任务的确定并不是参照当年的粮食产量(这可能是缘于操作上的困难)，往往是根据以前年度的平均产量来确定一个地区的粮食上交任务。在正常年份，由于农民手中还剩下能够维持生存的粮食，所以不会遭受饥饿的威胁，在丰收年份甚至还有少许余粮，但一旦粮食减产，农民则要负担减产的全部后果，在上交了公粮后的余粮很可能不足以维持生存，此时农民就会面临饥饿，即产粮区农民承担了农业生产的全部风险。

这种统购统销政策带来城乡之间的对立，后来出现很多地方的农民隐匿粮食，为了有效实行粮食的统购，在 1958 年开始了公社化运动，强制性地入社使得农业生产遭到破坏，到了 11 月初，入社农户占总农户数的 99.1%(赵德馨，1988)，公社成为最基本的经济单位，在完成征购任务上面显得更富有效率，使得从农村抽调资源更加彻底，基本上消灭了原来农民抵抗中央政策的手段。伴随着公社化运动的是公共食堂制度，这种制度最初的目的是为了有效地分配粮食，使农村粮食呈现均等化分配。但公共食堂使得当时对农民的激励降低到一个很低的水平，因为农民的最终收益与其努力程度几乎不相关，农业生产也因此遭到严重破坏，同时公共食堂的消费机制也不健全，使得后期粮食供给更加紧张，加剧了自然灾害的严重程度。

在随后的分析中，我们发现在自然灾害发生时农村地区受到的影响最大，但是不同地区之间的差异很大，这个成为本文研究的重点，我们想知道到底是什么因素造成地区之间在几乎相同的政策环境下而人口死亡率却有着天壤之别。林毅夫、杨涛(Lin and Yang，2000；下文简称林文)得出城市偏向系统是造成死亡率差异的主要因素，本文则囊括了该结论，更准确地说是产粮区和非产粮区①的划分才是主要因素。另外，森的食物获取权理论自提出后一直受到传统理论的非议，其中很重要的一点是森在他的著作中并没有将两者对于饥荒的解释能力进行对比，因此也就不能说明前者比后者更科学，本文将会对这两者的影响作对比，以说明到底谁更具解释力。再者，曹树基在2005年曾指出林文存在两个问题，一是他们的数据来自中国政府公布的数据，而这个数据是否真实还值得研究，并且还得考虑当时的行政区划的变动问题，二是林文的结论无法解释农村地区人口死亡率的巨大差异，本文是继林文之后对该问题的又一研究，我们所选取的变量和数据都能很好地避免或者解决这两个问题，所以也可以说，在将森的食物获取权理论用来解释中国1959—1961年自然灾害方面，本文算是较完备和系统地解释了

① 在本文中产粮区是指粮食调出区域，也就是粮食主产区，而非产粮区是粮食调入区，这两个概念对应后面的非缺粮区和缺粮区，在本文中这两组概念没有差异。

中国自然灾害发生时地区之间的差异,同时也对森的理论有一定的补充。

本文分为如下几个部分:一是引言,回顾了自然灾害发生时的背景;二是理论及文献回顾,简要介绍两种饥荒理论,对有关研究中国自然灾害的文献作简单介绍;三是数据及分析,对本文的样本数据进行简要的统计描述分析;四是模型及检验,主要运用Panel data 的双向固定效应方法来验证本文的假设;五是结论。

二、理论及文献回顾

对饥荒的研究最早可以追溯到亚当·斯密和马尔萨斯,他们都认为战争和天灾可以在某一特定区域大量损害农业生产,导致广泛的食物短缺,并最终引起饥荒,这便是传统的解释饥荒的食物供给量下降理论(Food Availability Decline, FAD),FAD理论后来得到延伸,凡是仅从食物供给总量方面来阐述饥荒发生的研究都归于该理论的解释范围,而不管造成食物供给下降的原因是人为因素还是非人为因素。FAD理论着重从供给方面来解释饥荒的发生,而忽略了食物分配上的差异,后来森在其影响广泛的著作中,提出了对该理论有力补充的食物获取权理论(Entitlement)。该理论考虑一个人的禀赋向量,它可能包括土地拥有量、劳动力、健康状况以及其他产权,他可以用其最初禀赋生产或购买食物,当这两种方式都不能获得足够的食物时,饥饿便产生了,当这种状况长期得不到缓解和大范围①存

① 这里有必要强调是大范围的发生才能称为饥荒,小范围的人由于食物短缺饿死在本文中不算作饥荒,虽然森的理论中指出即使是仅有分配体制的扭曲也可能造成饥荒,但在现实中,一个理性的政府的分配体制不太可能通过体制变革使得大范围的人在正常年份濒临饥饿的威胁。在后面的分析中将延续这一概念。

在时饥荒便发生了,这可能是由于禀赋向量的减少(直接食物获取权失败),也可能因为食物价格发生了不利变化(交易食物获取权失败),还应包括人为扭曲的食物供应体系。可以看出食物获取权理论的重点是从微观层面上考虑食物的分配对饥荒的影响,同时该理论也得到了经验上的验证。但值得说明的是,食物获取权并不是饥荒发生的必要条件,它有一个前提是食物供给量的大幅度下降(至少是局部),即在农业生产滑坡的情况下,如果存在食物获取权下降,其将对饥荒的发生产生巨大的加剧作用,而相反的情况下,粮食生产没有恶化,即使存在食物获取权下降,由于整个社会食物供给相对丰裕,不存在某一部分人的食物短缺,饥荒还是不会发生。

对这次自然灾害的原因的研究一直众说纷纭,既有从传统的 FAD 理论的角度来解释,也有用森的食物获取权理论来解释,还有学者将两者综合起来,考察两者的影响大小。在以往的研究中,有学者(范子英、孟令杰,2005)将其归结为 FAD、食物获取权和制度因素三个方面,由于制度因素的一个直接后果是分配体系的扭曲,其仍属食物获取权理论的解释范围,所以我们接下来的分析将按 FAD 和食物获取权两方面来回顾。

考虑到自然灾害发生时整个中国农业产出下降的事实,也有很多学者试图从体制上找出原因。林毅夫(Lin, 1990)提出“退社权”的丧失是导致农业产出下降的主要因素,由于农业生产中监督成本太大,产出的增加就只能依靠激励来实现,早期的合作化运动中的“退社权”成为替代生产监督的有效手段,但1958 年的公社化运动剥夺了农户的该项权力,使得唯一的监督手段消失了,农户的激励降到一个很低的水平,农业产出随之急剧下降;同样当时的工业化进程也扮演了一个重要的角色,Yang 和 Li(2005)指出当时的政府急于加快重工业化进程，从农村中抽调了大量的资源，要素市场和产品市场都极大地向城市倾斜，使得脆弱的农业生产遭到破坏，农业产出急剧下滑；考虑到当时特殊的消费机制——公共食堂，杨大利（Yang, 1996）和文贯中、张欣（Chang and Wen, 1997）都指出公共食堂的不理性消费是导致自然灾害发生的主要因素，粮食的过度消费使得后期出现严重的短缺，加上粮食调拨体系的脆弱（周飞舟，2003），使得食物得不到及时的补给，灾荒便在这些地方最早出现。

1959—1961年粮食减产虽是一个不争的事实，但仅此不能成为饥荒发生的充分条件，分配体制的扭曲是导致灾荒和地区之间死亡率差异的重要因素。新中国成立后实行的重工业策略要求形成与之配套的机制，其中一个很重要的便是低工资政策（林毅夫、蔡昉和李周，1994），但低工资政策实行的一个前提是不能大幅度降低城镇居民的生活水平，于是消费物资的价格被压缩，农产品相对于工业品的价格被人为地扭曲，城镇居民的食物得到制度上的保证，逐渐形成一个有效的城市偏向系统（Lin and Yang, 2000），当粮食减产时，这种系统使得城镇居民得到保障，农村居民则要承受粮食减产的全部影响；更加严重的是当时的领导人对农业生产过度乐观，加上"浮夸风"的盛行，对农业产出的征收在灾荒年份不减反增，使得农民可支配的粮食更加少，征购率的上升成为灾荒发生的一个重要因素（Bernstein, 1985）。

林文的理论可以用来解释在灾荒发生时城市为何几乎没受影响，而农村的死亡率却很高。但即使是这样，有些问题仍然无法解释，在城乡分割的情况下，农村的政策环境在一个省内基本相似，但为何各地的死亡率有着很大的区别。我们认为各地的自然禀赋不一样可能是主要原因。在产粮区之间，即使存在着产出上的差异，由于当时的余粮征购制和公社制，在完成粮食征购任务后可以认为它们之间不存在较大的差异。但是在产粮区和非产粮区（如产棉区），则可能存在很大的差异，后者在正常年份的粮食供给基本上靠国家的返销粮和调拨粮。①产棉区在丰收年份的粮食供给也基本上没太大的变化，这是因为为了出口和战备的需要，国家已经最大可能地对粮食实行了统购，粮食供给的总量不会有太大的变化，在进行城市粮食配给之后，用来返销农村的粮食量也不会变化太大，同时棉花作为一种重要的经济作物在 1953 年就实行了统购，并且 1958 年实行的公社制使得这种变化的可能性更小；而在农业歉收的年份，由于返销粮的数量是事先拟定好的，国家会按以前制定的数额返销缺粮区，所以这些地区被排除在粮食生产波动的影响范围之外，其粮食供给得到了体制上的保障。

我们假定在正常年份产粮区和非产粮区之间死亡率不会有太大的差异，因为两者都能得到足够维持生存的粮食，在我们选择的样本中，1957 年死亡率的方差为 9.47；在非正常年份，产粮区由于粮食总产量的下降而导致农民可支配粮食的减少，面临饥荒威胁的几率较大，死亡率也较大，而非产粮区却不受粮食减产的影响，死亡率较常年没有大的变动，两者死亡率的差异会很大，在我们的样本中 1960 年的方差为 100.85。在随后的分析中，城市偏向系统不是太显著，主要是因为我们的样本是以县为单位，其中的非农人口都只占很小的比重，随时间变化的幅度很小。

---

① 在 1955 年制定的对粮食的定产、定购和定销的“三定”政策中规定：农村中粮食不足的农户为缺粮户，包括不从事粮食生产的农户，国家对缺粮户分别制定粮食缺额进行统销的政策（焦贵玺等，1991）。

三、数据及分析

(一) 样本的选择

本文所选取的数据是江苏省 55 个县①从 1954 年到 1977 年的数据，从 1954 年开始主要是因为林文曾指出，1954 年前，由于战争和其他的社会破坏向稳定的社会过渡，造成死亡率的显著下降；选择 1977 年作为结束是因为 1978 年中国实行改革开放，许多计划体制下的政策在这一年改变。选择江苏省是因为如前文所述，江苏省在饥荒年份的死亡率相对较低，其政策相对较保守，可以认为其省内各地方对中央政策的执行力度差异不大，即回避了政策执行力度对死亡率的影响，达到简化分析的目的；选择以县作为样本是因为各市的行政区划变化较大。人口方面的数据来自江苏省统计局 1986 年的《江苏省人口统计资料汇编》，其他数据来自江苏农林厅 1982 年出版的《江苏省农业统计资料（1949—1980）》，全国的数据来自中国统计出版社 1999 年的《新中国五十年统计资料汇编》。

从图 1 可以看出 1959—1961 年全国死亡率的平均水平有一个较大的变动，说明这三年经历了一场大的灾荒，同期的江苏省的死亡率水平也从 1957 年的 1.026％上升到 1960 年的 1.841％，上升比例为 79.4％，而全国的该比例为 135.5％，可见江苏省的变动要缓和得多。在灾荒最严重的 1960 年，死亡率的全国平均水平是江苏省的 1.4 倍，对此可能的解释是江苏省的人均粮食产出虽然在饥荒年份有所下降，但是相对于全国水平还是较高，但数据支持相反的解释，无法从粮食产量来解释这种

---

① 其中丹徒、泰县、邗江、响水、金湖、灌南、淮阴、震泽和沙洲由于大部分数据缺失而剔除，所有的县都是按 1982 年的行政区划计算。

差异;特别是如果考虑到结转库存的影响,即当年的死亡率不仅受当年的人均粮食产量的影响,上年的人均粮食产量也会有滞后影响,1959 年江苏省的人均粮食产出比全国水平要低 8.5%,这样江苏省加总的粮食产出比全国平均水平要低,而其死亡率居然也比全国平均水平低。

灾荒年份死亡率越低的省份其政策的激进程度也越温和(范子英、孟令杰,2005),这是一个相反的推理过程。政策越激进的省份其内部政策执行力度的差异也越大,相应的死亡率的差异也越大。这样我们从数据中可以得出江苏省在饥荒年份的政策激进程度相对于全国来说要温和,其内部由于政策执行力度差异对死亡率差异的影响程度也很低。以 1960 年来看,全国的死亡率的方差为 223.9,而江苏省的死亡率的方差仅为 100.85,从这可以看出当年对中央激进政策的执行力度,江苏省低于全国的平均水平,这样,在我们的分析中,以江苏作为样本,其随机扰动误差较全国的要低,这也是本文为何选择江苏省作为样本的原因。

江苏省地处于长江三角洲,地形以平原为主,平原占全省总面积的 69%,主要有苏南平原、江淮平原、黄淮平原和东部滨海平原,并且有五大淡水湖中的太湖和洪泽湖,农业种植条件比较优越。除了广大的平原外,省内还有占全省面积 5%的低山和丘陵,主要是分布在西南部的低山丘陵、东北部的丘陵山地和西北部的丘陵。[①]另外,江苏省的气候具有过渡性,淮北地区年降雨量较少,而且集中于夏季,淮南地区年降雨量较多,并且分配均匀,由此导致淮北地区一般是一年两熟,而淮南地区有的达到一年三熟。[②]由于地形分布和人口分布的不同,各地的人均自然

---

① 杜闻贞主编:《中国人口(江苏分册)》,中国财政经济出版社 1987 年版,第 10 页。

② 江苏年鉴编纂委员会:《江苏年鉴》,南京大学出版社 1991 年版,第 3 页。

资源禀赋条件差异很大，再加上气候的差异，导致各地农作物种类和人均产量的差异。

（二）变量的选择

在当时的经济条件下，中国大部分的农民没有较多的财产，即使有一定的财产，但由于不存在自由市场，所以不会影响最终的死亡率，因此财产便不在本文的考虑范围内；同时由于各地的医疗水平基本上都处在一个很低的水平，影响死亡率的主要是营养状况，而营养状况是由人均卡路里摄入量决定的，这样死亡率可以用一个简单的函数表示：$DR = f(C, H)$，其中，DR 为死亡率，C 为卡路里摄入量，H 为医疗水平。由于人均卡路里摄入量取决于一个人的食物摄入量，这里会存在一定的差异，因为食物品种不同，其含有的卡路里也有较大的差异，但由于数据计算上的难度，同时为了推导简单，本文不考虑这种差异，从而卡路里摄入量与食物摄入量之间的关系为：$C = f(G)$，G 表示食物量。

粮食的统销制度规定：对农村部分地区进行粮食的返销，这些地区称为缺粮区。所谓缺粮区主要是由两部分组成，一是经济作物主产区，这些地区中大部分的粮食产出不能自给，另一个是传统的缺粮区，主要是土地贫瘠、自然禀赋条件差、单位面积的粮食产出很低的地方，但这样的划分还有一定的缺陷，比如有的地区虽然粮食单产很低，但是人口很少，人均粮食可能比较高，所以人口数量也应在考虑范围之内，因此我们选取人均耕地面积①来衡量一个地区人均自然禀赋状况。在粮食主产区，每

---

① 评审人指出，考虑到复种状况的差异，采用播种面积更符合论文要求，不过我们查找的数据指出，复种指数低的地区都是死亡率低的地区，复种指数低代表的是自然禀赋状况不好，按照文中的结论，这些地区接近缺粮区，饥荒年份的死亡率比较低，所以采用耕地面积并不影响本文的结论（见附表 1）。

年上交完征购粮后剩余的粮食是决定死亡率的关键因素，我们将这个变量作为度量FAD的尺度，这是因为粮食减产会导致该变量的直接减少，并且这是农民真正可以支配的粮食，所以该变量可以精确定义食物供给量的下降(FAD)，其对死亡率的影响便是FAD的解释力度。考虑到统销制度对城乡之间影响的差异，一个地区如果城镇人口较多，政府按照城镇人口分配的粮食也会较多，综合的死亡率也会较低，如果不考虑该变量，最后的结果可能是有偏的，所以最后引入林文的城市偏向系统，本文采用城镇人口的比重来衡量这一变量。这样我们可以将一个地区人均食物摄入量表示成：$G = f(R, \mathrm{IP}, \mathrm{POP}, \mathrm{CPP}, \mathrm{UP})$，$R$ 表示自然禀赋状况，IP表示经济作物种植面积占总种植面积的比重，POP表示人均耕地面积(耕地总面积/总人口)，CPP表示粮食征购后人均拥有的粮食数量，UP表示城市化率(非农业人口/总人口)。

我们将上面两个函数综合，得到 $\mathrm{DR} = f(H, R, \mathrm{IP}, \mathrm{POP}, \mathrm{CPP}, \mathrm{UP})$，即一个地区死亡率的高低会受到该地医疗水平、其他自然禀赋状况、经济作物比重、人均耕地面积、人均拥有粮食量以及城市化率的综合影响。

(三) 描述分析

表1是本文第四部分将要使用到的变量在省级水平上历年的值，从死亡率来看，1959年的死亡率有一个很大的上升，相对于1958年上升了55.9%，即在1959年的死亡率人口是1958年的1.5倍以上，这说明从1959年开始江苏省经历了一场大灾荒，1960年的死亡率均值达到最高，到1963年，死亡率才恢复到灾荒前的1956年的平均水平。城市化率在1960年达到最高，这主要是由于当时推行的重工业化战略对农村劳动力的需求使得大批劳动力从农村进入城市，从灾荒过后年份该指标的

下降可以看出，政府又将先前进入城市的劳动力遣散回原地。人均粮食在1959年相对于1958年下降20.3%，下降到每天不足一斤，1960年该指标有略微回升，但当年却是灾荒最严重的年份，这是因为当年的死亡率受当年粮食产量和上年粮食产量的综合影响，人均粮食到1964年才恢复到饥荒前的正常水平，由于饥荒发生后的达尔文现象和消费机制效率的改善，饥荒在1962年便停止了。经济作物播种面积比重从饥荒开始前的1957年开始下降，一直到1965年才逐渐回升，这主要是受当时政府对农业过度乐观，降低了复种程度，甚至闲置部分耕地的影响。人均耕地面积从1949年开始一直下降，但值得注意的是，人均耕地面积在1959年相对于1958年增加了0.002公顷，而同期耕地总面积下降了3.83%，这说明1959年爆发了严重的灾荒，导致很多人非正常死亡，1960年耕地总面积接着下降了1.6%，但是人均耕地只减少了0.59%，一直到1962年人均耕地面积才开始下降，也正是这一年灾荒停止了。

表1　江苏省历年各变量的值

年份	死亡率（‰）	城市化率（%）	人均粮食（斤）	经济作物播种面积比重（%）	人均耕地面积（1/10公顷）
1954	12.12	14.19	—	9.96	2.11
1955	11.66	14.00	—	10.29	2.07
1956	12.81	13.83	—	10.17	2.00
1957	10.04	14.89	357	9.33	1.92
1958	9.33	16.25	335	8.96	1.76
1959	14.55	17.73	267	8.71	1.78
1960	18.41	18.06	270	8.56	1.77
1961	13.35	16.45	252	7.28	1.77
1962	10.36	14.86	270	7.41	1.74
1963	9.04	14.49	313	8.05	1.69

（续表）

年份	死亡率（‰）	城市化率（%）	人均粮食（斤）	经济作物播种面积比重（%）	人均耕地面积（1/10公顷）
1964	10.13	14.24	373	9.58	1.66
1965	9.48	14.17	388	10.30	1.60
1966	8.05	13.99	410	10.28	1.56
1967	7.81	13.34	408	10.75	1.51
1968	7.65	13.25	404	10.68	1.46
1969	6.80	12.09	392	10.21	1.42
1970	6.85	11.43	411	9.84	1.38
1971	7.38	11.55	431	9.52	1.34
1972	6.84	11.54	429	9.92	1.32
1973	6.52	12.63	448	10.23	1.29
1974	6.61	12.08	443	10.21	1.27
1975	6.46	12.02	439	9.97	1.25
1976	6.48	12.15	456	9.60	1.23
1977	6.48	12.11	431	9.75	1.22

注：人均粮食是指从集体分得的口粮，用一个县当年的粮食产出总量减去上交的粮食量除以总人口，该数据直接从《江苏省农业统计资料（1949—1980）》得到。

资料来源：死亡率来源于《江苏省人口统计资料汇编》，人均粮食来源于《江苏省农业统计资料（1949—1980）》，其他的由样本数据计算得出。

四、模型及检验

（一）前提假设

为了进行实证分析，由于数据的缺失，我们作如下前提假设。

1. 粮食的消费机制没有差异

虽然在灾荒年份全省都实行公共食堂制度，但不可否认的是其中的消费效率会有差异，即在可消费的粮食量相同的情况下，由于消费效率的差异，其最终死亡率会有差异。但由于数据的限制，本文默认所有的地区其消费的效率是一样的。另外，公共食堂只是在灾荒年份才存在，其出现是灾荒最初发生的原因(Chang and Wen, 1997)，但由于没有县级水平公共食堂的具体数据，本文无法考虑该因素。

2. 缺粮区的逼近定义

如果给定一个标准来区分缺粮区和非缺粮区，则这个标准是主观的。为了避免这种人为的差异，本文没有严格定义缺粮区的判断条件，而是认为在一个省内，人均耕地面积越少或者经济作物播种面积比重越大的县市就越接近缺粮区，这是一个逼近的过程。

(二) 模型

本文采用面板数据(Panel data)双向固定效应方法，这主要有三个原因：一是普通的模型很可能存在自相关，而面板数据的固定效应可以有效地消除自相关；二是数据可能存在严重的多重共线性，而面板数据由于巨大的样本量可以降低多重共线性对回归结果的影响；另外是可以消除那些不随时间变动或者不随截面变动的因素的影响。其中上缴征购粮后人均粮食量的数据由于从 1957 年开始缺失，所以是一组非平衡数据(unbalanced panels)，而不是平衡数据(balanced panels)，面板数据方法对此有很好的支持。

建立基本模型如下：

$$\ln \mathrm{DR}_{it} = \beta_0 + \beta_1 C_i + \beta_2 Y_t + \beta_3 \mathrm{IP}_{it} + \beta_4 \ln \mathrm{POP}_{it} + \beta_5 \ln \mathrm{CPP}_{it} + \beta_6 \mathrm{UP}_{it} + \varepsilon_{it} \quad (1)$$

β_0 是公共截距，表明各县具有的共同形态，C_i 表示截面固定效应，是各县的地区性因素对死亡率的影响，尽管我们假定各县的政策基本上一致，但由于存在一些地区差异，如自然条件、人口素质等会对死亡率产生影响，所以我们用固定效应对此进行控制，Y_t 是某些变量的时间趋势对死亡率的影响，其他的变量含义与上文相同。

当使用面板数据来分析时可能会因为省略变量造成残差项序列相关，当省略的变量与文中的某变量相关时，则该变量的估计将是有偏的，为了解决这种自相关问题，需要引入因变量的滞后项，该代理变量包含了那些遗漏的变量对本期因变量的影响。为了考察灾荒年份各变量的影响，我们还构造了一个虚拟变量，即当年份是 1959、1960 或者 1961 时该变量取 1，其他取 0，将该虚拟变量和前面的变量交叉相乘得到新变量，该变量即可以度量灾荒年份各变量对死亡率的影响程度。从而，模型(1)转化为：

$$
\begin{aligned}
\ln \mathrm{DR}_{it} = {} & \beta_0 + \beta_1 C_i + \beta_2 Y_t + \beta_3 \mathrm{IP}_{it} + \beta_4 \ln \mathrm{POP}_{it} + \\
& \beta_5 \ln \mathrm{CPP}_{it} + \beta_6 \mathrm{UP}_{it} + \beta_7 \ln \mathrm{DR}_{it-1} + \beta_8 \mathrm{DIP}_{it} + \\
& \beta_9 \ln \mathrm{DPOP}_{it} + \beta_{10} \mathrm{Dln\,CPP}_{it} + \beta_{11} \mathrm{DUP}_{it} + \\
& \beta_{12} D\ln \mathrm{DR}_{it-1} + \varepsilon_{it} \qquad (2)
\end{aligned}
$$

在正常年份农户手中拥有足够粮食，所以 ln CPP 不会影响死亡率，即 β_5 不应该显著异于 0，同样的道理，我们预期 β_3、β_4、β_6 也不显著异于 0。在灾荒年份，农民上缴征购粮后的余粮对死亡率有显著影响，余粮越多死亡率越低，即$(\beta_5+\beta_{10})<0$；各地返销粮的数量对死亡率有显著影响，而该返销粮由该地是否为缺粮区和城市人口数量决定，前者会参考该地的人均耕地面积和经济作物播种面积比重，人均耕地面积越少或者经济作物播种面积比重越大的地方，成为缺粮区的可能性越高，相应的灾荒年份死亡率会较低。所以在回归结果中，我们预期 $(\beta_3+\beta_8)<0$、$(\beta_4+\beta_9)>0$、$(\beta_6+\beta_{11})<0$，同时 β_8、β_9、β_{10}、β_{11} 显著异于 0；以前年度死亡率会对当年死亡率产生显著影响，一个简

单的逻辑是上一年的死亡率会影响今年的粮食产量，而后者又会影响当年的死亡率，这样我们预期 β_{12} 显著异于 0，考虑到死亡率有一个比较明显的时间趋势，所以我们预期 β_7 也显著异于 0。

在灾荒年份，各变量对死亡率的影响程度随年份的不同会有变化，我们想知道在灾荒发生的早期、中期和末期最活跃的因素有哪些，以及各变量对灾荒年份死亡率影响的时间趋势。因此，我们构造三个虚拟变量：R_1、R_2、R_3，当年份为 1959 时，$R_1 = 1$，其他则为 0；当年份为 1960 时，$R_2 = 1$，其他为 0；当年份为 1961 时，$R_3 = 1$，其他为 0。将该虚拟变量与上述各变量交叉相乘得到 15 个交叉变量，模型(2)转化为以下模型：

$$\begin{aligned}\ln \mathrm{DR}_{it} = {} & \beta_0 + \beta_1 C_i + \beta_2 Y_t + \beta_3 \mathrm{IP}_{it} + \beta_4 \ln \mathrm{POP}_{it} + \beta_5 \ln \mathrm{CPP}_{it} \\ & + \beta_6 \mathrm{UP}_{it} + \beta_7 \ln \mathrm{DR}_{it-1} + \beta_8 R_1 \mathrm{IP}_{it} + \beta_9 R_1 \ln \mathrm{POP}_{it} \\ & + \beta_{10} R_1 \ln \mathrm{CPP}_{it} + \beta_{11} R_1 \mathrm{UP}_{it} + \beta_{12} R_1 \ln \mathrm{DR}_{it-1} \\ & + \beta_{13} R_2 \mathrm{IP}_{it} + \beta_{14} R_2 \ln \mathrm{POP}_{it} + \beta_{15} R_2 \ln \mathrm{CPP}_{it} \\ & + \beta_{16} R_2 \mathrm{UP}_{it} + \beta_{17} R_2 \ln \mathrm{DR}_{it-1} + \beta_{18} R_3 \mathrm{IP}_{it} \\ & + \beta_{19} R_3 \ln \mathrm{POP}_{it} + \beta_{20} R_3 \ln \mathrm{CPP}_{it} + \beta_{21} R_3 \mathrm{UP}_{it} \\ & + \beta_{22} R_3 \ln \mathrm{DR}_{it-1} + \varepsilon_{it} \qquad (3)\end{aligned}$$

其中，β_8 表示经济作物播种面积对 1959 年死亡率的影响，β_{13} 表示对 1960 年死亡率的影响，β_{18} 表示该变量对 1961 年死亡率的影响，其他以此类推，其余的变量含义与上文相同。我们构造这些交叉变量是考虑各指标在灾荒年份对死亡率影响的时间趋势，旨在考察各指标在灾荒年份中对哪一年影响最大，对其中特定年份的死亡率影响较大的又是哪些因素。表 2 列示了以下回归中的变量。

表 2　变量意义和相应的数据来源

变　量	变 量 意 义	数 据 来 源
ln DR	Log(总人口死亡率)，总人口死亡率＝包括城镇人口死亡率和农村人口死亡率	《江苏省人口统计资料汇编》
UP	城市化率，＝非农业人口/总人口	《江苏省人口统计资料汇编》
IP	经济作物播种面积比重，＝经济作物总种植面积/农作物总种植面积	《江苏省农业统计资料(1949—1980)》
ln POP	Log(人均耕地面积)，人均耕地面积＝耕地总面积/总人口	《江苏省农业统计资料(1949—1980)》《江苏省人口统计资料汇编》
ln CPP	Log(征购后人均拥有的粮食量)	《江苏省农业统计资料(1949—1980)》
D	饥荒年度虚拟变量，饥荒年份取 1，其他 0	
R_1	1959 年虚拟变量，1959 年取 1，其他年份取 0	
R_2	1960 年虚拟变量，1960 年取 1，其他年份取 0	
R_3	1961 年虚拟变量，1961 年取 1，其他年份取 0	

随后的分析我们以模型(2)和模型(3)作为基准模型，但需要对模型进行一些扩展，我们对两个模型同时做两个方面的扩展：首先，前面在引入因变量的滞后项时我们的理由是该变量的引入可以缓和自相关，所以在对模型(2)和模型(3)回归时我们首先剔除因变量的滞后项，然后再引入，以观察该变量的引入是否真的达到了预期的效果，我们分别计算各自的扰动自相关系数，预期因变量滞后项的引入可以降低该系数。其次，考虑到粮食收获季节和因变量死亡率之间会有一个时滞，当年的死亡率

不仅受当年粮食产量的影响，还与上年粮食产量有关，所以，我们增加与食物摄入量相关变量的滞后一期项，预期该滞后项的引入可以改善模型的拟合程度。

（三）计量结果及解释

我们采用的是双向固定效应估计，表 3 给出了对模型(2)的估计，第一组是省略了因变量滞后项和自变量滞后项的估计结果，第二组引入了因变量滞后项，从计算的扰动自相关系数可以看出，在引入了滞后项后，该系数从 0.372 变为−0.009，自相关得到改善。第三组是在第一组基础上引入自变量滞后项，调整 R^2 从 0.674 上升到 0.709，说明引入滞后项是必要的。第四组是在第三组基础上引入因变量滞后项，计算的结果得出与第二组同样的结论，因变量滞后项的引入降低了自相关。表 4 是对模型(3)的估计，从计量的结果来看，滞后项的引入得出了与模型(2)同样的结论。为了避免重复，对两个模型的解释都以第四组为标准。

表 3　基于模型(2)的各因素对死亡率的影响程度

变　量	(1)	(2)	(3)	(4)
UP(城市人口比重)	−0.007* (−3.119)	−0.004** (−2.072)	−0.016* (−3.302)	−0.012* (−2.789)
IP(经济作物播种面积率)	−0.129 (−1.480)	−0.206** (−2.563)	−0.206 (−0.601)	−0.494 (−1.576)
ln CPP(人均拥有粮食量)	−0.152* (−3.350)	−0.154* (−3.665)	0.035 (0.691)	0.013 (0.279)
ln POP(人均耕地面积)	0.108 (1.359)	0.120 (1.631)	0.303** (2.303)	0.232*** (1.935)
Ln DR_{t-1}(滞后一期死亡率)	—	0.413* (11.228)	—	0.441* (11.386)
UP×D(饥荒年份虚拟变量)	0.001 (0.258)	0.002 (0.578)	0.032* (4.313)	0.032* (4.708)

（续表）

变　　量	(1)	(2)	(3)	(4)
IP×D(饥荒年份虚拟变量)	−1.315* (−5.120)	−0.767* (−3.136)	−2.399* (−2.875)	−1.544** (−2.019)
ln CPP×D(饥荒年份虚拟变量)	0.256* (3.148)	0.170** (2.230)	−0.045 (−0.431)	−0.098 (−1.012)
ln POP×D(饥荒年份虚拟变量)	−0.090** (−2.508)	−0.118* (−3.540)	0.603** (1.970)	0.883* (3.152)
Ln DR_{t-1}×D(饥荒年份虚拟变量)	—	−0.088*** (−1.658)	—	−0.110** (−2.082)
UP_{t-1}(滞后一期城市人口比重)	—	—	0.005 (1.204)	0.005 (1.327)
IP_{t-1}(滞后一期经济作物播种面积率)	—	—	−0.027 (−0.321)	0.028 (0.358)
ln CPP_{t-1}(滞后一期人均拥有粮食量)	—	—	−0.322* (−6.324)	−0.243* (−5.177)
ln POP_{t-1}(滞后一期人均耕地面积)	—	—	−0.069 (−0.622)	0.039 (0.385)
UP_{t-1}×D(饥荒年份虚拟变量)	—	—	−0.029* (−4.816)	−0.028* (−5.039)
IP_{t-1}×D(饥荒年份虚拟变量)	—	—	0.972 (1.295)	0.721 (1.050)
ln CPP_{t-1}×D(饥荒年份虚拟变量)	—	—	0.338* (3.461)	0.290* (3.244)
ln POP_{t-1}×D(饥荒年份虚拟变量)	—	—	−0.710** (−2.320)	−1.036* (−3.694)
调整 R^2	0.674	0.722	0.709	0.758
对数似然值	200.883	295.317	253.468	354.221
扰动自相关系数 ρ	0.372	−0.009	0.357	−0.036

注：括号中为 t 值，* 表示显著性水平为 1%，** 表示 5%，*** 表示 10%。

资料来源：江苏省农林厅：《江苏省农业统计资料(1949—1980)》，1982 年；江苏省统计局：《江苏省人口统计资料汇编》，1986 年。

模型(2)的估计结果基本证实了我们的预期,IP、ln CPP 的系数都不显著,是因为这些变量代表了正常年份各指标对死亡率的影响,按照我们前面的分析,正常年份的死亡率与这些指标没有强的相关性;UP 和 ln POP 的系数能够在 10%的显著性水平下通过检验,一个可能的解释是一个地区城市人口比重大的话,政府对公共设施的投入较多,比如医疗设施等,这样便减少了正常年份的死亡率,而如果人均耕地面积较多的话,作为缺粮区的可能性便很小,政府投入也就很少,死亡率则较高,所以前者跟死亡率是反向的关系,后者是正向关系。各变量滞后项中只有 $\ln CPP_{t-1}$的系数是显著的,说明在正常年份上缴征购粮后人均拥有的粮食量能够降低次年的死亡率,虽然前文我们曾假定正常年份死亡率跟这些变量都不相关,但由于存在缺粮区和非缺粮区的差别,并且粮食的征购量是按上一年的产量确定的,所以如果是丰收年份,非缺粮区人均拥有的粮食量要多于缺粮区,而当时的营养水平不是很高,人们只是维持在一个温饱水平,所以该变量对死亡率有反向的影响。

模型(2)各变量及滞后项的交叉项中,ln CPP 的系数显著,而 $\ln CPP_{t-1}$的系数显著,说明在灾荒年份上缴征购粮后剩余的粮食对当年的死亡率没有显著影响,而对次年死亡率有影响,所以该变量的滞后项能够通过显著性检验,虽然该变量滞后项系数为正,但不说明剩余粮食对死亡率的影响是正的,ln CPP、$\ln CPP \times D$、$\ln CPP_{t-1}$和 $\ln CPP_{t-1} \times D$ 的系数之和才是该变量对灾荒年份死亡率的影响,该数字为−0.029,即剩余粮食能够缓和灾荒。城市人口比重在灾荒年份对死亡率的影响是负的,值得说明的是,在灾荒年份当年的城市化率对死亡率是正向的作用(UP 和 $UP \times D$ 系数之和),这是因为统销制度中对粮食的分配是依据上年的指标,所以如果一个地区城市人口越多,则人均分得的粮食越少，当年的死亡率会越高，但对次年的死亡率有反向的作用（UP_{t-1} 和 $UP_{t-1}\times D$ 系数之和）。经济作物播种面积比重是作为衡量缺粮区的一个指标，比重越高则成为缺粮区的可能性越大，所以在灾荒年份的死亡率越低，计量的结果验证了这种预期（IP、$IP\times D$、IP_{t-1} 和 $IP_{t-1}\times D$ 系数之和为负），上年的经济作物播种面积比重对今年的死亡率没有显著影响（IP_{t-1} 和 $IP_{t-1}\times D$ 系数不显著），并且是正向的关系，这可能是由于我们选取的样本中纯粹的经济作物产区很少，大部分地区都是既有经济作物又有粮食作物，所以当上年的经济作物比重很大时会减少上年的粮食产量，而上年的粮食产量对今年的死亡率有显著影响。人均耕地面积是作为衡量缺粮区的另一个指标，人均耕地面积越多则成为缺粮区的可能性越小，在灾荒年份死亡率就越高，计量的结果验证了这种预期（ln POP、$\ln POP\times D$、$\ln POP_{t-1}$ 和 $\ln POP_{t-1}\times D$ 系数之和为正），人均耕地面积和死亡率是正向的关系。

前文的分析曾指出，CPP 可以用来度量 FAD 的解释力度，该变量滞后项的交叉项显著即说明 FAD 理论在解释中国灾荒时是有效的，UP、IP 和 POP 分别是城市人口比重、经济作物播种面积比重和人均耕地面积，用来度量食物获取权理论的解释力度，这三个变量及滞后项的交叉项大部分通过了显著性检验，即说明森的食物获取权理论在解释中国灾荒时也是有效的。将 ln CPP 和 $\ln CPP\times D$ 及滞后项的系数相加即是该变量对灾荒年份死亡率的影响程度，同样可以将 UP、$UP\times D$、IP、$IP\times D$ 及滞后项的系数相加减去 ln POP 和 $\ln POP\times D$ 及滞后项的系数之和，将这两个相加后的数字进行对比即可以对 FAD 理论和食物获取权解释力度进行比较，前者为 −0.029，后者是 −1.442，可见食物获取权理论在解释中国灾荒发生后死亡率的差异方面更具说服力。

模型(3)构造了一组灾荒年份各年虚拟变量和各变量的交叉项，该交叉项可以用来衡量该变量对该年死亡率的影响。表4是对该模型的计算结果，因变量滞后项和自变量滞后项的引入与模型2相同，从第四组回归结果可以看出，UP、IP、ln POP、ln CPP的系数和显著性水平与模型(2)相比没有大的变化，为了避免重复，相同的部分不再解释。上年的城市化率对1959年($UP_{t-1} \times R_1$ 显著)和1960年($UP_{t-1} \times R_2$ 显著)的死亡率有显著影响，对1961年的死亡率没有显著影响($UP_{t-1} \times R_3$ 不显著)；当年的城市化率对灾荒各年的死亡率都有负的显著影响，并且两者对死亡率的影响都是递减的，这说明城市人口比重在灾荒发生的早期有着决定性的作用。当年和上年的经济作物播种面积比重(UP)对1959年和1960年的死亡率有显著影响，对1961年没有影响，但两者的影响方向有一个相反的时间趋势，当年的经济作物播种面积比重在1959年是正的影响，1960年是负的，而上年的经济作物播种面积比重的影响则相反。上缴征购粮后人均拥有的粮食(CPP)在灾荒年份早期对当年死亡率有缓和作用，但到中期呈现相反的影响，说明早期影响较大的是自留粮，而灾荒最严重时国家返销的粮食起到了决定性的作用；该变量滞后项的影响趋势相反，并且只在早期有显著影响。人均耕地面积(POP)及其滞后项对各年死亡率都有显著影响，两者的时间趋势也是相反的，并且在灾荒末期的影响最严重。

城市人口比重、经济作物播种面积比重和上缴征购粮后的人均粮食在灾荒发生早期对死亡率差异有决定作用，到末期这些因素都不起作用；而人均耕地面积在末期影响最大。这可以说明传统的缺粮区划分对灾荒的承受能力较强，而经济作物主产区的划分则较弱。

表 4　基于模型(3)的各因素对死亡率的影响程度

变　　量	(1)	(2)	(3)	(4)
UP(城市人口比重)	−0.007* (−3.248)	−0.004** (−2.143)	−0.014* (−3.075)	−0.012* (−2.935)
IP(经济作物播种面积率)	−0.140 (−1.645)	−0.218* (−2.836)	−0.220 (−0.653)	−0.535** (−1.797)
ln CPP(人均拥有粮食量)	−0.118* (−2.629)	−0.118* (−2.896)	0.080 (1.613)	0.039 (0.895)
ln POP(人均耕地面积)	0.108 (1.386)	0.115 (1.633)	0.256** (2.022)	0.222** (1.988)
Ln DR_{t-1}(滞后一期死亡率)	—	0.413* (11.739)	—	0.436* (12.129)
UP_{t-1}(滞后一期城市人口比重)	—	—	0.005 (1.313)	0.005 (1.467)
IP_{t-1}(滞后一期经济作物播种面积率)	—	—	−0.029 (−0.359)	0.020 (0.280)
ln CPP_{t-1}(滞后一期人均拥有粮食量)	—	—	−0.281* (−5.707)	−0.217* (−4.982)
ln POP_{t-1}(滞后一期人均耕地面积)	—	—	−0.091 (−0.856)	0.026 (0.276)
UP×R_1(1959 年虚拟变量)	−0.007 (−1.187)	0.006 (1.043)	0.020 (1.603)	0.079* (6.373)
IP×R_1(1959 年虚拟变量)	−1.748* (−5.002)	−0.268 (0.763)	−2.863 (−1.635)	3.180** (1.973)
ln CPP×R_1(1959 年虚拟变量)	−0.179 (−1.472)	−0.012 (−0.107)	−0.763* (−5.029)	−0.327** (−2.377)
ln POP×R_1(1959 年虚拟变量)	−0.060 (−1.224)	−0.096** (−2.155)	−0.967*** (−1.814)	−1.810* (−3.768)
Ln DR_{t-1}×R_1(1959 年虚拟变量)	—	0.472* (4.668)	—	0.700* (6.702)
UP×R_2(1960 年虚拟变量)	0.002 (0.370)	0.005 (1.031)	0.026* (2.657)	0.029* (3.302)

（续表）

变　　量	(1)	(2)	(3)	(4)
IP×R_2（1960 年虚拟变量）	−1.085** (−2.238)	−0.309 (−0.681)	−5.208* (−3.641)	−3.720* (−2.932)
ln CPP×R_2（1960 年虚拟变量）	0.829* (5.880)	0.728* (5.632)	1.077* (5.626)	0.841* (4.744)
ln POP×R_2（1960 年虚拟变量）	0.040 (0.807)	0.022 (0.491)	1.098* (2.974)	1.414* (4.321)
Ln DR_{t-1}×R_2（1960 年虚拟变量）	—	−0.080 (−1.163)	—	−0.141** (−2.096)
UP×R_3（1961 年虚拟变量）	0.008 (0.855)	0.005 (0.587)	0.021 (1.385)	0.013 (0.951)
IP×R_3（1961 年虚拟变量）	−0.264 (−0.571)	−0.176 (−0.420)	1.208 (0.718)	0.517 (0.341)
ln CPP×R_3（1961 年虚拟变量）	0.392* (2.765)	0.363* (2.664)	0.152 (0.689)	0.122 (0.616)
ln POP×R_3（1961 年虚拟变量）	−0.214* (−4.126)	−0.256* (−5.455)	2.854*** (1.792)	3.181** (2.264)
Ln DR_{t-1}×R_3（1961 年虚拟变量）	—	−0.359* (−5.261)	—	−0.369* (−5.587)
UP_{t-1}×R_1（1959 年虚拟变量）	—	—	−0.026* (−2.790)	−0.057* (−6.596)
IP_{t-1}×R_1（1959 年虚拟变量）	—	—	1.489 (0.888)	−3.284** (−2.161)
ln CPP_{t-1}×R_1（1959 年虚拟变量）	—	—	0.815* (5.775)	0.380* (2.960)
ln POP_{t-1}×R_1（1959 年虚拟变量）	—	—	0.867 (1.644)	1.651* (3.472)
UP_{t-1}×R_2（1960 年虚拟变量）	—	—	−0.025* (−2.606)	−0.026* (−3.140)
IP_{t-1}×R_2（1960 年虚拟变量）	—	—	3.717* (3.254)	2.943* (2.922)

（续表）

变　量	(1)	(2)	(3)	(4)
$\ln CPP_{t-1} \times R_2$（1960 年虚拟变量）	—	—	-0.337^{**} (−2.132)	−0.162 (−1.118)
$\ln POP_{t-1} \times R_2$（1960 年虚拟变量）	—	—	-1.074^{*} (−2.879)	-1.442^{*} (−4.364)
$UP_{t-1} \times R_3$（1961 年虚拟变量）	—	—	-0.019^{***} (−1.706)	-0.016^{***} (−1.680)
$IP_{t-1} \times R_3$（1961 年虚拟变量）	—	—	−1.782 (−1.043)	−0.975 (−0.629)
$\ln CPP_{t-1} \times R_3$（1961 年虚拟变量）	—	—	0.326 (1.441)	0.308 (1.541)
$\ln POP_{t-1} \times R_3$（1961 年虚拟变量）	—	—	-3.074^{***} (−1.931)	-3.469^{**} (−2.470)
调整 R^2	0.688	0.746	0.733	0.793
对数似然值	231.978	352.731	308.217	450.389
扰动自相关系数 ρ	0.359	−0.019	0.341	−0.015

注：括号中为 t 值，* 表示显著性水平为 1%，** 表示 5%，*** 表示 10%。
数据来源：同表 3。

（四）进一步的讨论

本文第一部分曾对统购统销制度进行详细的描述，该制度在第一个五年计划（1953—1957 年）中确立，虽然后来有过一些变动，但基本的操作原则没有改变。对农村中缺粮区的确定是依据该地区在 1953—1957 年中的粮食是否能够自给，对该缺粮区国家核定一个返销粮食的数量标准，以后的年份基本按照这个标准返销，并且由于信息传递的时滞和政治因素，返销粮的数量没有大的变化，所以统销制度对于以后年度的粮食分配起到了决定作用。在正常年份，几乎所有人都能够得到维持生存的粮食，所以统销制度对正常年份死亡率没有显著影响；在灾荒年份，缺粮区的民众有国家返销的粮食，供给得到保障，但非缺粮区粮食减产并且没有返销粮，所以两者死亡率会有差异，粮食统销制度起到决定作用。这样对统销制度的度量会有意义，从本部分第一节的分析中我们可以看出，有两个指标可以用来衡量缺粮区：经济作物播种面积比重和人均耕地面积，所以我们构造了一组三阶段的模型：

$$\ln DR_{54-58} = \beta_0 + \beta_1 IP_{54-57} + \beta_2 \ln POP_{54-57} + \varepsilon \quad (4)$$

$$\ln DR_{59-61} = \beta_0 + \beta_1 IP_{54-57} + \beta_2 \ln POP_{54-57} + \varepsilon \quad (5)$$

$$\ln DR_{62-77} = \beta_0 + \beta_1 IP_{54-57} + \beta_2 \ln POP_{54-57} + \varepsilon \quad (6)$$

其中，IP（经济作物播种面积比重）和 POP（人均耕地面积）取 1954—1957 年的平均值，DR_{54-58}是 1954—1958 年死亡率的均值，DR_{62-77}是 1962—1977 年死亡率的均值，这是饥荒发生前后的正常时期，我们预期模型（4）和模型（6）中的参数总体不显著；DR_{59-61}是 1959—1961 年死亡率的均值，模型（5）考察的是饥荒年份，按照我们前面的分析，统销制度对该时期死亡率有显著影响，所以我们预期模型（5）中的参数估计是显著的。同时为了从计量上验证这种时间分段的合理性，我们取 DR、IP 和 POP 各年的平均值，再进行 CHOW 检验，得出 1959 年是一个典型的邹氏转折点①，这说明时期的分段在计量上是有道理的。

表 5 是我们对模型（4）、模型（5）和模型（6）的估计结果，经济作物播种面积比重和人均耕地面积是度量缺粮区的指标，前者在前两个阶段都能在 5％的显著性水平下通过检验，这可能是缘于政府当时的经济模式对经济作物的需求要大于对粮食的需求，对经济作物产区的公共投入要大于粮食产区，而这些投入

① 需要说明的是，我们无法对 1961 年进行 CHOW 检验，因为灾荒年份数量太少，在计量上无法进行。

会影响当地的人口素质，例如对医疗的投入可以降低当地的人口死亡率；第二阶段(1959—1961年)该变量的显著性水平较其他两个阶段要高，可以认为该变量对饥荒年份的死亡率有重大影响；第三个阶段(1962—1977年)时期较长，并且随着经济发展人们的营养状况得到很大的改善，人口死亡率与粮食不是显著相关。三个模型中，只有前两个模型回归结果的 F 统计量通过检验，显著性水平也是第二个模型最高，同时前后两个模型调整的 R^2 都比第二个要低很多。人均耕地面积(POP)只在灾荒年份显著，但是显著性水平和死亡率的影响程度相比经济作物播种面积比重要低得多。所以当年对缺粮区的确定更多的是考虑该地经济作物的比重。可以看出在1954—1957年形成的粮食统销制度，特别是对农村地区缺粮区的确定对紧接下来的灾荒年份的死亡率有显著影响。

表5　统销制度对各时期死亡率的影响

变　量	ln DR (1954—1958年死亡率均值)	ln DR (1959—1961年死亡率均值)	ln DR (1962—1977年死亡率均值)
IP(经济作物播种面积率)	−12.009**	−50.386*	−5.829
(1954—1957年均值)	(−2.536)	(−2.809)	(−0.272)
ln POP(人均耕地面积)	−0.071	−0.119***	−0.129
(1954—1957年均值)	(−1.260)	(−1.823)	(−1.333)
调整 R^2	0.147	0.210	−0.009
F-统计值	5.582	6.909	0.772
P 值	0.006	0.002	0.467
CHOW 检验			
F 值	—	21.026	—
P 值	—	0.000	—

注：括号中为 t 值，*表示显著性水平为1%，**表示5%，***表示10%。
数据来源：同表3。

五、结　论

森的食物获取权理论和传统的食物供给量下降理论在解释中国灾荒时都是有效的，对两者的比较我们得出的结论和林文的结论一致，前者比后者能在更大程度上解释中国灾荒，前者的解释能力是后者的将近五十倍。但与林文有一点不相同，本文的结论中城市偏向系统显得不是太具解释能力，其系数相对于其他的变量要小得多，这主要是与样本的选择相关，林文选择的是中国省际面板数据，其中包括各大城市的人口，本文则剔除了该数字，主要的原因是历年来行政区划有很大的变动。

第一个五年计划基本上确立了后来持续几十年的计划体制中的基本制度，统购统销制度中对粮食的分配是中国居民获得食物的标准，该制度导致的结果便是森所提出的食物获取权的差异。城市居民首先得到了体制上的食物供给保障，食物获取权优于其他群体；其次是对农村中缺粮区的衡定，属于该地区的群体得到了配给城市居民后的粮食的分配权，获得的是次食物获取权；最后是粮食主产区的居民，他们获得的是最底层的食物获取权。所以当农业产出滑坡时，食物总量减少，这时食物的分配顺序首先是城市居民，然后是缺粮区居民，最后才是粮食主产区居民，即粮食主产区居民负担了粮食生产的全部风险。在灾荒发生的年份，粮食主产区的居民首先面临饥荒的威胁，相应的死亡率也较其他地区要高，或者说一个地区城市人口和缺粮区居民越多，其死亡率便越低，所以地区之间死亡率的差异是由制度造成的。如果遵循森理论的自由市场经济的前提，结果应该是相反，粮食减产后粮食价格相对升高，最先受到威胁的应该是城市居民，最后才是粮食主产区居民，所以这又是一种制度性扭曲。

本文的分析对这种制度性扭曲进行了经验上的验证，得出缺粮区制度对饥荒年份农村死亡率的差异影响显著。缺粮区中的经济作物主产区在灾荒的早期就非常显著，而传统缺粮区只是在饥荒末期才起作用；并且前者在灾荒年份对死亡率的总影响要比后者强得多。所以对经济作物生产区的划分决定了该地区的食物获取权利，而食物获取权利在灾荒年份对死亡率起到决定作用。

本文的结论中有一点还值得讨论，如果统计数据正确的话，那么传统的食物供给量下降理论和森理论都无法解释中国在1958年的秋天取得丰收，公社食堂对社员敞开供应粮食，因而等级制的粮食获取权对农民暂时失效的情况下，为何在1959年的春天普遍发生粮食短缺。显然，灾荒不是始于粮食生产的滑坡，也不是始于对农民的粮食获取权的进一步的收缩。这些理论也无法解释为何在1961年、1962年和1963年人均粮食仍显著低于1958年的人均粮食的情况下(表1)，也就是粮食生产并没有根本起色的情况下，并且在等级制的食物获取权没有废除的情况下，灾荒竟然结束了。由于大食堂始于1958年的秋天，终于1961年的年终，显然，从逻辑来说，大食堂的兴废对灾荒的来去的解释力，是单纯的粮食生产滑坡论和森的粮食获取权理论所无法完全取代的。但本文的结果表明，一旦灾荒(且不讨论饥荒的触发因素和消失因素)发生，则中国特有的等级制的食物获取权对灾荒会在城乡人口之间以及农村的粮食主产区、非主产区、经济作物区的人口之间作如何分布有较强的解释能力。

附表 1　1975 年各地区耕地复种指数表

地区(市)	复种指数(%)	地区(市)	复种指数(%)
南京市	206	扬州地区	209
徐州地区	163	南通地区	218
淮阴地区	194	镇江地区	226
盐城地区	200	苏州地区	244
全省平均		200	

资料来源:单树模、王维屏、王庭槐编:《江苏地理》,江苏人民出版社 1980 年版,第 109 页。

参考文献

Aird, J., 1982, "Population Studies and Population Policy in China", *Population and Development Review*, Vol. 8, No. 2:267—297.

Ashton, B., K. Hill, A. Pizza and R. Zeitz, 1984, "Famine in China, 1958—1961", *Population and Development review*, 10(4):613—645.

Banister, J., 1987, *China's Changing Population*, Stanford: Stanford University Press.

Berstein, T., 1984, "Stalinism, Famine, and Chinese Peasants: Grain Procurement During the Great Leap Forward", *Theory and Society*, 13(3):339—377.

Chang, G. and J. Wen, 1997, "Communical Dining and the Chinese Famine of 1958—1961", *Economic Development and Cultural Change*, 46(1):1—34.

Chen, Chu-yuan, 1982, *China's Economic Development: Growth and Structural Change*, Boulder: Westview.

曹树基:《1959—1961 年中国的人口死亡及其成因》,《中国人口科学》2005 年第 1 期。

Coale, A. J., 1981, "Population Trends, Population Policy, and Population Studies in China", *Population and Development*

Review, 7(1):267—297.

杜闻贞主编:《中国人口(江苏分册)》,中国财政经济出版社,1987年版。

范子英、孟令杰:《有关中国1959—1961年饥荒的研究综述》,《中国农村观察》2005年第1期。

国家统计局国民经济综合统计司:《新中国五十年统计资料汇编》,中国统计出版社,1999年版。

江苏省统计局:《江苏省人口统计资料汇编》,1986年。

江苏省农林厅:《江苏省农业统计资料(1949—1980)》,1982年。

江苏年鉴编纂委员会:《江苏年鉴》,南京大学出版社1991年版。

金辉:《"三年自然灾害"备忘录》,《社会》1993年第4—5合期。

焦贵玺等:《粮食流通概论》,中国商业出版社1991年版。

Johnson, D. G., 1998, "China's Great Famine: Introductory Remarks.", *China Economic Review*, 9(2):103—109.

Kung, J. and Justin Yifu Lin, 2003, "The Causes of China's Great Leap Famine, 1959—1961", *Economic Development and Cultural Change*, 52(1):51—73.

Kung, J., and L. Putterman, 1997, "China's Collectivization Puzzle: A New Resolution", *Journal of Development Studies*, 33:741—763.

Li, W. and D. T. Yang, 2005, "The Great Leap Forward: Anatomy of a Central Planning Disaster", *Journal of Political Economy*, 113(4): 840—877.

林毅夫、蔡昉、李周:《中国的奇迹:发展战略与经济改革》,上海三联书店1994年版。

Lin, Justin Yifu., 1990, "Collectivization and China's Agricultural Crisis in 959—1961", *Journal of Political Economy*, Vol. 98, No. 6: 1228—1252.

Lin, Justin Yifu, and D. T. Yang, 1998, "On the Causes of China's Agricultural Crisis and the Great Leap Famine", *China Economic Review*, 9(2):125—140.

Lin, Justin Yifu and D. T. Yang, 2000, "Food Availability, Entitlements and the Chinese Famine of 1959—1961", *Economic Journal*, 110 (460): 136—158.

柳随年、吴群:《"大跃进"和调整时期的国民经济(1958—1965)》,黑龙江人民出版社 1984 年版。

Osmani, S., 1995, "The Entitlement Approach to Famine: An Assessment", in K. Basu et al., (eds.), *Choice, Welfare, and Development: Essays in Honour of Amartya Sen*, Oxford: Clarendon Press.

Peng, X. Z., 1987, "Demographic Consequences of the Great Leap Forward in China's Provinces", *Population and Development Review*, 13 (4): 639—670.

单树模、王维屏、王庭槐:《江苏地理》,江苏人民出版社 1980 年版。

Sen, Amartya K., 1981, *Poverty and Famine*, Oxford, U. K.: Clarendon Press.

Walker, K. R., 1984, *Food Grain Procurement and Consumption in China*, New York: Cambridge University Press.

Yang, Dali L., 1996, *Calamity and Reform in China: State, Rural Society, and Institutional Change since the Great Leap Famine*, Stanford: Stanford University Press.

赵德馨:《中华人民共和国经济史(1949—1966)》,河南人民出版社 1988 年版。

周飞舟:《"三年自然灾害"时期我国省级政府对饥荒的反应和救助研究》,《社会学研究》2003 年第 2 期。

(本文在收入本书时有删节——编者注)

(原载《经济学(季刊)》2007 年第 6 卷第 2 期)

分工与农业组织化演进：基于间接定价理论模型的分析*

向国成
（湖南科技大学新兴古典经济学研究所）
韩绍凤
（湖南科技大学商学院）

一、导　论

与理论界把农业组织化狭义地理解为协会、农会、合作经济等团队化组织的发展不同（张晓山，2003），我们认为农业市场化也是农业组织化的重要方面。从一般意义而言，经济的组织化是相对于封闭、孤立、缺乏联系的自然经济状态而言的，在本质上是人与人之间相互联系、相互依赖关系的发展过程，是对自给自足的否定与超越。而人与人之间相互联系、相互依赖关系发展的重要社会经济基础是分工发展。因此，应该从分工角度来理解组织化的发展。我们认为组织化是指通过一定的社会经济组织形式与制度来协调社会经济分工，从而使之构成一个相互联系、相互依赖的有机整体的发展过程。在此意义上，组织化包

* 本文写作过程中得到了宋醒民、于立、黄有光的悉心指导，并吸收了两名匿名审稿人的许多宝贵意见，在此一并表示感谢。

括两个基本方面：一是组织的团队化，如企业、农会、协会等科层组织的发展；二是组织的市场化，如农民之间通过产品市场和要素市场建立起来的买卖关系。这两个方面既对立又统一，相互依赖，相互促进。把科斯（Coase，1937）关于"厂商是市场的替代物"的思想一般化，可以说团队是市场的替代物，也就是说，如果两个及以上本身有着市场联系的经济主体组成一个团队并把市场关系内部化，则团队取代了市场。在另一些情况下，我们也看到如果没有一定的团队化，没有相应的团队内的分工发展来提高生产和交易效率，一些经济主体根本就进入不了市场，建立不了与他人的市场联系，市场化就受到很大限制。因此，团队不仅是市场的替代物，也是发展市场的工具。丹尼尔·F. 斯普尔伯（Daniel F. Spulber，1999［2002］）立足于中间层模型，全面阐述了"厂商是协调消费者与供应商的市场制造者"的观点，其中，包含了团队化是发展市场工具的思想。立足对组织化的广义理解，再纵观改革开放的历程，在以家庭承包为基础、统分结合的双层经营体制背景下，中国农业组织化大致沿着集体经济→家庭经营→农业商业化→农业产业化→农民团队化的路线演进。①

对这一演进路线，理论界没有给出一个统一的理论解释；对构成这一路线各个环节的理论研究也还需要进一步完善。

（1）关于集体经济向家庭经营的转变。人民公社体制转向

---

① 我们对这一进程的概括主要是根据不同时期的热点或焦点问题。20 世纪 70 年代末 80 年代初是集体经济向家庭经营转变的时期；80 年代中后期，流通体制改革使农业商业化得到空前发展；进入 20 世纪 90 年代，随着剩余劳动力的大量转移，农业生产过程的商业化也得到发展，同时，农业产业化成为热点问题，随后，农民团队化成为一个焦点问题。这一进程并不否定以家庭承包责任制为基础的双层经营体制，同时也不能机械地把这样一种演进顺序作绝对化的理解，组织的团队化与市场化往往是相伴而行的。这一演进路线的主体由市场化和以企业为主体的团队化发展所构成。

家庭承包制是在没有多少理论准备的情况下展开的，是实践先行和诱致性制度变迁的典范。林毅夫(Lin，1988)建立了一个“工分制下的生产队模型”，认为生产队的管理者因为农业劳动监督费用太高，选择了一个较低的监督程度，而队员因为劳动计量不充分和报酬平均分配(不能真正做到按劳分配)，选择了偷懒。所以，农业劳动监督费用太高和对劳动者激励不足共同导致了集体经济中劳动效率的损失。周其仁(1994)认为集体经济对管理者激励不足，即管理者没有剩余权是导致农业劳动监督不足进而劳动无效率的根本原因。他们的分析是深刻的，但只能说明集体经济为什么会失败，并不能说明集体经济必然转向家庭经营。按周其仁的思想逻辑，既然把剩余权利界定给管理者可以提高效率，为什么改革不把剩余权利界定给管理者，而采取家庭承包制把它界定给农民？即使要把剩余权利界定给农民，为什么不把它界定给农民集体实行农民自治(类似南斯拉夫的企业自治)，而要把它界定给农民个体实行家庭承包制？

(2) 关于农业商业化。理论界对农产品和农业生产资料的市场化程度进行了大量的实证分析(常修泽、高明华，1998；陈宗胜，1999；习近平，2001)，但对农业生产过程的市场化缺少相应的理论解释。

(3) 关于农业产业化。理论界对它的内涵、特征、作用的分析是汗牛充栋，陈吉元等(2000)把农业产业化经营的基本内涵概括为“以国内外市场需求为导向，以提高经济效益为中心，以加工流通企业为依托，以农副产品生产基地为基础，发挥当地资源优势，对农业的支柱产业和优势产品实行区域化布局、专业化生产、企业化管理、社会化服务，产供销、贸工农一体化经营所形成的一种较为完整的产业系统”。而我们认为真正需要把握的要点主要有三个方面：一是农业产业链的延伸；二是龙头企业的出现；三是企业与农民经济关系的协调。这三个方面可归结为一个问题，即农业产业链延伸发展过程中的组织化问题，其核心是龙头企业的出现。没有龙头企业，产业链的延伸发展是很困难的；正是有了龙头企业，才需要协调企业与农民之间的经济利益关系。只有把握农业产业化的这种本质特征，才不至于迷失在浩如烟海的文献描述之中。理论界对于这一问题的分析更多的是基于经验总结，而缺少理论模型。

(4) 关于如何解决农民进入市场的交易费用问题，怎样提高农民在与龙头企业及政府打交道时的谈判能力问题，理论界提出了发展农业技术经济协会、农民合作经济组织等农民团队化的措施，但实际发展状况与人们的期望还有很大距离。既然合作经济等团队化组织如许多人论述的有这样那样的好处，那么，它们的发展为什么还会不尽如人意？这需要从理论上进行反思。

本文立足于分工演化，运用由杨小凯、黄有光（Yang and Ng，1995；杨小凯，1998）发展的间接定价理论模型对中国改革开放以来农业组织化的演进主线给出了一个统一的理论解释。本文以下内容是：第二节，间接定价理论模型及其适当扩展：一个分析框架；第三节，分工与农业组织化演进：统一的理论解释；第四节，结论。

二、间接定价理论模型及其适当扩展：一个分析框架

间接定价理论模型是由杨小凯和黄有光在科斯（Coase，1937）和张五常（Cheung，1983）的思想基础上发展出来的。这一理论模型假定有很多天生相同的消费者—生产者，每个人都可以从事两种有专业化经济的活动，一种是生产最终产品的活

动，一种是生产中间产品的活动。人们用资源生产没有直接效用的中间产品，一定是因为中间产品的使用可以提高最终产品的生产效率，这是一种迂回经济效果。关于最终产品和中间产品生产如何组织，这一理论模型包含自给自足、产品市场组织、中间产品生产者享有剩余权利的企业组织、最终产品生产者享有剩余权利的企业组织四种结构。其中，企业与非对称剩余权利可以将交易效率相对低的活动卷入分工，以避免对这类活动的投入产出直接定价所形成的高昂交易费用，这类活动价值的大小由剩余收益来反映。这就是间接定价理论，企业是间接定价的工具。这一点正是杨小凯和黄有光教授所特别强调的，他们的根本目的在于解释企业产生及其性质，他们的论文标题"企业理论与剩余权结构"说明了这一点。也许正是由于他们自己过于强调这一点，结果大大局限了整个间接定价理论模型的解释范围，人们还以为间接定价理论模型就是企业理论。其实不然，整个间接定价理论模型包括自给自足、市场、企业三类结构，本质上是关于最终产品与中间产品分工时产权组织实现形式及其演变的理论，解释企业产生及其性质的间接定价理论只是整个模型的一部分。正是由于他们把注意力集中在企业这种组织结构上，对市场组织结构就没有像对企业组织结构那样进行细分。事实上，产品市场组织可以进一步细分为"无合同的市场组织结构"与"有合同的市场组织结构"（这里的合同是指正式合同）。有合同的市场组织结构是一种广泛存在的组织形式，而要分析这种组织形式，需要引入风险因素。风险是影响组织结构的重要因素。奈特(Knight, 1921)认为企业制度就是一种典型的风险交换和分摊的组织，间接定价理论也包含了这层含义，因为剩余收益的正与负、多与少，最终要经过市场的"惊险跳跃"来确证，享有剩余权利的人承担了风险。此外，新兴古典经济学在间接定价理论模型之外深入探讨了由分工引起的协调可靠性问题，即风险的组织问题（Yang and Wills，1990；Yang and Ng，1993；Lio，1998）。我们将在间接定价理论模型的中间产品市场交易中考虑交易风险，对其做适当扩展。

（一）理论假设

（1）存在最终产品与中间产品的分工，每个专业都存在专业化经济。设 y、y^s、y^d、p_y 代表最终产品（如粮食）的自给量、销售量、购买量和价格，x、x^s、x^d、p_x 代表中间产品（如管理知识）的自给量、销售量、购买量和价格。

（2）有 M 个事前相同的消费者—生产者，每个人有 1 单位的劳动资源禀赋。设 l_y、l_x 代表生产最终产品和中间产品的劳动投入份额，即生产的专业化水平。

（3）存在交易费用与交易风险。设 k 代表最终产品的交易效率，t 仅代表完成中间产品交换的交易效率（这都是对购买者而言的，而且不包含与合同有关的任何成本）。在现实生活中最终产品和中间产品交易都存在风险，这里为了使问题分析简化，同时又不影响分析结果，假定只有中间产品交易存在市场风险。中间产品交易可分为有合同保证和无合同保证两类，无合同保证的中间产品交易面临着市场风险，即生产最终产品的人面临可能买不到中间产品的风险。如果买到中间产品，则最终产品生产可以顺利进行；如果买不到中间产品，则最终产品生产为 0。设买到中间产品的概率为 μ，买不到中间产品的概率为 $1-\mu$。对有合同保证的中间产品交易而言，虽然也面临道德风险问题，但毕竟有合同约束，与无合同约束比较，中间产品交易风险要小得多（如果第三方仲裁有效，道德风险就会更小），假设有合同约束时的市场风险为零，但需要为签订并执行合同支付一定成本，令 λ 为合同成本系数，有合同保证的中间产品交易效

率实际上是 $t-\lambda$。[①]

(4) 劳动的交易效率考虑了组织成本的影响。通过企业形式组织的生产，没有产品交易风险，但有劳动的道德风险，为此需要支付一定的组织成本，假设这已包含在以 r、s 分别代表的生产最终产品、中间产品的劳动的交易效率中。

(5) 每个人最多卖一种产品；不买并自给同种产品；如果她卖消费品，则她同时自给该消费品；除非她自给自足所有产品，否则她不自给中间产品。[②]

设有如下的效用函数和生产体系：

$$u = y + ky^d$$

$$\text{s.t} \quad y + y^s = (x + Tx^d)^a l_y^a \quad \text{（生产 } y \text{ 的专家的生产条件）}$$

$$x + x^s = l_x^b \quad \text{（生产 } x \text{ 的专家的生产条件）}$$

$$l_x + l_y = 1 \quad \text{（禀赋约束）}$$

其中，T 代表有无合同保证时的中间产品的交易效率，a 为生产 y 的迂回经济程度和专业化经济程度参数，b 为生产 x 的专业化经济程度参数，且 $a \in (0.5, 1)$，$b > 1$。最终产品和中间产品的组织有五种基本结构：(1)结构 A(自给自足)。(2)结构 D，由模式(x/y)和(y/x)组成(符号 x/y 表示生产—消费者卖 x 买 y，本文这类符号都以此类推)，一部分人专门生产中间产品，一部

① 这里的假设只是简化理论分析的需要，在实际生活中，作为卖者往往也承担了交易费用，或者交易费用由卖者和买者共同分担。同样，不仅买者面临市场交易风险，卖者也面临市场交易风险，如果存在"资产专用性"的锁定，中间产品的卖者实际上可能面临更大的市场交易风险，因此，从卖者角度也有要不要用合同来约束的问题。

② 这是文定理的一种表述，见杨小凯：《经济学：新兴古典与新古典框架》，社会科学文献出版社 2003 年版，第 155 页。

分人专门生产最终产品，通过产品市场来组织，且中间产品交易无合同保证，交易有市场风险。(3)结构 C，由模式(x/y)和(y/x)组成，一部分人专门生产中间产品，一部分人专门生产最终产品，通过产品市场来组织，中间产品交易有合同保证，但购买者需要支付一定的合同成本。(4)结构 E，由模式(l_x/y)和(y/l_x)组成，表示生产最终产品 y 的专家雇用工人在企业内专门生产中间产品 x，然后生产并出卖最终产品给生产中间产品的专家。(5)结构 F，由模式(l_y/y)和(y/l_y)构成，表示生产中间产品(如管理知识)的专家雇用生产最终产品的工人组成企业，用中间产品生产最终产品，工人生产并购买最终产品。其中，结构 A、结构 E、结构 F 的解可以直接利用间接定价理论模型中的结果(杨小凯，2003)①，在这里仅求结构 D 和结构 C。

(二) 角点结构均衡信息

1. 结构 D

对模式(x/y)，有 $x = x^d = y = y^s = l_y = 0$，它的决策问题是：

$$\text{Max}\, U_x = ky^d$$

$$\text{s.t.} \quad x^s = l_x^b,\ l_x = 1$$

$$p_x x^s = p_y y^d \qquad \text{(预算约束)}$$

其解为： $x^s = 1,\ y^d = p_x/p_y,\ U_x = kp_x/p_y$

对模式 (y/x) 有 $x = x^s = y^d = l_x = 0,\ l_y = 1$，且由于购买中间产品无合同保证，存在市场交易风险，它的决策问题是：

---

① 在杨小凯和黄有光 1995 年的文章中，交易系数设定为交易成本系数(transaction cost coefficient)，后来改用交易效率系数(transaction efficiency)，它们是此消彼长的关系，没有本质变化，但方便计算。所以，本文利用的是用交易效率系数计算出来的结果。

$$\text{Max}\,\text{EU}_y = E_y$$

$$\text{s. t.}\quad y + y^s = \begin{cases}(tx^d)^a, & \mu \\ 0, & 1-\mu\end{cases}$$

$$p_y y^s = p_x x^d \qquad\qquad \text{（预算约束）}$$

其解为：$x^d = (at^a p_y/p_x)^{1/(1-a)}$，$y^s = (at^a p_y/p_x)^{1/(1-a)} \cdot p_x/p_y$

$$y = \begin{cases}(1-a)(atp_y/p_x)^{a/(1-a)}, & \mu \\ 0, & 1-\mu\end{cases}$$

$$\text{EU}_y = E_y = \mu(1-a)(atp_y/p_x)^{a/(1-a)}$$

由市场出清条件 $M_x x^s = M_y x^d$、效用均等条件 $U_x = \text{EU}_y$ 以及人口规模等式 $M_x + M_y = M$（M_x 与 M_y 是结构 D 中售卖产品 x 和 y 的人数），可以解出结构 D 角点均衡时的人均真实收入：

$$U_{\text{D}} = a^a(1-a)^{1-a}(\mu^{\frac{1-a}{a}}tk)^a$$

令 $\rho = t - t\mu^{\frac{1-a}{a}}$，可把 $t\mu^{\frac{1-a}{a}}$ 视为考虑交易风险时的中间产品交易效率，那么，$t - t\mu^{\frac{1-a}{a}}$ 则是由交易风险导致的中间产品交易效率期望损失系数，设其等于 ρ，则有 $t\mu^{\frac{1-a}{a}} = t - \rho$。

$$U_{\text{D}} = a^a(1-a)^{1-a}[(t-\rho)k]^a$$

2. 结构 C

其模式(x/y)的解与结构 D 的中间产品生产者相同。对模式(y/x)，有 $x = x^s = y^d = l_x = 0$，$l_y = 1$，它的决策问题是：

$$\text{Max}\,U_y = y$$

$$\text{s. t.}\quad y + y^s = [(t-\lambda)x^d]^a$$

$$p_y y^s = p_x x^d$$

其解为：

$$x^d = [a(t-\lambda)^a p_y/p_x]^{\frac{1}{1-a}},$$

$$y^s = [a(t-\lambda)^a p_y/p_x]^{\frac{1}{1-a}} p_x/p_y$$

$$U_y = [a(t-\lambda)p_y/p_x]^{\frac{a}{1-a}}(1-a)$$

由市场出清条件 $M_x x^s = M_y x^d$、效用均等条件 $U_x = U_y$ 以及人口规模等式 $M_x + M_y = M$ (M_x 与 M_y 是结构 E 中售卖产品 x 和 y 的人数)，可以解出结构 C 角点均衡时的人均真实收入：

$$U_c = a^a(1-a)^{1-a}[(t-\lambda)k]^a$$

五个结构角点均衡时的人均真实收入如表 1：

表 1　人均真实收入

结构 A	结构 D	结构 C	结构 E	结构 F
$[b^b/(1+b)^{1+b}]^a$	$(1-a)^{1-a}\cdot[(t-\rho)ak]^a$	$(1-a)^{1-a}\cdot[(t-\lambda)ak]^a$	$(1-a)^{1-a}\cdot(s^bka)^a$	$(1-a)^{1-a}\cdot(ar)^ak^{1-a}$

(三) 超边际比较静态分析

对这五个角点结构进行超边际比较静态分析，可以得到不同参数条件下的全面均衡解。当 $\lambda > \rho$ 时，结构 C 始终劣于结构 D，因此，结构 C 不可能出现在均衡之中，可能的均衡结构出现在结构 A、结构 D、结构 E、结构 F 之间；当 $\lambda < \rho$ 时，结构 C 始终比结构 D 好，因此，结构 D 不可能出现在均衡之中，可能的均衡结构在 A、C、E、F 之间产生。表 2 汇总了这五种结构的全面均衡比较静态分析结果。

表 2　全面均衡及其超边际比较静态分析

ρ与λ的值	$\lambda<\rho$							
s和t、λ、ρ的值	$t-\lambda<s^b$				$t-\lambda>s^b$			
k相对于r、t、s、α、λ、ρ的	$k<k_1$		$k>k_1$		$k<k_4$		$k>k_4$	
值均衡结构	$k<k_2$	$k>k_2$	$k<k_3$	$k>k_3$	$k<k_2$	$k>k_2$	$k<k_5$	$k>k_5$
均衡结构	结构 A	结构 F	结构 A	结构 E	结构 A	结构 F	结构 A	结构 C
ρ与λ的值	$\lambda<\rho$							
s和t、λ、ρ的值	$t-\rho<s^b$				$t-\rho>s^b$			
k相对于r、t、s、α、λ、ρ的	$k<k_1$		$k>k_1$		$k<k_6$		$k>k_6$	
值均衡结构	$k<k_2$	$k>k_2$	$k<k_3$	$k>k_3$	$k<k_2$	$k>k_2$	$k<k_7$	$k>k_7$
均衡结构	结构 A	结构 F	结构 A	结构 E	结构 A	结构 F	结构 A	结构 D

其中当：$k_1=(r/s^b)^{\alpha/(2\alpha-1)}$，　　则结构 F = 结构 E；

$k_2=[b^b/\alpha r(1+b)^{1+b}]^{\alpha/1-\alpha}(1-\alpha)$，则结构 A=结构 F；

$k_3=b^b(1-\alpha)^{(\alpha-1)/\alpha}/\alpha s^b(1+b)^{(1+b)}$，则结构 A = 结构 E；

$k_4=[r/(t-\lambda)]^{\alpha/(2\alpha-1)}$，　　则结构 F = 结构 C；

$k_5=b^b(1-\alpha)^{(\alpha-1)/\alpha}/\alpha(t-\lambda)(1+b)^{(1+b)}$，

　　则结构 A=结构 C；

$k_6=[r/(t-\rho)]^{\alpha/(2\alpha-1)}$，　　则结构 D = 结构 F；

$k_7=b^b(1-\alpha)^{(\alpha-1)/\alpha}/\alpha(t-\rho)(1+b)^{(1+b)}$，

　　则结构 D=结构 A。

我们在杨小凯和黄有光归纳总结的基础上把全部命题扩充表述如下：

命题 1：当劳动及产品交易效率足够低时，自给自足是全面均衡；当劳动及产品交易效率足够高时，分工结构是全面均衡。

这一命题由 k 小于或大于 k_2、k_3、k_5、k_7 来说明。

命题 2：市场交易风险导致需要有更高的交易效率才能保证分工结构是全面均衡，所以，防范风险的制度设计是提高社会分工水平的重要保证。这一命题由 k_7 来说明。在 k_7 中分母包含了风险损失系数 ρ，它与交易效率成正相关关系。如果不存在交易风险损失系数 ρ，k_7 就会变小，分工结构 D 出现所要求的交易效率水平就会相应降低；如果交易风险损失系数 ρ 不仅存在，而且提高，k_7 就会变大，分工结构 D 出现所要求的交易效率水平就会相应提高。

命题 3：如果由交易风险导致的中间产品交易效率期望损失系数(ρ)小于中间产品交易的合同成本系数(λ)，无合同保证的中间产品交易效率 $(t-\rho)$ 高于生产中间产品的劳动的交易效率(s^b)，并且最终产品的交易效率(k)和无合同保证的中间产品交易效率 $(t-\rho)$ 较之用于生产最终产品的劳动的交易效率(r)足够高(即 $k>k_6$)，则无合同的市场组织结构(结构 D)是全面均衡。

命题 4：如果由交易风险导致的中间产品交易效率期望损失系数(ρ)大于中间产品交易的合同成本系数(λ)，包含合同成本的中间产品交易效率 $(t-\lambda)$ 高于生产中间产品的劳动的交易效率(s^b)，并且最终产品的交易效率(k)和有合同保证的中间产品交易效率 $(t-\lambda)$ 较之用于生产最终产品的劳动的交易效率(r)足够高(即 $k>k_4$)，则有合同的市场组织结构(结构 C)是全面均衡。

有合同的市场组织结构是现代市场经济中很重要的经营组织结构，供应链、战略联盟等都是这样一种组织结构的具体形式。正如威廉姆森(2002)所说："企业、市场以及与此有关的各种签订合同的行为，都是重要的经济制度，也是一系列令人眼花缭乱的组织创新过程的产物。"

命题 5：如果劳动交易效率高于包含风险损失（或合同成本）在内的中间产品交易效率，分工则通过劳动市场和企业制度来组织。否则，分工则通过中间产品与最终产品市场来组织。

这是因为，当生产中间产品（如管理知识）的劳动（即管理劳动）交易效率高于包含风险损失（或合同成本）在内的中间产品（即管理知识）交易效率，即当 $t-\rho < s^b$（或 $t-\lambda < s^b$）时，市场组织结构 C（或结构 D）不是全面均衡的可能解，全面均衡解出现在企业结构（结构 E、结构 F）和自给自足结构（结构 A）之间。只要交易效率足够高，企业结构就是全面均衡。即使中间产品的劳动交易效率低于包含风险损失（或合同成本）在内的中间产品交易效率，即当 $t-\rho > s^b$（或 $t-\lambda > s^b$）时，只要生产最终产品的劳动交易效率高于包含风险损失（或合同成本）在内的中间产品交易效率（即 $k < k_4$ 或 $k < k_6$），不需要进行生产中间产品劳动交易的企业结构 F 是全面均衡。

命题 6：当企业在全面均衡中出现时，如果生产最终产品的劳动交易效率（r）低于生产中间产品的劳动交易效率（s），则最终产品专家是企业老板，享有剩余权利，结构 E 是全面均衡；否则，则中间产品专家（如管理专家）是企业老板，享有剩余权利，结构 F 是全面均衡。

命题 6 正是杨小凯和黄有光强调的企业与非对称剩余权利可以将交易效率相对低的活动卷入分工，以避免对这类活动的投入产出直接定价所形成的高昂交易费用，这类活动价值的大小由剩余收益来反映。这就是间接定价理论。

当我们完整而不是局部地看待这一理论模型时，它不仅仅是一个企业理论模型，实际探讨的是出现最终产品与中间产品分工时产权实现的组织结构与形式问题，企业作为间接定价工具只是整个理论模型的一部分，它揭示了：当交易效率足够低和

(或)交易风险足够高时,产权将采取自给自足的直接实现形式;当交易效率足够高和(或)交易风险足够低时,产权将采取分工的实现形式;在分工的实现形式中又分为直接定价形式和间接定价形式,当只有最终产品,或者出现了中间产品与最终产品的分工但劳动交易效率低于产品交易效率时,产权将通过中间产品和最终产品市场直接定价来实现,否则,产权将以剩余权利的形式通过劳动市场和企业制度间接定价来实现。①

间接定价理论模型也丰富了经济组织演进理论。在间接定价理论模型中包含自给自足、无合同市场结构、有合同市场结构、最终产品生产者享有剩余权利的企业结构和中间产品生产者享有剩余权利的企业结构五种基本组织形式。应该看到,自从有了最终产品与中间产品的分工,人类经济的组织活动在物质形态上主要围绕最终产品和中间产品的分工而展开,并在一定的历史阶段演化成商业化和企业化的发展。可以把结构D、结构C视为商业化发展,结构E、结构F视为企业化发展。从历史角度来看,间接定价理论模型在整体上反映了人类经济组织结构从自给自足向商业化与企业化演进的历史主线,并揭示了这一演进过程的内在逻辑:(1)中间产品的出现是经济组织向商业化、企业化演进的重要物质基础。如果没有中间产品的出现,没有迂回化生产,最终产品的劳动生产力很低,没有多少剩余产品,这时,人类社会就难以向商业社会转型。(2)存在专业化经济(包括规模经济)的报酬递增机制,是驱动最终产品与中间产品分工的基本动力。(3)交易

---

① 杨小凯指出,在通过中间产品和最终产品市场组织的结构中,没有企业和劳动市场存在,"剩余索取权和剩余控制权在双方是对称分布的",也就是说,产权采取直接定价的实现形式。参见《经济学:新兴古典与新古典框架》,社会科学文献出版社2003年版,第153页。

效率的提高和风险防范机制的设计使最终产品与中间产品的分工得以实现。(4)产权主体在综合考虑专业化经济、交易效率、市场风险的基础上将选择最有利的组织结构,或市场化,或企业化,抑或自给自足。

三、分工与农业组织化演进:统一的理论解释

(一) 人民公社制的解体:剩余权利主体缺失与内生交易费用膨胀

林毅夫(Lin, 1988)在《中国农业改革中的家庭承包制:理论与实证研究》一文中对人民公社为什么解体给出了正式的理论模型。他为了研究人民公社生产队体制向家庭承包制转变的缘由与效果,构建了一个"工分制的生产队模型",认为生产队中劳动激励或者说劳动者的努力程度是管理者所实施的监管程度的函数,由于在农业中提供有效监管的成本太高,从而不能准确计量劳动者的劳动贡献,导致工分份额与贡献份额不对称,不能做到真正的按劳分配。所以,生产队的劳动激励不足。相反,家庭承包制使每个劳动者享有剩余权利,克服了计量劳动者努力程度的困难,从而人民公社必然解体并转向家庭承包制。应该说这是关于人民公社解体的最早的正式理论模型,不过,在肯定这一点的时候,我们也发现其理论阐述过程中的一点瑕疵。这就是作为"工分制的生产队模型"参照物的不是家庭承包制,而是"私人农场"或其他私人经济组织。①因此,人民公社解体并转向私人农场而不是家庭承包制才是理论逻辑更为合理的结论。

① 私人农场与家庭承包制之间还是存在一定的差别,前者以土地私有制为基础,可以存在雇佣劳动关系;后者以土地公有制为基础,在当时的中国也不允许有雇佣劳动关系。

如果认为在当时的中国，由于土地公有制和意识形态的原因，私人农场不是选项，那么，把私人农场作为“生产队模型”的参照物就没有多少实际意义，还不如直接把家庭承包制作为“生产队模型”的理论参照物。也就是说，用“工分制的生产队模型”与私人农场的效率对比来说明人民公社解体并向家庭承包制转变在理论的逻辑链条上似乎存在一定的缺陷。

要说明人民公社必然解体，其实不必与私人农场比较，如果以土地公有制为基础的不同组织结构的比较能够说明至少有一种结构比人民公社的效率高，那么，人民公社从经济上看就必然要解体。根据间接定价理论模型，这种比较可以从两个基本方面进行：一是有没有真正合格的产权主体或剩余权利主体，一般而言有产权主体的体制在效率上要优于无产权主体的体制；二是产权（或者利益）的组织实现形式。前者为根本，后者是派生，如果允许自由选择，产权主体总是会找到最有利的产权（或者利益）组织实现形式。在土地公有制基础上，农业生产经营活动体制既可以采取无产权主体的体制，如人民公社中无论是管理者还是生产者都没有合法的剩余权利；也可以采取有产权主体的体制，如家庭承包制。周其仁（1994）强调剩余权利对经济效率的重要性，认为人民公社的生产队体制对管理者激励不足，即管理者没有剩余权是导致农业劳动监督不足进而劳动无效率的根本原因。按照这一观点来推论，即使不与家庭承包制比较，如果把剩余权利赋予管理者（也就是管理者承包），并且继续采取生产队的组织形式（即产权与利益的组织实现形式不变），经济效率也会因为管理者的监管程度提高而提高。从间接定价理论模型来看，也就是在团队生产中，当管理者的管理劳动交易效率相对较低时，把剩余权利赋予管理者，让剩余权利发挥作用，对管理者的管理劳动进行间接定价，可以促进效率提高（见命题 6，结构F)。[①]因此,在土地公有制基础上,总是可以找到有产权主体的体制来替代无产权主体的体制,像管理者承包、家庭承包等都是可以选择的方案。

对问题还可以作进一步的分析,理论上可以假设存在另一种无产权主体的组织形式,即生产队把土地承包到每个家庭,采取家庭生产而非集体生产的方式,每个家庭全部农产品都交公,没有剩余权利,一个家庭的净收入是根据每个家庭交公的农产品占生产队全部农产品的份额来分配,姑且称这种形式为无产权家庭生产组织。而在人民公社体制下,生产劳动由集体组织,一个家庭的净收入是根据每个家庭的劳动工分占生产队全部劳动工分的份额来分配,姑且称这种形式为无产权集体生产组织。由于这两种结构都没有产权主体,如果要对它们的经济效率进行比较,只能通过比较它们的利益组织实现形式来说明。从图1我们看到生产队成员分为两大类,一类是管理者,如生产队的书记、队长、副队长、会计等,他们从事农业生产活动的规划、考核、协调、计量、分配等工作,提供的是管理知识与管理劳动,属于提供中间产品及生产中间产品劳动的范畴;另一类是生产者,直接从事农产品的生产,是从事最终产品生产的农业劳动者。这里存在中间产品生产与最终产品生产的分工。假定在这两种组织形式中,管理者有相同的激励[②],那么,经济效率就取决于组织成本与生产者的劳动状态。从组织成本来看,在无产权集

① 可以把间接定价理论模型中的企业理论看作是一种团队化理论,在生产队的农业劳动中,存在管理劳动与生产劳动的分工,管理劳动的监管与考核更加困难,管理劳动的交易效率一般低于生产劳动的交易效率,如果要选择生产队体制,把剩余权利赋予管理者是合理的。

② 尽管他们不是合法的剩余权利主体,但是,正如周其仁(1994)指出的,他们享有一定的监管者特权,占有提拔、子女招工等方面的先机,虽然不能说这有多么强的激励作用,但还是或多或少地存在。

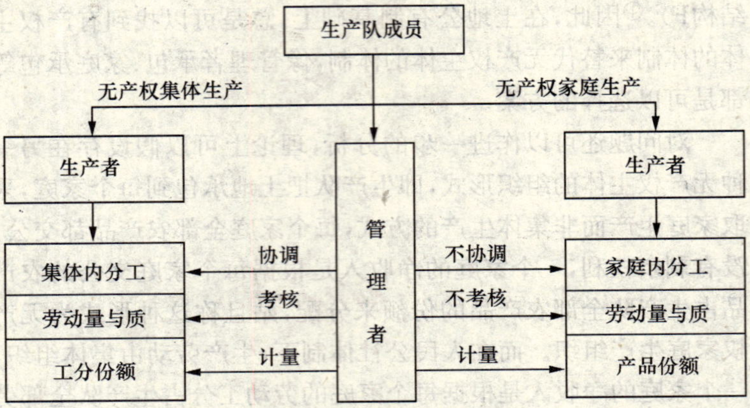

图 1　两类无产权主体生产组织的比较

体生产组织中，管理者要对生产劳动在集体范围内进行分工协调，而在无产权家庭生产组织中，生产劳动分工由家庭成员自行安排；前者按工分份额来分配，要求尽可能对每个人的劳动数量与质量给予准确考核，也就是要求对劳动过程进行监管，而后者按产品份额来分配，只看劳动结果，不管劳动过程，不需要对劳动的数量与质量进行考核。①毫无疑问，在组织成本上，无产权家庭生产组织要比无产权集体生产组织低。从生产者的劳动状态来看，在无产权集体生产组织中，正如林毅夫指出的，由于监管成本太高，导致工分份额与贡献份额不对称，不能做到真正的按劳分配，生产者就有很强的“偷工减料”的机会主义行为动机；而在无产权家庭生产组织中，产品份额就是贡献份额，直接决定家庭净收入的分配比例，这对生产者的偷工减料行为有较强的约束。用间接定价理论模型来审视，按工分份额分配在本质上是生产队

① 人民公社对管理者也是按工分份额分配，管理者的工分份额一般是按生产队平均工分额上浮一定比例。

(严格讲应该是政府或国家)"购买"生产者生产农产品(或最终产品)的劳动,是生产最终产品劳动的交易;按产品份额分配在本质上是生产队"购买"生产者生产的农产品(或最终产品),是最终产品的交易。在一般情况下,农产品的交易效率要比生产农产品劳动的交易效率高。人类历史上地租形式由劳役地租向实物地租、货币地租转化也说明了这一点。①通过这种对比,应该可以说在经济效率上无产权家庭生产组织要胜过无产权集体生产组织。

我们经历过人民公社的集体劳动,在这里仅举两个隐性地降低劳动质量的例子来说明农业劳动的交易效率低。在人民公社体制下,栽秧是按亩计算工资或工分,在技术上要求秧的行间距一般是3—6寸。在田埂较远的地方,生产队长不能用肉眼一下看出秧的行间距,若要确定秧的行间距、考核劳动质量,他就必须下到田间来。实际上他很难时刻做到这一点,因而当把秧插斜一点,在视觉上形成前后紧簇的感觉时,站在田埂上就不能准确判断秧的行间距。结果离田埂近的地方是3—6寸,而离田埂远的地方就变成了4—7寸或5—7寸。又例如在稻田和棉田里除草,也是按亩来计算工资或工分。众所周知,秧苗、棉苗栽下去后不久的第1、2道除草工作很重要,如果除草不净,它就会与秧苗、棉苗争夺肥料、阳光与水分,等到它与秧苗、棉苗"齐头并进"时再除之,一方面于事难补,农作物生长已受到影响,另一方面需要投入更多的劳动力。但社员为了在一定时间内完成更多的面积,往往是在生产队长容易看到的田的四周,除草比较干净,而到了田中间则是"锄草不除根"。所以在收获的时候,野草比棉花树还高,稗子比禾稻还深。这与缪尔达尔对南亚农业生产的描述有惊人的

① 这不意味在任何条件下都没有农业劳动交易,果真这样,农业中就不会有雇佣劳动制度。但是,应该看到,由于农业劳动交易效率低,即使有劳动交易,也是小规模的,这就是为什么农业中流行家庭经营的根本原因。

相似,“他们(是指农业工人——引者注)即使表面上十分繁忙,但在实际中却不愿为产出作出非常有效的贡献”(缪尔达尔,1992)。

劳动质量损失是人民公社时期劳动效率和农业产出损失的主要原因,这一点可以通过家庭承包责任制改革后农业的高速发展来反证。劳动对农业增长的贡献可以从劳动投入数量和劳动质量两个方面进行分析。劳动投入数量一般用总劳动时间(即劳动力数量乘以人均劳动时间)来衡量,而劳动质量很难找到直接的衡量指标,可以用劳动总贡献扣除劳动力数量贡献和人均劳动时间贡献后的余量来反映。根据林毅夫(1994)的估计,在1978—1984年间,劳动对农业增长的总贡献是51.41%,其中,劳动人数增加能解释农业增长的4.52%,46.89%要由家庭承包责任制改革带来的劳动生产率的提高来解释。在46.89%中扣除人均劳动时间的贡献,余下的就是劳动质量的贡献。人均劳动时间在改革后是否增加了呢?在人民公社时期已出现了农民“一天的工作时间大约是10个小时,接近一个人劳动时间的生理极限”的情景(郭熙保,2002),改革后人均劳动时间在此基础上要再延长,实际上没有多少余地,而且农作物的复种指数由1978年的151.0%下降到1984年的146.9%(林毅夫,1994),农业劳动任务减少。所以,不能认为改革后的人均劳动时间比改革前长。1978—1985年间农业就业量净增2 275万人,年均增长率为1.17%(武力,2003);如果假定改革前后的农业人均劳动时间相差不大,那么,总劳动时间的年均增长率大约也是1.17%;再假定没有劳动质量的提高,劳动时间的平均生产率还与改革前相当,那么,劳动力数量对农业增长的贡献大约应是7个百分点(1.17乘以6年),而林毅夫的估计只有4.52个百分点。这说明改革后的人均劳动时间比改革前要短,人均劳动时间与农业增长负相关。因此,46.89%的贡献率应视为农业劳动质量提高的结果。由此反观生产队的劳动低效率，则主要应归因于劳动质量的损失。劳动质量损失正说明生产农产品的劳动交易效率不高。劳动效率及农业产出的损失在本质上是生产队成员争夺分工好处的机会主义行为造成的内生交易费用。

通过上述对比分析，自然可以得出人民公社体制必然解体的结论。因为不仅可以找到有产权主体的体制来替代它，甚至还可以找到无产权主体的体制来替代它。从间接定价理论模型来看，人民公社之所以必然解体，首先是在这个团队中没有一个合格的产权主体，剩余权利作为企业家才能的定价机制不能充分发挥作用；其次，在这个团队成员利益的组织实现形式上，试图对交易效率低的农业管理与生产劳动进行直接定价，但由于监管者激励不足及监管成本太高，对劳动直接定价不可行，结果平均主义大行其道，减少动数量、降低劳动质量的机会主义行为到处盛行。人民公社作为一种团队分工结构，不仅不能获得专业化经济报酬递增的好处，反而为不断膨胀的内生交易费用所困。一言蔽之，剩余权利主体的缺失使不当的利益组织实现形式所蕴含的机会主义行为得以膨胀，导致了无法承受的内生交易费用，最终使人民公社彻底解体。

（二）家庭承包制的选择：明确剩余权利主体与向自给自足回归

上述分析说明，没有剩余权利主体的组织结构一定是低效率的。为了解决剩余权利主体的缺失，可供选择的组织形式大致有土地家庭私有制、农民自治制、管理者承包制、家庭承包制等。家庭承包制只是其中的一种可能性，这种可能性为什么会成为当时的必然选择？

土地家庭私有制由于众所周知的原因，在路径依赖上显然不具有可选择性。

农民自治制实际上是农民集体承包。这里，剩余权利的界定与分配将有三个环节。首先，自然是农民集体享有剩余权利。其次，农民集体也需要从事管理活动的管理者，对于管理者劳动如何定价？由于对管理者活动的监督与考核存在困难，比较可行的办法是由农民集体赋予管理者一定的剩余收益权实行间接定价，于是产生了农民集体与管理者之间的剩余权利瓜分与分配的问题。这一问题直接关系到作为衡量企业家价值的剩余权利定价机制能否真正地发挥作用，围绕管理者的剩余收益比例将会展开频繁的讨价还价。再次，当管理者享有一定的剩余收益权后，如何来组织生产劳动并使自己的剩余收益最大化？一种方式是按劳分配，为此，对生产劳动进行监督与考核需要付出一定的成本；另一种方式是向家庭承包，管理者把自己享有的一部分剩余收益再赋予承包家庭，以达到对监督费用的节约。尽管在管理者与承包家庭之间也产生了剩余收益分配的讨价还价，但只要管理者让渡的这部分收益小于监督费用，就会采取家庭承包的方式。另外，管理者为了自己的剩余收益最大化，主观上总是想把劳动任务交给那些生产能力更强的人，但是在农民自治的情况下，管理者并没有充分行使这种权利的空间，因为农民才是主人，有天然的劳动与就业权利。所以，在农民自治的情况下，企业家价值的间接定价机制并不能得到充分的发挥，经过多次承包后，农民自治实际上最终可能会演变为家庭承包。

管理者承包制就像国有企业的承包改革一样，把剩余权利界定给生产队长或以生产队长为主的领导集体。如果管理者承包，他们就应该在投资决策、生产经营、产品定价、劳动力使用等方面享有决定权。这样做有一个明显的好处，那就是可以实现许多理论工作者倡导的类似农场（这就是一种农业企业）的规模化经营。我们的问题是，既然管理者承包有利于实现农业的规模化经营，为什么当初不把剩余权利界定给管理者？在当时的背景下，我国工业化和城市化的程度还很低，农民进城就业的机会很少，如果管理者要通过减少劳动力来使自己剩余收益最大化，那么，剩余劳动力去哪里？这就成了一个社会稳定问题。再者，宪法规定农村土地是集体所有，每个人享有同等的就业与劳动权利，管理者在法律上没有解雇农民的权利。因此，管理者在使用多少劳动力、雇不雇用谁上并没有充分的决定权。在农产品的生产和定价上，管理者同样没有决定权，这些权利最终还是掌握在国家和政府的手中。在当时，也没有资本市场，银行的商业化程度很低，管理者即使发现了良好的市场机会，也难以从资本市场和银行获得筹措资本的支持。剩余控制权与剩余收益权是一对孪生兄弟，剩余控制权是剩余收益权的保证，剩余收益权是剩余控制权的目标。当管理者由于经济的、法律的原因不能充分行使剩余控制权时，剩余收益作为企业家（管理者）价值的定价机制并不能充分发挥作用。无论是农民自治还是管理者承包，都是团队内分工的组织结构，一个没有剩余权利主体的团队分工结构一定是低效率的；同样，即使有剩余权利主体，但剩余权利不能充分发挥作用的团队分工结构也会是低效率的。此外，即使管理者承包，在如何组织生产劳动并使自己的剩余收益最大化上，也面临着与农民自治一样的困境。管理者承包最终也可能会演变为家庭承包。

农民自治和管理者承包都是类似于企业的科层组织，存在团队内部的分工，在这种组织结构下，一要有剩余权利主体，二要有剩余权利发挥作用的条件，只有这样，团队组织才可能是有效率的。当剩余权利作为企业家的间接定价机制在中国农业中还不能充分发挥作用时，农民自治和管理者承包都不是经济上的合理选择。

从人民公社的生产队体制向家庭承包制转变，一方面把剩余权利界定给了农民个体;另一方面管理劳动和生产劳动都集中在一个人(把一个家庭看作一个人,不考虑家庭内分工)身上,实行无分工的组织结构,本质上是向自给自足结构回归。把剩余权利界定给农民,在当时的生产决策、产品定价、资本筹措上面临着与管理者承包同等的约束条件,剩余权利也不能充分发挥作用。正因如此,那么,就应该尽量避免选择那些会“天然”地产生内生交易费用的组织结构。尤其在劳动力市场没有发育,农业劳动交易效率比较低的情况下,更应该避免。根据宋洪远提供的资料,在1978年12月中共十一届三中全会召开以后,全国各地主要采取了联产和不联产的两类生产责任制,“不联产的责任制一般是在生产队统一计划、统一经营的情况下,将农活包给作业组和个人,生产队向承包者规定在一定时期内必须按质完成的作业数量和应得工分,超额完成的给予奖励,完不成任务或质量不合格的扣减工分报酬……联产的责任制是在生产队统一经营、统一核算的情况下,把承包者的利益与生产的最终成果直接挂钩,包产内的产量由生产队统一分配,超产奖励,减产受罚。联产责任制主要有专业承包、包产到组、包产到户、包产到劳等形式。比如包产到组是将土地、劳力、耕畜、农机固定到作业组织,制定出产量、用工和生产费用指标,由作业组承包完成,完成任务后包产部分上交生产队统一分配,由生产队按原定指标拨付生产费用和工分。后来,各种形式的联产责任制逐步演变为包产到户和包干到户,其中尤以包干到户最受欢迎”(宋洪远,2000)。这里的经济根源就在于当劳动及产品交易效率足够低时,自给自足是全面均衡(见命题1)。实行家庭承包制是向自给自足回归,没有管理劳动与生产劳动的分工与交换,管理劳动和生产劳动集于一身,剩余权利的实现首先取决于农民自身努力的程度,“交足国家的,留足集体的,余下都是自己的”,从而形成足够强的激励机制，避免了内生交易费用产生的风险。家庭承包制正是在劳动及产品交易效率低、剩余权利不能充分发挥作用的条件下农民对内生交易费用最小化组织结构的合理选择。此外，把土地平等地承包给每个农民除体现土地集体所有的法律意义外，在经济上还包含了每个农民天生相同且都可能成为企业家的含义，这也最大限度满足了农民对平等(包括起点平等)、就业和自尊的需求。

(三) 农业商业化的发展：生产过程市场化与无合同市场组织结构

1984 年之前，农村改革的重点是在全国逐步推广家庭承包责任制，奠定农业发展的微观基础，但并没有从根本上触及传统的计划经济体制。1984 年是关键的一年，该年启动了对计划经济体制的改革，随后对农业采取了缩小指令性计划、废除统购统销体制、实行价格"双轨制"、引导农民跨区域流动、放松对非公有制经济发展的管制和允许土地协商转包等诸多措施。这些措施是对农民的"松绑"，大大提高了经济活动的交易效率，为农民发挥聪明才智提供了广阔舞台，市场作为引导农民投资决策和资源配置的机制开始真正发挥作用，农业商业化构成了 20 世纪八九十年代农业组织化演进的重要组成部分。农业商业化首先是农产品交易市场化①，但更能深刻反映农业商业化程度是农业生产过

① 常修泽、高明华(1998)认为中国 1997 年农产品交易市场化程度达到 77.20%；习近平(2001)认为 1998 年中在 50%—75%之间；陈宗胜(1999)认为 1994 年达到了 91.5%。尽管不同学者的估算方法和结果不同，但都能放映我国农产品的商业化有了很大程度的发展。根据中共中央政策研究室与农业部共同组成的农村固定观察点办公室公布的《全国农村社会经济典型调查数据汇编》(1986—1999 年，第 3—4 页)的资料计算，全国农户(指被调查的)平均的主要农产品的出售数量与产量之比，到 1999 年，除粮食、牛羊肉分别为 41.5%、78.8%外，猪肉、家禽、禽蛋、奶类、水产品都在 80%以上，分别是 (转下页)

程的市场化(樊亢、戎殿新,1994)。关于农业生产过程的市场化,主要从中间产品投入市场化和农业生产环节市场化来分析。

从中间产品投入来看,反映农业生产过程市场化的指标是农业投入物的外购率。生产性固定资产是重要的中间投入品,农户拥有的生产性固定资产主要有役畜、种畜、产品畜、大中型铁木农具、农林牧渔业机械、工业机械、运输机械、生产用房等。假设其中役畜、种畜、产品畜是自给的,其他均为外购,根据农户年末拥有的生产性固定资产原值计算,1999 年是 1986 年的 5.8 倍,固定资产投入的外购率从 1986 年的71.1%上升到 1999 年的 86.7%(《全国农村社会经济典型调查数据汇编》,2001)。如果加上农户购买的流动性生产资料,农业投入物的外购比率将更高。全国平均每个农户购买的化肥数量 2001 年是 1983 年的 1.4 倍,饼肥为 0.44 倍,农药为 1.53 倍,农用薄膜为 4.26 倍,生产用燃料为 11.21 倍(《中国农村住户调查年鉴》,2002)。这既反映了农业生产迂回程度的提高,也反映了迂回程度的市场化水平提高。在实行家庭承包制的初期,农业固定资产随着生产队的解体而损失,在集体经济中曾经发挥作用的农用机械及动力为人力和畜力所替代,生产的迂回程度降低,这在一定程度上是向最终产品和中间产品都自给自足的结构回归。但是,随着改革的深入,中青年农业劳动力向城市转移导致了农户对中间投入品需求的增加,承包期长期化稳定了农民对投资的剩余权利的预期,专业商人的出现、市场及其秩序的建设提高了产品

(接上页)82.5%、95.5%、91.7%、98.4%、98.2%。以村(被调查村)为单位计算的全国平均的农产品出售数量与产量之比,棉花、油料、糖料、麻类、烟叶、茶叶、药材、蚕茧、水果、蔬菜、木材、毛竹、林产品分别是 88.7%、55.1%、101.2%、100%、96.1%、91.9%、95.2%、99.4%、76.5%、60.8%、56.1%、40.2%、58.6%(农村固定观察点办公室,2001:487—489)。这些数据既反映农产品商业化程度整体上比较高,又反映不同农产品的商业化程度存在差异。

交易效率，这些因素共同作用深化了农户与中间产品生产者之间的社会分工，农户与中间产品生产者之间的分工是通过农产品市场与中间产品市场来组织的，剩余权利对称分布其间。

从农业生产环节来看，农业生产环节的劳务外购（或者叫劳务外包）也得到发展。①最初，劳务外购是以互换劳动的形式出现，这主要于农忙季节发生在亲戚、邻里和朋友之间。但随着农村劳动力的进一步转移，农户兼业化得到发展，更多老人和妇女投入农业劳动之中，越来越多的家庭仅依靠自身的劳动力不足以有效地完成承包土地的生产经营，产生了对中间生产环节服务的需求，而一些精明的农民也发现在一定的市场容量下购买农用机械承包他人的整田、收割等任务变得有利可图。于是，出现了一些农户支付一定货币把农业生产的一些环节如育苗、整田、收割等任务包给他人来完成的现象。在北方的小麦收获季节，收割机大规模跨区域耕作就是典型事例。劳务外购由最初的互换劳动发展为货币与劳务的交换，是农业商业化、货币化发展的重要表现。这种现象在美国等发达国家是比较普遍的，“有专门从事农田耕作的农耕公司，代为撒药防虫的服务公司，代为收获作物的收割公司，承包家畜防役治病的兽医公司等，这几乎是工业分工日趋细密的历史过程在农业中的重演”（樊亢、戎殿新，1994）。尽管我国当前农业生产环节的市场化不能与美国等国家相提并论，但随着农村劳动力的转移、中间产品与劳务的交易效率提高，农业生产经营的产前、产中、产后各环节的分工与市场化必将进一步发展。

农业投入物的外购率提高，农业生产中间环节的劳务外包，

① 我们认为有必要把购买劳务与购买劳动力区别开来。购买劳务仍然保持买卖者之间的市场关系，并没有形成企业内雇主与雇员之间的不对称的剩余权利关系；而购买劳动力则不同，形成了企业内雇主与雇员之间的不对称的剩余权利关系。

绝大多数情况都是无合同市场组织结构。从命题3来看，当由交易风险导致的中间产品交易效率期望损失系数小于中间产品交易的合同成本系数，无合同保证的中间产品交易效率高于生产中间产品的劳动的交易效率，且最终产品的交易效率和无合同保证的中间产品交易效率较之用于生产最终产品的劳动的交易效率足够高时，农业生产过程的市场化就会采取无合同市场组织结构。

（四）农业产业化的兴起：龙头企业出现与有合同市场组织结构

如前所述，农业产业化的要点主要是农业产业链的延伸、龙头企业的出现、龙头企业与农民经济关系的协调。其中，龙头企业是农业产业化发展的最主要标志；正是有了龙头企业，才需要协调企业与农民之间的经济利益关系。

1. *农业企业化的发展：龙头企业出现*

在农业产业化发展过程中，农业产业链不断延伸，中间产品和最终产品日益丰富起来，它们之间的分工也越来越复杂化。从命题5来看，如果劳动交易效率高于包含风险损失（或合同成本）在内的中间产品交易效率，分工及剩余权利的实现就会通过劳动市场和企业制度来组织。正因如此，20世纪90年代以来，随着要素市场尤其是劳动力市场不断完善，劳动交易效率不断提高，龙头企业在农产品的加工与流通环节如雨后春笋般发展起来了，根据牛若峰（2002）的资料，农业产业化经营组织的数量1996年有11 824个，1998年有30 344个，2000年发展到66 000个，其中绝大部分是龙头企业带动的。

2. *龙头企业与农民的关系：有合同市场组织结构*

龙头企业促进了农产品加工工业的发展，农民生产的产品日益转化为龙头企业的中间产品，农民和龙头企业成为上下游的关系。龙头企业为了保证稳定的原材料来源，农民为了避免进入市场的交易费用与风险，龙头企业与农民之间的分工通过有合同的市场结构来组织，“公司(＋基地)＋农户”的合同型农业产业组织得到发展，像订单农业、承租返包等都是这一类型的具体组织形式。这里，农民和龙头企业之间的分工主要是通过产品市场来组织，只是中间产品交易有合同保证。

(1) 订单农业。这是一种比较普遍地通过购销合同来协调龙头企业与农户分工的组织形式，合同主体一方是为数众多的农户或代表农户的基层组织，另一方是从事生产加工、销售与服务的龙头企业。这种组织形式通过一定的购销合同关系来实现小农生产与大农经营的结合(向国成等，2002)。

(2) 承租返包。虽然“承租返包”的具体内容因地、因企而异，但其基本结构是相似的：①龙头企业为了获得稳定、优质的农产品原料，通过乡(镇)、村组织，在农民同意的基础上，支付一定的费用向农户承租土地，取得了一定时期决定土地用途的权力；②龙头企业对土地进行规划整治，然后再划块承包给农户，承可者既可以是原土地承包者，也可以是其他人；③龙头企业承担向农户提供种子、技术与管理服务和保证按一定价格收购农产品的义务，农户则按企业的要求进行生产与管理，承担把全部产品卖给企业的义务；④若农户承担生产产品的直接生产费用如农药、肥料及劳动力成本等，将根据卖给企业的产品产量和合同规定的价格获得收益，否则，农民按承包土地的数量和产品产量获得报酬(耿明斋，2000；马晓河、韩俊等，2000)。“承租返包”不是一般的购销合同。龙头企业如果只与农户签订产品购销合同，一般不向农户提供技术、管理和土地整治等方面的服务，也没有掌握土地用途的决定权，尤其是在农户不履行合同的时候，企业没有更换土地承包主体的权力，所以，一般的购销合同对农户的约束力不强。但在“承租返包”方式下，如果农户拒绝承担合同规定的义务，龙头企业则有更换土地承包主体的权力，享有充分的“退出权”，从长远利益上对农户形成了强有力的约束。因此，合同关系一旦形成，对双方都具有强有力的约束，容易得到贯彻落实。马晓河、韩俊等（2000）甚至认为“承租返包”将农业变成了企业的“第一车间”，将农民变成了“工人”，进行企业化管理。尽管如此，我们认为农民毕竟还不是龙头企业的职工，企业向农户购买的是作为生产最终产品的中间产品——农产品原料，而不是农户的劳动力和劳动，龙头企业与农户仍是一种市场交易关系。龙头企业为什么不直接购买农户的劳动力，而是购买用来生产最终产品的中间产品？为什么不采取企业形式或无合同约束的市场形式，而要与农户保持一种有合同约束的市场交易关系？

从命题 4 看，当由交易风险导致的中间产品交易效率期望损失系数大于中间产品交易的合同成本系数，包含合同成本的中间产品交易效率高于生产中间产品的劳动的交易效率，并且最终产品的交易效率和有合同保证的中间产品交易效率较之用于生产最终产品的劳动的交易效率足够高时，则有合同的市场组织结构（即结构 C）就会得到发展。

（五）农民团队化的困境：内生交易费用的制约与土地、户籍制度改革

在农业商业化和企业化的发展中，作为分散农户面临新的矛盾：一是在进入市场时，单个农户面临外生交易费用这座大山的阻挡，以至于根本无力进入市场；二是在面向企业时，与龙头企业谈判处于弱势地位，似乎无力保护和争取自身应有的权利。[①]20 世纪

① 不仅如此，农民的剩余权利还受到政府代理人侵蚀。“据农业部统计，1992 年农民负担的村提留和乡统筹费为 420 亿元，人均 47.38 元，占上年农民人均纯收入的 7.87%，高于国务院的规定 2.87 个百分点；除此之外，农民承担的各项社会负担达 120 亿元，人均 13.6 元，占上年农民人均纯收入的 2.3%，两项合计占上年农民人均纯收入的 10.17%”（宋洪远，2000）。

90 年代以来，农民的团队化（或狭义的组织化）成为理论与实践关注的焦点之一。为此，理论界大力倡导发展合作经济组织，因为这有利于节省外生交易费用和提高农民谈判能力。如果以合作经济组织作为农民团队化的典型代表，那么，农民团队化的困境就是合作经济组织的困境。而合作经济组织在本质上还是企业①，所以，农民团队化的困境本质上就是农民企业化的困境。

根据魏道南、张晓山（1998）的资料，1996 年底全国农村的专业合作组织发展到 150 万个，而其他学者提供的资料显示，1999 年底全国农村的专业合作组织是 140 万个（李惠安，2000）。浙江是我国农村专业合作经济组织发展比较快的地方，根据黄祖辉等（2002）的调查，到 2000 年底浙江各类农民专业合作组织只有 2 667 家，会员 20.18 万，占全省农户的 1.88%，平均每个农民专业合作组织的会员规模只有 75.6 人。尽管不同学者的数据有差异，但都说明我国农村合作经济组织的覆盖率不高。不仅如此，这些专业合作组织中初步形成规模、运行比较规范的大约只有 14 万个，若以前述 140—150 万为基础，大约相当于农村合作经济组织总量的10%。②根据农业部 1995 年“百业百村”调查，合作经济组织职能发挥好、中、差的比重为 30.4%、62.9%、6.7%（罗必良等，2002）。所以，从整体上看，我国农村合作经济组织的满意率也不高。既然农村合作经济组织有利于降低交易费用，提高农民的谈判能力，为什么农民开展合作经济组织的积极性不高？什么因素制约了农民创办并加入合作经济组织的积极性？我们认为，农村合作经济作为农民团队化（或农民企业化）发展的组织形式，在节省

① 正如杜吟棠（2002）的书名《合作社：农业中的现代企业制度》。

② 《中国农业年鉴 2000》，中国农业出版社 2000 年版，第 123 页。

外生交易费用、提高谈判能力的同时，也面临着内部成员争夺分工好处的机会主义行为以及由此产生的内生交易费用的制约。也就是说，合作经济组织面临着节省外生交易费用与产生内生交易费用的两难冲突。正是对可能产生的内生交易费用的预期，农民在加入合作经济组织时往往表现得理性而谨慎。如果理论上只看到合作经济组织可以节省外生交易费用而无视内生交易费用的产生，就会对农民加入合作经济组织时表现出来的迟疑、犹豫、拒绝，甚至退出感到困惑不解，进而无法解释我国农村合作经济组织发展为什么会步履维艰！尤其当合作经济组织以模糊产权为基础，剩余权利作为企业家才能的间接定价机制不能充分发挥作用时，农民更是望而生畏、退避三舍！

根据阿尔钦和德姆塞茨(Alchian and Demsetz，1972)的总结，企业有多种类型，包括古典企业、利益分享企业、社会主义企业、公司、共有的非营利企业、合伙制企业等。在他们看来，企业作为团队组织不可避免地面临劳动的监管与计量问题，从而需要监督者。接下来的问题是，谁来监督监督者或者怎样使监督者有监督的动力？对这一问题的不同解决方法，决定了不同类型企业产生内生交易费用的大小，进而也决定了不同类型企业的适应范围和生命力。他们认为最好的解决办法是赋予雇主与监督者剩余权利，而在各种类型的企业中，古典企业是最有效的，其他类型的企业都无法有效地解决团队中因计量困难而引起的偷懒问题。[①]也就是说，古典企业相对而言是一种最少产生

---

① 古典企业具有如下特征：(1)联合投入的生产；(2)有几个投入所有者；(3)作为契约的一方共享所有联合投入契约；(4)它拥有对任何投入契约进行再谈判的权利，并可独立于与其他所有者的契约；(5)它拥有剩余权利；(6)它拥有出售剩余权利的权利。见 Alchian 和 Demsetz(1972:783)。

内生交易费用的团队组织。这也正是间接定价理论模型中的企业类型。当我们看到一种最少产生内生交易费用的团队组织在中国农村发展尚且困难的时候，就不难理解那些更可能产生内生交易费用的合作经济组织为什么会发展迟缓。

可以把家庭农场看作是农业中的古典企业，有剩余权利主体，存在雇佣劳动关系。到1999年，在被调查的高收入农户中，平均每个农户有1.51个长期雇佣劳动力，有1.24个临时雇佣劳动力，支付的年雇佣工资总额为1 661.83元(《全国农村社会经济典型调查数据汇编》,2001:341)。这既说明中国家庭农场有一定的发展，也说明它的规模还很小。之所以形成这种局面，一方面土地流转市场使一些农户扩大了土地经营规模，产生了对雇佣劳动力的需求，同时，农村劳动力市场发展提高了农业生产劳动力的交易效率，使得一定的劳动交易变得有利可图，从而存在雇佣劳动关系的家庭农场得到一定的发展。另一方面当一个善于经营的农民需要扩大经营规模的时候，实际上又没有完善的土地与资本市场来满足其需要。首先，从农村土地制度来看，土地在法律上是集体所有(实质上还是国家所有)，农民并没有真正的继承权与转让权，也就是说，农民不能按土地市场价格买卖承包土地。因此，现在发生在农民之间的土地转让许多是临时性、小规模的，往往是出去打工的农民把土地暂时转让给那些从事农业生产经营的人，转让时间的长短取决于农民外出打工的时间长短。再加上人多地少的约束，有经营才能的农民要想扩大家庭农场的土地经营规模不是一件轻而易举的事情。其次，从农村资本市场来看，受家庭小规模经营的制约，家庭需要的资本规模一般达不到规模经济的要求，金融机构办理农民小额信贷无利可图，结果20世纪90年代以来，中国正规金融机构基本上退出了农村市场。这可从民间借贷情况得到印证。根据温铁军(2001)的调查材料,民间借贷的发生率高达95%,高利息的民间借贷发生率达到了85%。总之,无论土地市场还是资本市场,都难以满足最少产生内生交易费用的家庭农场的发展需要,农民的企业家才能不能得到充分发挥,从而家庭农场规模还很小。

在家庭承包制基础上发展家庭农场尚且困难重重,那么,要在家庭承包制基础上发展更为复杂、更容易产生内生交易费用的合作经济组织,其难度与进程也就可想而知。像传统的供销合作社等合作经济组织以公有产权为基础,由于产权模糊,不存在剩余权利定价机制或者这一机制不能充分发挥作用,从而不能抑制团队内生交易费用的膨胀,效率很低,旨在服务于农业和农民的目的难以实现。所以,在农民团队化的发展上,我们认为今后应把着力点放在最少产生内生交易费用的家庭农场上。[①]发展家庭农场,无疑需要进一步转移农村劳动力,因此,按自由、平等的原则尽快改革城乡户籍制度是非常必要的。发展家庭农场,根本出路可能还在于土地制度改革,似乎一切问题都与土地制度有着千丝万缕的联系。金融机构之所以退出农村市场,是因为农村家庭这一微观基础的经营规模太小,与其打交道没有规模经济,交易效率太低。而家庭经营规模之所以小,除人多地少这一禀赋条件外,就是农民对承包土地没有完整的产权,不享有继承、抵押、转让等权利。没有这些权利,当一个农民真正要彻底离开农村时,不能从土地上得到任何收益,就像一个考上大

① 理论界大力倡导发展农村合作经济组织来节省外生交易费用和提高农民谈判能力,实际上家庭农场规模扩大也具有同样的效果。发展合作经济组织是以当前家庭数目为前提,是一种静态发展思路;而发展家庭农场正是要减少未来农业人口与家庭数目,是一种动态发展思路。这两种思路应该统一起来,以发展家庭农场为重点。

学的农村学生离开农村一样。也就是说，没有完整的产权，仅有的承包权是不能折现的，那么，要获得土地的未来收益，就只能继续保留承包权。这样就制约了农村土地的流转，进而制约了家庭土地经营规模的扩大。没有完整的产权，土地就不能成为农民相对廉价地发展家庭农场与合作经济组织的物质基础。如果甲村的一个农民要与乙村的一个农民合作，需要用土地入股作为合作基础，但是，土地是集体的，个人根本就没有土地入股的权利，那么，农民之间的自愿合作就无法展开。没有完整的产权，农民连抵押土地获得资本的机会也没有，土地市场与资本市场就不能互动发展。我们认为，为了促进家庭农场发展，可以土地承包的既成事实为基础，实行土地永佃制，除土地名义上还是国有之外，把土地的完整产权都赋予农民。①

当农民拥有土地的完整产权时，农业的微观基础将由家庭承包转向家庭农场。由于土地产权清晰，剩余权利机制能够充分发挥作用，产权主体将会根据最终产品及其劳动、中间产品及其劳动的交易效率与风险选择有效的经营组织形式与经营规模。其中，由于产权完整而清晰，能够抑制内生交易费用的膨胀，以家庭农场为基础的合作经济组织也将得到良好发展。日本合作经济组织的成功发展是一个很好的例证。到 1980 年，日本的“综合农协”有 4 528 个，“专业农协”有 5 191 个，参加农协的农户有 466.1 万户，会员有 788.5 万人，合作组织对农户的覆盖率达到 100％(张宝珍，1995)。

---

① 香港回归前，土地归英国皇室支配，但公民可以通过支付一定的费用取得 99 年或永久使用权，可以继承、转让与抵押，相当于永佃制，这种土地制度成为香港经济发展的重要基础。以土地承包的既成事实为基础实行土地永佃制，可采用收取一定费用的办法来平衡无地与有地、少地与多地农户之间的利益关系。这需要另行研究。

四、结　论

(1) 间接定价理论模型把专业化经济、交易风险和交易费用融为一体，不仅仅是一个企业理论模型，企业作为间接定价工具只是整个理论模型的一部分。该模型在本质上是探讨出现最终产品与中间产品分工时产权实现的组织结构与形式问题，同时在整体上又反映了人类经济组织结构从自给自足向商业化与企业化演进的历史主线，并揭示了这一演进过程的内在逻辑。

(2) 从分工角度理解农业组织化，它是组织团队化与组织市场化的辩证统一。改革开放以来，在以家庭承包为基础、统分结合的双层经营体制背景下，中国农业组织化沿着集体经济→家庭经营→农业商业化→农业产业化→农民团队化的路线演进，间接定价理论模型可以对这一演进路线给出统一的理论解释。这是改革开放提高交易效率、促进分工演化的结果，是农民对中间产品、最终产品及劳动的交易效率与风险进行综合比较后，选择剩余权利赖以实现的最优组织结构的结果。

(3) 在林毅夫和周其仁的分析基础上，我们认为剩余权利主体的缺失使不当的利益组织实现形式所蕴含的机会主义行为得以膨胀，导致了无法承受的内生交易费用，最终使人民公社彻底解体。

(4) 通过对土地私有、农民自治、管理者承包和家庭承包等组织形式的比较，我们认为家庭承包制正是在劳动及产品交易效率低、剩余权利不能充分发挥作用的条件下农民对内生交易费用最小化组织结构的合理选择，尽管它在一定程度上是向自给自足结构回归。

(5) 随着土地、劳动力和资本等要素市场的逐步发展，交易效率的提高，农户生产经营职能重新走向分工是必然趋势。农业投入和农业生产环节市场化程度的提高、龙头企业与合同型农业组织的发展都是农业组织化发展的具体表现，在本质上是农民综合比较最终产品及其劳动、中间产品及其劳动的交易效率与风险后选择最有效的产权实现形式的必然结果。

（6）提高农民团队化程度的合作经济组织发展受困于内生交易费用的制约，家庭农场是一种最少产生内生交易费用的团队组织，在农民团队化发展上，今后应把着力点放在家庭农场的发展上。为此，应以土地承包的既成事实为基础，实行土地永佃制，为家庭农场的发展奠定土地制度基础，以此为基础的合作经济组织也将会得到良好发展。

（7）在间接定价理论模型中包含无合同市场结构、有合同市场结构、最终产品生产者当老板的企业结构和中间产品生产者当老板的企业结构，每种组织结构都有各自存在的条件，没有一个在任何条件下都是最优的均衡结构。所以，在当前制度创新中，不必用一种方式去否定另一种方式，应尊重人们的自愿选择，应该允许产业组织形式多样化、多元化，允许各种方式相互竞争、相互比照、相互借鉴，以形成比较完善的农业产业组织体系（向国成等，2002）。

参考文献

Alchian, A. A. and H. Demsetz., 1972, "Production, Information Costs and Economic Organization", *American Economic Review*, 62(5): 777—795.

Cheung, S., 1983, "The Contractual Nature of the Firm", *Journal of Law and Economics*, 26(1):1—21.

Coase, R., 1937, "The Nature of the Firm", *Economica*, 4(16): 386—405.

陈宗胜:《中国经济体制市场化进程研究》,上海人民出版社 1999 年版。

陈吉元、彭建强、周文斌:《21 世纪中国农业与农村经济》,河南人民出版社 2000 年版。

常修泽、高明华,《中国国民经济市场化的推进程度及发展思路》,《经济研究》1998 年第 11 期。

杜吟棠:《合作社:农业中的现代企业制度》,江西人民出版社 2002 年版。

耿明斋:《河南科迪食品集团土地"承租返包"模式研究》,《中国农村经济》2000 年第 7 期。

丹尼尔·F. 斯普尔伯著,张军译:《市场的微观结构》,中国人民大学出版社 2002 年版。

樊亢、戎殿新:《美国农业社会化服务体系》,经济日报出版社 1994 年版。

郭熙保:《农业剩余劳动力及其转移问题:理论思考与中国的经验》,《世界经济》2002 年第 12 期。

冈纳·缪尔达尔著,谭力文、张卫东译:《亚洲的戏剧:对一些国家贫困问题的研究》,北京经济学院出版社 1992 年版。

黄祖辉、徐旭初、冯冠胜:《农民专业合作组织发展的影响因素分析——对浙江省农民专业合作组织发展现状的探讨》,《中国农村经济》2002 年第 3 期。

Knight, F., 1921, *Risk, Uncertainy and Profit*, Chicago: Hart, Shaffner and Marx.

林毅夫:《制度、技术与中国农业发展》,上海三联书店、上海人民出版社 1994 年版。

Lin, J. Y., 1988, "The Household Responsibility System in China's Agricultural Reform: A Theoretical and Empirical Study", *Economic Development and Cultural Change*, 36(3):S199—S224.

Lio, M., 1998, "Uncertainty, Insurance, and Division of Labor", *Review of Development Economics*, 2(1):76—89.

罗必良、李孔岳、王京安、吴忠培:《农业产业组织:演进、比较与创新》,中国经济出版社 2002 年版。

李惠安:《99 农村专业合作经济组织国际研讨会论文集》,中国农业出版社 2000 年版。

马晓河、韩俊等:《野力模式:农业产业化的新探索》,《中国农村经济》2000 年第 2 期。

诺斯著,陈郁、罗华平译:《经济史中的结构与变迁》,上海三联书店 1991 年版。

牛若峰:《中国农业产业化经营的发展特点与方向》,《中国农村经济》2002 年第 11 期。

奥尔森著,陈郁、郭宇峰、李崇新译:《集体行动的逻辑》,上海三联书店、上海人民出版社 1995 年版。

宋洪远:《改革以来中国农业和农村经济发展政策的演变》,中国经济出版社 2000 年版。

武力:《改革开放前后人力资源配置及效率比较研究》,《中国人口科学》2003 年第 2 期。

魏道南、张晓山,《中国农村新型合作组织探析》,经济管理出版社 1998 年版。

温铁军:《农户信用与民间借贷研究》。http://www.cei.gov.cn/forum50/doc/50cyfx/200107311731.htm。

威廉姆森著,段毅才、王伟译:《资本主义经济制度——论企业签约与市场签约》,商务印书馆 2002 年版。

习近平:《论中国农村市场化进程测度》,《经济学动态》2001 年第 11 期。

向国成:《对"承租返包"的经济学分析——一个分工理论的启示》,《中国农村观察》2002 年第 5 期。

向国成、肖国安、李媛媛:《论我国农业组织模式发展的阶段性及当前的选择》,《中国软科学》2002 年第 6 期。

杨小凯:《经济学:新兴古典与新古典框架》,社会科学文献出版社 2003 年版。

Yang, X. and Y-K. Ng, 1995, "Theory of the firm and Structure of Residual Rights", *Journal of Economic Behavior Organization*, 26(1): 107—128;中文见杨小凯:《经济学原理》,中国社会科学出版社 1998 年版,第 114—139 页。

Yang, X. and Y-K. Ng, *Specialization and Economic Organization, a New Classical Microeconomic Framework*, Amsterdam: North-Holland, 1993. 中文版见张玉钢译:《专业化与经济组织》,经济科学出版社 1999 年版。

Yang, X. and I. Wills, 1990, "A Model Formalizing the Theory of Property Rights", *Journal of Comparative Economics*, 14(2):177—198.

周其仁:《中国农村改革:国家与土地所有权关系的变化——一个经济制度变迁史的回顾》,《中国社会科学季刊(香港)》1994 年总第 8 期。

张宝珍:《日本农业保护政策的特点及作用》,《世界经济》1995 年第 12 期。

张晓山:《提高农民的组织化程度　积极推进农业产业化》,《农村合作经济经营管理》2003 年第 2 期。

(原载《经济学(季刊)》2007 年第 6 卷第 2 期)

近代外国在华投资：规模与效应分析*

杨德才

（南京大学经济系）

鸦片战争后，外国资本紧随坚船利炮来到了中国，外国在近代中国的投资帷幕便由此拉开。从投资者的角度来说，国外投资最基本的动机是资本所有者追求其资产组合价值或资产净值最大化的愿望。资本逐利，追求价值的最大化本无可厚非，然而，近代外国在华的投资则是在列强强迫中国签订并接受不平等条约的背景下发生的，因而，这种外国投资的性质有了很大的变异。尽管近代中国政府允许外国在华直接投资办厂（即外国投资在华取得合法权）是在签订了《马关条约》之后，但事实上，西方列强在华的投资早在鸦片战争后便已开始。那么，近代外国在华规模究竟有多大？这些外国投资盈利情况怎样？它们对近代中国本土企业的成长与发展产生了怎样的影响？甚至，它们对近代中国经济的发展又产生了哪些深远的影响呢？本文将对这些问题逐一进行研究。

一、外国投资作用：意见与争论

所谓外国投资（Foreign Investment），是从投资的接受国来

* 本文为第五届中国经济学年会入选论文，感谢匿名审稿人的中肯而又富有启发性的评论。

讲的，是指来自本国(或称为母国)之外的资本所从事的投资行为；而如果站在投资者所属的国家来讲，则又称为国外投资，是指从投资者所属的国家之外获得资产的行为。外国投资一般包括外国直接投资(Foreign Direct Investment)和外国间接投资(Foreign Indirect Investment)两种基本形式，其中最为主要的是外国直接投资(简称 FDI)。直接投资一般涉及工厂和土地等生产资料的所有权，如兴办工厂、开发房地产等活动，而间接投资则主要涉及债券、银行贷款和证券(股票)等金融资产，不直接参与生产。如果股票所有权使股东控制了厂商的经营活动，股票投资也可以认为是直接投资。

赫伯特·G.格鲁贝尔认为，造成外国直接投资的动机是很复杂的，除了追求资产价值的最大化外，还有其他的动机。这些动机可能牵涉到外在性或与市场的不完全性有关系，而通过在国外投资、成为跨国公司，它们会顺次被内在化或者被消除掉。另外，厂商之所以要从事外国直接投资，还在于它们要控制产品质量和保持商业秘密。外国直接投资最后一个主要原因涉及政府政策造成的扭曲。①

外国投资行为虽然是与西方列强的对外侵略活动同步发生的(甚至更早)，但对外国投资行为的经济研究则是在 20 世纪中叶以后，关于外国投资对东道国经济发展的影响，争论颇多，难以统一：一派持支持赞成的态度，另一派则持反对批评的观点。②

持支持赞成态度的认为，外国投资可以补充东道国可用资源供给，如储蓄、外汇、政府财政收入和人力资本技能等与获得

---

① 伊特韦尔等编，陈岱孙译：《新帕尔格雷夫经济学大辞典》第二卷，经济科学出版社 1996 年版，第 432 页。

② 迈克尔·P.托达罗，黄卫平等译：《经济发展》，中国经济出版社 1999 年版，第 527—530 页。

增长和发展目标应有的资源水平的差距。例如，在一个简单的“储蓄—投资缺口”模型中，哈罗德—多马模型提出国内储蓄率 s 与产出增长率 g 之间存在直接关系，用方程式表示为 $g = s/k$，其中，k 是国内资本产出比率。如果希望的国民产出增长率 g 定为每年 7%，而资本—产出比率是 3，则必需的年储蓄率是 21%（因为 $s = gk$）。比如，如果国内所能够动员的储蓄率只有国内生产总值的 16%，则可以说存在 5%的“储蓄缺口”。如果一国可以用外国投资弥补这个缺口，它就可能很好地达到预定的增长率。持支持赞成态度的还认为，外国投资除了为东道国提供金融资源和新工厂外，而且还提供了“一揽子”所需资源，包括管理经验、企业家能力和技术技能，这可以通过培训计划和在工作中学习的方式被转移到当地国家。他们认为，这种知识、技能和技术的转移对接受国而言是富有生产效益的。

对外国投资持反对批评的观点，原因是多方面的。在经济方面，外国投资并不能弥补东道国经济发展的资本缺口，尽管外国投资会提供资本，它们也可能降低储蓄和投资率。这是由于它们会通过与东道国签订排他性的生产协定而窒息竞争，不能将大量的利润再投资，并以高利率贷款给东道国。外国投资提供的管理、企业家技能、思想、技术等对促进当地这些资源的发展可能是微不足道的，而且可能由于外国投资所创办的公司（尤其是那些进行国外投资的跨国公司）垄断了国内市场，从而窒息了国内企业家的发展，实际上阻碍了这些资源的发展。此外，外国投资所创办的公司可能会压抑国内企业家和运用它们的先进技术等，抑制当地小企业的出现和发展，从而损害东道国的经济。最后，从政治的角度看，极端的情况是外国投资所创办的公司，甚至可能用回扣的直接手段贿赂最高阶层的政府官员或其他重要人员，从而在各个阶层的政治决策中能够发挥相当大的影响，阻碍东道国经济效益、社会福利最大化的实现。

上述关于外国投资作用的争论，是针对一个主权完整的东道国而言的。虽然不能肯定地说对一个主权完整的国家而言，外国投资尽是正面的积极的效应，但是至少外国投资对东道国经济发展所产生的正效应是主要的。而在近代，外国投资的大量进入显然不是在中国主权完整的状态下发生的，它们受到领事裁判权、协定关税等特权的庇护，那么，享有特权的外国投资对近代中国经济发展究竟产生了怎样的影响，就需要客观、具体地分析。

二、外国直接投资及其热潮

（一）甲午战争前的外国直接投资

直接投资最基本的特征就是直接从事生产活动。外国在近代中国的投资首先是从直接投资开始的。从直接投资的规模、方向和影响上来看，近代外国在华投资明显地以甲午战争为界线，分为前后两个时期。

鸦片战争以后，随着西方列强对华侵略范围的不断扩大和它们获得的特权越来越多，它们在华因直接投资而设立的各种工厂、企业也越来越多，涉及的行业主要是航运业、船舶修造业、农副产品加工业、服务性轻小工业和公用事业等。其中在鸦片战争后到19世纪60年代中期期间，外国投资的重点是航运业和船舶修造业，成立了许多后来比较著名的船厂和轮船公司，如祥生船厂、香港黄埔船坞公司、耶松船厂、旗昌轮船公司、怡和洋行、太古洋行等。从60年代到80年代期间，外国投资相对集中于农副产品加工业，投资兴办了许多砖茶厂、缫丝厂、轧花厂、制糖厂等。在80年代后至1894年，外国投资的重点是公用事业和杂项工业，如在租界内开办自来水、自来火、电光公司等，还投资兴办酿酒、制药等工业。这样，到甲午战争前，外国在华直接投资设立的工业企业，据估计，共有 191 个[①]，其中，船舶修造业和出口商品加工业 116 个，印刷厂 13 个，食品加工业 23 个，公用事业 8 个，化学工业 11 个，建筑及杂项工业各 10 个。到 1894 年，据估计，外国在华工业资本总额近 2 000 万元，投资总额近 2 800万元（约折合 1 424.5 万美元）；航运业投资总额约为 1 334.3万美元。具体如表 1 所示。

表 1　甲午战争前外国直接投资估计(1894 年)　　单位：万元

业别		资本额	投资额
工业投资	船舶修造业	494.3	811.2
	砖茶制造业	400.0	560.0
	机器缫丝业	397.2	517.3
	进出口加工业	149.3	193.8
	一般轻工业	379.3	491.0
	公用事业	152.3	204.5
	合　计	1 972.4	2 777.8（约为 1 424.5 万美元）
航运业投资			1 334.3 万美元
总　计			2 758.8 万美元

资料来源：孙毓棠(1981)，第 116 页；许涤新、吴承明(1990)，第 133 页。

从表 1 可以看出，甲午战争前，外国在华直接投资的产业主

① 赵德馨(1988)，第 76 页。关于外国投资到甲午战争前在华创办的工业企业准确数字，争论颇多。据孙毓棠研究，到甲午战争前，外国投资在华创办的工业企业计 88 个（孙毓棠、汪敬虞主编：《中国近代工业史资料》第一辑，第一册，科学出版社 1957 年版，第 242—247 页）。还有人认为其数量应为 103 个（费正清编：《剑桥中国晚清史》下册，中国社会科学研究院历史研究所编译室译，中国社会科学出版社 1993 年版，第 40 页）。

要集中于船舶航运业和农副产品加工业，其目的是直接为进出口贸易服务。这一时期，外国在华投资之所以相对集中于上述两个产业，是因为当时这两个产业的市场比较大，每个产业中具体的每个工厂投资规模则不需要太大，但利润率却很高，利润比较丰厚。①表 2 是甲午战争前某些年份外国在华直接投资创办的部分企业的盈利状况。

表 2　甲午战争前在华外国直接投资创办企业的获利状况

企业名称	年　代	资　本	利　润	利润率	股票附息率
香港黄埔船坞	1886	1 562 500 元	375 049 元	24.0%	16%
公司	1893	1 562 500 元	322 386 元	20.6%	14%
祥生船厂	1891.5—1892.4	800 000 两	139 903 两	17.5%	12%
	1893.5—1894.4	800 000 两	138 964 两	17.4%	12%
耶松船厂	1892.7—1893.6	750 000 两	101 128 两	13.5%	9%
	1893.7—1894.6	750 000 两	157 259 两	21.0%	11%
美查兄弟有限	1889.11—1890.10	275 000 两	32 471 两	11.8%	10%
公司	1892.11—1893.10	275 000 两	15 796 两	5.7%	—
老德记药房	1892	120 000 元	21 422 元	17.9%	7%
新上海制冰厂	1893	36 000 两	5 138 两	14.3%	9%
上海大英自来	1874	150 000 两	23 121 两	15.4%	11%
火房	1889	200 000 两	43 476 两	21.7%	12%
	1894	200 000 两	49 456 两	24.7%	12%
上海自来水公司	1884	119 639 镑	4 885 镑	4.1%	4%
	1890	143 926 镑	55 630 两	9.1%	8%
	1894	144 000 镑	71 355 两	10.7%	9%

资料来源：历年《北华捷报》载各企业营业报告与股东年会报告。转引自孙毓棠(1981)，第 118 页。

① 关于外国在华投资的盈利状况，学术界的观点并不完全一致。有的（尤其是我国的老一辈经济史学家）认为很高，有的（如我国新生代经济史学研究者和一些国际著名的从事中国经济史学研究的学者）认为其实并不是很高。究竟是高还是低，在本文后面的部分将作出分析。

(二) 甲午战争后的外国直接投资

这一时期,外国在华投资的规模有明显增加,其直接投资涉及的产业主要有:制造业、矿冶业、铁路航运业和房地产业等。投资的范围也由甲午战争前集中于东南部沿海和租界而不断地向内地拓展,几乎遍及各地。投资的目的在于生产就地销售的商品。外国在华产业资本1913年较1894年增长二十余倍,1920年较1894年增长近三十倍,①从而形成了外国投资中国的热潮。

制造业方面的直接投资主要投资于纺织、面粉、卷烟、造船及农副产品加工等,在华直接设厂制造生产。根据汪敬虞先生的研究,在1895—1913年间,外国直接投资创办了115个工厂企业,投资总额为4 807.8万元。其中,英国24个,投资总额为1 069.3万元;日本36个,投资总额为1 868.9万元;俄国37个,投资总额为907.6万元;德国、法国和美国分别为6个、4个和6个,各自的投资总额分别为361.9万元、258.1万元和311.0万元;另外还有其他国家的企业2个,投资总额为31.0万元。②至于1895—1913年间外国直接投资在制造业内部各产业间的分布状况,如表3所示。

表3　制造业外国直接投资分布状况(1895—1913年)

	家数	投资额(万元)	占制造业比重(%)
造船工业	7	289.5	6.02
纺织工业	16	1 251.5	26.03
其中:棉纺织	12	1 082.6	22.52
缫丝	4	168.9	3.51

① 赵德馨(1988),第116页。

② 许涤新、吴承明(1990),第548页。

（续表）

	家数	投资额(万元)	占制造业比重(%)
食品工业	69	2 355.6	49.0
其中：面粉	43	1 035.9	21.55
卷烟	4	383.2	7.97
榨油	11	536.2	11.15
其他工业	23	911.2	18.95

资料来源：汪敬虞，《中国近代工业史资料》第2辑上册，中华书局1962年版，第7—11页。

外国投资兴办的制造业中，资本主要集中于棉纺织业和面粉业，两者投资额占整个制造业投资总额的44.07%。棉纺织业又主要以投资办纱厂为主，1897—1914年间，仅英、美、德、日四国在华纱厂投资额就达916.6万元。其中著名的纱厂有英国的怡和纱厂、老公茂纱厂和日本的日信纱厂、上海纺绩公司等。面粉业以俄商和日商的直接投资为主，截止到1913年，外国在华投资所办的面粉厂达43家，投资总额达1 035.9万元。其中，俄商工厂35家、日商工厂6家，各自的投资额分别为700.2万元、264.7万元。

在1895—1913年间，外国在华用于矿冶业方面的投资总额达4 996.9万元，设立厂家计32个。用于矿冶业方面的直接投资总额超过制造业，使得矿冶业成为甲午战争之后外国直接投资最多的产业，这其中又以英国商人投资最多，达3 793.0万元。据研究，外国投资在中外煤矿投资总额中所占比重，1906年为84.8%，1913年为79.6%，1919年为60.6%。在煤矿开采方面，1913年中国煤总产量为1 288万吨，其中，机械采煤767.8万吨，而外国资本控制的7大煤矿（开滦、焦作、抚顺、本溪湖、华德、井陉、临城）在煤总产量和机械采煤量中分别占46.8%和78.4%。外国投资在近代中国铁矿业与冶铁业中，几乎达到了完全垄断的程度，其中在1900—1925年间，生铁与铁矿产量接近100%都被外资控制着。

甲午战争后，以铁路航运业为主的运输业是在外国直接投资的所有产业中增长最快、比重最大的产业。据统计，外国在华运输业的投资由1894年的13.3百万美元增加为1914年的335.6百万美元，增长24倍，其所占外国在华投资总量的份额由1894年的12.2%上升到34.9%。①外国对中国航运业的直接投资在甲午战争前即已开始，甲午战争后继续增长，1894年前，在华外国轮船公司有14家，1895—1913年新设14家，1914—1930年又设立15家。在中国各通商口岸进出中外轮船总吨位中，外轮1897年占76.8%，1916年占77.6%，1926年占80.0%。1911年，在长江轮运总吨位中，中国最大的轮船公司招商局与外国太古、怡和、日清三大轮船公司相比较，只占16.2%。然而，这一时期在铁路航运业中增长最快的并不是航运业，而是对铁路业的投资。截止到1914年，外国直接投资于铁路航运业的总资本额为335.6百万美元，而其中铁路业投资即达292百万美元。关于外国在华铁路投资的具体情况，吴承明先生作了非常深入的研究，其研究结论大致如表4所示。

表4　1914年外国在华铁路直接投资估计

单位：里程（公里）、投资估计（百万美元）

国别	铁路名称	建筑年代	里程	投资估计
俄	中东铁路	1898—1903	1721	189.3
德	胶济铁路	1899—1904	446	15.0
法	滇越铁路	1903—1909	464	32.0
日	南满铁路	1899—1903	1 105	49.0
英	广九铁路（英段）	1907	36	6.7
	合　计		3 772	292.0

资料来源：吴承明，《帝国主义在旧中国的投资》，人民出版社1955年版，第168页。

① 许涤新、吴承明(1990)，第529、540页。

外国人在中国占有土地和建造房屋也是一种直接投资，这种直接投资行为同样在甲午战争前即已发生，只是在甲午战争后增长更为迅速而已。据仅仅对英、美、法、日、德五国在华房地产业投资的估计，1902 年投资总额约为 79.6 百万美元，而至 1914 年则已达 225.3 百万美元，为 1902 年的 2.83 倍，增长还是比较快的。

外国在近代中国的直接投资，在甲午战争前多以中小资本为主，许多外国中小资本借助于不平等条约的保护，试图通过在华的直接投资、获取高额利润，迅速度过资本积累阶段，寻求更大的扩张，因此，甲午战争前，从总体上看，直接投资的规模并不很大。而甲午战争后，外国在华直接投资的总量增长很快，其投资特点也由起先的中小资本唱主角渐变为具有垄断性质的大公司（如英国的怡和洋行、日本的南满铁道株式会社等）来投资扩张，因而增长很快。由于垄断生产经营、多元化经营、规模经营，一般获利程度都不错，平均利润率大致在 10%—15%之间。

三、外国间接投资与日俱增

外国在近代中国的投资，从总量上来看，甲午战争前以直接投资为主，而甲午战争后虽然直接投资额比战前增长了很多，但在外国投资总量中其所占的比重则是下降的，更主要地是以间接投资为重。吴承明先生在对甲午战争前外国在华投资的估计中，其中直接投资的有：航运业、工业、贸易业、其他商业等，它们各自占外国投资总额的比重分别为：11.17%、11.93%、35.12%、4.55%，即直接投资占总投资的 62.77%。而间接投资有：银行业[①]、保险业、政府贷款等，其各自占外国投资总额的比重对应的是：23.52%、5.02%、8.69%，间接投资占总投资额的37.23%。[②]间接投资量明显小于直接投资量。而甲午战争后，这种情况发生了非常大的变化。

甲午战争前外国在华的间接投资首先是从设立银行开始的。鸦片战争后，外国在华设立的第一家银行是东方银行（初名Oriental Bank，1851年改称Oriental Banking Corporation）分行[③]，是由英国人设立的。期后，英国人又设立了有利银行（原为Chartered Bank of Asia，1858年与Mercantile Bank of India，London and China合并，改组为Chartered Mercantile Bank of India，London and China）和麦加利银行（Chartered Bank of India，Australia and China，亦称渣打银行）分行。这期间最著名的、发展最快的银行是由几个在华的英国大商人1865年发起成立于香港的汇丰银行，该银行原定注册资本为500万港元，而实际注册资本则不到一半，然而，经过短暂的发展，其拥有资本额迅速增长，1883年增资至750万元、1890年增资至1 000万元；同时它还在汉口（1868年）、天津（1880年）和北京（1885年）开设了分行。[④]后来在中国开设银行的还有法、德、日等国。截止到1894年，在中国共有8家外资银行，它们的资本及投资额估计如表5所示。

---

① 关于外国在东道国银行业的投资，究竟应看作直接投资还是间接投资，学术界的观点并不一致。本文采用的是现代外国投资的相关理论及主要观点，将其视为间接投资的一部分。

② 许涤新、吴承明（1990），第133页。

③ 关于Oriental Bank、Oriental Banking Corporation，中文有译为丽如银行、金宝银行和东亚银公司的。

④ 孙毓棠：《抗戈集》，中华书局1981年版，第146—147页。

表 5　甲午战争前外资银行在华投资估计(1894 年)

银行名称	资本额	在华投资额估计		
		比重	投资额	折合美元
呵加剌	1 000 000 镑	1/2	500 000 镑	2 450 000
有利	7 500 000 镑	1/4	1 875 000 镑	9 187 500
麦加利	800 000 镑	1/3	350 000 镑	1 715 000
汇丰	15 000 000 港元	全部	15 000 000 港元	7 500 000
德华	5 000 000 两	全部	5 000 000 港元	3 500 000
大东惠通	300 000 镑	1/3	100 000 镑	490 000
中华汇理	2 219 000 港元	全部	2 329 000 港元	1 164 500
横滨正金	4 500 000 日元	1/2	4 094 000 日元	2 087 940
合计				28 094 940

资料来源:许涤新、吴承明(1990),第 127 页。

甲午战争前在外国间接投资中还有对保险业的投资和对中国政府的放贷。按吴承明先生的估计,到 1894 年止,在华设有机构的保险公司共有 9 家,投资总额合计 5 992 800 美元。①同一时期,外资银行或洋行还通过向中国政府放贷的形式进行间接投资,以获取利息。依据徐义生统计,自 1853 年至 1894 年共有贷款 46 笔,到 1894 年尚有 7 笔未清偿,仅这 7 笔未清偿的放贷,估计折合即达 10 380 349 美元②,可见当时通过放贷向中国进行间接投资的数量也并不很小。

甲午战争后,从外国对华投资的构成来看,间接投资有不断上升的趋势,在外国投资总额中的份额明显增长许多。有论者认为,从 1894 年到 1913 年间,中国长期资本流入量中外国对中国政府的贷款占据很大份额,1895、1912、1913 年,外国对中国

① 许涤新、吴承明(1990),第 128 页。
② 许涤新、吴承明(1990),第 132 页。

的贷款约占长期资本流入量的78%，而这三年外国对中国的直接投资只占20%左右。①目前，关于甲午战争后外国在华间接投资占这一时期外国总投资的比重，学术界争论还颇多，但是，不管间接投资具体的比重究竟是多少，有一点却是可以肯定的，即外国间接投资的份额上升是比较迅速的。

甲午战争后直到第一次世界大战，中国政府总是面临着赔款抑或财政正常开支的沉重压力，为了维持政府的正常运转，中国政府决定大举外债，向外国借款，因而，也就为外国的间接投资提供了市场，使得当时以向中国政府提供贷款方式进行的间接投资的数额，占到了外国在华投资总额的一半以上。根据徐义生的统计，从甲午战争到第一次世界大战为止，中国历届政府向外国举借的贷款总额（单位：库平银两）分别如下②：

	笔数	贷款额	实收额
清政府所贷(1894—1911)	112	1 203 825 452.94	660 535 961.08
北洋政府及南方政府(1911—1914)	77	565 986 935.89	347 300 073.28
合　　计	189	1 769 812 388.83	1 007 836 034.36

另据吴承明先生研究统计，从19世纪60年代中期至中华人民共和国建立前，外国通过向中国历届政府提供贷款（这里仅指军事财政贷款）方式进行的间接投资总额即达2 500.3百万美元③，具体情况如下（单位：百万美元）：

---

① 王利华：《近代外人对华投资的影响因素剖析》，《南开经济研究》1997年第2期。

② 这里所列出的贷款额系指有明确记载、可以统计到的数字，而一些资料不详的则不包括在内（徐义生(1962)，第52、240页）。

③ 吴承明(1985)，第47页。

时　期	国外贷款总额	年均贷款额
1865—1902	286.4	7.5
1903—1914	238.3	19.9
1915—1930	304.1	19.0
1931—1936	35.8	6.0
1937—1941	635.9	127.2
1942—1948	999.8	142.8
合　计	2 500.3	29.8

对铁路业及其他实业的间接投资。根据宓汝成的研究，截止到1914年底，外国对近代中国铁路建设进行间接投资（即贷款）修筑的铁路里程为4 846公里，占当时铁路总里程的50.65%。具体而言，甲午战争后由外国间接投资修筑的铁路主要有：京奉铁路（英）、京汉铁路（英、法）、粤汉铁路（美、英、德、法）、津浦铁路（英、德）、吉长铁路（日）、广九铁路（英）等。投资国家除了美、英、德、法、日外，还有俄、比、荷等国，而以英国最多。第一次世界大战后，日本超过英国。从1898年至1927年，外国对中国的铁路贷款重要的有63笔。在对中国铁路进行间接投资的同时，外资还对当时的其他实业进行了间接投资，如煤矿、铁矿、通讯、航运等。发生在清政府覆亡前的除铁路以外的著名实业间接投资有：1899年的萍乡煤矿借款、1902年的汉阳铁厂借款、1908年的邮传部借款和汉冶萍借款、1910年的井陉煤矿借款等。到北洋政府时期，外国对中国实业的间接投资依然继续着，但与晚清时期有一个共同的特征，即在外国间接投资的总额中，绝大多数的对中国间接投资的份额是以中国政府军事、财政借款的方式发生的，实业性借款在北洋政府时期外国间接投资总额中占有1/4左右的比重。如整个北洋政府时期，实业借款额共计只占当时借款总额的23%左右，而在贷款的实收

总额中也只占29%左右。[①]

在甲午战争后与日俱增的间接投资热潮中，外国的在华银行扮演了十分重要的角色，对间接投资的持续上升起了推波助澜的作用。正因为如此，甲午战争后，外国在华银行业发展很快。1895—1914年间，新设的西方银行约有十家，分支机构四十余处，尚有日本在华银行和中日合资银行，加上分支机构近三十处。这一时期在外国对华进行间接投资中最为活跃的银行是汇丰银行与华俄道胜银行。这样，到1914年，包括银行业、保险业在内的外国金融业在中国的投资估计总额为75 572 000美元。[②]

四、利润率、资本成本与资本吸收能力[③]

资本逐利、增殖的本性决定了资本的流动方向。在西方近代工业文明已经比较发达的时候，中国则还停留在传统落后的农业文明里，生产力低下、商业经济落后、社会贫困、人口众多，但所有这些在投资者的眼里却尽是商机，因为与此相对应的必然是资本短缺而投资空间大、劳动力与资源丰富而廉价、市场广阔而盈利机会多。也就是说，在这样的地区进行投资将会有一

① 北洋时期的总借款额为1 336 996 790.11银元，其中，铁路借款为232 326 594.97银元，占总借款额的17.34%；航运电信借款额为38 913 570.60银元，占总借款额的2.90%；工矿借款总额为38 135 413.58银元，占总借款额的2.85%。在上述总借款额中，北洋政府实收到贷款976 414 254.08银元，上述三大实业实际收到的贷款分别为：214 264 993.52、35 538 675.19、34 399 378.45银元，各占北洋政府实收到贷款总额的21.89%、3.63%、3.51%（徐义生（1962），第242—243页）。

② 许涤新、吴承明(1990)，第536页。

③ 本节分析参考了王利华先生发表在《南开经济研究》1997年第2期上的《近代外人对华投资的影响因素剖析》一文的部分内容。

个非常不错的预期利润率。预期利润率的高低成为影响资本流向的最为重要的因素。此外，资本成本、资本的吸收消化能力、社会政治的稳定程度等都影响到资本的流动。

虽然投资于中国市场的预期利润率很高，但资本的流动及其变动趋势显然更受到实际利润率的影响，实际利润率成为外国投资额和投资方向的最终决定因素。更何况，在近代中国从事投资的外国资本绝大多数是民间私人投资呢？私人投资对实际利润率高低更是十分敏感。仅以 1913—1914 年为例，在英国对华投资总额中，属于民间资本的投资总额即达 1 610 百万美元，数量很大。①再如美国，在其对外的投资总额中，长期的情况是民间投资的份额超过政府或国家投资的份额，即使到 20 世纪初，这种状况也没有改变，如 1914 年、1919 年、1924 年和 1930 年，政府或国家投资的份额仅占美国所有对外投资总额的 30％、27.8％、27.8％和 20％，国家投资份额不断下降，民间投资份额却不断上升。②虽然近代中国的潜在市场比较大，潜在需求也不小，但是，从已有的资料可以看出，外国在华直接投资所办的一些企业其实际利润率却并不高，远远低于预期利润率。如表 6 所示。

表 6　1872—1932 年中国几个行业外企利润率各区间分布状况(％)

利润占净值的％*(区间)	外贸行业	保险业	银行业	运输业	公用事业	制造业	其他	全部投资
亏损	5.0	0.8	1.7	7.3	3.2	10.4	6.8	5.0
0—4.99	10.0	3.3	6.8	9.1	4.8	18.3	22.7	10.3

① Svedberg, P., 1978, "The Portfolio-Direct Composition of Private Foreign Investment in 1914 Revisited", *Economic Journal*, 88(352): 763—777.

② 转引自宫崎犀一等(1990)，第 63 页。

（续表）

利润占净值的%*（区间）	外贸行业	保险业	银行业	运输业	公用事业	制造业	其他	全部投资
5—9.99	45.0	10.6	37.3	40.0	32.3	20.0	34.1	25.9
10—14.99	20.0	16.3	32.2	23.6	32.3	21.7	15.9	22.6
15—19.99	15.0	17.9	13.6	18.2	14.5	12.2	6.8	14.4
20—24.99	0.0	20.3	1.7	0.0	9.7	7.0	6.8	9.0
25—29.99	0.0	13.0	1.7	0.0	3.2	4.3	2.3	5.2
30 以上	5.0	17.9	5.1	1.8	0.0	6.1	4.5	7.5
总数	100.0	100.0	100.0	100.0	100.0	100.0	100.0	100.0
0—10	60.0	14.7	45.8	56.4	40.3	48.7	63.6	41.2
0—15	80.0	31.0	78.0	80.0	72.6	70.4	79.5	63.8
序号	20	123	59	55	62	115	44	478

说明：* 利润是根据现代会计方法重新计算的，如折旧和坏账被视作花费；净值不仅包括实收资本，而且还包括所有结余。公开发表的利润数据未将折旧扣除，资本只包括实收资本，如表 2 孙毓棠先生使用公布的利润和资本数据。再如孙毓棠先生计算出，1879 年上海煤气公司的利润率为 23.4%（见孙毓棠，《中国近代工业史资料》第 1 卷，科学出版社 1957 年版，第 181 页），而根据现代会计方法计算的结果却是 14%。

资料来源：《北华捷报》，1873—1933 年；王利华：《近代外人对华投资的影响因素剖析》，《南开经济研究》1997 年第 2 期。

由表 6 可知，1872—1932 年间在华直接投资的外国企业所获利润率大多在 5%—20%之间，其中，约 41%的企业利润率在 10%以下，64%左右的企业利润率低于 15%，对华直接投资利润率达到 25%或在其上的大约只占总数的 13%。值得注意的是，制造业的利润率极低，其半数左右的利润率低于 10%。根据表 7，可以算出外国企业在中国的加权平均利润率为 13.38%。而 1908—1937 年英国国内直接投资的利润率并不比在中国从事直接投资的利润率低多少，有的年份甚至还比中国高。美国情形稍有不同，1900—1914 年美国国内制造业直接投资的利润率较低，而 1919—1928 年其制造业的利润率却有大幅度提高，1919 年甚至高达 18.3%，如表 7 所示。

表 7　英国与美国国内直接投资的利润率(%)

年份	英国		美国	年份	英国		美国	年份	英国		美国
	所有股本	普通股	(制造业)		所有股本	普通股	(制造业)		所有股本	普通股	(制造业)
1900			8.34	1912	10.88	14.47	6.20	1926	10.81	14.06	12.4
1901			7.72	1913	11.53	16.08	6.16	1927	10.84	14.07	9.5
1902			8.25	1914	10.37	13.72	5.60	1928	10.74	13.77	11.0
1903			7.57	1915	12.39	17.46		1929	10.56	13.44	
1904			6.45	1916	12.93	17.86		1930	8.68	10.55	
1905			7.09	1917	12.88	17.43		1931	5.73	6.18	
1906			8.34	1918	13.67	18.62		1932	5.72	6.41	
1907			7.90	1919	14.60	19.92	18.3	1933	6.69	7.92	
1908	6.83	8.38	6.07	1920	13.24	17.58	12.3	1934	8.04	9.80	
1909	7.74	9.40	6.89	1921	6.81	7.75	2.9	1935	9.05	11.51	
1910	9.35	11.97	7.26	1922	9.05	11.18	10.2	1936	10.62	13.66	
1911	9.95	12.82	7.10	1923	9.94	12.67	11.2	1937	12.10	15.83	
				1924	10.68	13.77	10.0				
				1925	11.37	14.91	12.1				

资料来源:(1) Hargreaves Parkinson, 1938, "British Industrial Profits", *The Economist*, Dec. 17:597—603;

(2) E. I. Epstein and R. A. Gordon, Feb. 1939, "Profits of Selected American Industrial Corporations, 1900—1914", *Review of Economic Statistics*: 122—128;

(3) Ralph C. Epstein, 1934, *Industrial Profits in the United States*, New York:56;

(4) 王利华:《近代外人对华投资的影响因素剖析》,《南开经济研究》1997 年第 2 期。

根据表7可以计算出，1908—1937年间英国全部资本的平均利润率为10.13%，普通资本的平均利润率为13.11%；1900—1928年间美国制造业投资的平均利润率为8.68%。对照它们在华直接投资所获得的利润率或平均利润率，近代外国在华直接投资的实际利润率并不像预期的那样高，与在其国内投资相比也未见得高出很多。

在实际的投资中，投资的实际利润率低于预期利润率是经常发生的一种很正常的经济现象，不正常的是，一些外国投资者发现，其在华投资获得的实际利润率甚至也并不比在他自己的国家投资所获得的利润率高，这对他们后来决定资本的流向影响很大。如1920—1938年间驻华英美烟公司的账面利润率在14%左右①，而同期前后美国卷烟工业年均利润率亦达13.9%。②

资本成本对资本的流向也有重要的影响。一般而言，资本成本的高低受资本的可获得程度、市场分割或市场一体化程度、汇率风险、货币状况和国别风险（包括政治局势、政府政策、文化差异等）等因素的影响。中国的投资环境不太理想，可供投资用的资金不多（即资本可获得程度不高），资本市场发育不良且处于分割状态，货币单位繁杂，政治动荡不安，与西方存在很大的文化差异，等等，所有这些因素都促使资本成本提高，从而降低了资本收益率，最终导致较低的投资额。这里仅以资本的可获得程度、市场分割和市场一体化程度对资本成本的影响为例，说明资本成本对投资决策的影响。

资本成本等于权益资本和债务资本的加权平均成本，即

---

① 上海社会科学院经济研究所编：《英美烟公司在华企业资料汇编》第四册，中华书局1983年版，第1597页。

② E. B. Alaerfer，1957，*Economics of American Industry*，New York：636.

$$K = k_e[E/(E+D)] + k_d[(1-T)D/(D+E)]$$

上式中，K 表示企业资本的加权平均成本或资本成本，k_e 表示税后权益资本成本，k_d 表示税前债务资本成本，T 表示边际税率，E 表示权益资本的市场价值，D 表示债务资本的市场价值。此式表明，资本成本不仅受权益资本成本的影响，而且也受债务资本成本的影响。这两种资本成本都受资本市场各种风险的影响。

国内企业的资本可获得程度是由国内资本市场的供给和需求决定的，国内企业按其最佳资本结构（即资本成本最低时的债务资本和权益资本的比例）筹集资金，但由于筹集的资本仅限于国内市场，当筹集的资本绝对额超过一定水平时，边际资本成本就会上升。进行国际投资的企业其资金来源不限于某一国内市场，它们除在母国市场筹资外，还在国际资本市场和所在国资本市场筹资。若国际资本的可获得程度高，企业不仅能在资本结构不变的条件下增加集资能力，而且还能筹集到成本比国内企业更低的资本。

因此，资本可获得程度和资本市场一体化程度越高，资本成本就越低，资本预算越多，投资额就会增加；反之，较低的资本可获得程度和资本市场被分割必然带动资本成本上升，减少资本预算，投资额也就必然会降低。

近代中国由于未能形成较为成熟的资本市场、由存款积蓄转化而来的资本不多、将十分有限的储蓄转化为投资的机制也很不健全，加之中国实行银本位而西方发达国家实行金本位，使得中国货币无法纳入国际货币体系，从而致使在近代中国的市场上筹资的成本一直很高。此外，近代中国的政治高风险、中西文化的差异以及中国普遍的排外情绪都增加了外国在华投资的资本成本，甚至有时有些外国直接投资的企业也会出现在亏损状态下经营的情形。[①]

除了上述的实际利润率、资本成本的影响外，一国对资本的吸收能力的大小也直接关系到资本的盈利程度和后续资本的流动方向。一般来讲，影响资本吸收能力大小的主要因素有：人口的数量、消费需求、人力资本质量、生产力水平、民族文化传统等。

人口数量与消费需求对投资的影响主要表现在产品的市场需求和产品市场实现等方面。古典经济学家马尔萨斯、西斯蒙第等对此早有论述。人口的多少直接关乎产品市场需求的多少，两者一般是成正比的。也正因为这个原因，在中国的大门被打开之后，外国的资本与商品蜂拥而入。同样，在历史上，以英国为代表的西方发达国家的绝大多数国外投资投向了美洲，是因为在美洲的开发过程中，有大量的移民人口进入了美洲，从而创造了极大的市场需求。近代中国虽然有四万万之众，但并未产生很大的市场需求。

有人将近代中国未产生巨大市场需求、进而未引致外国投资规模迅速上升的原因，部分归结为伴随着西方坚船利炮未能形成一个向中国移民的热潮。我们认为，这个分析有失偏颇。事实上，移民也是一种投资，移民热潮之所以能形成是因为移民移往的国家或地区能够提供更多、更好的创业与盈利机会。近代中国之所以未形成外国人移往中国的热潮，是因为中国不具备这样的条件或机会。没有移民的国家或地区，其市场需求的扩大可以借助于内在的原居民消费需求的扩大而扩大。一国居民消费需求的扩大，受到诸如人均国民收入、居民可支配收入、边际消费倾向等因素的影响，近代中国消费需求不旺，显然与中

---

① 侯继明：《关于外人在华投资的"压迫论"（1895—1937 年）》，载《中国近代经济史研究资料》第 5 辑，上海社会科学院出版社 1986 年版，第 111—129 页。

国的贫弱以及居民可支配收入低关联在一起的。没有旺盛的市场需求，意味着产品市场价值实现的难度加大，从而影响到投资者生产能力的利用和发展，直至影响其盈利和投资意愿。

人力资本质量对资本的吸收能力大小影响最为直接，低水平的人力资本质量直接影响着生产力水平的发挥与发展，相反，高质量的人力资本却可以产生良好的"溢出"效应并获得一个增长"余值"，进而产生示范效应，促进投资的进一步增长。近代中国不论是在甲午战争前还是在其后，人力资本的状况不仅没有得到多大改善，反而因社会的动荡而每况愈下，这样的人力资本状况决定了其对外国投资的吸收能力将是十分有限的。

一个民族的文化传统也影响着资本的吸收能力。中国几千年一以贯之的农本思想、小农意识、自给自足的自然经济等，使得中国文化传统对外来势力具有很强的排斥性，既影响了外国投资设厂，又影响了市场扩大。

实际利润率、资本成本以及资本吸收能力的大小、高低对外国直接投资的影响十分巨大，在这些因素共同作用下，外国在华投资的方向作出了比较大的调整，即间接投资在总投资中的份额持续上升。①这是因为有利于外国在华进行间接投资（主要是借款）的因素更多，主要有：

利率高。以借款为主的外国间接投资，几乎全部是以高利率为条件的。外国向中国提供的贷款，年利率一般是4%—

① 关于近代外国在华投资的比例，即直接投资与间接投资孰重孰轻的问题，学术界的观点并不一致，有不少学者认为直接投资的份额更多一些，如雷麦认为，直接投资占总投资的份额1902年为63.9%，1914年为67.3%；吴承明认为，直接投资占总投资的份额1902年为65.1%，1914年为66.3%。但也有不少学者的观点正好与他们相反，认为间接投资的份额更多。本文作者将外国的借款视为间接投资，因而，也持间接投资份额更多一些的观点。我们认为，之所以出现判断观点上的相左，是因为每个学者在分析时候的统计口径不一致而造成的。

5%，铁路借款则有不少高达7%，而到第一次世界大战期间，更是高达8%—10%。这样的利率即使在当时的国际金融市场上，也属于比较高的。

回扣大。除了比较高的利息收入外，回扣高也是外国间接投资不断增长的一个重要原因。高额的回扣也构成了外国投资者的利润。当时回扣小者为5.875%、大者为17%。如1896年的“英德借款”1 600万镑是按94%实付，债券分两部分发行，1 000万镑于该年3月按98.75%发售，600万镑于同年9月按99%发售；发行银行获得77.5万镑的现实利润(即回扣)。再如“善后大借款”，总额为2 500万镑，按84%付款，债券按90%发行，发行的银行团净赚150万镑，手续费约30万镑。[①]

风险小。直接投资由于绝大多数是自己投资、自己经营，生产出来的产品能否迅速实现其价值或有多少能实现其价值，却不是由自己决定的，而是由市场来决定，因而存在一定的市场风险。而间接投资尤其是借款，由于是以国家信用做担保、由当时中国最为稳定的几个大的税种的税收来做抵押担保，因而，风险很小。风险小而收益高，外国投资者又何乐而不为呢？

成本低。由于直接投资需要调研、组织、设计和管理，所以相应地需要支付各项费用，致使生产成本中非直接生产性成本不断上升。而间接投资因为并不涉及生产与管理，因而，省去了直接投资所需支付的一切交易成本、管理成本和监督成本等，有利于投资总收益的提高和增长。

利润率、资本成本与资本吸收能力对直接投资的抑制，利息与回扣、风险与成本对间接投资的诱致，使得外国投资的结构在甲午战争后发生了明显变化：直接投资份额下降，间接投资份额

---

① 许涤新、吴承明(1990)，第567—568页。

上升。但是，这种变化也不是绝对的，不论是直接投资还是间接投资的变动都是非线性的、无规律的，呈现不规则的变动，究其原因，恐怕与近代中国尤其是民国建立之后的中国现实国情关联在一起的。由于近代中国是个政治动荡不安的国家，而且市场又被严重分割，极高的政治风险和不良的市场状况决定了外国对华投资变动的可能趋势。

五、外国投资增长中的中资企业发展

在外国投资的不断增长中，中资企业发展状况又呈现怎样一种情景呢？对外国投资增长背景下的中资企业发展情景的分析，有助于全面认识外国投资的性质与效应。事实上，国内绝大多数经济史学家将近代与日俱增的外国投资定性为经济侵略，并将其视为阻碍近代中国经济发展的因素之一。①而很少或几乎没有学者认为外国投资只是一种经济行为，是资本逐利增殖本性的外在表现，其对近代中国的经济发展也有正效应。实际上，应对近代外国在华投资的性质与效应做出具体分析，不可概而论之，否则，将很难辨明是非曲直。

首先，分析外国在华投资总额占其国际投资总额的比例。到第一次世界大战结束之前，英国无疑是世界上最为强大的国家，其对外投资构成了当时国际投资的最主要部分，如 1885 年、1900 年和 1913 年，主要国家对外投资额分别为 12 000、22 000

---

① 近代外国投资被定性为经济侵略，持这种观点的学者有：吴承明（许涤新、吴承明，1990）、汪敬虞（汪敬虞主编：《中国近代经济史》，人民出版社 2000 年版）、郑友揆（1984）等。而国外的研究者则持相反的观点，认为并非仅仅是经济侵略，如侯继明（Hou Chi-ming，1965，*Foreign Investment and Economic Development in China*，*1840—1937*，Cambridge，Mass：Harvard University Press）、费正清（费正清编：《剑桥中国晚清史》，中国社会科学出版社 1993 年版）等。

和 44 000 百万美元，其中英国分别占 7 000、11 000 和 18 300 百万美元；其次是法国，其对应年份的投资额分别为 3 500、5 600 和8 700 百万美元①。既然英法两国是当时世界上对外投资最多的国家，那么，只要分析这两个国家对外投资在世界范围内地区的分布，便可对其在华投资的性质做出一个一般性的、浅层次的判断。表 8 为 19 世纪末至 20 世纪初英法两国对外投资的地区投资额分布状况。

表 8　19 世纪末至 20 世纪初英法对外投资的地区分布

单位：百万美元，%

地　区	英国（1896 年）	法国（1902 年）
欧　洲	1 250(10.4)	4 100(70.6)
北美洲	2 250(18.8)	150(2.6)
美　国	1 550	100
加拿大	700	50
拉丁美洲	1 250(10.4)	650(11.2)
大洋洲	1 600(13.3)	n.(n.)
亚　洲	1 700(14.2)	200(3.4)
印度、锡兰	1 450	…
中　国	150	150*
非　洲	1 900(15.8)	700(12.1)
其他地区	2 050(17.1)	…
合　计	12 000(100)	5 800(100)

注：* 包括法属殖民地和菲律宾的大约 3 000 万美元。

资料来源：转见宫崎犀一等（1990），第 58 页。

根据表 8 可以计算出，1896 年英国对华投资数量只占其对外投资总额的 1.25%，1902 年法国对华投资数量也只占其对外投资总额的 2.07%；到 1914 年第一次世界大战爆发前，英

① Brown，M. B.，1974，*Economics of Imperialism*，Penguin：171.

国、法国、德国和美国等几个主要国家对华的投资额分别为600、150、250和50百万美元，各占其对外投资总额的3%、1.66%、4.31%和1.43%。[①]从19世纪末到20世纪40年代前，上述几个国家对外投资主要分布如下：英国集中在北美洲和亚洲、法国和德国集中在欧洲和美洲、美国集中在北美洲和拉丁美洲。英国在亚洲进行国际投资的分布具体状况如表9所示。

表9 19世纪末至20世纪40年代前英国在亚洲国际投资分布

单位：百万美元，%

地　　区	1896年	1914年	1938年
印度、锡兰	1 450(85.29)	1 850(52.11)	3 050* (35.47)
中　　国	150(8.82)	600(16.90)	850(9.88)
亚　　洲	1 700(100.00)	3 550(100.00)	8 600** (100.00)

注：* 包括缅甸在内。 ** 还包括大洋洲在内。

资料来源：根据宫崎犀一等(1990)，第58—60页表格数字计算而得。

根据表9也能看出，英国在亚洲地区进行的国际投资中，其对中国的投资所占份额一直不是很高，最高的时候也未超过20%。一般来讲，要通过投资对一个国家进行经济侵略，则侵略国应集中其国际投资的绝大多数份额投资于被侵略国，否则，要形成经济侵略将是比较困难的。是不是由于中国经济的存量过分薄弱、是不是由于中国近代工业文明太少，而只需要较少的投资就可以形成经济侵略并控制中国的经济命脉呢？这需要进行进一步的探讨后方能回答，但如果对照英国在印度的投资情况，将更有利于问题的深入分析和思考。

其次，分析外国在华投资的结构与行业分布。正像前面分析所指出的一样，外国投资的结构分为直接投资与间接投资，如

---

① 宫崎犀一等(1990)，第59页。

果将外国金融机构向中国政府提供的贷款视为投资，那么，甲午战争后外国在华的间接投资比例是不断上升的。就这些以贷款形式出现的间接投资而言，由于附有十分苛刻的政治条件，使得中国政府在获得这些借款后，实际上跌入了别人早已设计好的陷阱，被人左右，任人宰割。从这个角度而言，以贷款为主要方式的外国间接投资具有很强的欺骗性、奴役性和侵略性。这一点是不容置疑的！

但是，从另一个角度来看，在近代中国的外国投资中，不论是直接投资还是间接投资，其投资的主体始终是外国的民间资本而非外国的国家或政府资本，甚至许多附有苛刻条件的借款也是由外国民间资本扮演主角的。既然是民间资本成为了外国投资的主体，而民间资本除了最具有资本的原初特性（即逐利、增殖）外，还有一个特点就是分散性与盲目性。分散性与盲目性这一特点决定了民间资本的投资不可能是有意识的、有目的地去对一个国家进行经济侵略，其在东道国某些行业投资的相对集中，很可能是因为这个行业的产品或服务有着非常强烈的市场需求或严重的供给不足，即有很好的市场利润前景。在市场利润这个杠杆的引导下，资本迅速在某些行业聚集，形成对一国某些重要行业或部门的控制与垄断。如果外国的投资及其聚集，仅此而已，这仍只能视为市场的自发行为而非目的性很强的经济侵略。当然，必须要看到的是，近代外国投资的大量进入是在不平等条约保护下并享有许多经济政治特权的背景下发生的，这就使得外国投资的性质有了很大的变异，因此，从这个角度而言，近代外国在华的投资具有一定的侵略性。

表 10 为近代外国在华的外资厂矿和中外合办厂矿的情况，从这个表中大致可以看清外国投资在华的行业、地区分布，由此可以对外国在近代中国的投资是否形成经济侵略、进而控制中

国经济命脉做出自己的判断。

表10　1895—1913年设在中国的外资厂矿和中外合办厂矿的国别、产业、地点和创办资本的规模

		厂矿数				创办资本(1 000中国元)			
		外资(A)	中外合办(B)	A+B	占总数的%	外资(A)	中外合办(B)	A+B	占总数的%
国别	英国	28	9	37	27.21	25 465	24 216	59 681	48.16
	法国	4	2	6	4.41	2 986	1 609	4 515	4.38
	德国	9	3	12	8.82	6 534	1 147	7 681	7.45
	日本	35	14	49	36.03	19 829	6 501	26 330	25.53
	俄国	9	8	17	12.50	3 866	2 782	6 648	6.44
	美国	6	2	8	5.88	2 551	689	3 240	3.14
	其他	5	2	7	5.15	3 028	1 950	4 978	4.83
合计		96	40	136	100.00	64 259	38 894	103 153	100.00
行业	采矿	10	22	32	23.53	18 533	31 436	49 969	48.44
	工程与造船	7	0	7	5.15	2 895	0	2 895	2.81
	电力与自来水	16	3	19	13.97	10 772	742	11 514	11.16
	纺织	12	4	16	11.76	10 325	2 190	12 515	12.13
	食品	34	5	39	28.68	15 126	2 022	17 148	16.62
	其他	17	6	23	16.91	6 608	2 504	9 112	8.83
合计		96	40	136	100.00	64 529	38 894	103 153	100.00
地点	江苏	33	11	44	32.35	18 501	5 121	23 622	22.90
	直隶	7	6	13	9.56	4 645	24 309	28 954	28.07
	湖北	8	2	10	7.35	3 576	1 609	5 185	5.03
	山东	5	1	6	4.41	3 503	92	3 595	3.49
	满洲	37	16	53	38.97	18 680	5 332	24 012	23.28
	其他	6	4	10	7.35	15 354	2 431	17 785	17.24
合计		96	40	136	100.00	64 259	38 894	103 153	100.00

（续表）

		厂矿数				创办资本(1 000 中国元)			
		外资(A)	中外合办(B)	A+B	占总数的%	外资(A)	中外合办(B)	A+B	占总数的%
创办资本规模	不到 100 000	2	5	7	5.15	120	288	408	0.40
	100 000—249 999	32	15	47	34.56	5 021	2 213	7 234	7.01
	250 000—499 999	30	7	37	27.21	11 623	3 132	14 755	14.30
	500 000—999 999	17	6	23	16.91	12 887	4 088	16 975	16.46
	1 000 000—4 999 999	14	5	19	13.97	20 622	7 541	28 163	27.30
	超过 5 000 000	1	2	3	2.21	13 986	21 632	35 618	34.53
合计		96	40	136	100.00	64 259	38 894	103 153	100.00

资料来源：根据汪敬虞编：《中国近代工业史资料，1895—1914 年》第二辑第一册，中华书局 1962 年版，第 2—13 页计算。转引自费正清编：《剑桥中国晚清史》下册，中国社会科学出版社 1993 年版，第 41—42 页。

表 10 清楚地显示出，甲午战争后直到第一次世界大战爆发前，外国在华投资行业比较多的为采矿业和食品业，采矿业占外国在华设厂总数和投资总额的对应份额分别为 23.53％与 48.44％，食品业则为 28.68％与 16.62％。除掉外国直接投资设厂和中外合资办厂外，其余的份额应该是属于包括官办资本企业在内的中资企业的，这样算来，在甲午战争后，采矿业中有 76.47％的企业和 51.56％的投资额、食品业中有 71.32％的企业和 83.38％的投资额是属于中资企业的，外国投资在最为集中的两个产业上都未达到绝对垄断的地步，由此可见，外国投资即使有经济侵略，也没有曾经论述和想象的那么严重。

最后来看外国投资不断增长背景下的中资企业发展情况。学者侯继明认为，随着外国人在 1895—1937 年间增加了其工业投资，“中国经济的现代部分出现了华人企业与外国企业长期共存的情况……（而这种）共存……表明，从长远看，（华人企业）能够与(外国企业)发展一样快。”①学者高家龙在研究了 1890—1930 年英美烟公司与南洋烟草公司的竞争、发展情况后，认为这两家公司不仅仅是竞争对手，而且都是非常成功的大企业，是由于两者的直接竞争导致了它们的成功。②甲午战争后，由于外国人取得了在华投资办厂的合法权，从而导致了在许多产业中都存在着中外企业竞争的情况：棉纺市场上有华人申新纱厂与日本内外棉株式会社之间的竞争；纺织机械市场上有华人大隆机器厂与两个美国制造业者——萨科—洛厄尔机器厂和维定机器厂之间的竞争；火柴市场上有大中华火柴股份有限公司与两个外国的公司——瑞典火柴公司和日本铃木会社之间的竞争；图书和出版市场上有两个华人出版社——商务印书馆和中华书局与英人兆祥洋行之间的竞争；肥皂、制碱与肥料市场上有华人永利制碱公司和五洲皂药厂与英国利华兄弟公司、卜内门洋碱有限公司和帝国化学工业公司之间的竞争；水泥市场上有华人广东水泥厂与在香港的英国青洲英妮公司之间的竞争；钢铁市场上有华人汉阳铁厂与日本在鞍山和本溪的南满株式会社之间的竞争；烟草市场上有华人的南洋兄弟烟草公司与外国的英美烟公司之间的竞争；等等。中资企业与外资企业之间的竞争几乎遍及当时中国的各个产业与行业。

虽然创办企业和发展企业的市场环境充满了竞争和不确定性，但是市场尤其是企业发展的活力也正来源于此。如果没有竞争，企业就将失去发展的动力。表面上看，似乎没有外资企业的进入和竞争，中资企业就可以从从容容地去发展，并能最大化

---

① Hou Chi-ming, 1965, *Foreign Investment and Economic Development in China, 1840—1937*, Cambridge, Mass.: Harvard University Press: 138—139.

② 高家龙:《中国的大企业——烟草工业中的中外竞争》，商务印书馆 2001 年版，第 318 页。

地从事资本积累而逐步扩大。但事实上，在外资企业进入还不是很多的甲午战争前，中资企业并没有发展起来。更有，如果没有外资企业的进入及其对中国利权的攫取，中国政府能否进行允许中国人办企业的制度变迁还不可预测！几千年一以贯之的“重农抑商”制度安排决定了中资企业即使没有外资企业的市场竞争与压力也将很难发展起来。中国的历史实际上早已为此做出了最好的注释。反观甲午战争后市场竞争日益加剧的情景下，反而是近代史上中资企业成长与发展比较好的时期（如表11所示），实在值得深思！

表11　1895—1913年开业的中资制造业和采矿业的企业数和创办资本(按行业)　资本单位：1 000中国元

行　业	企业数	占总数的%	创办资本	占总数的%	平均资本
煤矿	42	7.65	14 508	12.06	345
金属采矿和冶炼	39	7.10	7 565	6.29	194
金属加工	15	2.73	2 787	2.32	186
公用事业(水电)	46	8.38	21 600	17.96	470
水泥	3	0.55	2 620	2.18	873
砖瓦	12	2.19	651	0.54	543
陶器	7	1.28	772	0.64	110
玻璃	10	1.82	3 429	2.85	343
火柴	26	4.74	3 444	2.86	132
蜡烛、肥皂	18	3.28	805	0.67	45
轧花	3	0.55	280	0.23	93
纺纱	19	3.46	10 454	8.69	550
织布、印染	27	4.92	1 261	1.05	47
缫丝	97	17.67	11 584	9.63	119
毛织	7	1.28	5 215	4.34	745
麻织	4	0.73	1 000	0.83	250
其他织布	6	1.09	732	0.61	122

（续表）

行　业	企业数	占总数的%	创办资本	占总数的%	平均资本
碾米	9	1.64	1 012	0.84	113
制面	53	9.65	8 622	7.17	163
榨油	28	5.10	4 752	3.95	170
纸烟、烟草	20	3.64	1 378	1.15	69
其他食品	15	2.73	3 111	2.59	207
造纸	14	2.55	5 929	4.93	424
印刷	6	1.09	1 160	0.97	193
鞣革	11	2.00	4 608	3.83	419
其他	12	2.19	1 009	0.84	84
合计	549	100.00	120 288	100.00	219

资料来源：根据汪敬虞编：《中国近代工业史资料，1895—1914 年》第二辑第二册，中华书局 1962 年版，第 869—920 页计算。

从表 11 来分析，中资企业不仅行业分布十分分散，而且资本规模都不大。若从企业数量来看，中资企业最为集中的行业依次是缫丝、面粉、煤矿和公用事业（水电）；而若从资本规模来看，中资企业资本集聚最多的行业又依次是公用事业（水电）、煤矿、缫丝和纺纱。综合来看，在企业数和创办资本这两方面，中资企业大部分集中在纺织业等轻型制造业（共 160 个，占企业总数的 29.14%；资本额共 30 246 000 中国元，占总资本的 25.14%）和食品加工业（计 125 个，占企业总数的 22.76%；资本额共 18 875 000 中国元，占总资本的 15.69%）这类行业。采矿业占总企业数的 14.75%，占总资本的 18.35%。对照表 10，如果仅从企业数量与资本数量分布而言，中资企业与外资企业呈现了类似的特征。如果从投资的总规模和企业的平均资本来比较，则中资企业与外资企业的差别似乎也不是很大。具体如表 12 所示。

表12 1895—1913年中资、外资*企业规模比较

资本单位:1 000中国元

创办资本规模	企业数量及各占份额				资本数量及各占份额				平均资本规模	
	企业数		占总数的%		创办资本		占总数的%			
	中资	外资	中资	外资	中资	外资	中资	外资	中资	外资
10 000—49 999	214		38.98		5 899		4.90		28	
50 000—99 999	89	2	16.21	2.08	7 052	120	5.86	0.19	79	60
100 000—249 999	104	32	18.94	33.33	17 732	5 021	14.74	7.81	170	157
250 000—499 999	85	30	15.48	31.25	29 901	11 623	24.86	18.09	352	387
500 000—999 999	40	17	7.29	17.71	27 980	12 887	23.26	20.06	700	758
1 000 000—4 999 999	17	14	3.10	14.58	31 725	20 622	26.37	32.09	1 866	1 473
5 000 000以上		1		1.04		13 986		21.77		13 986
合　计	549	96	100.00	100.00	120 288	64 259	100.00	100.00	219	669

注:*外资企业不包括中外合资企业。

资料来源:根据费正清编:《剑桥中国晚清史》下册,中国社会科学出版社1993年版,第41—42、48页表格资料计算而得。

综合表10、表11和表12来看,在甲午战争后外国投资绝对量明显增多的情况下,中资企业发展的速度和规模是非常快的,外国投资对中资企业发展的挤压之势似乎也并未形成,或即使已经形成但并不十分严重,而且,这种挤压似乎更应该理解为构建在不平等条约基础之上的市场竞争。中国的经济史学家们认为这种形式的中外竞争是不平等的,并列出了外资企业较中资企业拥有的有利条件,如易于获得外资、尖端技术、企业人才、管理效率以及政治和外交特权等以证明这种观点。但国外的学者则不赞成此观点，认为中外竞争是平等的，他们也承认外资企业可能拥有上述各种优势，但他们又认为这些优势被中资企业所拥有的有利条件抵消了。侯继明认为，外资企业具有“更多的资本，更大的资本密集程度，先进的技术，不受官方干涉”等优势，但中资企业也独享某些优势，如“了解本地情形、民族主义和企业易于转向”[①]。帕金斯认为，外资企业可能“资本成本较低……但是这一优势被华人企业中更廉价的劳动力成本和更大的劳动强度所抵消”[②]。吉尔伯特·罗兹曼认为，外国投资有利于中资企业的仿效行为发生，并且认为，“任何企业家只要能有效地制造并销售其产品，就能获取利润。外国企业家在现代技术、信贷以及对国际市场行情的掌握方面，优于中国企业家，但中国企业家在雇佣劳动力、获得本地产销信息方面同样也优于外国企业家。中外企业家究竟谁最有优势，实际上要取决于变幻莫测的市场情况。”[③]关于竞争平等与否的争论虽然难以达成一致，但甲午战争后中资企业的蓬勃发展却是有目共睹的事实。基于以上的分析，似乎可以得出一个一般性的结论：在外国投资与日俱增的情形下，中资企业的发展不仅未受到太大的约束和阻滞，而且在外资企业扩张的冲击下也成长迅速。

六、近代外国在华直接投资的效应

外国间接投资由于绝大部分是以借款的形式出现的，这样的外国投资加重了中国经济发展的灾难，具有很强的掠夺性，对

---

① Hou Chi-ming(1965).

② Perkins, Dwight H., 1975, *China's Modern Economy in Historical Perspective*, Stanford University Press: 45.

③ 吉尔伯特·罗兹曼(1988)，第423页。

近代中国经济发展没有任何的正效应可言，因而，不再予以分析。至于以铁路借款等“实业借款”形式出现的间接投资，虽然也具有一定的负面效应，但由于这些间接投资对近代中国基础设施的改善和供给、对中国实业的发展有一定的促进作用，所以，将其连同外国直接投资的效应一并加以分析。

外国直接投资是紧随坚船利炮来到中国的，由外国直接投资而创设的外资企业，是中国大地上出现的第一批使用机器生产的近代工业文明。尽管外国直接投资对近代中资企业的正常成长有一些影响，“尽管有外资企业和进口商品的竞争”，但也应该看到，“中国现代部门的工业仍在扩展”①，外国在华投资在客观上对中国近代生产力的产生和发展，对中国早期工业化的启动和发展，对中资企业的成长和壮大，对市场的扩大和市场制度的建设等也是有推动力的，②因而，具有积极的正面效应。

1. 资本的溢出效应

外国投资增加了中国社会的资本流量，有利于缓解近代中国社会资本的短缺。由于资本严重不足，导致中国资金市场求大于供，银行放款利率居高不下。根据日本人的调查，1910 年中国银行放款利率一般在 10%左右，最高达20%。③这时工厂融通资金的主要来源是钱庄。辛亥革命以前，上海钱庄放款年利率大抵在 7.2%—12%左右，银根紧张时甚至在 20%左右。上海以外的各埠钱庄放款利息“多数比上海为高”④。1920 年左右，中国一些城市放款利率又有所上升。从北洋政府财政部档

---

① 吉尔伯特·罗兹曼(1988)，第 420 页。

② 陈谦平等:《近代英国在华直接投资评析》，载吴景平等主编:《近代中国的经济与社会》，上海古籍出版社 2002 年版。

③ 严中平(1955)，第 144 页。

④ 严中平(1955)，第 146—147 页。

案材料看，当时京、津一带资金短缺，“所有各项利率均较前增高”。其中以“救济农工”标榜的农工银行，1917 年以来放款利率最高为 18%，而到 1921 年时这一上限已升至 21.6%。[①]高利率一方面侵蚀原有的产业资本，另一方面又吸引社会资金流向流通领域，而使生产领域资本形成更加不足。这样形成一个“低资本形成—低收入—低储蓄能力—高利率—低资本形成”的恶性循环。而从资金的需求者，即生产企业角度来看，甲午战争后近代工业发展最快的是棉纺织业，其中纺纱业的发展又超过织布业，其原因之一是创办纺纱厂“资本可以稍轻”，其规模可以“随其资本之大小而设立”[②]，对于资本实力微薄的实业家来说，选取纺纱厂作为投资对象，就不难理解其苦衷。与此形成鲜明对照的是同一时期英国银行贷款利率的低下。当时在华英国银行的放款利率一般在 4%—8%之间，[③]而英国国内银行的放款利率在 1900—1908 年间更低，平均不过 3.4%[④]。大量价格低廉的外国资本的流入为中国“现代化经济部门筹措了很大一部分资金”[⑤]，这些资金对近代中国经济发展的促进作用是不言自明的。

2. 技术与管理技能的正外部效应

所谓技术的正外部效应主要是指投资主体在从事生产或其他经济行为时，并非有意转让或传播其技术，而是在其经济行为中自然输出技术及其引起的技术提高。它的主要形式有：在外

① 中国第二历史档案馆编：《中华民国史档案资料汇编》第三辑，金融(一)，江苏古籍出版社 1991 年版，第 420—424 页。

② 张国辉(1988)。

③ 张继凤(1982)。

④ 转见严中平(1955)，第 161 页。

⑤ 侯继明：《外国投资和经济现代化》，载张仲礼主编：《中国近代经济史论著选译》，上海社会科学院出版社 1987 年版，第 52 页。

国投资企业受过训练并有经验的人员流动、外国投资者的竞争压力迫使当地生产厂家提高自己的技术水平、仿效外国投资者的新产品和新工艺等。所谓管理技能的正外部效应是指东道国可以借助外国所设公司的人员流动，使东道国有关人员获得管理经验；借助东道国企业模仿与之竞争的外国投资者的管理技术，提高组织技能。吉尔伯特·罗兹曼说：外国直接投资“能使中国企业家学会新的技术，借到资金且仿效外国企业的一套经营管理程序”①。

3. 进口替代效应的增强

鸦片战争以后，洋货进口不断增加，机制品市场日益扩张。在洋货行销的刺激下，中国的仿洋机制品工业产生了。洋货多销一分，利益多外流一分，于是商战、实业救国思潮掀起，民族替代工业纷纷崛起。而外国在华直接投资则进一步增强了这种进口替代效应。以卷烟业为例，卷烟是近代中国进口之大宗商品，民国以后进口值增长较快，从民国初年的每年 1 000 多万元增长至 20 世纪 30 年代的 6 000 多万元；尤其是英美烟公司在华经营的成功，刺激了国货卷烟工业的规模也不断扩大，从民国初年的十余家，发展到 20 世纪 30 年代的一百多家，成为中国近代民族工业的一大支柱产业。其他如肥皂、造纸、电灯、酸碱、铅笔、化妆品、电扇、甘油等国货工业都是以进口替代的形式切入市场而发展起来的。据 1936 年《中国经济年鉴》记载，中国近代工业有食品、棉纺织、碱、酸、盐等 18 个主要行业，其中 14 个是进口替代行业，占主要行业总数的 77.8%。再对国货工业的地域分布进行分析，这一情况将会看得更加清楚：口岸地区，特别是上海，是外国在华直接投资的主要地区，而民族工业的产值也在 50%

① 吉尔伯特·罗兹曼(1988)，第 423 页。

左右，是近代民族工业无可争议的经济中心。进口替代民族工业的发展是与外国直接投资设厂的刺激有着密切关联的。

4. *交通等基础设施建设的带动效应与溢出效应*

基础设施供给的多少直接影响到一国的经济发展，基础设施的建设与改善不仅可以降低经济发展的交易成本、运输成本，而且还可以获得积聚效应、规模效应。中国传统的运输工具是木帆船，而随着外国投资航运业，以蒸汽为动力的轮船开始在中国出现，从而引发了中国航运业的一场革命：汽船开始逐步取代帆船。据研究，到 19 世纪 60 年代，帆船与汽船各半；至 90 年代，帆船运载量只占总吨数的 1/30，并继续呈现不断减低的趋势。轮船在运载量和速度上均优于帆船，对市场的扩大以及运输成本的下降是很有利的。再如铁路建设，从 1903 年至 1907 年，外国直接投资兴建的铁路计 3 772 公里，外国间接投资（即中国政府借款）修建的铁路为 4 846 公里，在外国投资的带动下，中国政府也开始自筹资金增加铁路的供给，这样，到 1913 年，中国建成通车的铁路里程达 9 854 公里，改变了二十多年前中国无一寸铁路的局面。[①]铁路的建设与通车，既给铁路沿线的经济发展带去了商品经济观念、扩大了市场，又方便了货物的运输、节约了成本。由于铁路建设对经济发展的成效显著，此后的中国政府继续利用内外资进行建设，以增加铁路的供给。据史载，到 20 世纪 30 年代，国内共建筑铁路 16 972 公里，其中，13 353公里归当时中国政府所有。“在这 13 353 公里铁路的投资中，45.5%是外国贷款的，由六七个国家在近四十年内提供的贷款总额累计达 5 400 万英镑。”[②]此外，外国投资在租界内和通商口岸城市对自来水、煤气、电力等公共基础设施的建设与供给，

---

① 安格斯·麦迪森(1999)，第 77 页。

② 郑友揆(1984)，第 53 页。

也带动了中国政府对其他“自开商埠”及非通商口岸以至所有城市公共基础设施的建设与供给，促进了城市本身以及近代城市化的发展。

至于外国投资基础设施建设的溢出效应更加明显。由于外国投资的地域相对集中，使得其基础设施产品的供给也相对集中于以上海为代表的几个大城市。这些大城市基础设施因不断得到外国投资而日益改善，也为中资企业的发展提供了便利而可以乘机“搭便车”，对中资企业外部成本的降低至关重要。由于这个原因，所以可以看到，近代兴起的中资企业绝大多数都集中在以上海为主的几个大城市，而这正是外国投资基础设施的溢出效应有利于中资企业发展的表证。当然，还应该看到中资企业在上海等地相对集中的另一个重要原因，即安全感的影响。由于“中国的企业家们感到条约口岸是一个能够提供商业安全和有效生活方式的世外桃源，在这些避风港里，他们通过对制造业的投资不仅能保持自己的财富，而且享有更大的自由去支配这些财富”①，所以导致了中资企业在地理空间上的相对集中。

关于外国投资的效应问题，吉尔伯特·罗兹曼的这段论述也是很有启发的。“成千上万的中国地方企业所使用的工具依然主要是依靠人力而不是资本。他们通过经纪人和商人组成的网络交换产品，有一整套的城镇和乡村各级市场，乡村市场是定期逢集的。而手工业生产始终与农田耕作的忙闲相关。中国企业家不得不去等待良好的条件来组织以工厂为基础的生产，这些条件包括：适宜的技术、与其他行业（房地产、金融、商业）一样有吸引力的利润、需有充足的低利率贷款以购买机器设备。以上条件只有条约口岸才具备，西方人在那里也有开办银行或其他企业的自

① 吉尔伯特·罗兹曼(1988)，第420页。

由。有这些自由的口岸市场和大规模的外国公司的存在，中国企业才会有刺激和榜样组织起来，否则什么也谈不上。”①

虽然外国直接投资具有非常明显的示范、溢出与积聚等效应，但众所周知，外国直接投资所产生的这些效应能否发挥出来、对东道国的民族产业和企业能否产生带动作用，主要取决于东道国民族企业的投资能力、投资冲动。一位外国学者在比较中、日、俄三国近代经济发展历史时认为，三国都有吸引、利用和控制外资的问题，日、俄在“利用那些可能成为剥削他们的人这方面较为成功”，而中国由于“较弱的政治结构”，造成很大的损失。②所谓中国“较弱的政治结构”，当然是指近代中国的半殖民地化，但也包括担负领导近代中国经济发展重任的软弱的中国政府。由于软弱的中国政府没有承担起领导经济发展的重任，不仅导致了外资利用的无序混乱，而且还导致稀缺资源的长期非优化配置，从而造成近代中国产业市场的结构严重失衡。而日本、俄国由于有一个强大的政府，其通过产业政策、投资政策等经济制度设计安排，不仅充分地利用了外国投资来促进本国经济的快速发展，而且还迅速地实现了工业化，摆脱了也一度如中国似的任人欺凌的境地。近代，由于中国主权的不完整，由于缺少一个强大的中央政府，尽管外国在华的投资数量不少，但中国并未借此发展起来，像日本、俄国那样较为成功地利用外国投资的好运始终没有在近代中国降临。

尽管外国投资未能阻止近代中国本土企业的成长，尽管外国投资具有多方面的正效应，但是，在分析近代外国在华投资效应时，则不能不注意外资的进入是在不平等条约的庇护下发生的，更不能不注意外资的进入及其对东道国资源的肆意采伐是

① 吉尔伯特·罗兹曼(1988)，第422页。

② Elvin，Mark(1982)。

一种赤裸裸的强权侵略。近代外国在华投资其本意是为了实现其在中国盈利的长期化，并在每次列强侵华战争中扮演着极不光彩的角色，推波助澜，助纣为虐。然而，即使面临着极其不利的政治、经济环境，中资企业在外国投资的刺激下，依然似滚滚长江东逝水般而不可遏制地成长并壮大起来了，这是外国投资者所没有想到的，因此，从这个角度而言，近代外国在华投资在客观上又推动了中国经济的进步。

参考文献

安格斯·麦迪森:《中国经济的长远未来》，新华出版社 1999 年版。

陈谦平等:《近代英国在华直接投资评析》，载吴景平等主编《近代中国的经济与社会》，上海古籍出版社 2002 年版第 239—256 页。

Elvin, M.:《中日俄近代早期经济增长的比较》，《经济学术资料》1982 年第 5 期。

高家龙:《中国的大企业——烟草工业中的中外竞争》，商务印书馆 2001 年版。

宫崎犀一等:《近代国际经济要览·16 世纪以来》，中国财政经济出版社 1990 年版。

Hou, C., 1965, *Foreign Investment and Economic Development in China, 1840—1937*, Cambridge, Mass.: Harvard University Press.

侯继明:《外国投资和经济现代化》，载张仲礼主编:《中国近代经济史论著选译》，上海社会科学院出版社 1987 年版，第 50—78 页。

吉尔伯特·罗兹曼:《中国的现代化》，江苏人民出版社 1988 年版。

迈克尔·P. 托达罗:《经济发展》，中国经济出版社 1999 年版。

Perkins, D., 1975, *China's Modern Economy in Historical Perspective*, Stanford: Stanford University Press.

上海社会科学院经济研究所:《英美烟公司在华企业资料汇编》第四册，中华书局 1983 年版。

孙毓棠:《抗戈集》，中华书局 1981 年版。

Svedberg, P., 1978, "The Portfolio-Direct Composition of Private Foreign Investment in 1914 Revisited", *Economic Journal*, 88(352): 763—777.

王利华:《近代外人对华投资的影响因素剖析》,《南开经济研究》1997年第2期。

吴承明:《中国资本主义与国内市场》,中国社会科学出版社1985年版。

许涤新、吴承明:《中国资本主义发展史》第2卷,人民出版社1990年版。

徐义生:《中国近代外债史统计资料(1853—1927)》,中华书局1962年版。

严中平:《中国棉纺织史稿》,科学出版社1955年版。

伊特韦尔等:《新帕尔格雷夫经济学大辞典》第二卷,陈岱孙译,经济科学出版社1996年版。

张国辉:《中国棉纺织业1895—1927年的发展和不发展》,载《中国社会科学院经济研究所集刊》第10集,中国社会科学出版社1988年版。

张继凤:《略论百年来我国利率的变迁》,《金融研究》1982年第4期。

赵德馨:《中国近代国民经济史教程》,高等教育出版社1988年版。

郑友揆:《中国的对外贸易和工业发展(1840—1948)》,上海社会科学院出版社1984年版。

(原载《经济学(季刊)》2007年第6卷第3期)

区域一体化、经济增长与政治晋升*

徐现祥

（中山大学岭南学院）

李　郇

（中山大学地理科学与规划学院）

王美今

（中山大学岭南学院）

一、引　言

建立全国统一开放的市场是我国经济转轨的重要目标之一。从我国区域开放实践看，一方面，我国区域间恶性竞争、重复建设、市场保护等市场分割问题一直比较突出（银温泉和才婉如，2001）；另一方面，国内区域经济一体化（regional integration）的出现以及增多已成为一个重要现象，比如长三角和泛珠三角目前的自发实践。因此，一个有意思的问题是，在我国经济转轨过程中，为什么有些省区选择市场分割，而有些省区

* 感谢 *Tuzawz Liang*（梁志成）、李杰、周泳宏、吴玉鸣、傅十和与匿名审稿人的评论和建议，以及贺茉莉的出色助研工作。本文的研究得到广东省自然科学基金项目（05300601）、广东省哲学社会科学规划项目（05D-06）和中山大学“985 工程”产业与区域发展研究哲学社会科学创新基地的资助，在此表示感谢。

却开始致力于区域经济一体化？现有文献大致从以下两个方面展开：

主流的解释是从财政分权的视角探索我国市场分割的根源。众多文献将我国市场分割归因于分权改革，如沈立人和戴园晨（1990）、Young（2000）、银温泉和才婉如（2001）、平新乔（2003）、林毅夫和刘培林（2004）等。但大量文献也揭示，财政分权为地方政府发展当地经济提供了适宜的激励，如Qian和Weingast（1997）、Qian和Roland（1998）和Jin等（2005）等。

最新文献的进展是从地方政府官员所面临的政治激励展开的，如Maskin等（2000）、Blanchard和Shleifer（2000）、周黎安等（2005）和Li和Zhou（2005）等。自20世纪80年代初，我国地方官员升迁标准由过去以政治表现为主变为以经济绩效为主。周黎安（2004）进一步明确指出，在这种政绩观下，“地政官员合作困难的根源并不主要在于地方官员的财税激励及其他们所处的经济竞争性质，而是在于嵌入在经济竞争当中的政治晋升博弈的性质”，并尝试从政治晋升博弈出发对我国的市场分割和恶性竞争等问题给出一个全新的解释。但是，如果说，政治晋升博弈中的政府官员不愿意合作，那么，为什么同样面临晋升竞争的某些省区却选择了区域经济一体化？其实，张军（2005）已明确指出，在这种政绩观下，地方官员为增长而竞争，会带来地方保护主义、重复建设等问题，但是区域之间的“贸易”联系却是不断加强的。①

---

① 国务院发展研究中心最近组织的一项全国性的调查表明，无论是企业还是非企业单位都认为，二十多年来，地方保护的严重程度呈现逐步减轻之势（李善同等，2004）。大量实证文献都发现，我国市场分割程度是不断下降的，较详细的综述请参阅朱希伟等（2005）。另外，桂琦寒等（2004）较好地综述了度量市场分割程度的方法。

总之，现有文献主要是从地方政府所面临的财政、政治激励的角度论述我国市场建设问题，正如 Jin 等(2005)所明确指出的，这两种研究思路是互补的。但这两种思路还没有系统研究以下问题：面临相同的激励，为什么有些省区选择市场分割，而有些却开始致力于区域经济一体化。沿着后一条思路，本文从中央政府按照经济绩效晋升地方政府官员的假设出发，构建了一个简单的地方政府官员晋升博弈模型，证明了理性的地方政府官员为了晋升最大化，既可能会选择市场分割也可能会选择区域经济一体化，具体选择因条件而异，从而为地方政府在区际关系的迥异行为提供了一个具有内在一致性的解释。具体而言，在中央政府按照经济绩效晋升地方政府官员的情况下，当地方政府官员的努力具有正外部性或正溢出效应时，地方政府官员会理性地选择区域一体化，从而将正溢出效应内部化，获得更快的经济增长以及更高的晋升可能性；反之，当存在负外部性或负溢出效应时，地方政府官员会理性地选择市场分割，从而将负溢出效应外部化，以免殃及自身经济增长以及相应的晋升可能性。基于长三角的实证分析支持理论模型的预测。

本文从政治激励的角度探索中国地方政府在区际关系上的行为，但政治激励并不是中国特有的现象。比如转轨经济体俄罗斯同样存在这一情形，Blanchard 和 Shleifer(2000)发现，中俄对地方政府的政治激励不同，由此带来财政分权的经济绩效迥异。再比如美国也存在政治激励，Besley 等(1995)和 Besley 等(2005)从理论和实证两个方面分析了美国各州州长连任可能性(各州间的政治竞争)与其经济政策、经济绩效之间的关系，发现二者显著正相关。

本文的模型类似于 Bester 和 Güth(1998)、Possajennikov(2000)和 Bolle(2000)，但解决的问题完全不同。Bester 和

Güth(1998)、Possajennikov(2000)和 Bolle(2000)提供了一个简洁的处理偏好内生的方法,并基于该方法探索理性的经济活动主体为什么会选择利他行为。本文模型的基本假设更多地来源于中国的经验观察,采用他们所开创的方法,探索理性的地方政府官员,为了晋升最大化,是选择区域一体化还是市场分割。当然,Bester 和 Güth(1998)、Possajennikov(2000)和 Bolle(2000)的工作更具有一般性,但通过引入新的因素——基于中国的经验观察修正原模型的基本假设——完全可能得到一些新的结论或解释一些新的现象。

以下部分的结构安排是:第二部分是模型;第三部分是实证;最后是结论性评述。

二、模　型

(一) 基本假定

1. 经济增长与政治晋升

我们考察由 n 个相邻区域构成的经济体。经济体存在一个中央政府,它雇用 n 个同质的地方官员管理其下辖的 n 个区域。

由于无法观察到每个地方官员的努力程度,中央政府依据每个区域经济增长的快慢升迁任免该地方政府官员。简单起见,我们把经济体的地方官员晋升函数表示为

$$v = g \tag{1}$$

(1)式中,v 和 g 分别表示地方官员晋升的可能性和经济增长速度。(1)式的经济含义非常直观,地方官员管辖区域的经济增长速度越快,其得到晋升的可能性就越大。就我国而言,自20 世纪 80 年代初,我国地方官员激励方式发生重大变化,官员升迁的考核标准由过去以政治表现为主变为以经济绩效为主,

形成了今天流行的基于地方经济发展的可度量的政绩观。周黎安等(2005)以及 Li 和 Zhou(2005)采用我国省级官员晋升数据发现,省级官员在任期间的平均增长速度对其晋升有显著的正的影响。

每个地方政府官员都是理性的,为晋升而展开两两竞争。为追求晋升最大化,地方政府官员尽可能促进本地区的经济增长。①张军(2005)把这种现象称之为我国地方官员"为增长而竞争"。假定地区 i 的经济增长取决于地方官员 i 的努力程度 $(x \geqslant 0)$,即

$$\overline{g}_i = mx - x^2 \tag{2}$$

其中,$m > 0$,是常数。(2)式表明,在一定范围内,区域的经济速度随着地方官员努力程度的增加而提高。确切地说,地方官员的努力每增加一单位,经济增长速度就会提高 $(m - 2x)$ 单位。该假定是合理的,原因有二:一是无论新古典经济增长理论还是新经济增长理论都证明了经济增长的引擎是技术进步,因此,经济速度不可能随着地方官员努力程度的增加而一直提高。二是大量增长文献揭示了政府行为确实影响到经济增长速度,如 Rebelo(1991),特别是 Easterly(2005),基于欠发达国家实践给出了大量证据。

地方官员的努力存在外部性,即地方官员 i 的努力能够影响到其他区域的经济增长速度。大量的经济增长文献揭示了外部性对经济增长的影响,如 Romer(1986)和 Lucas(1988)等。同理,其他地方政府官员的努力也会影响到区域 i 的经济增长。

---

① 我们也无须否认,在一些地方的确可能出现"官员出数字,数字出官员"的问题,可如果数字全是"吹"出来的,像 20 世纪 50 年代流行的"浮夸风"那样,我想我们的经济早就因为数字的膨胀而崩溃了,还能坚持到今天?(张军,2005,第 135 页)

由于晋升竞争是成对进行的，我们假定区域 i 的经济增长速度也受到其竞争对手努力程度 $(y \geqslant 0)$ 的影响，即

$$g_i = \theta xy \tag{3}$$

其中，$\theta \in (-1, 1)$ 是常数，度量竞争对手的努力对区域 i 的经济增长速度的影响程度。限制 $|\theta| < 1$ 旨在强调区域 i 经济增长主要是靠自身的努力，周黎安(2004)也采取同样的限制。显然，$\theta = 0$，则经济体里不存在外部性。当 $\theta \in (0, 1)$ 时，竞争对手的努力有利于区域 i 的经济增长，即存在正外部性或正溢出效应；当 $\theta \in (-1, 0)$ 时，竞争对手的努力不利于区域 i 的经济增长，即存在负外部性或负溢出效应。

式(2)和式(3)相加，则得到区域 i 的经济增长表达式，即

$$g_i = \overline{g}_i + g_i = mx - x^2 + \theta xy \tag{4}$$

地方政府官员 i 的竞争对手 j 也会为追求晋升最大化而尽可能促进本地区 j 的经济增长。由于地方政府官员是同质的，地区 j 的经济增长速度就可以表示为

$$g_j = my - y^2 + \theta yx \tag{5}$$

在基于经济绩效的人事考核体系下，中央政府根据经济增长速度晋升地方官员，众多的地方官员为晋升而展开竞争。由式(1)、式(4)和式(5)可知，地方政府官员 i 和 j 的晋升可能性可以表示为

$$v_i = g_i,\ v_j = g_j$$

2. 地方政府官员的偏好

地方政府官员关注的是晋升。因此，地方政府官员 i 和 j 的偏好 U 定义为

$$U_i = v_i + \alpha v_j,\ U_j = v_j + \beta v_i,\ -1 \leqslant \alpha \leqslant 1,\ -1 \leqslant \beta \leqslant 1 \tag{6}$$

显然，当$\alpha=\beta=0$时，则表明地方政府官员只关注自己晋升的可能性；当α，$\beta>0$时，则表明不仅关注竞争对手的升迁，而且竞争对手的升迁能够增进自身的福利；当α，$\beta<0$时，则表明竞争对手的升迁会降低自身的福利。基于此，本文依据α的大小，对地方政府官员i在处理区域关系的选择定义如下：当$\alpha>0$时，地方政府官员j的晋升能够增进地方政府官员i的福利，称地方政府官员i偏好区域一体化的发展战略。当$\alpha<0$时，地方政府官员j的晋升将降低地方政府官员i的福利，称地方政府官员i偏好市场分割的发展战略。同理，地方政府官员j在处理区域关系上也有上述两种选择。

显然，市场分割和区域一体化都是地方政府通过发展经济获得晋升的策略。在以下具体分析中，我们首先视α和β给定，考察地方政府官员最优的努力水平；然后分析地方政府官员为了实现晋升最大化，是选择区域一体化还是市场分割，还是因条件而异。

需要强调的是，这并不同于经济文献中的一般做法。通常，人们是给定刻画经济活动主体偏好的效用函数，然后考察经济活动主体效用最大化的行为。在本文，首先给定地方官员的偏好，地方政府官员选择最优的努力程度，官员的努力关系到该地区的经济增长并最终决定其晋升的可能性；然后考察，为了实现晋升最大化，地方政府官员是选择区域一体化还是区域市场分割，从而将其偏好内生，如图1所示。我们这么做是可行的，地方政府官员为了实现晋升最大化，完全可以有时偏好区域一体化，有时偏好市场分割。其实，这正是Bester和Güth(1998)、Possajennikov(2000)、Bolle(2000)所开创的一种内生偏好的方法。

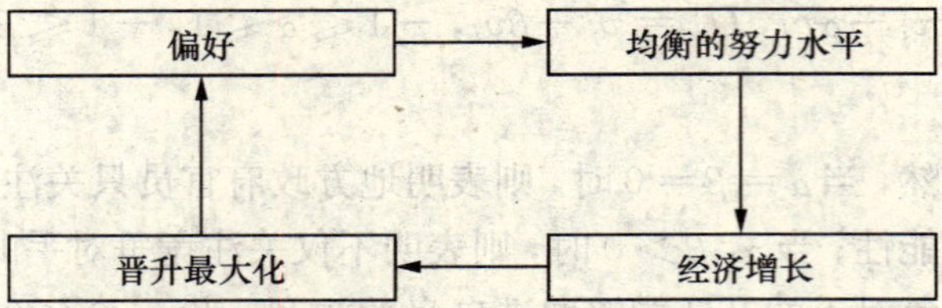

图 1　地方政府内生偏好

(二) 基准模型

所谓基准模型是指 $\alpha=\beta=0$ 的情形。在这种情形下，地方政府官员既不会选择区域一体化也不会选择市场分割。

当 $\alpha=0$ 时，地方政府官员 i 晋升函数等同于其效用函数，即

$$U_i=v_i=mx-x^2+\theta yx$$

地方政府官员 i 效用最大化的条件是

$$\frac{\partial U_i}{\partial x}=0\Rightarrow m-2x+\theta y=0 \tag{7}$$

由于地方政府官员 i 和 j 为了晋升而竞争，(7)式显然是地方政府官员 i 最优努力程度的反应函数。同理，我们可以得到，当 $\beta=0$ 时，地方政府官员 j 最优努力程度的反应函数为

$$m-2y+\theta x=0 \tag{8}$$

联立(7)式和(8)式就得到了地方政府关于 i 和 j 均衡的努力程度和均衡的晋升可能性，即

$$\bar{x}=\bar{y}=\frac{m}{2-\theta},\ v_i(\bar{x},\bar{y})=v_j(\bar{x},\bar{y})=\left(\frac{m}{2-\theta}\right)^2 \tag{9}$$

(9)式表明，两个理性的地方政府官员为晋升展开竞争，当均衡时，最优努力程度相同，晋升可能性相同。

（三）一般情形

所谓一般情形是指，$\alpha \neq 0$ 且 $\beta \neq 0$。在一般情况下，地方政府效用最大化问题可以表示为 $\max\limits_{x} U_i = v_i + \alpha v_j$。

需要强调的是，在我们构造的经济体里，地方官员的努力存在外部性。在基准情况下，地方官员显然无法把这种外部性内部化；但在一般情形下，则存在这种可能性。因为，当 $\alpha \neq 0$ 时，地方官员 i 的努力对地区 j 增长速度的影响 θyx 就通过 i 对竞争对手的关注（αv_j）进入自己的效用函数。这时，地方官员 i 在实现自身效用最大化的过程中，必然会考虑这种外部性。

在一般情形下，地方政府官员 i 效用最大化的条件是

$$\frac{\partial U_i}{\partial x} = 0 \Rightarrow m - 2x + \theta y + \alpha\theta y = 0 \tag{10}$$

(10)式显然是地方政府官员 i 最优努力程度的反应函数。与(7)式相比，(10)式等式右边多了一项 $\alpha\theta y$，它反映了地方政府官员 i 考虑到了其自身的努力对地区 j 经济增长的影响。

同理，我们可得地方政府官员 j 最优努力程度的反应函数为

$$m - 2y + \theta x(1+\beta) = 0 \tag{11}$$

联立(7)式和(8)式就可得地方政府 i 和 j 的均衡努力程度，即

$$x^* = m\frac{2+\theta(1+\alpha)}{4-\theta^2(1+\alpha)(1+\beta)}$$

$$y^* = m\frac{2+\theta(1+\beta)}{4-\theta^2(1+\alpha)(1+\beta)} \tag{12}$$

(12)式具有很强的经济含义，我们将其概括为命题1。

命题1：当 $\theta \neq 0$ 时，地方政府官员最优的努力程度具有以下性质：

① $\frac{\partial x^*}{\partial \beta} > 0$；$\frac{\partial y^*}{\partial \alpha} > 0$；

② 当 $\theta\alpha > 0$ 时，$x^*(\alpha, \alpha) = y^*(\alpha, \alpha) > \bar{x} = \bar{y}$；

③ 当 $\theta\alpha < 0$ 时，$x^*(\alpha, \alpha) = y^*(\alpha, \alpha) < \bar{x} = \bar{y}$。

证明：由(12)式显然可得①。当 $\alpha = \beta$ 时，(12)式可以表示为 $x^*(\alpha, \alpha) = y^*(\alpha, \alpha) = m/[2-\theta(1+\alpha)]$，与(9)式比较可得②和③。证毕。

命题1中的①揭示了，当存在外部性时，竞争对手越关注，地方官员越努力。这符合人们的直观认识。通常，人们越被别人关注，越要好好表现，这样才可能在竞争中胜出。

命题1中的②和③揭示了，当地方政府可以把其外部性内部化时，可能会出现的四种结果。具体而言，当经济体里存在正外部性时（$\theta > 0$），如果进行区域一体化，即 $\alpha > 0$，则地方政府官员均衡的努力水平高于基准水平；反之，如果进行市场分割，即 $\alpha < 0$，则地方政府官员均衡的努力水平将低于基准水平。当经济体里存在负外部性时（$\theta < 0$），如果两个地区进行市场分割，即 $\alpha < 0$，则地方政府官员的努力程度大于基准水平；而进行区域一体化合作，即 $\alpha > 0$，则地方政府官员的努力程度将低于基准水平。

地方政府官员关注其竞争对手晋升，是否会提高自身晋升可能性呢？命题2给出了回答。

命题2：当 $\alpha = \beta$ 且 $\theta \neq 0$ 时，$v_i = v_j$ 且 $\frac{\partial v_i(x^*(\alpha, \alpha), y^*(\alpha, \alpha))}{\partial \alpha} > 0$；

当 $\alpha < \beta$ 且 $\theta \neq 0$ 时，$v_i(x^*(\alpha, \beta), y^*(\alpha, \beta)) > v_j(x^*(\alpha, \beta), y^*(\alpha, \beta))$。

证明：当 $\alpha = \beta$ 时，$x^*(\alpha, \alpha) = y^*(\alpha, \alpha) = m/[2-\theta(1+\alpha)]$，代入晋升函数，得 $v_i = v_j = m^2(1-\alpha\theta)/[2-\theta(1+\alpha)]^2$，对 α 求

导即得前半部分的结论。当 $\alpha \neq \beta$ 时，把 x^* 和 y^* 代入晋升函数可得，$v_i - v_j \geqslant [m^2\theta^2(\beta-\alpha)(1-\alpha\beta)]/[4-\theta^2(1+\alpha)(1+\beta)]^2$。因此，当 $\beta > \alpha$ 且 $\theta \neq 0$ 时，$v_i > v_j$。证毕。

命题2揭示了，地方政府官员在晋升竞争中相互关注对方的晋升，对自身晋升可能性的影响大致有两种情况。第一种情况是，当两个地方政府官员相互关注的程度一样时，在均衡情况下，二者的晋升可能性是一样的。这时，如果两个地方政府选择区域一体化，那么二者的经济增长将更快，从而比不选择区域一体化的其他地方政府官员具有更多的晋升可能性，即当 $0 < \alpha = \beta$ 时，$v_i(\bar{x}, \bar{y}) = v_j(\bar{x}, \bar{y}) < v_i(x^*, y^*) = v_j(x^*, y^*)$。其实，如果我们根据地方政府官员在晋升竞争中的相互关注程度把 n 个地方政府官员划分为几大类，第一种情况揭示了，每类地方政府官员的晋升可能性是一样的，但不同类的地方政府官员的晋升可能性是不一样的，它随着相互关注程度的增加而增加。另外一种情况是，在晋升竞争中，地方政府官员更多地关注竞争对手的晋升，会降低自身的晋升可能性、增进对手的晋升可能性。这也是文献里通常强调的，合作者具有偏离的动机，就本文而言，每个地方政府官员为了自身晋升最大化有降低关注对手程度的动机。需要强调的是，这并不意味着地方政府在晋升竞争中一定选择市场分割。因为，由第一种情况可知，一群选择市场分割的地方政府官员，大家的晋升可能性皆比较低，这时如果一个地方政府选择区域合作而获得更大晋升可能性，那么其他地方政府官员也会理性地选择合作，结果区域一体化地区在晋升竞争中脱颖而出。当然，在区域一体化的地方政府间，如果一个地方政府选择市场分割从而获得更大晋升可能性，那么其他地方政府官员也会理性地选择市场分割，从而区域一体化的地区在晋升竞争中土崩瓦解。

(四) 晋升最大化的发展战略

在均衡时,地方政府官员的努力程度及其晋升可能性皆取决于竞争双方的偏好参数 α 和 β,即对不同发展战略的偏好程度。在本部分,我们将着重考察地方政府选择哪种类型的发展战略才能够在晋升竞争中胜出,即寻找使地方政府晋升最大化的 α^* 和 β^*。

在晋升竞争中,地方政府官员 i 和 j 的偏好参数分别是 α 和 β。为了表达的方便,我们把地方政府官员 i 的晋升函数表示为 $R(\alpha, \beta) \equiv v_i(x^*(\alpha, \beta), y^*(\alpha, \beta))$,其中 $R(\cdot, \cdot)$ 中的第一、二个参数分别是地方政府官员 i 和 j 的偏好参数。显然,这时地方政府官员 j 的晋升函数就可以表示为 $R(\beta, \alpha)$,即晋升竞争是一个对称博弈。

我们将采用进化稳定策略(evolutionarily stable strategy, ESS)来刻画地方政府官员在晋升竞争中能够实现晋升最大化的发展战略。所谓进化稳定策略是指,地方政府官员的偏好参数 α^* 满足

$$R(\alpha^*, \alpha^*) \geqslant R(\alpha, \alpha^*), \ \forall \alpha \in [-1, 1] \tag{13}$$

当 $R(\alpha^*, \alpha^*) = R(\alpha, \alpha^*)$ 时,

$$R(\alpha^*, \alpha) > R(\alpha, \alpha) \tag{14}$$

(13)式表明,在一群偏好参数为 α^* 的地方政府官员中,选择 α^* 最利于晋升,其他选择不会带来更多的晋升机会。(14)式表明,即使其他选择与选择 α^* 一样能够带来相同的晋升可能性,选择 α^* 仍然是最优反应,因为当其他地方政府官员选择 α 时,选择 α^* 的地方政府官员将获得更大的晋升可能性。联合起来,(13)式和(14)式其实揭示了,进化稳定策略构成了在晋升竞争中能够经得起“优胜劣汰”选择的稳定状态,即进化稳定均衡。

进化稳定策略是由 Smith 和 Price(1973)提出的一个基本

均衡概念，能够较好地刻画地方政府晋升竞争的情况。因为，在中央政府根据经济绩效晋升地方政府官员的过程中，如果选择 α^* 的地方政府官员具有很大的晋升可能性，其他地方政府官员就会学习模仿，那么选择 α^* 的一群地方政府官员就在晋升竞争中胜出。

到底哪种类型的发展战略才能够在晋升竞争中胜出呢？命题 3 给出了回答。①

命题 3：当 $\theta \in (-1, 0) \cup (0, 1)$ 时，$\alpha^* = \theta/(2-\theta)$ 是唯一的进化稳定策略。

命题 3 揭示了，地方政府在晋升竞争中所选择的发展战略因条件而异。具体而言，当地方政府官员的努力具有正外部性或正溢出效应时，地方政府官员会理性地偏好于区域一体化，从而将正溢出效应内部化，获得更快的经济增长以及更高的晋升可能性；反之，当存在负外部性或负溢出效应时，地方政府官员会理性地偏好于区域间市场分割，从而将负外部性外部化，以免殃及自身经济增长以及相应的晋升可能性。

命题 3 为长三角城市在 20 世纪 80 年代和 90 年代两种截然不同的选择提供了一个内在逻辑一致的解释，即长三角城市间溢出效应的变化。在 20 世纪 80 年代，中央极力推进长三角一体化，1984 年国务院还成立上海经济区规划办公室。但各个地方政府却选择了市场分割，比如 Young(2000)在其论文中所列举的我国省区采取地方保护、进行各种贸易战的例子，几乎都来源于长三角。到了 1989 年，上海经济区规划办公室被撤销，长三角第一次整合热潮就此结束。但进入 20 世纪 90 年代，长三角却自发地选择了区域一体化。1992 年，14 个城市发起成立

① 证明见附录。

了长三角14城市经济协委(办)主任联席会议①,1997年,14个城市政府又自发组成长江三角洲经济协调会,到2003年,该组织已有16个正式成员。周边的一些城市也纷纷表示要加入这一轮的长三角一体化进程。地方政府的迥异行为根源于长三角城市间溢出效应的变化。"在20世纪80年代,长江三角洲地区可谓群龙无首,领先发展的江浙地区互不买账,更不把上海放在眼里。浦东开发结束了这一离心状态——以上海为龙头、江浙为腹地,长江三角洲地区的经济结构、市场体系、基础设施和城市布局之间的合作分工趋势日益明显。"(洪银兴和刘志彪,2003,第99页)

命题3同时还揭示了,地方政府官员选择的区域一体化程度与市场分割的程度并不是对称的。当经济体里存在负外部性或负溢出效应时,区域间市场分割的程度会随着负外部性程度的增加而增加,最严重时,α^* 接近 $-1/3$,即 $\inf \alpha^* = -1/3$;当经济体里存在正外部性或正溢出效应时,区域间一体化程度会随着正外部性程度的增加而增加,最大时,α^* 接近1,即 $\sup \alpha^* = 1$。这表明,当经济体里的正外部性足够大时,地方政府自下而上的区域一体化行为几乎就可以建立起全国统一开放的大市场。②

在命题3的基础上,可以得到两个有意义的推论:

推论1:当 $\theta \in (-1, 0) \cup (0, 1)$ 时,$x^*(\alpha^*, \alpha^*) > \bar{x}$ 总成立。

证明:当 $\theta \in (-1, 0)$ 时,$\alpha^* = \theta/(2-\theta) < 0$。因此,$\theta\alpha^* > 0$。

---

① 这14个城市是,上海、无锡、宁波、舟山、苏州、扬州、杭州、绍兴、南京、南通、常州、湖州、嘉兴和镇江。

② 当 $\alpha^* = 1$ 时,每个地方政府的偏好是一样的,而且对其他地方政府官员晋升的偏好程度恰好等于对自己晋升的偏好程度,即 $U_i = v_i + v_j$, $\forall i$。

由命题1可知，$x^*(\alpha^*,\alpha^*)>\bar{x}$。当$\theta\in(0,1)$时，$\alpha^*=\theta/(2-\theta)>0$。因此，$\theta\alpha^*>0$。由命题1可知，$x^*(\alpha^*,\alpha^*)>\bar{x}$。证毕。

推论1其实是对命题1的精练。它揭示了，在中央政府按照经济绩效晋升地方政府官员的情况下，如果经济体里存在正外部性，地方政府官员为了晋升最大化则会理性地选择区域一体化，尽量把正外部性内部化，这时均衡的努力程度大于基准的努力程度；反之，地方政府官员则会理性地选择区域市场分割，尽量把负外部性外部化，这时均衡的努力程度也大于基准的努力程度。这表明，在基于经济增长绩效的人事考核体系下，无论地方政府官员是选择市场分割还是区域一体化都会努力工作。从这种意义上说，中央基于经济绩效晋升地方政府官员能够有效地激励地方政府官员努力工作。①其实，这一点正是文献的最新进展所强调的，如Li和Zhou(2005)、周黎安等(2005)等。张军(2005)更是明确指出，基于经济绩效晋升地方政府官员解决了我国经济增长的动力和动能问题。

推论2：当$\theta=\{\theta_1,\theta_2\}$且$\theta_1>0\geqslant\theta_2$时，经济体将分为一体化和非一体化区域，且$g(\alpha^*(\theta_1),\alpha^*(\theta_1))>g(\alpha^*(\theta_2),\alpha^*(\theta_2))$；$v(\alpha^*(\theta_1),\alpha^*(\theta_1))>v(\alpha^*(\theta_2),\alpha^*(\theta_2))$。

由命题3和命题2显然可得推论2。推论2明确了地方政府官员在区际关系上晋升最大化的发展战略的绩效。具体而言，它不仅指出，当经济体里同时存在正、负外部性时，一部分地方政府官员则会理性地选择一体化，而另外一部分则选择非一体化，从而经济体里出现一体化区域与非一体化区域并存的现象；而且明确指出，一体化区域将比非一体化区域增长得更快，从而

① 这为我国各级地方政府整日忙于改善当地投资环境、招商引资，甚至经营城市等提供了一个脚注。

一体化区域的地方政府官员具有更多的晋升可能性。①这与新经济增长文献中的结论是一致的，如 Rivera 和 Romer(1991)证明了发达国家间的经济一体化能够提高经济增长速度。

三、实 证 分 析

本文的实证分析还是初步的，因为我们暂时还无法直接从命题 3 出发实证分析我国地方政府在区际关系上的行为。尽管如此，推论 2 还是为实证检验本文的理论预测提供了一种可能性。基于此，本部分重点实证分析地方政府官员选择区域一体化是否具有更多的晋升可能性。考虑到 Li 和 Zhou(2005)、周黎安等(2005)已经发现，我国省级官员在任期间的平均增长速度对其晋升有显著的正的影响，我们将重点实证分析，地方政府官员选择区域一体化时，是否可能取得更高的平均经济增长。

(一) 实证模型

结合式(4)、式(5)与实证经济增长文献中的通常做法，我们把区域 i 的平均增长速度表示为

$$g^{i}_{t,\,t+T} = mx - x^{2} + \theta xy + \beta\ln(ay^{i}_{t}) + X^{i}\Psi \tag{15}$$

式(15)中，$g^{i}_{t,\,t+T}$ 是区域 i 在 t 到 $t+T$ 期的平均增长速度；等式右边的前三项其实就是式(4)、式(5)，刻画地方政府官员的努力程度；ay^{i}_{t} 是区域 i 在初始时刻 t 的人均 GDP；$X^{i}=(\ln x^{i}_{1},\ \ln x^{i}_{2},\ \cdots,\ \ln x^{i}_{K})'$ 是刻画区域 i 稳定状态的列向量(一组对数形式的控制变量)；β 和 $\Psi=(\alpha_{1},\alpha_{2},\cdots,\alpha_{K})'$ 是参数。其实，如果 $\beta<0$，则式(15)就是著名的 Barro 回归方程。因此，每个区域

① 毋庸置疑，一体化的市场将会带来自由贸易论者所强调的部分或全部好处。

为式(15)所刻画意味着,每个区域的经济增长速度与其自身初始状态到其稳定状态的差距大致成反比。采用式(15)刻画每个区域的经济增长是比较符合实际的。因为,跨国趋同文献揭示了在跨国层面上存在条件β趋同,具有代表性的文献。如 Barro 和 Sala-i-Martin(1992)、Mankiw 等(1992);国内大量文献揭示了,不仅我国省区间存在条件β趋同(蔡昉等,2002);而且地级及以上城市间也存在趋同(徐现祥和李郇,2004)。

由式(15)和推论 2 可得命题 4[①],

命题 4:当$\theta=\{\theta_1, \theta_2\}$且$\theta_1>0\geqslant\theta_2$时,

$$g^i_{t,\,t+T}-g^{-i}_{t,\,t+T}=\gamma \mathrm{dum}+\beta\ln\left(\frac{ay^i_t}{ay^{-i}_t}\right)+(X^i-X^{-i})\Psi, \quad (16)$$

其中,$\gamma>0$;$-i$表示区域i以外的其他经济体;dum 是对地方政府官员努力的一种度量,具体取值是,当一体化区域与非一体化区域比较时为 1,其他为 0。

证明:由推论 2 可知,当$\theta=\{\theta_1, \theta_2\}$且$\theta_1>0\geqslant\theta_2$时,经济体分为一体化区域,记为$A=\{j\mid\theta^j=\theta_1\}$,和非一体化区域,记为$B=\{j\mid\theta^j=\theta_2\}$。设$i\in A$,则$-i\in A$或$-i\in B$。(15)式代入(16) 式得$g^i_{t,\,t+T}-g^{-i}_{t,\,t+T}=m(x-y)-(x^2-y^2)+\beta\ln(y^i_t/y^{-i}_t)+(X^i-X^{-i})\Psi$。当$-i\in A$时,由命题 1 可知,地方政府官员$i$和$-i$的均衡努力水平相等,因此$\{m(x-y)-(x^2-y^2)\}=0$。不妨记$\gamma\mathrm{dum}=m(x-y)-(x^2-y^2)$,其中$\mathrm{dum}=0$,$\forall\gamma$。当$-i\in B$时,由推论 2 可知,$\{m(x-y)-(x^2-y^2)\}$是大于零的常数,同样可表示为$\gamma\mathrm{dum}=m(x-y)-(x^2-y^2)$,其中$\mathrm{dum}=1$,$\gamma>0$。证毕。

---

① 命题 4 与徐现祥和李郇(2005)中的命题 2 类似。

命题 4 的经济含义值得我们强调。一是它提供了一种度量地方政府官员均衡努力程度的可能性，尽管我们在模型中已经求出均衡状态的努力水平，但是在实证分析中，我们很难直接度量它。二是提供了一个考察市场一体化与经济增长、官员晋升的实证分析框架。(16)式中，等式左边刻画的是区域间平均增长速度的差距，显然，如果等式右边中的系数 γ 显著大于零，则表明地方政府官员选择区域一体化有利于本区域的经济增长，从而有利于自身的晋升。三是它保持了 Barro 回归方程的基本性质。如果在(15)式中 $\beta < 0$ 成立，那么在(16)式中显然也成立。考虑到本文主题，我们最关心的系数当然是 γ，预期 $\gamma > 0$。

(二) 实证分析对象与数据来源

实证分析对象是我国的长三角地区。选择长三角地区主要是因为，长三角地区不仅是我国经济发展发展水平最高的区域，而且围绕着长江口形成了一个发展的自然整体；1992 年，长三角 14 个市经协委(办)发起成立长三角 14 城市经协委(办)主任联席会，开始了自下而上的一体化进程，1997 年，14 市政府通过平等协商，自愿组成新的协调组织——长江三角洲城市经济协调会，目前是我国区域一体化发展最好的地区。[①]基于此，全国省区可分为一体化区域和非一体化区域，[②]前者包括江苏、浙江和上海；后者是全国的其他省区。

本文所采用省区数据全部来源于刘明兴和章奇整理的《1970—1999 中国经济增长数据》，样本区间是 1992—1999 年。[③]

---

① 关于长三角一体化的详细发展历程请参阅徐现祥和李郇(2005)。

② 泛珠三角是 2003 年底提出，2004 年开始实践的。考虑到本文采用的是 2004 年以前的数据，我们还是把泛珠三角的 9 省区视为非一体化区域。

③ 数据库的原始样本区间本来是 1970—1999 年，选择 1992—1999 年是因为长三角一体化的实践始于 1992 年。

该数据库包括港澳台、西藏和海南以外的 28 省区①,由于(16)式采用的是横向比值,我们实证分析中的样本是 378 个($C_{28}^2=378$),其中一体化区域的是 3 个($C_3^2=3$),非一体化区域的是 300 个($C_{25}^2=300$),跨区的是 75 个($C_3^1C_{25}^1=75$)。

(三) 回归结果

在实证分析中,我们把(16)式具体表示为

$$g_{t,\,t+T}^{i}-g_{t,\,t+T}^{-i}=c+\gamma\mathrm{dum}+\beta\ln\left(\frac{ay_t^i}{ay_t^{-i}}\right)+\alpha_1\ln\left(\frac{s^i}{s^{-i}}\right)+\alpha_2\ln\left(\frac{\mathrm{FDI}^i}{\mathrm{FDI}^{-i}}\right)+\alpha_3\ln\left(\frac{\mathrm{TCI}^i}{\mathrm{TCI}^{-i}}\right)+\varepsilon \quad (17)$$

其中,g、s、FDI 和 TCI 分别表示 1992—1999 年间平均的人均实际收入的增长率、投资率(资本形成总额占 GDP 比重)、外商投资与 GDP 之比和发展战略选择指数②;ay 是 1992 年的人均实际 GDP。回归结果见表 1。

由表 1 中的回归方程(1)可知,与命题 4 预期的一致,γ 显著为正。具体而言,在 1992—1999 年间,长三角一体化区域的平均增长速度显著比全国其他非一体化区域高 1.1 个百分点。

当引入初始收入水平等控制变量后,由回归方程(2)可知,γ 仍然能够通过显著水平为 1% 的检验,而且大小几乎没有变化。就控制变量而言,与实证分析我国省区趋同文献中的发现完全一致,$\ln(ay)$ 的回归系数显著为负,即我国省区间存在条件趋同;其他控制变量如 ln(FDI)、$\ln(s)$ 和 ln(TCI) 也是显著的,而且回归系数的符号与现有文献的发现一致。另外,随着这些

① 重庆仍然被视为四川的一部分。

② 发展战略选择指数是按照各省各工业部门总产值加权计算的工业技术选择指数。

表 1　回归结果

	(1)	(2)	(3)	(4)	(5)	(6)	(7)	(8)
省区固定效应	无	无	有	有	有	有	有	有
dum	0.011 (7.4)***	0.015 (6.4)***	0.016 (3.5)***		0.016 (2.7)***	0.016 (3.2)***		0.015 (3.0)***
dum7891				0.020 (4.2)***			0.030 (6.6)***	
dum9299				0.027 (5.5)***			0.036 (5.8)***	
The Inverse Mill's Ratio					−0.014 (−2.4)**			−0.008 (2.8)***
ln(*ay*)		−0.027 (−11.2)***	−0.037 (−14.3)***	−0.028 (−15.2)***	−0.046 (−9.2)***			
ln(*y*)						−0.011 (−6.2)***	−0.007 (−5.9)***	−0.020 (−5.1)***
ln(FDI)		0.010 (15.5)***	0.012 (17.8)***	0.009 (20.1)***	0.013 (14.1)***	0.013 (12.4)***	0.009 (18.7)***	0.017 (9.7)***
ln(*s*)		0.038 (6.0)***	0.063 (9.6)***	0.043 (10.3)***	0.078 (8.7)***	0.027 (2.6)***	0.020 (4.3)***	0.024 (2.5)**

（续表）

	(1)	(2)	(3)	(4)	(5)	(6)	(7)	(8)
省区固定效应	无	无	有	有	有	有	有	有
ln(TCI)		−0.008 (−2.5)**	−0.01 (−3.6)***	−0.006 (−2.0)**	−0.003 (−0.7)	0.008 (1.5)	0.009 (5.8)***	0.019 (3.1)***
Adj-R^2	0.04	0.54	0.71	0.58	0.71	0.54	0.47	0.55
F	18.0***	88.7***	29.7***	333***	29.4***	14.8***	21.6***	19.0***
N	378	378	378	756	378	378	756	378
H_0: dum7891 =dum9299				7.7***			2.8*	

注：括号内是 t 值；***、**、* 分别表示通过显著水平为1%、5%和10%的检验；(5)和(8)是采用 Heckit 法估计。

常见控制变量的引入，回归方程的拟合度从4%上升到54%。

考虑到在实证分析中如果忽视各个省区的个体固定差异，回归结果可能是有偏的（Islam，1995），我们进一步估计28个省区的固定效应。具体做法是，在式(17)中，以 $\sum c_i d_i$ 取代 c 刻画每个城市的固定效应，d_i 的取值是，在横向比较中，与 i 相比的为1，其他为0。[①]从回归方程(3)看，与回归方程(2)对比，引入各省区固定效应后，γ 仍然能够通过显著水平为1%的检验，而且大小几乎没有变化。控制变量仍然显著，回归系数确实都发生了变化，回归方程的拟合度也上升到71%。

不可否认，长三角一直是我国经济增长较快的地区之一。回归方程4揭示了，长三角在自发选择区域一体化之前的增长速度就比其他地区高，但选择区域一体化后，增长速度比其他地区更高。在回归方程4中，我们把各省区的数据追溯到1978年。考虑到长三角在1978—1991年间没有自发选择区域一体化，而在1992—1999年间自发选择了区域一体化，从而构成一个两阶段的面板数据，样本个数是756(2×378=756)，采用广义最小二乘法的估计结果见表1中的回归方程4。从回归结果看，长三角在选择一体化之前，其增长速度显著地比其他地区高2个百分点，选择一体化之后，比其他地区高2.7个百分点；而且由表1中最后一行的Wald检验可知，二者显著不同。这表明，尽管长三角一直保持了快速增长，但自发选择区域一体化后，增长速度比其他地区更高，大致提高了0.7个百分点。其他控制变量与回归方程2和3相比，并没有发生实质性变化。

总之，回归方程(1)到(4)揭示了，长三角的地方政府官员自

---

① 徐现祥和李郇(2005)在考察长三角一体化对区域协调发展时采取了这种做法，Engel和Rogers(1996)在考察美国、加拿大间边界效应时也采取了这种做法。

1992年自发选择区域一体化实践后，平均增长速度显著比全国其他非一体化区域高。

（四）稳健性检验

上小节中的回归结果是否稳健？我们将从以下三个方面进一步验证。

1. 一体化的内生性问题

实证分析旨在考察地方政府官员选择区域一体化时，是否能取得更高的经济增长。为了实现这一点，我们不得不处理地方政府选择一体化的内生性问题。因为，加入一体化并不是随机选择的，而是满足一定条件时（比如命题3），地方政府才会选择，这是典型的由样本选择所带来的偏差问题。我们运用Heckman(1979)的两步法（the two step procedure），即通过构造逆米尔斯比率（The Inverse Mills Ratio）对地方政府的自我选择进行控制。[①]

回归方程(5)报告了引入逆米尔斯比率的回归结果。[②]逆米尔斯比的t值为−2.4，能够通过显著水平为5%的检验，这意味着，确实存在样本选择问题，回归方程(3)的估计结果有偏。但是，当我们控制了地方政府的自我选择行为后，回归结果没有发生实质性的变化。γ仍然能够通过显著水平为1%的检验，而且大小根本没有变化；控制变量大都显著，只是回归系数略微变化；回归方程的拟合度也没有发生变化，仍然为71%。

---

① 在计量经济学文献中，这种方法也被称之为Heckit方法（Wooldridge，2005，第589页）。

② Probit的回归结果为$P(\text{dum}=1\mid z)=\Phi(z\hat{\alpha})$，其中$z\hat{\alpha}=-2.1+\underset{(4.2)}{0.85}\ln(ay)-\underset{(-1.3)}{0.07}\ln(\text{FDI})-\underset{(-3.1)}{1.75}\ln(s)-\underset{(-3.0)}{0.8}\ln(\text{TCI})+\underset{(2.4)}{0.57}\text{share}$，share是全国28个省区通过铁路运输的省间贸易的比重，转引自叶裕民(2000)中的表1，原始数据是根据1998年《中国交通年鉴》计算。括号内是Z值。LR统计量是75，能够通过显著水平为1%的检验。

2. 实际GDP增长速度与实际人均GDP增长速度

考虑到Li和Zhou(2005)、周黎安等(2005)采用的是实际GDP增长率,而不是实际人均GDP增长率,我们同样采用实际GDP增长率为被解释变量,回归结果见回归方程(6)到(8)。需要明确的是,在回归分析中,由于被解释变量是实际GDP增长率,相应的初始水平也就是各省区1992年的实际GDP。

采用实际GDP增长率度量经济绩效,结果并没有发生实质性变化。与回归方程(3)相比,回归方程(6)同样揭示了,γ能够通过显著水平为1%的检验,而且大小没有变化;控制变量没有发生多少实质性变化,唯一的变化是,ln(TCI)的回归系数不显著或者符号与现有文献中的发现相反。与回归方程(4)相比,回归方程(7)同样揭示了,尽管长三角一直保持了快速增长,但自发选择区域一体化后,增长速度比其他地区更高,大致提高了0.6个百分点。就其他控制而言,也没有发生多少实质性变化。

在回归方程(8)中,我们还是运用Heckman(1979)的两步法对地方政府的自我选择进行控制。① 从回归方程看,逆米尔斯比的t值为−2.8,能够通过显著水平为5%的检验,确实存在样本选择问题,但是回归结果并没有发生任何实质性变化。

3. 基于江浙沪下辖的城市样本

确切地说,长三角一体化是江苏中部的8市、浙江北部的7市和上海市的实践,并非江苏、浙江全部城市的实践。因此,江苏、浙江和上海本身就可以划分为由16个城市组成的一体化区域和其他8个地级城市组成的非一体化区域。这时,样本总数

① *Probit*的回归结果为$P(\text{dum}=1\mid x)=\Phi(x\hat{\beta})$,其中$x\hat{\beta}=-3.8+\underset{(7.1)}{1.77}\ln(\text{FDI})-\underset{(-6.3)}{0.76}\ln(\text{FDI})-\underset{(-1.2)}{0.69}\ln(s)-\underset{(-6.4)}{2.17}\ln(\text{TCI})+\underset{(5.3)}{1.59}\text{share}$,括号内是Z值。*LR*统计量是130,能够通过显著水平为1%的检验。

是 276 个,其中一体化区域的是 120 个($C_{16}^{2}=120$),非一体化区域的是 28 个($C_{8}^{2}=28$),跨区的是 128 个($C_{16}^{1}C_{8}^{1}=128$)。本部分所采用的原始数据是市区人均 GDP,样本区间是 1992—2002 年,其中 1998 年以前的数据来源于《新中国城市 50 年》,1999—2002 年的数据来自《中国城市统计年鉴》(2000—2003)。由于没有找到样本区间内按可比价格计算的 GDP,GDP 是按照名义价格计算的。回归结果见表 2。

表 2　基于城市样本的回归结果

	(9)	(10)	(11)	(12)	(13)
城市固定效应	无	无	有	无	有
dum	0.017 (2.4)**	0.029 (5.3)***	0.031 (6.2)***		
dum9297				0.016 (2.3)**	0.017 (2.5)**
dum9702				0.044 (6.6)**	0.044 (7.5)***
ln(ay)		−0.057 (−11.2)***	−0.056 (−12.4)***	−0.54 (−10.7)***	−0.059 (−11.9)***
Adj-R^2	0.02	0.353	0.63	0.20	0.44
F	5.9**	68.7***	19.9***	46.0***	17.8
N	276	276	276	552	552
$H0$:dum9297 =dum9702				25.7***	64.3***

注:括号内是 t 值;***、**、* 分别表示通过显著水平为 1%、5% 和 10% 的检验。

由回归方程(9)可知,与基于省区样本的回归结果一致,γ 显著为正,仍然在 0.015 左右。具体而言,在 1992—2002 年间,长三角一体化的 16 个城市的经济增长比其他城市显著高了 1.7 个百分点。

当引入初始人均收入水平后，如回归方程(10)所示，$\gamma=0.03$，而且能够通过显著水平为1%的统计检验。$\ln(ay)$的回归系数显著为负，即江苏、浙江和上海下辖的24个地级及以上城市间存在趋同。这与我国趋同文献中的发现是一致的，徐现祥和李郇(2004)已经发现我国202个地级及以上城市间存在绝对趋同。当进一步引入各城市固定效应后，如回归方程(11)所示，与回归方程(10)相比，回归结果没有发生任何实质性变化。

考虑到1997年，长三角城市成立了长江三角洲城市经济协调会，进一步推动长三角地区一体化进程，我们把样本区间限定为1992—1997年和1997—2002年，从而构成一个面板数据，采用广义最小二乘法的估计结果见表2中的回归方程(12)和(13)。从回归结果看，在成立长江三角洲城市经济协调会之前，长三角一体化的16个城市的经济增长比其他城市显著高了1.7个百分点左右，但成立之后，比其他城市显著高4.4个百分点，提高了2.7个百分点。由表2中最后一列的Wald检验可知，这种变化是显著的。这表明，随着一体化进程的推进，一体化地区的经济增长速度更快，从而地方政府获得更多的晋升可能性。显然，这与命题2相吻合。

至此，我们可以得出结论，长三角的地方政府官员自发选择区域一体化实践后，平均增长速度显著比全国其他非一体化区域高，而且这个发现是稳健的。结合Li和Zhou(2005)、周黎安等(2005)的实证发现，我们可以推论出，在当前的政绩观下，长三角的地方政府官员选择区域一体化实践后确实可获得更高的晋升可能性。①

① 《南方周末》先后在《政坛瞩目"苏州现象"》(2004年11月18日)和《任职中西部的东部高官们》(2006年7月6日)中报道了这种现象。

(五) 直接的微观证据

作为补充，我们将进一步考察，如果地方政府官员选择市场一体化，消除地方保护、市场分割，那么企业的经济收益是否显著增加，从而为上面的结论提供直接的微观证据。

世界银行和中国国务院发展研究中心在 2003 年发起的一次关于地方保护的调查中特意询问了企业如下的问题，如果消除地方保护主义，经济产出将会发生怎样的变化？龚冰琳等(2005)基于 12 个省区 1 101 家企业的回答，发现，如果消除地方保护、市场分割，那么企业总收入(等于产品价格与销售量的乘积)预计将平均增长 3.5%—9%，每个省区的情况如表 3 所示。

表 3　预计平均收入增长率

省　份	企业数量	平均收入增长率(%)
贵　州	92	9.12
江　苏	47	8.74
青　海	22	7.98
河　南	71	7.61
云　南	73	7.57
湖　南	186	6.98
上　冻	105	6.84
陕　西	74	6.41
四　川	110	5.04
福　建	64	4.36
上　海	83	3.91
黑龙江	84	3.51

数据来源：龚冰琳等(2005)表 5。

以上分析表明，直接的微观证据与本文基于长三角所发现的宏观层面的证据是一致的。因为，在地方政府官员选择市场一体化、消除地方保护的过程中，如果企业的经济收益预计显著增加了，那么我们有理由相信经济体在宏观层面上的经济绩效也应随之改善，从而地方政府的财政收入和政治晋升可能性也应随之提高。

四、结论性评述

建设全国统一开放的大市场是我国经济转轨的重要目标之一，但在转轨过程中，不仅存在市场分割问题，而且还存在区域一体化现象。理性的地方政府何时选择市场分割，何时选择区域一体化？本文从地方政府官员晋升竞争的角度展开讨论。

在理论上，我们构造了一个简单的地方政府晋升博弈模型，证明了在中央根据经济绩效晋升地方政府官员的情况下，地方政府官员为了晋升最大化，既可能选择市场分割也可能选择区域一体化，因条件而异，从而为地方政府官员在区际关系上的迥异行为提供了一个具有内在逻辑一致性的解释。另外两个结论也值得强调。一是我们证明了中央基于经济绩效晋升地方政府官员能够有效地激励地方政府官员努力工作，为现有的实证文献(Li and Zhou，2005；周黎安等，2005 等)提供了理论基础。另一个是，我们还证明了，当条件成熟时，理性的地方政府会自发地选择区域一体化，而且最终几乎可以成就全国统一开放的大市场。

在实证上，考虑到 Li 和 Zhou(2005)、周黎安等(2005)已经发现省级官员在任期间的平均增长速度对其晋升有显著的正的影响，我们着重分析，已选择区域一体化的地方政府是否取得了更快的经济增长。以长三角为例，我们发现，长三角的地方政府官员自 1992 年选择区域一体化实践后，平均增长速度显著地比全国其他非一体化区域高，而且我们采用 Heckman(1979)两步法克服了样本选择所带来的偏差，该发现是稳健的。这意味着，与理论模型的预期一致，当条件成熟时，地方政府官员选择区域一体化可获得更快的经济增长、更高的晋升可能性。

当然，本文的实证分析还是初步的。如何从政治晋升的角度直接检验地方政府在区际关系上的行为，还有待进一步研究。

附录：命题 3 的证明分为以下六步：

第一步　证明当 $\theta \neq 0$ 时，$\frac{\partial R}{\partial \alpha}=0$ 的内点解是 $\alpha^{*}=\frac{\theta}{2-\theta}$ 或 $\alpha^{*}=-\frac{\theta+2}{\theta}$。

$R(\alpha, \beta)$ 对 α 求导，令一阶条件 $\frac{\partial R}{\partial \alpha}=0$，整理得

$$\frac{\theta}{2+\theta(1+\alpha)}+\frac{2\theta^{2}(1+\beta)}{4-\theta^{2}(1+\alpha)(1+\beta)}=\frac{\theta+\theta^{2}(1+\beta)}{2+\theta(1-\alpha)-\theta^{2}\alpha(1+\beta)} \tag{A1}$$

令 $\alpha^{*}=\alpha=\beta$，(A1) 式整理可得，当 $\theta \neq 0$ 时，$\alpha_{1}^{*}=\frac{\theta}{2-\theta}$，$\alpha_{2}^{*}=-\frac{\theta+2}{\theta}$。

第二步　证明 $\alpha_{2}^{*}=-\frac{\theta+2}{\theta}$ 不是进化稳定策略。

当 $\alpha_{2}^{*}=-\frac{\theta+2}{\theta}$ 时，$R\left(\alpha,-\frac{2+\theta}{\theta}\right)=\frac{m^{2}}{4}$，$\forall \alpha$，满足(13)式，但不满足(14) 式，因为 $R\left(-\frac{2+\theta}{\theta}, \alpha\right)>R(\alpha, \alpha) \Rightarrow 0>\frac{1-\alpha \theta}{[2-\theta(1+\alpha)]^{2}} \Rightarrow \alpha \theta>1$。矛盾。

第三步　证明边界值 $\alpha=1$ 不是进化稳定策略。

$R(1, 1) = \frac{m^2}{4(1-\theta)} \geqslant R(\alpha, 1)$，$\forall \alpha$。显然 $R(1, 1) \geqslant R(\alpha, 1)$ 并不总是成立，即不满足(13)式。

第四步　证明当 $\theta = 0$ 时不存在进化稳定策略。当 $\theta = 0$ 时，$R(\alpha, \beta) \equiv \frac{m^2}{4}$，不满足(14)式。

第五步　证明当 α^* 是进化稳定策略时，α^* 唯一，且 $\alpha^* = \frac{\theta}{2-\theta}$。由以上四步显然可得。

第六步　证明当 $\theta \in (-1, 0) \cup (0, 1)$ 时，$\alpha^* = \frac{\theta}{2-\theta}$ 是进化稳定策略。当 $\alpha^* = \frac{\theta}{2-\theta}$ 时，(13) 式 $R\left(\frac{\theta}{2-\theta}, \frac{\theta}{2-\theta}\right) \geqslant R\left(\alpha, \frac{\theta}{2-\theta}\right)$ 等价于

$$\frac{m2\theta^2(2+\theta)(2-\theta)[\theta(1+\alpha)-2\alpha]^2}{16(1-\theta)[\theta^2(1+\alpha)+2\theta-4]^2} \geqslant 0 \qquad \text{(A2)}$$

显然，当 $\theta \in (-1, 0) \cup (0, 1)$ 时，对 $\forall \alpha$，(A2)式恒成立。另外，(A2)式同时还揭示了，当 $\alpha \neq \alpha^*$ 时，$R\left(\frac{\theta}{2-\theta}, \frac{\theta}{2-\theta}\right) > R\left(\alpha, \frac{\theta}{2-\theta}\right)$ 恒成立。这表明(14)式成立。证毕。

参考文献

Blanchard, O. and A. Shleifer, 2000, "Federalism with and without political centralization: China versus Russia", NBER Working Paper 7616.

Barro, R. and X. Sala-i-Martin, 1992, "Convergence", *Journal of Political Economy*, 100(2): 223—251.

Besley, T. and A. Case, 1995, "Incumbent Behavior: Vote-Seeking,

Tax-Setting, and Yardstick Competition", *American Economic Review*, 85(1):25—45.

Besley, T., T. Persson and D. Sturm, 2005, "Political Competition and Economic Performance: Theory and Evidence from the United States", NBER Working Paper 11484.

Bester, H. and W., 1998, Güth, "Is Altruism Evolutionarily Stable?", *Journal of Economic Behavior and Organization*, 34(2): 193—209.

Bolle, F., 2000, "Is Altruism Evolutionarily Stable? And Envy and Malevolence?", *Journal of Economic Behavior and Organization*, 42(1): 121—124.

蔡昉等:《制度、趋同与人文发展》,中国人民大学出版社 2002 年版。

Easterly, W. 著,姜世明译:《在增长的迷雾中求索》,中信出版社 2005 年版。

Engel, C. and J. Rogers, 1996, "How Wide Is the Border?" *American Economic Review*, 86(5):1112—1125.

桂琦寒、陈敏、陆铭、陈钊:《中国国内商品市场趋于分割还是整合?》工作论文,http://www.essrc.org/luming/Article/Index.asp, 2004。

龚冰琳、徐立新、陈光炎:《中国的地方保护主义:直接的微观证据》,《经济学报》2005 年第 1 卷第 2 辑。

Heckman, J., 1979, "Sample Selection Bias as a Specification error", *Econometrica*, 47(1):153—161.

洪银兴、刘志彪:《长江三角洲地区经济发展的模式和机制》,清华大学出版社 2003 年版。

Islam, N., 1995, "Growth Empirics: A Panel Data Approach", *Quarterly Journal of Economics*, 110(4):1127—1170.

Jin, H., Y. Qian and B. Weingast, 2005, "Regional Decentralization and Fiscal Incentives: Federalism, Chinese Style", *Journal of Public Economics*, 89(9—10):1719—1742.

Li, H. and L. Zhou, 2005, "Political Turnover and Economic Performance: The Incentive Role of Personnel Control in China", *Journal of Public Economics*, 89(9—10):1743—1762.

李善同、侯永志、刘云中、陈波:《中国国内地方保护问题的调查与分析》,《经济研究》2004 年第 11 期。

林毅夫、刘培林:《地方保护和市场分割:从发展战略的角度考察》,北京大学中国经济研究中心内部讨论稿 No. C2004015, 2004。

刘明兴、章奇, 2005, "China's Economic Growth Data: 1970—2002", http://www.fed.org.cn/data_private.asp。

Lucas, R., 1988, "On the Mechanics of Economic Development", *Journal of Monetary Economics*, 22(1):3—42.

Mankiw, N, D. Romer and D. Weil, 1992, "A Contribution to the Empirics of Economic Growth", *Quarterly Journal of Economics*, 107(2):407—437.

Maskin, E., Y. Qian and C. Xu, 2000, "Incentives, Information, and Organizational Form", *Review of Economic Studies*, 67(2):359—378.

Possajennikov, A., 2000, "On the Evolutionary Stability of Altruistic and Spiteful Preferences", *Journal of Economic Behavior and Organization*, 42(1):125—129.

平新乔:《政府保护的动机与效果——一个实证分析》,北京大学中国经济研究中心内部讨论稿 No. C2003032, 2003。

Qian, Y. and B. Weingast, 1997, "Federalism as a Commitment to Preserving Market Incentives", *Journal of Economic Perspectives*, 11(4):83—92.

Qian, Y. and G. Roland, 1998, "Federalism and the Soft Budget Constrain", *American Economic Review*, 88(5):1143—1162.

Rebelo, S., 1991, "Long-Run Policy Analysis and Long-Run Growth", *Journal of Political Economy*, 99(3):500—521.

Rivera, L. and P. Romer, 1991, "Economic Integration and Endogenous Growth", *Quarterly Journal of Economics*, 106(2):531—555.

Romer, P., 1986, "Increasing Returns and Long-Run Growth",

Journal of Political Economy, 94(5):1002—1037.

Smith, J. and G. Price, 1973, "The Logic of Animal Conflict", *Nature*, 246:15—18.

沈立人、戴园晨:《我国"诸侯经济"的形成及其弊端和根源》,《经济研究》1990 年第 3 期。

Wooldridge, J., *Introductory Econometrics: An Modern Approach* (2nd Edition),清华大学出版社 2005 年版。

徐现祥、李郇:《中国城市经济增长的趋同分析》,《经济研究》2004 年第 5 期。

徐现祥、李郇:《市场一体化与区域协调发展》,《经济研究》2005 年第 12 期。

叶裕民:《中国区际贸易冲突的形成机制与对策思路》,《经济地理》2000 年第 11 期。

银温泉、才婉如:《中国地区间市场分割成因和治理》,《经济研究》2001 年第 6 期。

Young, A., 2000, "The Razor's Edge: Distortions and Incremental Reform in the People's Republic China", *Quarterly Journal of Economics*, 115(4):1091—1135.

张军:《中国经济发展:为增长而竞争》,《世界经济文汇》2005 年第 4—5 期。

周黎安:《晋升博弈中政府官员的激励与合作》,《经济研究》2004 年第 6 期。

周黎安、李宏彬、陈烨:《相对绩效考核:中国地方官员晋升机制的一项经验研究》,《经济学报》2005 年第 1 卷第 1 辑。

朱希伟、金祥荣、罗德明:《国内市场分割与中国的出口贸易扩张》,《经济研究》2005 年第 12 期。

(原载《经济学(季刊)》2007 年第 6 卷第 4 期)

集聚与分散：新经济地理学模型与城市内部空间结构、外部规模经济效应的整合研究*

陈良文　杨开忠

（北京大学政府管理学院）

一、问 题 的 提 出

对经济活动空间集聚现象的解释长期以来一直是城市与区域经济学及其相关学科的核心任务之一，但长期以来，受微观经济学发展、数学工具、计算机模拟技术等的限制，对经济集聚现象的解释一直没有很好地模型化。无论是 Thunen(1826)的农业区位模型还是 Aloson(1964)的土地租金模型，都是在给定经济活动中存在一个中心之后，再分析经济活动的空间特征，实际上都是在非均质空间下进行的分析，无法解释在均质空间中为什么会产生经济向中心集聚的现象。20 世纪 70 年代以来，随着微观经济学、公共经济学、计算机模拟技术、运筹学等的发展，城市与区域经济学领域涌现出了一大批解释经济集聚现象的理

* 本文受到国家自然科学基金重点项目“我国区域城镇化管理的系统研究”（项目资助号：70433002）资助。作者感谢张庆华博士的有益讨论和修改意见，感谢谢燮博士在数值模拟方面的讨论和建议，还要感谢两位匿名审稿人详细的评论和意见。

论模型，形成了一个新的学术高潮。由于导致经济空间集聚的机制是多种多样的，不同的理论模型从不同的机制着手进行解释，但最终的结论都是，即使是在均质空间下，经济自身的力量也会导致经济活动空间分布的不均衡性。其中，Krugman(1991a)等经济学家发展出的新经济地理学具有一定的代表性。

Krugman(1991a)较早地将Dixit和Stiglitz(1977)的垄断竞争模型应用于区域经济学领域，提出了新经济地理学模型的基本框架。其模型的核心集聚力量是消费者对商品的多样性偏好、地区之间运输成本以及厂商内部规模经济同时构成的金融外部性(Pecuniary Externalities)，其模型基本的集聚原理为：集聚在一个区域的厂商越多，当地生产的产品种类越多，在消费者多样性偏好和正的运输成本假设之下，这意味着该地区工业品价格指数更低，这样有更多的工人被吸引到这个区域；工人数量的增加，形成了对差异产品的更大需求，吸引了更多的厂商搬迁到该地区，这样最终会形成经济活动的非均衡分布、出现经济活动的中心—边缘格局。在Krugman之后，M. Fujita，A. Venables，G. Ottaviano，D. Puga等对新经济地理学基本模型做了进一步的拓展，并出现了一批针对新经济地理学模型的实证研究[Davis and Weinstein(1996，1999)，Hanson(1997，1998)等]。

虽然新经济地理学模型对经济活动空间集聚现象具有较好的解释力，但由于新经济地理学模型仅关注地区之间的运输成本，而把各地区(城市)自身视为一个个的点，忽视各地区(城市)内部的空间结构、通勤成本以及土地市场。实际上，城市内部空间结构对经济的集聚程度会有比较大的影响，城市内部的通勤成本、高房价、环境污染等一般被视为导致集聚不经济的因素，显然，新经济地理学模型完全忽视此类因素不尽合理。

与此同时，新经济地理学模型所反映的集聚机制仅仅是金融外部性，忽视了其他类型的外部规模经济，特别是厂商之间的外部规模经济效应。而实际上，自马歇尔以来，知识外溢等外部规模经济效应一直为集聚经济的相关研究所重视，显然，新经济地理学模型对此的忽视与经济现实并不吻合。

正是由于新经济地理学模型面临上述非常关键的两类缺陷，因此，将城市内部空间结构和其他类型的集聚机制整合入新经济地理学模型框架便显得尤为必要。

对于第一类整合，目前已有一些学者进行了非常有益的尝试。Helpman(1995)较早地在新经济地理学模型中引入住宅消费，但并没有对城市内部空间结构进行全面考虑。Brackman等(1996)将不同企业之间的拥挤效应引入新经济地理学模型当中，虽然没有考察城市内部的空间结构，但通过引入拥挤效应将经济中的分散力量纳入模型框架之中，修正了标准的新经济地理学模型。Tabuchi(1998)将Krugman的模型和Aloson的土地租金模型进行了较为全面的整合，在新经济地理学模型框架中引入了城市内部的通勤成本和住宅消费，将消费者的多样性偏好视为经济的集聚力量，而将城市内部通勤成本和住宅消费视为分散力量，模型结论显示经济活动的集聚程度会低于Krugman的标准模型，且当地区间运输成本趋于零时，无论模型中的参数如何赋值，经济活动在两个地区之间的平均分布即分散状态是长期均衡。最近，Anas(2002)将城市内部空间结构纳入新经济地理学模型的框架，并考察了最优城市规模，模型的结论显示，随着城市总人口规模的增加，最优的城市规模不断缩小，即经济的集聚程度不断降低，最终会趋向于所有的经济活动将会完全的分散，每个企业将会单独的布局在一个地区，Anas将此过程称为逆集聚(De-agglomeration)过程。显然，Tabuchi(1998)和Anas(2002)模型的结论都与现实经济世界并不相符：

$$M = \left(\sum_{i}^{N} c_i^{(\delta-1)/\delta} \right)^{\delta/(\delta-1)} \tag{2}$$

其中，c_i 表示消费者对第 i 类制造业产品的消费量，$\delta \geqslant 1$ 是各类制造业产品之间的替代弹性，N 是所有制造业产品的种类，CES 形式的效用函数表明了消费者对制造业产品存在多样化偏好。

假设农业产品为计价单位，其价格标准化为 1，第 i 类制造业产品的价格为 p_i，距离 CBD 地区为 k 处的地租水平为 $r(k)$、向 CBD 地区的通勤成本为 $T(k)$，地区 1 代表性工人的工资水平为 w_1。同时，假设地租为缺位的土地所有者获得。则地区 1 代表性工人面临的预算约束为

$$\sum^{N_1} c_{i1} p_{i1} + \sum^{N_2} c_{i2} p_{i2}/\tau + r(k)S(k) + A + T(k) = w_1 \tag{3}$$

在约束(3)下最优化工人的效用函数可得住房和农业产品的消费量分别为

$$S(k) = \frac{\gamma[w_1 - T(k)]}{r(k)} \tag{4}$$

$$A = (1-\mu-\gamma)[w_1 - T(k)] \tag{5}$$

同时，令 c_{11} 和 c_{12} 分别代表地区 1 工人对地区 1 生产的代表性制造业产品和地区 2 生产的代表性制造业产品的消费量，p_1，p_2 分别为地区 1 生产的代表性产品和地区 2 生产的代表性产品的价格，则根据效用最大化可以求出：

$$\frac{c_{11}}{c_{12}} = \left(\frac{p_2}{p_1 \tau} \right)^{\delta} \tag{6}$$

(二) 生产

下面，我们转向生产者行为，假设经济中劳动总量标准化为 1，其中$(1-\mu)$的比例为农民，且农民在两个地区之间平均分布，

每位农民生产一单位的农产品，因此各地区农业的产量即农民的收入为

$$Y_A = \frac{(1-\mu)}{2} \tag{7}$$

制造业中每个企业都是对称的，使用相同的技术，劳动是唯一的投入要素，企业从事生产需要投入一定的固定成本，表明企业具有内部规模经济。在标准的新经济地理学模型中，企业的生产过程仅考虑内部规模经济，而忽视了企业相互之间的外部经济。

为了弥补传统新经济地理学模型的缺陷，我们在企业的生产过程中引入企业之间的正向外部规模经济效应，即多个企业在空间上的集聚有利于企业之间的知识外溢，从而提高各个企业的产出效率。生产过程之中的外部规模经济效应的系统研究源自马歇尔（Marshall，1890），Ohlin（1933）和 Hoover（1936）等进一步发展相关研究，Mills（1967）和 Henderson（1974）将其较早地引入城市经济学领域，作为城市形成和发展重要的向心力来考虑，之后 Chipman（1970），Abdel-Rahman 等（1990），Michael，Perrot 和 Thisse（1996），Black 和 Henderson（1999），Au 和 Henderson（2005）等大量研究都将马歇尔的外部规模经济效应视做重要的经济集聚力量。

我们用以下的生产函数体现企业内部规模经济和相互之间的正向外部规模经济效应，由于企业是对称的，因此我们仅考虑一个地区的代表性企业，公式中将不再显示企业的下标：

$$x_1 = A(N_1)l_1 - \alpha \tag{8}$$

其中，x_1 表示地区 1 代表性企业的产出，l_1 为劳动投入，N_1 表示地区制造业企业的总量，$A(N_1)$是外部规模经济效应函数且 $A'(N_1) > 0$，集聚于一个地区的制造业企业数量越多，则单位

劳动的边际产出越高，表明了企业之间的正向外部性。α 为企业的固定成本，表明企业平均成本随产量的增加不断下降，用于衡量企业内部规模经济。每个企业都将企业之间的外部规模经济视为给定的，因此决策时不考虑自身行为对外部规模经济程度的影响。为简便起见，我们给出 $A(N_1)$ 的显性形式①：

$$A(N_1)=N_1^{\varepsilon},\ \varepsilon\geqslant 0 \tag{9}$$②

由制造业企业的生产函数可以求出其劳动投入关于产出的函数：

$$l_1=\frac{\alpha+x_1}{A(N_1)}=N_1^{-\varepsilon}(\alpha+x_1) \tag{10}$$

则地区 1 代表性制造企业的利润为

$$\pi_1=p_1x_1-w_1N_1^{-\varepsilon}(\alpha+x_1) \tag{11}$$

由于制造业产品的替代弹性和需求价格弹性均为 δ，因此厂商利润最大化意味着：

$$p_1\left(\frac{\delta-1}{\delta}\right)=w_1N_1^{-\varepsilon} \tag{12}$$

将(12)式代回(11)式并根据制造业企业的均衡利润为零，可以求出制造业企业的均衡产量：

$$x_1^{*}=\alpha(\delta-1) \tag{13}$$

将(13)式代入(10)式可以求出制造业企业的均衡劳动投入：

① Black 和 Henderson(1999)、Au 和 Henderson(2005)等的研究均采取此种函数形式衡量外部规模经济效应。

② $\varepsilon=0$ 表明不存在外部规模经济效应，ε 越大表明外部规模经济效应越强，ε 是衡量外部规模经济效应强弱的指标。

$$l_1^* = N_1^{-\varepsilon}(\alpha\delta) \quad (14)$$

假设地区 1 和地区 2 的制造业工人分别为 L_1、L_2，且满足 $L_1+L_2=\mu$，因此，地区 1 均衡的企业数量（由于企业存在内部规模经济，因此一类产品只有一个企业生产，因此均衡企业数量即为均衡的制造业产品种类）为

$$N_1 = \frac{L_1}{N_1^{-\varepsilon}(\alpha\delta)} \Rightarrow N_1^* = \left(\frac{L_1}{\alpha\delta}\right)^{\frac{1}{1+\varepsilon}} \quad (15)$$

（三）城市内部空间结构

先考察地区 1 的城市内部空间结构。根据城市内部区位均衡的一阶条件：

$$r'(k)S(k)+T'(k)=0 \Leftrightarrow r'(k)S(k)=-T'(k) \quad (16)$$

该区位均衡是城市地租模型的标准一阶条件，表明地租与通勤成本之间存在替代关系，地租随距离 k 的下降意味着通勤成本随 k 的上升。

同时由式(4)可知：

$$S(k)r(k)=\gamma[w_1-T(k)] \quad (4')$$

将(16)式与(4′)式左右两端相除，得：

$$\frac{r'(k)}{r(k)} = \frac{-T'(k)}{\gamma(w_1-T(k))} \Leftrightarrow \gamma \mathrm{dlog}\, r(k) = \mathrm{dlog}(w_1-T(k)) \quad (17)$$

(17)式表明地租随距离 k 的变化率等于工人可支配收入［即 $w_1-T(k)$］随距离 k 的变量率除以 γ，假设城市中心 CBD 地区的地租水平为 r_0，则可以给出城市地租函数：

$$r(k)=r_0(1-T(k)/w_1)^{1/\gamma} \quad (18)$$

这样，由(4)式和(18)式可以求出 k 处均衡的住房消费：

$$S(k)=\frac{\gamma(w_1-T(k))}{r(k)}=\frac{\gamma(w_1-T(k))}{r_0(1-T(k)/w_1)^{1/\gamma}},\tag{19}$$

则区位 k 的人口密度为

$$\frac{1}{S(k)}=\frac{r_0(1-T(k)/w_1)^{\frac{1}{\gamma}-1}}{\gamma w_1}\tag{20}$$

假设区域 1 内的城市边界为$[-b_1, b_1]$，城市边界处地租水平等于农业地租，即 $r(b_1)=r_A$。所有工人都居住在城市边界之内，因此地区 1 内的城市总工人数量为

$$L_1=\int_0^{b_1}\frac{2\pi k}{S(k)}\mathrm{d}k=\frac{2\pi r_A\int_0^{b_1}k(1-T(k)/w_1)^{\frac{1}{\gamma}-1}\mathrm{d}k}{\gamma w_1(1-T(b_1)/w_1)^{\frac{1}{\gamma}}}\tag{21}$$

(四) 两区域均衡

首先，考虑工人在两地区之间区位选择的均衡。由(12)式、(15)式可知两地区制造业产品的价格之比为：

$$\frac{p_2}{p_1}=\frac{w_2N_2^{-\varepsilon}}{w_1N_1^{-\varepsilon}}=\frac{w_2}{w_1}\left(\frac{L_2}{L_1}\right)^{\frac{\varepsilon}{1+\varepsilon}}\tag{22}$$

将(22)式代入(6)式，可求出地区 1 工人对两地区代表性制造业产品的消费量之比为

$$\frac{c_{11}}{c_{12}}=\left(\frac{p_2}{p_1\tau}\right)^{\delta}=\left(\frac{w_2}{w_1\tau}\right)^{\delta}\left(\frac{L_2}{L_1}\right)^{\frac{\varepsilon\delta}{1+\varepsilon}}\tag{23}$$

定义地区 1 制造业产品的价格指数 $I_1$① 为

---

① 价格指数的引入详见 Krugman(1991a)，此处不再详细推导。

$$I_1 = \left(\sum_{i=1}^{N} p_i^{1-\delta} \right)^{\frac{1}{1-\delta}} = \left[N_1 p_1^{1-\delta} + N_2 (p_2/\tau)^{1-\delta} \right]^{\frac{1}{1-\delta}} \tag{24}$$

将(12)式、(15)式代入(24)式得：

$$I_1 = \left[\left(\frac{L_1}{\alpha\delta} \right)^{\frac{1-\varepsilon+\varepsilon\delta}{1+\varepsilon}} \left(\frac{w_1 \delta}{\delta - 1} \right)^{1-\delta} + \left(\frac{L_2}{\alpha\delta} \right)^{\frac{1-\varepsilon+\varepsilon\delta}{1+\varepsilon}} \left(\frac{w_2 \delta}{(\delta - 1)\tau} \right)^{1-\delta} \right]^{\frac{1}{1-\delta}} \tag{25}$$

由(1)式、(4)式、(5)式、(23)式、(25)式可知地区 1 和地区 2 之间的间接效用之比为

$$\frac{U_1}{U_2} = \frac{\left\{ \frac{\mu[w_1 - T(k)]}{I_1} \right\}^{\mu} \left\{ \frac{\gamma[w_1 - T(k)]}{r(k)} \right\}^{\gamma} [(1-\mu-\gamma)(w_1 - T(k))]^{1-\mu-\gamma}}{\left\{ \frac{\mu[w_2 - T(k)]}{I_2} \right\}^{\mu} \left\{ \frac{\gamma[w_2 - T(k)]}{r(k)} \right\}^{\gamma} [(1-\mu-\gamma)(w_2 - T(k)]^{1-\mu-\gamma}} \tag{26}$$

将(26)式在 $k = b_1, b_2$ 处取值并化简得：

$$\begin{aligned} \frac{U_1}{U_2} &= \frac{w_1 - T(b_1)}{w_2 - T(b_2)} \frac{I_2^{\mu}}{I_1^{\mu}} \\ &= \frac{w_1 - T(b_1)}{w_2 - T(b_2)} \left[\frac{L_1^{\frac{1-\varepsilon+\varepsilon\delta}{1+\varepsilon}} (w_1/\tau)^{1-\delta} + L_2^{\frac{1-\varepsilon+\varepsilon\delta}{1+\varepsilon}} w_2^{1-\delta}}{L_1^{\frac{1-\varepsilon+\varepsilon\delta}{1+\varepsilon}} w_1^{1-\delta} + L_2^{\frac{1-\varepsilon+\varepsilon\delta}{1+\varepsilon}} (w_2/\tau)^{1-\delta}} \right]^{\frac{\mu}{1-\delta}} \end{aligned} \tag{27}$$

定义 $f = L_1/(L_1 + L_2) = L_1/\mu$，即地区 1 工人占两地区工人总数的比例，则(27)式可以简化为

$$\frac{U_1}{U_2} = \frac{w_1 - T(b_1)}{w_2 - T(b_2)} \left[\frac{f^{\frac{1-\varepsilon+\varepsilon\delta}{1+\varepsilon}} (w_1/\tau)^{1-\delta} + (1-f)^{\frac{1-\varepsilon+\varepsilon\delta}{1+\varepsilon}} w_2^{1-\delta}}{f^{\frac{1-\varepsilon+\varepsilon\delta}{1+\varepsilon}} w_1^{1-\delta} + (1-f)^{\frac{1-\varepsilon+\varepsilon\delta}{1+\varepsilon}} (w_2/\tau)^{1-\delta}} \right]^{\frac{\mu}{1-\delta}} \tag{28}$$

工人在两个地区之间的区位选择均衡由(28)式决定，当两

个地区都有工人分布，即 $f \in (0, 1)$ 时，$\frac{U_1}{U_2} = 1$ 为区位选择均衡，表明代表性工人无论是在地区 1 居住还是在地区 2 居住，其效用水平都是一样的；当所有工人集中于区域 1 时，即 $f = 1$ 时，$\frac{U_1}{U_2} \geqslant 1$ 为区位选择均衡，表明即使所有的工人都集中在地区 1，地区 1 的效应水平还高于地区 2，因此工人也没有动机在两地区之间进行迁移；同理，$f = 0$ 时，$\frac{U_1}{U_2} \leqslant 1$ 为区位均衡。

接下来，考虑两地区之间收支均衡，地区 1 所有工人的可支配收入（除去通勤成本后的收入）总额为 $\int_0^{b_1} [w_1 - T(k)] \cdot \frac{2\pi k}{S(k)} \mathrm{d}k = \phi_1 w_1 L_1$，将 $S(k)$、L_1 的表达式代入，可以求出其中 $\phi_1 = \frac{\int_0^{b_1} k(1 - T(k)/w_1)^{1/\gamma} \mathrm{d}k}{\int_0^{b_1} k(1 - T(k)/w_1)^{\frac{1}{\gamma}-1} \mathrm{d}k}$，$\phi_1$ 衡量工人可支配收入占工资的比重，其取值范围为 0 到 1 之间。由(7)式可知地区 1 农民的总收入为 $\frac{1-\mu}{2}$，因此地区 1 的总收入为

$$Y_1 = \frac{1-\mu}{2} + \phi_1 w_1 L_1 \tag{29}$$

假设用 z_{11} 衡量地区 1 收入在地区 1 生产的制造业产品上的消费与地区 1 收入在地区 2 生产的制造业产品上的消费之比，z_{12} 衡量地区 2 收入在地区 1 生产的制造业产品上的消费与地区 2 收入在地区 2 生产的制造业产品上的消费之比。则可知：

$$z_{11} = \left(\frac{N_1}{N_2}\right)\left(\frac{p_1}{p_2/\tau}\right)\left(\frac{c_{11}}{c_{12}}\right) = \left(\frac{L_1}{L_2}\right)^{\frac{1-\varepsilon+\varepsilon\delta}{1+\varepsilon}} \left(\frac{w_1 \tau}{w_2}\right)^{1-\delta} \tag{30}$$

$$z_{12}=\left(\frac{N_1}{N_2}\right)\left(\frac{p_1/\tau}{p_2}\right)\left(\frac{c_{21}}{c_{22}}\right)=\left(\frac{L_1}{L_2}\right)^{\frac{1-\varepsilon+\varepsilon\delta}{1+\varepsilon}}\left(\frac{w_1}{w_2\tau}\right)^{1-\delta} \tag{31}$$

则两地区的收支平衡意味着：

$$w_1L_1=\mu\left[\left(\frac{z_{11}}{1+z_{11}}\right)Y_1+\left(\frac{z_{12}}{1+z_{12}}\right)Y_2\right] \tag{32}$$

$$w_2L_2=\mu\left[\left(\frac{1}{1+z_{11}}\right)Y_1+\left(\frac{1}{1+z_{12}}\right)Y_2\right] \tag{33}$$

(32)式左边是地区 1 所有工人的工资收入，右边是地区 1 和地区 2 对地区 1 生产的制造业产品的总消费。

至此，我们可以得出由 11 个方程组成的均衡方程组，其中，需要求解的内生变量也为 11 个，分别为 b_1，b_2，w_1，w_2，Y_1，Y_2，z_{11}，z_{12}，L_1，L_2，f：

$$\begin{cases}
L_1=\int_0^{b_1}\frac{2\pi k}{S(k)}\mathrm{d}k=\dfrac{2\pi r_A\int_0^{b_1}k(1-T(k)/w_1)^{\frac{1}{\gamma}-1}\mathrm{d}k}{\gamma w_1(1-T(b_1)/w_1)^{\frac{1}{\gamma}}} & \text{(eq1)}\\
L_2=\int_0^{b_2}\frac{2\pi k}{S(k)}\mathrm{d}k=\dfrac{2\pi r_A\int_0^{b_2}k(1-T(k)/w_2)^{\frac{1}{\gamma}-1}\mathrm{d}k}{\gamma w_2(1-T(b_2)/w_2)^{\frac{1}{\gamma}}} & \text{(eq2)}\\
Y_1=\dfrac{1-\mu}{2}+\dfrac{\int_0^{b_1}k(1-T(k)/w_1)^{1/\gamma}\mathrm{d}k}{\int_0^{b_1}k(1-T(k)/w_1)^{\frac{1}{\gamma}-1}\mathrm{d}k}w_1L_1 & \text{(eq3)}\\
Y_2=\dfrac{1-\mu}{2}+\dfrac{\int_0^{b_2}k(1-T(k)/w_2)^{1/\gamma}\mathrm{d}k}{\int_0^{b_2}k(1-T(k)/w_2)^{\frac{1}{\gamma}-1}\mathrm{d}k}w_2L_2 & \text{(eq4)}\\
z_{11}=\left(\dfrac{L_1}{L_2}\right)^{\frac{1-\varepsilon+\varepsilon\delta}{1+\varepsilon}}\left(\dfrac{w_1\tau}{w_2}\right)^{1-\delta} & \text{(eq5)}
\end{cases}$$

$$
\begin{cases}
z_{12} = \left(\frac{L_1}{L_2}\right)^{\frac{1-\varepsilon+\varepsilon\delta}{1+\varepsilon}} \left(\frac{w_1}{w_2\tau}\right)^{1-\delta} & \text{(eq6)} \\
w_1 L_1 = \mu\left[\left(\frac{z_{11}}{1+z_{11}}\right)Y_1 + \left(\frac{z_{12}}{1+z_{12}}\right)Y_2\right] & \text{(eq7)} \\
w_2 L_2 = \mu\left[\left(\frac{1}{1+z_{11}}\right)Y_1 + \left(\frac{1}{1+z_{12}}\right)Y_2\right] & \text{(eq8)} \\
L_1 + L_2 = \mu & \text{(eq9)} \\
f = L_1/(L_1+L_2) & \text{(eq10)} \\
\frac{U_1}{U_2} = \frac{w_1 - T(b_1)}{w_2 - T(b_2)}\left[\frac{f^{\frac{1-\varepsilon+\varepsilon\delta}{1+\varepsilon}}(w_1/\tau)^{1-\delta} + (1-f)^{\frac{1-\varepsilon+\varepsilon\delta}{1+\varepsilon}} w_2^{1-\delta}}{f^{\frac{1-\varepsilon+\varepsilon\delta}{1+\varepsilon}} w_1^{1-\delta} + (1-f)^{\frac{1-\varepsilon+\varepsilon\delta}{1+\varepsilon}}(w_2/\tau)^{1-\delta}}\right]^{\frac{\mu}{1-\delta}} & \\
\begin{cases} \geqslant 1,\ f=1 \\ =1,\ f\in(0,\ 1) \\ \leqslant 1,\ f=0 \end{cases} & \text{(eq11)}
\end{cases}
$$

三、外部规模经济效应的定性分析

在 Tabuchi(1998)不含马歇尔外部规模经济效应的模型当中，由于引入了城市内部空间结构，增加了经济的分散力，模型结论显示当地区间运输成本为零时，不论模型中的其他参数如何取值，经济活动在两地区之间的平均分布是长期均衡，即从长期来看，经济不会出现集聚现象，该结论是 Tabuchi(1998)模型的主要结论，显然该结论与经济现实并不相符。

在我们的模型当中，由于将外部规模经济效应作为经济的集聚力量引入，即使地区间运输成本为零，Tabuchi(1998)模型的结论不再成立，即分散不再是唯一均衡。

令 $\tau=1$，代入(eq11)式、(eq5)式、(eq6)式可知：

$$\frac{U_1}{U_2}=\frac{w_1-T(b_1)}{w_2-T(b_2)} \tag{34}$$

$$z_{11}=\left(\frac{L_1}{L_2}\right)^{\frac{1-\varepsilon+\varepsilon\delta}{1+\varepsilon}}\left(\frac{w_1}{w_2}\right)^{1-\delta}=z_{12} \tag{35}$$

将 $z_{11}=z_{12}$ 代入(eq7)式、(eq8)式并将两式左右两端分别相除,可得:

$$\frac{w_1L_1}{w_2L_2}=z_{11}=\left(\frac{L_1}{L_2}\right)^{\frac{1-\varepsilon+\varepsilon\delta}{1+\varepsilon}}\left(\frac{w_1}{w_2}\right)^{1-\delta}\Rightarrow\frac{w_1}{w_2}=\left(\frac{L_1}{L_2}\right)^{\frac{\varepsilon(\delta-2)}{(1+\varepsilon)\delta}} \tag{36}$$

由(36)式可知:

$$\frac{\mathrm{d}(w_1/w_2)}{\mathrm{d}(L_1/L_2)}=\frac{\varepsilon(\delta-2)}{(1+\varepsilon)\delta}\left(\frac{L_1}{L_2}\right)^{\frac{2\varepsilon\delta}{(1+\varepsilon)\delta}}\begin{cases}>0,\ \delta>2\\=0,\ \delta=2\\<0,\ \delta<2\end{cases} \tag{37}$$

由于 $\frac{\mathrm{d}(w_1/w_2)}{\mathrm{d}(L_1/L_2)}$ 与 $\frac{\mathrm{d}(w_1/w_2)}{\mathrm{d}f}$ 符号相同,因此(37)式可以改写为

$$\frac{\mathrm{d}(w_1/w_2)}{\mathrm{d}f}\begin{cases}>0,\ \delta>2\\=0,\ \delta=2\\<0,\ \delta<2\end{cases} \tag{37'}$$

同时,由(eq1)式和(eq2)式可知,$\partial L_1/\partial b_1>0$, $\partial L_2/\partial b_2>0$,即城市工人数越多,城市边界越宽,因此城市边界地区向CBD的通勤成本 $T(b_1)$ 和 $T(b_2)$ 分别随着城市工人数 L_1 和 L_2 的增加而增加。因此:

$\delta>2$ 时,$f\uparrow\rightarrow\frac{T(b_1)}{T(b_2)}\uparrow$, $\frac{w_1}{w_2}\uparrow$,因此 $\frac{\mathrm{d}(U_1/U_2)}{\mathrm{d}f}$ 的符号不确定,取决于 δ, ε, γ 等参数的值以及通勤成本函数 $T(k)$ 的具体形式。如果出现 $\frac{\mathrm{d}(U_1/U_2)}{\mathrm{d}f}>0$ 状况,经济最终会稳定于集聚状态,即制造业工人将完全集中于区域 1 或区域 2。

从以上分析，我们可以得出：

定理 1：在引入城市内部空间结构和外部规模经济效应的模型当中，在地区间运输成本为零的条件下（$\tau = 1$），经济活动在两地区之间的平均分布不再是唯一的稳定均衡，当 $\delta > 2$ 时，稳定的均衡状态取决于经济中的其他参数。即：即使没有地区间运输成本，经济也可能会集聚。

四、数 值 模 拟

第三部分仅对运输成本为零的特殊情形进行了定性分析，为了对模型结果有更直观的了解，同时分析不同参数条件下的均衡结果，接下来我们通过数值模拟的方法求解方程组（eq1）—（eq11）。为了求解方便，我们给出通勤成本函数的形式为 $T(k) = tk$，t 为衡量单位距离的通勤成本。

数值模拟的程序如下：首先对参数赋值，同时对内生变量 $f \in [0, 1]$ 赋一个值，代入（eq1）—（eq10）式，并利用 matlab 程序求出内生变量 b_1，b_2，w_1，w_2，Y_1，Y_2，z_{11}，z_{12}，L_1，L_2 的解，并将 f 的值和其他内生变量的解代入（eq11）式，求出 $\frac{U_1}{U_2}$ 的值，每赋一次 f 值就求出一个 $\frac{U_1}{U_2}$ 的值，我们在 $[0, 1]$ 间按从小到大的顺序对 f 不断赋值，然后根据求出的每个 $\frac{U_1}{U_2}$ 的值判断此 f 取值是否达到均衡。判定是否达到均衡的条件为：我们定义两区域之间的均衡为一个地区的工人没有动机搬迁到另一个地区去，则如果给定的 $f \in (0, 1)$，则 $\frac{U_1}{U_2} = 1$ 时达到均衡状态，即两地区工人效用完全相等，工人没有动机从一个地区搬迁到另一个地区去；如果 $f=0$，则$\frac{U_1}{U_2}<1$时达到均衡，即如果所有工人都集聚在地区 2，并且地区 2 的效用高于地区 1，则地区 2 的工人没有动机搬到地区 1，此时，即使两地区效用不相等也达到空间均衡；同理，如果 $f=1$，则$\frac{U_1}{U_2}>1$时达到均衡。

(一) 外部规模经济效应(ε)对集聚程度的影响

本文在标准新经济地理学模型的基础上引入了城市内部空间结构和外部规模经济效应，我们首先考察外部规模经济效应对经济集聚程度的影响。

为了考察外部规模经济效应对经济集聚程度的影响，我们从大到小不断调整外部规模经济效应指数 ε 的值，ε 取值大表明外部规模经济效应强，ε 取值小表明外部规模经济效应弱，我们分别取 $\varepsilon=0.5$，0.1，0 三种情形，$\varepsilon=0.5$ 表明经济中外部规模经济效应较强，$\varepsilon=0.1$ 表明经济中的外部规模经济效应一般，$\varepsilon=0$ 表明经济中不存在外部规模经济效应。

根据既有研究和经验值，其他参数取值如下：$\delta=2.5$，$\mu=0.3$，$\gamma=0.5$，$t=1$，$r_A=10$，地区间运输成本 τ 值取 0.9。①模拟结果显示，当 $\varepsilon=0.5$ 时，经济中存在三个均衡，即 $f=0$ 时$\frac{U_1}{U_2}<1$，$f=0.5$ 时$\frac{U_1}{U_2}=1$，$f=1$ 时$\frac{U_1}{U_2}>1$，其中分散均衡

① 我们对参数赋值进行如下说明：首先，参数的取值只是相对的数值，并不代表绝对值的含义，如我们可以将农业地租 r_A 取值为 10，也可以取值为 100，但这并不影响我们分析的结论，因为我们此处考查的主要是 $\delta=2.5$，ε 取值不同时，经济集聚程度的差异，如果我们取 $r_A=100$，得出的结论仍然不变：即随着 ε 取值上升，经济集聚程度会上升，并会出现经济完全集聚的情形；其次，我们的参数取值充分借鉴了现有的相关研究，以确保可比性，此部分的参数取值与 Tubchi (1998) 的取值完全一致。以后各部分研究的参数取值参见此说明。

($f=0.5$)不是稳定均衡①,只有经济完全集聚于区域 1 或完全集聚于区域 2 的均衡是稳定均衡,即完全集聚是经济的稳定均衡,但稳定状态时经济是集聚于区域 1 还是区域 2 取决于经济的初始状态;当 $\varepsilon=0.1$ 时,经济中同样存在三个均衡,并且分散均衡也不稳定,只有完全集聚是稳定均衡,但与 $\varepsilon=0.5$ 的情形相比,$f=0$ 时$\frac{U_1}{U_2}$的值更高,而 $f=1$ 时$\frac{U_1}{U_2}$的值更低,说明随着外部规模经济效应的下降($\varepsilon=0.5$ 下降到 $\varepsilon=0.1$),经济的集聚程度会有所降低;当 $\varepsilon=0$ 时,即经济中不存在外部规模经济效应,此时经济中只有一个均衡,即 $f=0.5$ 时$\frac{U_1}{U_2}=1$,并且这一均衡是稳定的,说明当经济中不存在外部规模经济效应时,经济活动会趋向于在两地区之间平均分布而不再集聚于某一区域。因此数值模拟的结果显示,外部规模经济效应会提高经济的集聚程度。

具体模拟结果如图 1 所示,图中横轴为 f 数值,纵轴为两地

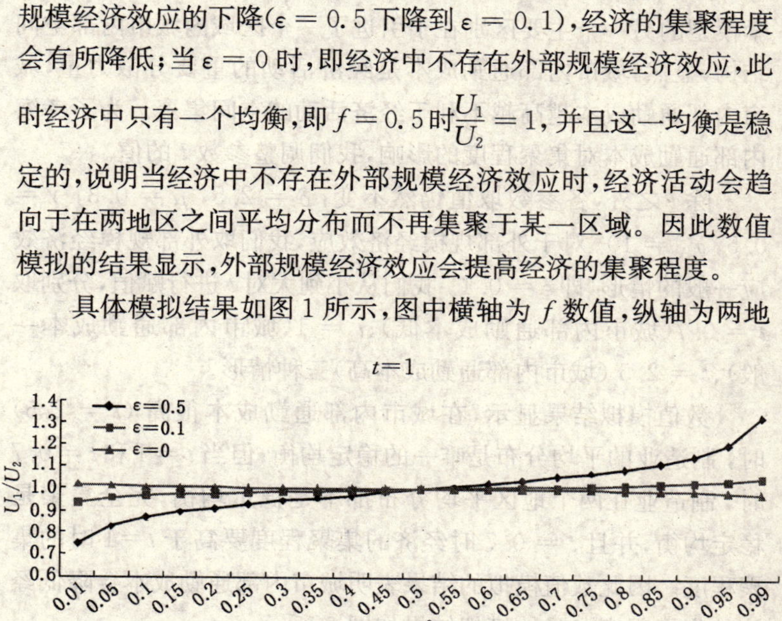

图 1 数值模拟结果:ε 对集聚程度的影响

---

① 因为 $f<0.5$, $\frac{U_1}{U_2}<1$,所以地区 1 的工人会往地区 2 迁移,导致 f 下降,最终会收敛到 $f=0$ 的情形,反之,当 $f>0.5$ 时,地区 2 的工人会向地区 1 迁移,最终会收敛到 $f=1$ 的情形。

区之间的效用之比，根据均衡的判定条件决定各种条件下均衡的数量和稳定性质。

此外，为了考察更为细致，我们可以调整其他参数，如 δ，τ 等的取值，模拟的结果同样显示外部规模经济效应越强，经济的集聚程度越高，限于篇幅，不再报告详细结果。

(二) 城市内部通勤成本(t)对集聚程度的影响

除引进外部规模经济效应之外，本文与标准的新经济地理学模型的另一个主要区别在于引进了一个区域内城市内部空间结构，显然，城市内部通勤成本是经济活动的重要分散力量，城市内部通勤成本越高越不利于经济活动的空间集聚。为了考察内部通勤成本对集聚程度的影响，我们调整参数 t 的值。

除 t 之外，各参数取值仍然不变：$\delta = 2.5$，$\mu = 0.3$，$\gamma = 0.5$，$r_A = 10$。对于外部规模经济效应，我们取外部规模经济效应一般的情形，即 $\varepsilon = 0.1$。我们从小到大对 t 进行赋值，分别取 $t = 0.7$(城市内部通勤成本低)、$t = 1$(城市内部通勤成本一般)、$t = 2.5$(城市内部通勤成本高)三种情形。

数值模拟结果显示，在城市内部通勤成本很高 ($t = 2.5$) 时，制造业的平均分布是唯一的稳定均衡；但当 $t = 1$ 和 $t = 0.7$ 时，制造业在两个地区平均分布都不是稳定均衡，完全集聚是稳定均衡，并且 $t = 0.7$ 时经济的集聚程度要高于 $t=1$ 时的集聚程度。因此数值模拟的结果表明城市内部通勤成本会降低经济的集聚程度。具体模拟结果如图 2 所示。

同样，我们可以调整其他参数，如 δ，τ 等的取值，基本的结论仍然是城市内部通勤成本越低，经济的集聚程度越高。限于篇幅，不再报告详细结果。

(三) 外部规模经济效应和城市内部通勤成本的交互作用

在本部分(一)中，我们保持城市内部通勤成本不变，考察外

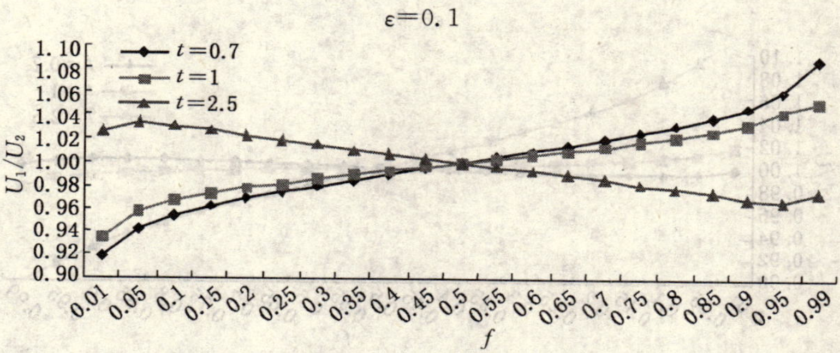

图 2　数值模拟结果：t 对集聚程度的影响

部规模经济效应对经济集聚程度的影响；在本部分(二)中，我们保持外部规模经济效应不变，考察城市内部通勤成本对集聚的影响。在这一部分，我们同时调整 t 和 ε 的参数值。

其他参数取值仍然保持不变，即：$\delta=2.5$，$\mu=0.3$，$\gamma=0.5$，$\tau=0.9$，$r_A=10$。我们分别考察 $\varepsilon=0$ 和 $\varepsilon=0.5$ 两种情形，t 的取值仍然是 0.7，1，2.5 三种情形。

1. $\varepsilon=0$ 的情形

在没有外部规模经济效应的情形下，$t=0.7$ 时完全集聚是稳定均衡，$t=1$ 和 2.5 时，经济在两地区平均分布是稳定均衡，因此数值模拟的基本结论仍然是内部通勤成本会降低经济的集聚程度。

同时，我们与(二)的比较可以看出，在没有外部规模经济效应情形下，$t=1$ 时，集聚不再是稳定均衡，而 $t=0.7$ 时集聚虽然仍然是稳定均衡，但集聚的程度要低于 $\varepsilon=0.1$ 的情形。因此，该数值模拟结果显示，即使在城市内部通勤成本一般的情形下，如果没有外部规模经济效应，经济也会趋于分散。具体的模拟结果如图 3 所示。

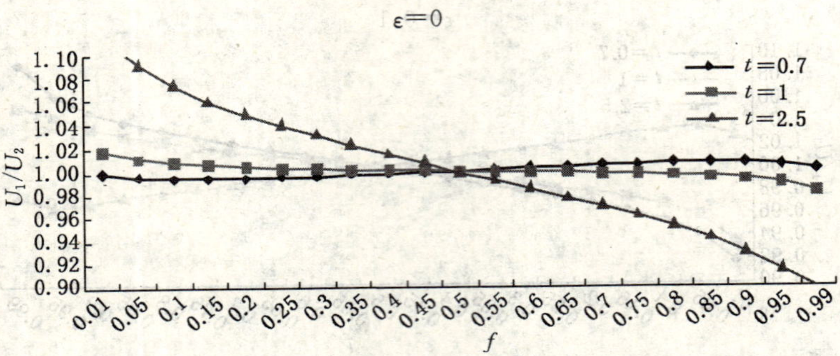

图 3　ε＝0 的情形

2. ε＝0.5 的情形

我们将外部规模经济效应程度进一步提高，取 $\varepsilon = 0.5$，结果显示，$t = 2.5, 1, 0.7$ 时，制造业平均分布都不再是稳定均衡，完全集聚是稳定均衡。将模拟结果与 4.2 部分相比较可以看出，即使是 $t = 2.5$ 时完全集聚也是稳定均衡，因此说明即使在通勤成本很高时，只要外部规模经济效应足够强，经济也可能会集聚的。具体模拟结果如图 4 所示。

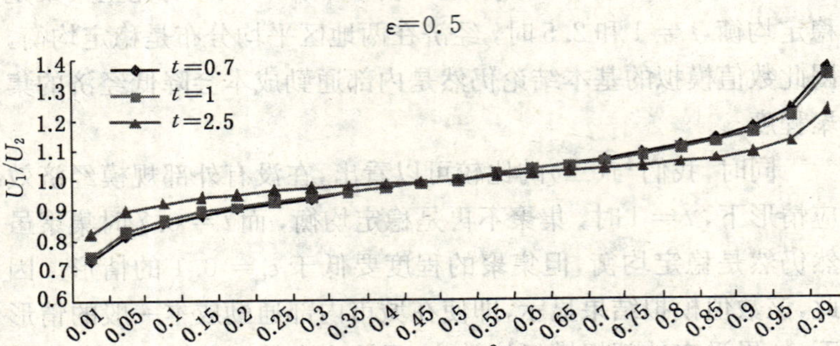

图 4　ε＝0.5 的情形

五、结　论

在引进城市内部空间结构和外部规模经济效应后，新经济地理学模型更加接近经济现实，模型的结论也显示作为分散力量的城市内部通勤成本和作为集聚力量的外部规模经济效应对经济集聚程度的影响非常显著，在不同的情形下，经济集聚的程度会有所不同，因此相对于标准的新经济地理学模型而言，新的模型对经济现实的解释力更强，也解决了 Anas(2002)等提出的新经济地理学模型集聚机制过于单一的问题。

第四部分的数值模拟也很好地验证了模型的理论预期，模拟结果显示外部规模经济效应会显著增加经济的集聚程度，而城市内部通勤成本会降低经济的集聚程度，说明将此两类因素引入新经济地理学模型是非常必要的。此外，文中的定理 1 也说明：即使在地区间运输成本为零的条件下，只要外部规模经济效应足够强，经济也可能会走向集聚的，因此说明随着经济发展和技术进步，即使地区间运输成本不断降低，经济也不一定会趋于分散。

参考文献

Abdel-Rahman, H. and M. Fujita, 1990, "Product Variety, Marshallian Externalities, and City Sizes", *Journal of Regional Science*, 30(2): 165—183.

Alonson, W., 1964, *Location and Land Use*, Cambridge, MA: Harvard University Press.

Anas, A., 2004, "Vanishing Cities: What does the New Economic Geography Imply about the Efficiency of Urbanization?", *Journal of Economic Geography*, 4(2): 181—199.

Anas, A. and K. Xiong, 2003, "Intercity Trade and the Industrial Diversification of Cities", *Journal of Urban Economics*, 54(2):258—276.

Black, D. and J. Henderson, 1999, "A Theory of Urban Growth", *Journal of Political Economy*, 107(2):252—284.

Brakman, S., H. Garretsen and C. van Marrewijk, 2001, *An Introduction to Geographical Economics*, Cambridge: Cambridge University Press.

Brakman, S., H. Garretsen, R. Gigengack, C. Van Marrewijk and R. Wagenvoort, 1996, "Negative Feedbacks in the Economy and Industrial Location", *Journal of Regional Science*, 136(4):631—651.

陈良文、杨开忠:《集聚经济的六类模型:一个研究综述》,《经济科学》2006 年第 6 期。

Chipman, J., 1970, "External Economies of Scale and Competitive Equilibrium", *Quarterly Journal of Economics*, 84(3):347—385.

Au, C. and J. Henderson, 2005, "Are Chinese Cities Too Small?", Working Paper, Brown University.

Davis, D. and D. Weinstein, 1996, "Does Economic Geography Matter for International Specialization?", Mimeo, Harvard University.

Davis, D. and D. Weinstein, 1999, "Economic geography and regional production structure: an empirical investigation", *European Economic Review*, 43(2):379—407.

Dixit, A. and J. Stiglitz, 1977, "Monopolistic Competition and Optimum Product Diversity", *American Economic Review*, 63(3):297—308.

Duranton, G. and D. Puga, 2004, "Microfoundations of Urban Agglomeration Economies", in Henderson J. and J. Thisse(eds.), *Handbook of Regional and Urban Economics*, volume 4. Amsterdam: North Holland.

Helpman, E., 1995, "The Size of Regions" Working Paper No. 14-95, The Foerder Institute for Economic Research, Tel-Aviv University.

Fujita, M., P. Krugman and A. Venables, 1999, *The Spatial Economy: Cities, Regions and International Trade*, Cambridge, Massachusetts: The MIT Press.

Hanson, G., 1997, "Increasing Returns, Trade and the Regional Structure of Wages", *Economic Journal*, 107(440):113—133.

Hanson, G., 1998, "Market Potential, Increasing Returns, and Geographic Concentration" NBER Working Paper, No. 6429.

Henderson, J., 1974, "The Sizes and Types of Cities", *American Economic Review*, 64(4):640—656.

Hoover, E., 1936, *Location Theory and the Shoe and Leather Industries*, Cambridge, MA: Harvard University Press.

Krugman, P., 1991a, "Increasing Returns and Economic Geography", *Journal of Political Economy*, 99(3):483—499.

Krugman, P., 1991b, *Geography and Trade*, Cambridge, MA: MIT Press.

Krugman, P. and A. Venables, 1995, "Globalization and the Inequality of Nations", *Quarterly Journal of Economics*, 110(4):857—880.

Marshall, A., 1890, *Principles of Economics*, London: Macmillan.

Michel, P., A. Perrot and J. Thisse, 1996, "Interregional Equilibrium with Heterogeneous Labor", *Journal of Population Economics*, 9(1): 95—114.

Mills, E., 1967, "An Aggregative Model of Resource Allocation in a Metropolitan Area", *American Economic Review*, 57(2):197—210.

Ohlin, B., 1933, *Interregional and International Trade*, Cambridge, MA: Harvard University Press.

Ottaviano, G. and J. Thisse, 2004, "Agglomeration and Economic Geography", in Henderson, J., and J. Thisse(eds.) *Handbook of Regional and Urban Economics*, volume 4. Amsterdam: NorthHolland.

Venables, A., 1996, "Equilibrium Locations of Vertically Linked Industries", *International Economic Review*, 37(2):341—359.

Tabuchi, T., 1998, "Urban Agglomeration and Dispersion: A Synthesis of Alonso and Krugman", *Journal of Urban Economics*, 44(3): 333—351.

（原载《经济学(季刊)》第7卷第1期）

生产性公共开支经济中政府债务的福利损失*

林细细　龚六堂

（北京大学光华管理学院）

一、引　言

国债问题始终是经济学领域的一个重要问题。围绕着李嘉图等价定理能否成立这一问题，经济学者对最优国债进行了热烈的讨论，Barro(1974)对这一定理进一步完善和发展，提出了著名的巴罗-李嘉图等价。如果李嘉图等价定理成立，则政府发行公债和征税其实没有差别。考虑到比例税将造成税收超额负担，Chamley(1981，1986)、Lucas(1990)和 Turnovsky(1996)的文章中得到的结论是在比例税情形下，最优的资本收入税为零，政府成为净债权人。

与此同时，一些学者则认为李嘉图等价在经济现实中并不成立。比如经济中不存在无限生命的个体、经济个体不具有理性预期，但这些论调从经济理论研究而言则过于草率和武断。但是，当消费者异质性、金融市场不完备等经济假设在经济理论

*　本项目研究受国家社会科学基金资助。

中得到充分关注时，李嘉图等价定理不成立的论调也多起来。具有代表性的文章为 Woodfood(1990)和 Aiyagari(1994)，后者在消费者异质性和市场存在借贷约束下，提出公债具有自我保险的作用，能够放松借贷限制。而在其后，Aiyagari(1995)更进一步提出了 Chamley 的结论并不成立，最优资本税不为零。此后，Aiyagari 和 McGrattan(1998)则把宏观经济模型数量化，通过美国经济的数值模拟，提出美国的最优债务存量水平为 2/3，这一数目刚好为美国战后的平均水平。他们还认为当样本经济债务存量偏离最优债务存量水平时，福利损失非常小，不会超过千分之一。Floden(2001)在他们的基础上，进一步考虑转移支付的作用，结果与他们的结论基本保持一致，只是 Floden 发现转移支付的福利作用比公债大。

但是这些文章都有一个共同的不足之处：没有考虑政府对生产的影响。而政府对生产的影响无论在理论研究还是在实证研究方面都得到了一定的认可。在已有的文献研究中，一种考虑的是存量形式即公共资本参与生产，而另一种形式则是流量形式即公共开支参与生产。本文采用的后一种形式，即 Barro (1990)中所提出的生产函数形式，考虑到现实经济中有一部分政府公共开支对生产没有直接影响，我们在文章中将公共开支分为消费性公共开支和生产性公共开支，后一种公共开支才对生产有直接影响。由于在经济中，增长效应(growth effect)都比较大，因此，如果考虑了内生经济，则福利变化可能将很大，我们也将在文章中检验这一经济直观成立与否。

尽管中国的公债历史可以追溯到封建社会，但是从我们研究的对象而言，则集中在新中国成立以来的债务情况。新中国从 50 年代就开始发行国内公债，先是“人民胜利折实公债”后是“国家经济建设公债”，此外还有向苏联举借的外债。中国的理论界对这些公债的作用都持较为肯定的态度，不过从80年代恢复发行公债以来，大家对公债的看法就出现了褒贬不一，公债也因此成为财政领域一个热门话题。1998年实行的积极财政政策和此后实行的双稳健政策，公债发行数量大幅度地增加，这引起了许多经济学者的极大关注，理论界关于债务发行数量是否合理从几个债务指标展开了激烈的讨论。如贾康和赵全厚(2000)从理论上认为国债规模与国债效应存在一个倒U型关系，这导致了最优债务规模的存在。另一方面，他们从中国经济统计中的实证数据得到国债的债务指标，对比国际上这些债务指标经验值，得出中国国债依存度严重超标而国债负担率又远未超标这一悖论，并对此进行解释。他们持有的观点是现实的国债规模被低估，因为忽略了国家的或有负债。周佰成等人(2002)则从国债的偿债率、依存度和累积负担率三个指标出发，以国际上这些指标的经验值作为基准，建立国债发行的最优规模。刘溶沧和马拴友(2001)从中国的实证数据出发，考虑了赤字、国债与经济增长的关系。这些文章尽管做出了一定的学术贡献，但是，他们在讨论时，只局限于参照国际的一些经验标准或从短期的一些计量指标展开，而并没有从长期一般均衡和经济模型数量化的角度来考虑这个问题，另外，他们对国债的考虑并没有从直观上给出国债造成福利损失有多大。林细细和龚六堂(2007)在 Aiyagari 和 McGrattan(1998)文章的基础上，结合中国经济现状，对中国国债政策进行福利分析。结果发现在中国目前的样本经济状态(1978—1998)下，较大量发行公债并未带来很大的福利损失，尽管这个损失数额比 Aiyagari 和 McGrattan(1998)的结论来得大。但该文章没有考虑政府公共开支对生产的影响。

本文在林细细和龚六堂(2007)的基础上，结合中国实际，考虑了生产性公共开支的内生经济中，经济中最优的债务规模及福利影响。由于我们的模型是建立在封闭经济下，因此我们考虑的债务为国内公债，即不包含外债。我们发现，由于政府公债的正效应在中国目前的情形下较小，从而不足以抵消其负的效应，因此，最优的公债水平将为负。但是，我们发现，目前较大规模地发行政府公债，其福利损失将非常大。相对于中国样本经济，债务存量每提高 10%，将产生 2%左右的福利损失。这一结论与林细细和龚六堂(2007)差别很大，公债问题需要引起足够重视。

从结构上作如下安排，第二部分为模型部分，我们建立基本模型并讨论政府公债的作用。第三部分我们对模型进行参数化并说明模型计算方法。第四部分为数值模拟部分，我们得出数值模拟结果，并讨论结果的敏感性(Robust)。第五部分为政策分析部分，我们分析现行公债政策带来的福利影响。最后我们得出本文的结论，并指出文章的一些不足之处。

二、模　型

具有无限生命的经济个体，为了分析的方便，我们将其数量标准化为连续统 1。每个人提供一单位劳动，但其劳动生产力 e_t 则存在着外在的冲击。每个人当期的 e_t 独立同分布，每个 e_t 在时间上遵循马尔可夫过程。为了简化分析，我们将平均的劳动生产力标准化，即 $E(e_t)=1$。每期劳动者的劳动生产力加总后为固定常数，不随着时间 t 的变化而发生变化，这样就不存在加总的不确定性。经济中不存在保险市场(或者说保险市场效率低下)，不过每个人可以交换两种无风险资产，即资本和政府公债。但是，在要素市场上，则是完全竞争。于是，当经济处于稳定增长时，在平衡增长路径上，尽管由于劳动生产力的冲击使得个人的消费、收入和财富将存在着波动，但是，人均收入、消费和财富将不变，且存在着一个稳定的分布。

与 Aiyagari 和 McGrattan 不同的是，我们考虑了现实经济中政府公共开支对生产的重要作用，在生产中改变了生产函数，采用 Barro(1990)的生产函数形式，即 $y_t = AK_t^{\alpha} g_t^{1-\alpha}$，其中，$y_t$、$K_t$、$g_t$ 分别为人均产出、人均资本存量和人均政府公共开支。这种生产性的政府公共开支为纯公共产品，政府仅仅发生支出，无从体现其报酬①。当要素市场和产品市场为完全竞争时，我们得到：

$$w_t = (1-\alpha)AK_t^{\alpha} g_t^{1-\alpha}, \ r_t = \alpha AK_t^{\alpha-1} g_t^{1-\alpha} - \delta$$

其中，w_t 和 r_t 分别为 t 期的工资和资本回报率，δ 为资本折旧率。

消费者有两种收入来源，即资产收入和劳动收入。这些收入缴纳完税收，用于消费后剩余的资产留到下期。此外，消费者则面临着借贷约束限制，即其每期资产不能为负。消费者的即期效用函数为 $c_t^{1-v}/(1-v)$，其中，v 为风险回避系数，c_t 为消费者在 t 期的消费。消费者最大化其一生的效用，其面临的问题可以描述如下：

$$\max_{\{c_t, a_{t+1}\}} E\left[\sum_{t=0}^{\infty} \beta^t c_t^{1-v}/(1-v) \,\middle|\, a_0, e_0\right]$$

约束条件为

$$c_t + a_{t+1} \leqslant (1+r)a_t + w_t e_t - T_t$$

$$c_t \geqslant 0, \ a_t \geqslant 0, \ t \geqslant 0, \ a.s.$$

其中，a_t 为消费者在 t 期拥有的资产，T_t 为消费者获得收益后

① 这是一种典型的财政起源于公共需要的看法，即政府取得收入是“取之于民，用之于民”，是为了提供市场无法有效提供的公共产品，公共产品在这里即体现为生产性公共开支。

缴纳的定额税收，β 为效用的主观贴现因子。

我们认为政府是个仁慈的政府，他没有任何私人目的，且具有承诺能力（commitment），政府的目标和消费者的目标一致：最大化消费者的一生总效用。政府可以通过发行公债和收税取得收入，但是需要偿还到期的债务本息和发生一些政府公共开支，这些公共开支对生产具有一定的作用（体现在生产函数上）。于是，政府的预算约束方程为：

$$T_t + B_{t+1} = g_t + (1+r)B_t$$

其中，B_t 为政府在 t 期发行的非状态偶发性公债。

当市场达到均衡时，$A_t = B_t + K_t$。其中，A_t 为经济中消费者拥有的资产总和。

为了较好地描述最优的债务规模，首先需要找一个指标来刻画。我们采用相对数指标，即政府公债占总产出的比重。与 Aiyagari 和 McGrattan 不同的是，我们在内生经济的模型框架下引入了公共开支①，为了较好说明经济状况，我们建立下面的引理。

引理 1：在上述经济中，消费者进行最优化选择后，总消费、总资产、工资、总政府公共开支、税收、政府公债等人均总量指标占总产出的比重保持不变时，经济在平衡增长路径上。

这条引理的证明比较容易。根据平衡增长路径定义，各个总量指标沿着固定的增长率增长，只要令它们的增长率均为经济增长率，我们的引理自然得到证明。

通过引理 1，我们将上述最优化问题进行转化为相对数指

① Barro(1990)给出这种生产函数，该加总生产函数出现在于政府公共开支参与生产时产生外部性。

标。记 $\tilde{c}_t=\dfrac{c_t}{y_t}$，$\tilde{c}_t=\dfrac{a_t}{y_t}$，$\tilde{w}_t=\dfrac{w_t}{y_t}$，$k_t=\dfrac{K_t}{y_t}$，$\tau_t=\dfrac{T_t}{y_t}$，$b_t=\dfrac{B_t}{y_t}$，$\gamma_t=\dfrac{g_t}{y_t}$。当经济处于稳定增长时，$r$，$k_t$，$\tilde{w}_t$，$\tau_t$，$b_t$，$\gamma_t$ 均为固定常数，我们省略其时间下标。此时的经济增长率①用 ϕ 表示，于是 $y_t=y_0(1+\phi)^t$。

从生产者行为得到，$r=\alpha/k-\delta$，$\tilde{w}=1-\alpha$，$k=(A\gamma^{1-\alpha})^{-1/\alpha}$。

政府的预算约束变为：

$$\tau+(\phi-r)b=\gamma \tag{1}$$

记 $\tilde{a}_t=\tilde{k}_t+b_t$，消费者的优化问题

$$V(\tilde{a}_0\mid e_0)=\max_{\{\tilde{c}_t,\,\tilde{a}_{t+1}\}} y_0E\left[\sum_{t=0}^{\infty}\beta^t(1+\phi)^{(1-v)t}\,\tilde{c}_t^{1-v}/(1-v)\mid\tilde{a}_0,\,e_0\right]$$

受约束于

$$\tilde{c}_t+(1+\phi)\,\tilde{a}_{t+1}\leqslant(1+r)\,\tilde{a}_t+\tilde{w}_t-\tau$$

$$\tilde{c}_t\geqslant 0,\ \tilde{a}_t\geqslant 0,\ t\geqslant 0,\ a.s. \tag{2}$$

建立函数方程的 Lagrange 方程

$$L(\tilde{c}_t,\,\tilde{a}_{t+1},\,\phi\mid\tilde{a}_t,\,e_t)=\tilde{c}_t^{1-v}/(1-v)+$$
$$\beta(1+\phi)^{(1-v)}E_tV(\tilde{a}_{t+1},\,e_{t+1})+\mu_{1t}\,\tilde{a}_{t+1}+\mu_{2t}\,\tilde{c}_t \text{②}$$
$$+\lambda_t((1+r)\,\tilde{a}_t+\tilde{w}_t-\tau-\tilde{c}_t-(1+\phi)\,\tilde{a}_{t+1})$$

这样得到一阶条件：

---

① 这里的经济增长率是由整个经济系统内生决定的，而非外生给定。我们接下来将会涉及这方面内容。

② 为了简化分析，在求解中，我们省略了常数 y_0，这影响不到优化的结论。

$$\tilde{c}_t: \tilde{c}_t^{-v} = \lambda_t - \mu_{2t} \tag{3}$$

$$\tilde{a}_{t+1}: \beta(1+\phi)^{(1-v)} E_t V_1'(\tilde{a}_{t+1}, e_{t+1}) = (1+\phi)\lambda_t - \mu_{1t} \tag{4}$$

和松弛条件：

$$\lambda_t \geqslant 0, (1+r)\tilde{a}_t + \tilde{w}_t - \tau - \tilde{c}_t - (1+\phi)\tilde{a}_{t+1} \geqslant 0,$$

$$\lambda_t((1+r)\tilde{a}_t + \tilde{w}_t - \tau - \tilde{c}_t - (1+\phi)\tilde{a}_{t+1}) = 0,$$

$$\mu_{1t} \geqslant 0, \tilde{a}_{t+1} \geqslant 0, \mu_{1t}\tilde{a}_{t+1} = 0,$$

$$\mu_{2t} \geqslant 0, \tilde{c}_t \geqslant 0, \mu_{2t}\tilde{c}_t = 0,$$

另外，由包络引理得到：

$$V_1'(\tilde{a}_t, e_t) = \lambda_t(1+r) \tag{5}$$

由方程(3)、方程(4)和方程(5)得到：

$$\beta(1+\phi)^{(1-v)}(1+r)E_t(\tilde{a}_{t+1}^{-v} + \mu_{2t+1}) = (1+\phi)(\tilde{c}_t^{-v} + \mu_{2t}) - \mu_{1t}$$

即

$$(1+\phi)(\tilde{c}_t^{-v} + \mu_{2t}) \geqslant \beta(1+\phi)^{(1-v)}(1+r)E_t(\tilde{c}_{t+1}^{-v} + \mu_{2t+1})$$

不等号在 $\tilde{a}_{t+1} = 0$ 时成立，即借贷限制起作用时。上式简化为

$$(\tilde{c}_t^{-v} + \mu_{2t}) \geqslant \beta(1+r)/(1+\phi)^v E_t(\tilde{c}_{t+1}^{-v} + \mu_{2t+1}) \tag{6}$$

通过求解上述优化问题，我们将得到资产的决策规则，即 $\tilde{a}_{t+1} = \mathscr{R}(\tilde{a}_t, e_t; r, b, \gamma, \tau)$ 时，将该决策规则同劳动生产力冲击形成的马尔可夫过程，我们就可以用来计算关于资产和劳动生产力冲击的稳定联合分布，我们将这个分布函数记为 $H(\tilde{a}_t, e_t; r, b, \gamma, \tau)$。在得到稳定的静态分布基础上，我们将得到此时的人均资产，即 $\bar{a} = \iint \mathscr{R}(\tilde{a}_t, e_t; r, b, \gamma, \tau) dH = \overline{\mathscr{R}}(r; b, \gamma, \tau)$，这个人均资产表明了稳定状态下社会对资产的供给。而稳定状态下社会对资产的需求包括两个部分，即政府公债和企业生产

所需的资本。从而有 $\bar{a}=b+k(r)$。在政府税收、公债和生产性公共开支给定的条件下，我们将可以得到均衡的资本存量、利率和经济增长率。

如果一个经济满足下列条件，我们称为市场均衡：(1)存在一个稳定分布；(2)要素市场出清，即生产所需的资本和劳动恰好为市场的供给量；(3)消费者最优化条件得到满足；(4)政府预算平衡。

让我们转向政府。如果政府追求的目标是在固定生产性公共开支占总产出的比率①的基础上合理选择政府债务水平。于是，我们从要素市场的均衡条件可以得到固定的利率水平和资本产出比率。我们继续考虑(6)式，当劳动生产力波动较大时，借贷限制在每期起作用。这样，当经济处于稳定增长时，在稳定分布中，将有一个正的测度满足借贷限制。将(6)式两边按照稳定分布取期望，得到：

$$\beta(1+r)/(1+\phi)^{v}<1 \text{ 即 } \phi>(1+r)^{1/v}\beta^{1/v}-1 @\phi_0$$

从这个式子我们得到一个有趣的结论，即在劳动生产能力存在异质性的情况下，借贷限制约束加剧了经济增长。借贷约束越强，经济增长越快；反之，则经济增长速度越慢。ϕ_0 为最低的经济增长率，即借贷约束不起作用时的经济增长率。结合要素市场均衡利率方程，我们得到：

$$\phi_0=[\beta(1+\alpha A^{1/\alpha}\gamma^{(1-\alpha)/\alpha}-\delta)]^{1/v}-1$$

于是，我们得到最低经济增长率与生产性公共开支比率的变化关系：

---

① 这种假定有一定的现实依据。只有社会有较大产出时，政府才能拿出更多的财政资金来发生支出。反之，则财政支出将减少。而消费性支出与生产性支出往往呈固定比例，尽管我们这里先忽略消费性公共开支。而且，从政策执行来看，线性关系比较直观，容易得到议会(人大)审批通过。

$$\frac{d\phi_0}{d\gamma}=\frac{1-\alpha}{v}(1+\alpha A^{1/\alpha}\gamma^{(1-\alpha)/\alpha}-\delta)^{1/v-1}\beta^{1/v}A^{1/\alpha}\gamma^{(1-2\alpha)/\alpha}。$$

因为主观贴现因子小于 1，生产函数中资本份额为小于 1 的常数，而折旧率也是小于 1 的常数，风险回避系数为正数，因此，我们得到最低经济增长率与生产性公共开支呈正相关关系。这样，为了保证有正的最低经济增长率，生产性公共开支水平不能太低，即不能低于 $\gamma_0=(1+\beta\delta-\beta)^{\alpha/(1-\alpha)}(\alpha\beta)^{-\alpha/(1-\alpha)}A^{-1/(1-\alpha)}$。

下面，我们来考虑公债的作用。将政府预算约束方程(1)和 $\tilde{a}_t=\tilde{k}_t+b_t$ 代入(2)式，我们得到新的约束方程：

$$\tilde{c}_t+(1+\phi)\tilde{k}_{t+1}\leqslant(1+r)\tilde{k}_t+\tilde{w}_t-\gamma,\ \tilde{k}_{t+1}\geqslant-b \quad (7)$$

我们用(7)式代替(2)式，求解稳定分布下的消费者最优化问题。根据偏好的局部非饱和性原理，(7)式的第一个不等式在没有借贷约束情况下必然成立。但是，在存在借贷约束的情况下，如果劳动生产力波动太大，导致最低的劳动生产力所创造的收入足够小①，为了满足消费额必须非负这个约束条件，在低劳动生产力的情况下，借贷约束起作用，即 $\tilde{k}_{t+1}=-b$。因此，增加发行政府公债实际上起到放松借贷约束条件这一作用。在其他条件不变的情况下，发行公债越多，用以缓冲劳动生产能力波动带来的收入冲击的能力将越大；这也就意味着消费将更加平滑，因此福利将得到改善。从另外一个角度看，借贷约束放松，消费者的收入波动将越小，而这种波动将转嫁到资本市场上，使得资本市场波动更大。这种大波动使经济处于较动荡状态，从而影响到经济的长期增长。即体现了 Ramey 和 Ramey(1995)所得到的

① 当 $r>\phi$ 时，要使消费非负，则 $\tilde{k}_t\geqslant-\tilde{w}_t e_{\min}/(r-\phi)$，结合借贷约束条件，当 $b\leqslant\tilde{w}_t e_{\min}/(r-\phi)$，起作用(binding)的债务存量的这个约束条件，债务存量越大，约束将越少。

结论，波动与经济增长率成反比。这从消费者预算约束的欧拉公式更好理解。由于借贷约束限制越少，也将意味着消费者最优化的欧拉公式中更容易取等号，亦即经济增长率越趋向最近经济增长率。于是经济增长率下降，在其他条件不变的情况下，这将造成福利的下降。图 1 让我们更为直观地了解债务存量变化对经济增长率造成的影响。在图 2 中，当 b 从 0.5 提高到 3 时，资本供给曲线向右移动，这使得均衡时经济增长率下降。

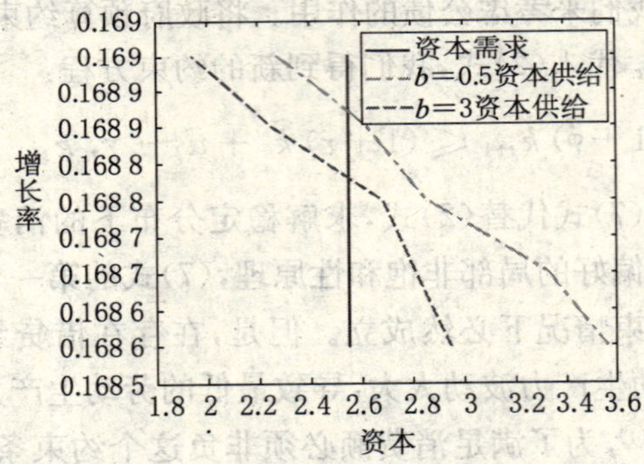

图 1　债务存量与经济增长率

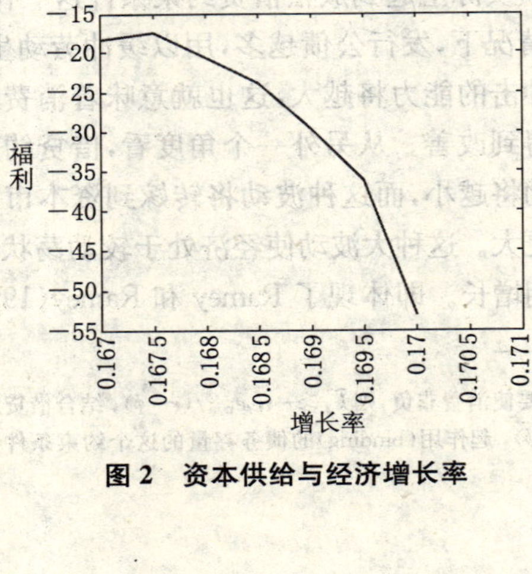

图 2　资本供给与经济增长率

债务存量提高尽管将造成经济增长率下降，从而导致社会福利损失。不过我们从消费者的新预算方程(7)式也发现，由于经济增长率的提高，将使得补偿经济增长的资本减少，使得消费者留有更多的消费，这将提高消费的福利。图 2 为给定债务存量下，经济增长率发生变化导致的福利变化。我们也发现，一味地提高经济增长率并不一定会增加社会福利。经济增长率与社会福利形成一个倒 U 型的曲线。

因此，政府公债的发行从其正外部效应而言，可以提高消费率，改善社会福利。但是，政府公债的发行也存在着一定的负外部效应。首先，由于发行公债提高资产流动性，这降低了经济增长率。其次，从平衡预算的角度而言，发现公债需要用税收来补偿，如果用总额税形式，则将对所有消费者收取同样数量的税收，这将加剧低收入者的负担，加剧他们收入的不稳定。此外，如果采用比例税形式时，则还将造成税收的超额负担。

正因为这些正负效应之间的权衡为最优债务存量的确定提供了一个存在的合理理由。作为福利标准，我们采用功利主义的观点，从经济稳定状态出发，利用次优框架(Second-best)，考虑政府为了使得消费者福利最大化时，应如何选择公债水平和税收政策。即最大化目标函数

$$\Omega = \iint V(a, e)\mathrm{d}H(a, e)$$

为了有效衡量最优债务存量带来的福利收益，我们采用卢卡斯(Lucas, 1990)的方法，即在其他条件不变的情况下，考虑消费者达到样本经济时，其增加的消费水平占消费者目前消费水平的比重，如果为正，即为消费者没有达到最优债务水平时的福利损失，反之即为福利收益。

为了更好地对经济现状进行模拟，我们在第三部分将对模

型进行拓展，并在拓展的基础上对经济参数进行赋值。

三、参数化及计算方法

(一) 参数取值

为了更好地模拟现实经济，我们将模型进一步拓展。在政府税收方面，我们用比例税代替第二部分的模型里面的总额税①，政府对资产和劳动同时征税，τ_w 为工资税税率，τ_a 为资产税税率。而劳动供给具有一定的弹性，消费者可以选择劳动的时间，但是消费者面临着时间约束。为了方便起见，我们将消费者的总时间标准化为 1，l_t 表示为消费者在 t 期选择的休闲数量。消费者的效用函数为 $(c_t^{\xi} l_t^{1-\xi})^{1-v}/(1-v)$，$\xi$ 为效用中的消费份额。消费者的预算约束方程为

$$\tilde{c}_t + (1+\phi)\tilde{a}_{t+1} \leqslant (1+(1-\tau_a)r_t)\tilde{a}_t + (1-\tau_w)\tilde{w}_t e_t(1-l_t) + \chi_t$$

其中，χ_t 为政府给予消费者的转移支付占产出的比重。

政府的公共开支分为两个部分，即消费性公共开支和生产性公共开支，政府预算约束方程为

$$\tau_a r\tilde{a}_t + \tau_w \tilde{w}_t N_t + b_{t+1} = \gamma_t + \gamma_t^c + (1+r)b_t + \chi_t$$

其中，γ_t^c 为政府在 t 期的消费性公共开支占产出的比重。

类似于前面的分析，我们在次优框架得到经济稳定状态下的稳定分布，并从而得到消费者对资产的供给和劳动的供给。然后

① 在经济现实中的税收主要以比例税存在，因此我们数值模拟时采用比例税。由于比例税形式将带来税收的超额负担，因此公债水平提高后，相比总额税情形，采用比例税时公债带来的福利成本将提高。

根据市场均衡条件得到此时的经济增长率和劳动供给量，进而得到给定财政政策下的社会福利值 $\Omega = \iint V(a, e)\mathrm{d}H(a, e)$。

在此基础上，我们按照中国的一些实际情况对设定模型中的参数进行校正。我们考虑的样本经济为 1978—1998 年这二十年中国的宏观经济指标。资本产出率、资本折旧率、人均实际经济增长率、国债余额、人均实效劳动时间，这几个数据我们采用林细细和龚六堂(2007)的数值，分别 3.4、0.066 5、0.07、0.043 2和 0.24。劳动生产力的马尔可夫过程为

$$\ln e_{t+1} = \rho \ln e_t + \zeta_{t+1},\ \zeta_{t+1} \sim N(0,\ \sigma^2)$$

我们采用林细细和龚六堂(2007)取值，$\rho = 0.8$ 和 $\sigma = 0.06$。

我们采用 Barro(1990)的生产函数，关于生产函数参数的估计，我们采用反推的方法。在我们中国生产函数估计方面，尽管存在一定的争议，但是工资份额所占比重较低，这是一个不可否认的现实，于是，我们采用工资份额为 0.4，这也就意味着 $\alpha = 0.6$，这个数值和张军及邹至庄等人的结果基本保持一致。政府生产性公共开支 γ 我们采用 0.06，而消费性公共开支(将具有生产性的公共开支和转移支出排除在外) γ^c 我们采用 0.085 3，政府转移支出 χ 采用 0.022。这三个政府决策变量的数据来源于《中国统计年鉴 2001》和《中国统计年鉴 2005》中 1978—1998 年中国政府支出和政府税收资料进行相应的平均。风险回避系数方面，我们试验性采用 $v = 1.5$。

在此基础上，我们通过数值模拟得到其他参数值。首先，由下列两式得到样本经济的利率和税率。

$$\alpha = (r + \delta)k$$

$$\tau(1 - \alpha) + \tau r k + g b = \gamma + \gamma^c + \chi + (1 - \tau) r b$$

得到 $r = 0.11$，$\tau = 0.217$。

在消费者进行最优化选择时，如果存在着内点解，则以下条件得到满足

$$E(\tilde{c}_t) = \frac{\xi}{1-\xi}E(\tilde{w}e_t l_t)$$

而 $N = 1 - E(e_t l_t)$，$\tilde{w}N = (1-\tau)(1-\alpha)$

由资源约束条件，我们得到

$$E(\tilde{c}_t) = 1 - \gamma - \gamma^c - (g+\delta)k$$

于是，我们得到 $\xi = 0.2826$。

在这些参数设置的基础上，我们通过市场均衡条件得到 $\beta = 0.9939$。

总之，我们采用的参数列举如下：$\alpha = 0.6$，$\delta = 0.0665$，$g = 0.07$，$\chi = 0.022$，$\gamma^c = 0.0853$，$\gamma = 0.06$，$v = 1.5$，$\beta = 0.9939$，$\rho = 0.8$，$\sigma = 0.06$，$\xi = 0.2826$

（二）计算方法

我们采用 matlab 软件进行数值模拟计算。对于劳动生产力的马尔可夫过程，我们采用广为采纳的方法，即 Tauchen (1986)的做法，将其离散化为 7 个状态空间。

在我们采用的次优框架下，福利分析相应于每个债务负担率水平下的比较静态分析。即在给定的政府政策变量①下，计算均衡时我们采用如下方法。在给定一个经济增长率水平和劳动者的休闲水平(可以得出市场对劳动时间的需求)，我们可以资本存量的相对水平(相对于产出，下同，可以简单称之为资本的需

① 即政府生产性公共开支、消费性公共开支、政府转移支付和公债水平给定进行分析。

求水平)和工资水平,然后根据政府的预算平衡方程,我们得到税率水平。在此基础上,我们采用值函数迭代的方法求解动态规划方程,从消费者的最优化决策得到消费者对资产的供给水平和对劳动时间的供给水平。如果这两个供给和需求水平各自相等,那我们就得到了均衡的经济增长率水平和休闲水平,进而计算此时的福利水平。如果这两个市场没有同时达到均衡,那么我们需要改变经济增长率和休闲水平,直至两个市场达到均衡为止。

四、数值模拟结果

(一)福利评价标准

我们在具体经济的模拟中,由于在效用函数中,涉及休闲与劳动的替代,因此,我们需要固定或休闲其中一个要素,然后进行福利比较。为了跟没有休闲的效用函数比较,我们采用的标准是固定休闲。即通过我们得到的样本经济模型的数值与其他债务存量下的福利值,固定样本经济的休闲,通过这两个福利值换算出消费的福利收益或损失。

即若样本经济下均衡的消费和休闲流为 c_s^A 和 l_s^A,稳定分布为 λ^A,而另一经济的消费和休闲流为 c_s^B 和 l_s^B,稳定分布为 λ^B,假定从样本经济变为 B 经济的福利收益为 u。则

$$\int E_t V(\{(1+u)c_s^A,\ l_s^A\}_{s=t}^{\infty})\mathrm{d}\lambda^A = \int E_t V(\{c_s^B,\ l_s^B\}_{s=t}^{\infty})\mathrm{d}\lambda^B$$

当 $u > 0$ 时为福利收益,反之为福利损失。

(二)福利结果

在参数化的基础上,我们改变政府债务存量得到相应的福利值,进而我们进行最优债务分析。我们采用的福利基准为样本经济状况(1978—1998 年这一经济阶段宏观经济的福利状况)。以

此为参照，我们列举出债务存量从－1到0.5水平时的福利变化、消费比率（消费占产出的比例）、工作时间比率、利率、税率和经济增长率。从数值计算结果我们发现，在中国的经济参数下，政府公债的自我保险作用较小，不足以抵消公债提高造成的挤出效应和征收比例税造成的税收超额负担，最优的债务存量为负值①。从我们得到的结论来看，福利收益或损失比 Aiyagari 和 McGrattan(1998)要大很多，他们的结论从0到67%的债务存量变化的福利损失或收益还不到0.1%，而林细细和龚六堂(2007)则在外生技术进步的经济中得到，相比样本经济，当债务存量由样本经济水平提高到50%时，福利损失则仅将近1%。但是我们得到的福利情况则是如果将债务存量由样本经济提高到10%，福利损失为1.461 6%；20%的债务存量比例时，福利损失为3.974 6%；到50%的债务存量时，福利损失为10.623 3%。这些结果我们在图3中反映出来，在该图中，福利值的单位为1%，福利收益为0处，即样本经济处我们用一横线标出。从这些福利值来看，提高债务存量需要相当谨慎，因为其福利影响实在太大，因此有必要对我国政府公债政策进行足够的关注。

在图4中，随着债务存量提高，利率降低，这是由于提高公债负担率加剧了资本市场的风险，在内生增长的经济中，资本积累将增加。于是，资本回报率下降，即利率降低。这个结论跟 Aiyagari 和 McGrattan(1998)结论截然不同，这是由于 Aiyagari 和 McGrattan(1998)中资本市场不能通过增长效应释放出来，因此使得资本存量相应下降。由于随着公债负担率提高，经济增长率下降，于是，消费者的收入拿去补偿经济增长的资本将减少，这增加了当期消费，于是消费率提高，这在图5中得到反

① 整个福利收益的曲线应为倒U曲线，为了直观比较中国目前债务变化造成的福利影响，我们没有给出完整曲线。

映。而随着消费水平提高,休闲的边际效用提高,休闲提高,工作时间减少,图 6 也反映了这种关系。图 7 表明政府债务存量提高,税率增加。因为债务提高从政府预算角度来看意味着政府需要收取更多的税收,故税率相应提高。与我们前面的理论分析保持一致,提高政府公债存量降低经济增长率,我们从图 8 中直观地得出这一结论。

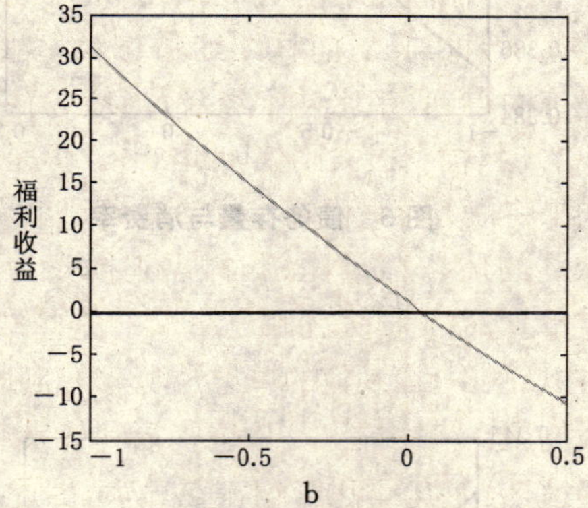

图 3　债务存量与福利收益

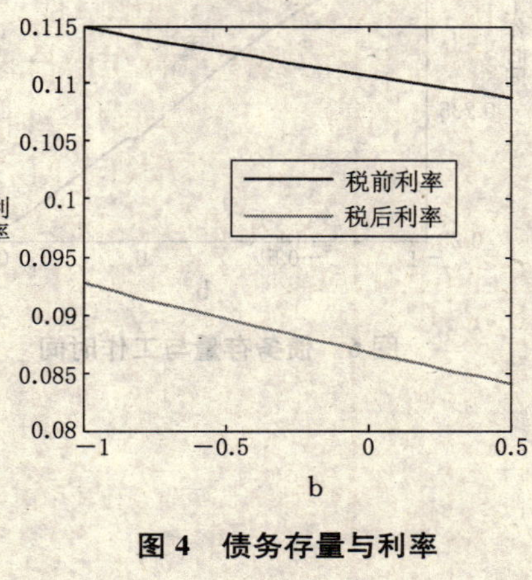

图 4　债务存量与利率

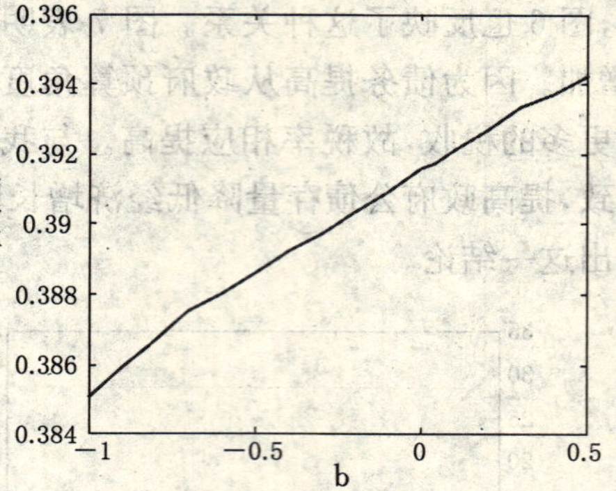

图 5　债务存量与消费率

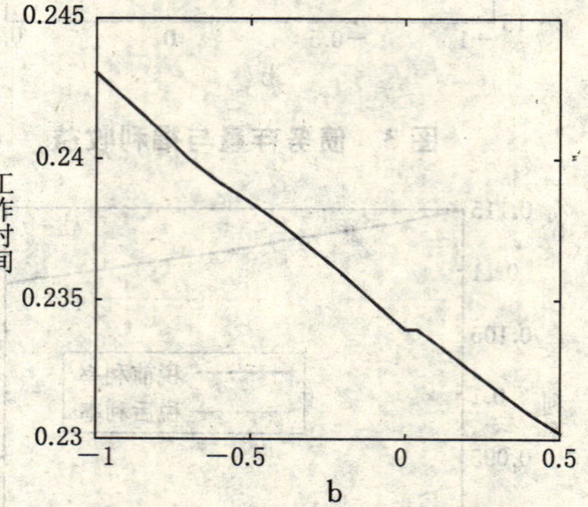

图 6　债务存量与工作时间

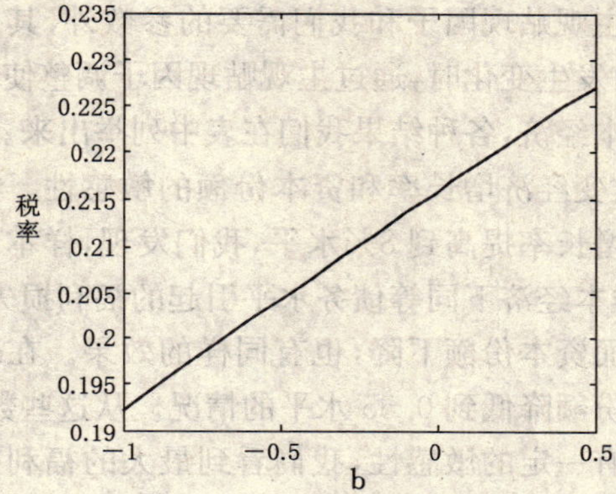

图 7　债务存量与税率

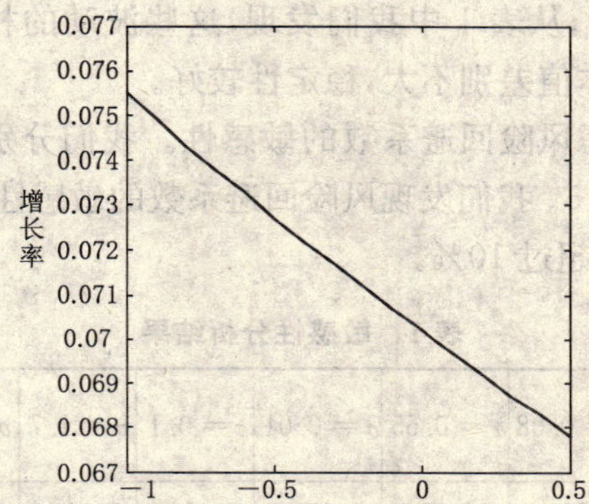

图 8　债务存量与经济增长率

为了更好地理解我们结论的可靠性，我们将在下一部分进行敏感性分析，即改变我们模型所依赖的参数，理解这些参数变化导致的福利影响。

（三）敏感性分析

本部分主要考虑我们得到的结论对于参数的敏感性。即我们假定除了主观贴现因子和我们需要的参数外，其他参数保持不变，当参数发生变化时，通过主观贴现因子调整使得其他经济变量符合样本经济，各种结果我们在表中列举出来。

首先，改变经济增长率和资本份额的敏感性。如果将样本经济的经济增长率提高到8%水平，我们发现，样本经济的增长率增加，与样本经济下同等债务水平引起的福利损失相比，其数值将较大。而资本份额下降，也有同样的效果。在表1中我们列举出资本份额降低到0.55水平的情况。从这些数值来看，这两个参数具有一定的敏感性，我们看到最大的福利损失不会超过10%。

其次，变动劳动生产力的波动，我们选取标准差为0.1和0.01两种情形，从表1中我们发现，这些波动的相比而言敏感性较差，跟样本值差别不大，稳定性较好。

最后，考虑风险回避系数的敏感性。我们分别取值为 $v=1.7$、1.1和0.5。我们发现风险回避系数的敏感性也是比较大，但是基本没有超过10%。

表1　敏感性分析结果

债务存量	样本经济	$g=0.08$	$\alpha=0.55$	$\sigma=0.01$	$\sigma=0.1$	$v=1.7$	$v=1.1$	$v=0.5$
0.1	1.461 6	1.738 9	1.457 5	1.375 3	1.424 9	1.319 1	1.635 7	2.428 4
0.2	3.974 6	4.412 0	4.119 7	3.727 8	3.917 7	3.567 6	4.394 7	6.421 4
0.3	6.297 0	7.038 9	6.565 0	6.078 5	6.385 3	5.787 9	7.301 7	10.274 0
0.4	8.450 7	9.653 8	8.643 1	8.337 0	8.810 5	7.945 9	9.812 4	13.976 6

注：表中的数据单位均为百分之一，且均为福利损失，为了方便，我们省略负号。

(四) 政策分析

从数值模拟的结果，我们得到在考虑了政府公共开支对生产产生影响的内生经济中，政府公债存量水平的变化对福利影响极大。相比样本经济，债务存量增加到 10%时，福利损失约为 1.5%；而提高到 20%，则福利损失约为 4%；提高到 30%时，福利损失则为 6%；提高到 40%时，福利损失约为 8%。总之，债务存量每提高 10%，将产生 2%左右的福利损失。因此，对公债大量发行的恐慌是有必要的。

那么，究竟我国从 1998 年开始以来实行的积极财政政策①，公债发行幅度增加导致公债存量上升会造成多大的福利影响呢？为了更为准确地研究这个问题，我们把改变了的财政政策详细考虑进去。我们注意到：1999 年至 2004 年，政府的消费性公共开支和转移支出发生了一定的变化，消费性公共开支从 8.53%增加到 8.63%，而转移支出从 2.2%降低至 1.07%，当我们把这个因素考虑进去时发现，相比原先的样本经济，目前的债务存量水平能够带来福利收益，而且福利收益较大，相比维持在 4.32%的债务存量水平，福利收益为 17.358 6%。而债务存量达到 20%时，则还有 12.314 3%的福利收益，即使债务存量水平达到 40%，其福利收益为 6.937 5%。总之，单纯考虑转移支付和政府消费性公共开支变化后的债务存量水平发生变化的福利影响时，我国目前大规模的发行公债相比以前而言，则仍然是一个较好的帕累托改进，有较大的福利收益。

但是，我们不能忽略一个事实：1999 年以来，我国政府的生产性公共开支比重急剧下降，1999 至 2004 年生产性政府公共开支下降至 3.731%。由于政府生产性公共开支影响经济的内生增长率，生产性公共开支减少将导致经济增长率急剧下降至 4%，自然而然，社会福利也将发生巨大的变化。在与样本经济

① 2003 年改为双稳健财政政策，公债发行额和存量继续增加。

同样的债务存量水平下，目前的财政政策的福利损失则达到87.486 5%——如此巨额的福利损失！不过，我们发现在这种经济下，改变债务存量造成的福利损失不是太大。如相比样本经济，当债务存量达到40%时，福利损失也仅为88.263 3%。即改变债务存量水平而保持其他财政政策不变时的福利损失不超过1%。于是，在这种经济中，政府改变生产性公共开支要相当谨慎，因为这种增长效应(growth effect)有时会很大。不过，这与目前社会上一直呼吁的政府公共开支过大并不矛盾，因为那主要是针对于政府白白浪费在消费性公共开支上和生产性公共开支效率低下而提出的。

五、结　论

本文的主要贡献是在Aiyagari和McGrattan(1998)的理论模型基础上，考虑了生产性公共开支对经济增长的影响。在此基础上，我们利用中国的经济参数进行实证分析，结果发现，在中国，尽管巴罗-李嘉图等价定理不能成立，这为存在最优公债提供一个合理存在理由，但是比较公债的正负效应，我们发现最优公债仍然为负。由于我们的目标放在目前中国讨论较多的大规模发行公债问题，因此我们主要集中在样本经济(1978—1998)基础上，讨论公债水平发生改变后带来的福利影响。而由于生产性公共开支将产生巨大的增长效应，政府公债提高降低了经济增长率，这产生很大的负福利效应，这一结果与Aiyagari和McGrattan(1998)、林细细和龚六堂(2007)差别较大，政府目前较大规模的发行公债需要相当谨慎！

而且假如我们将变化的政府开支和转移支出考虑进去，我们发现，其实目前的公债规模相比以前的样本经济，其福利损失将更大,达到 87%以上!因此,我们有必要将大规模发行公债视为洪水猛兽。

但是,本文仍然存在着一些需要改进的地方。首先,我们没有考虑国债的利率期限结构,而这个问题则是目前讨论较多的一大热点,如果将利率期限考虑进去,其福利影响将会如何?其次,我们考虑的是一个封闭经济的情形,如果拓展到开放经济,在经济大国和经济小国中,债务存量的变化又将带来怎样的福利影响?最后,假如我们进一步考虑分级财政,中央政府和地方政府都能发行公债,那结果又将如何?尽管中国目前没有地方政府发行公债,假如我们能够提出一些合理的理论解释,则将为地方发行公债与否提供一个较好的理论依据。

参考文献

贾康,赵全厚:《国债适度规模与我国国债的现实规模》,《经济研究》2000 年第 10 期。

林细细,龚六堂:《中国债务的福利损失分析》,《经济研究》2007 年第 1 期。

刘溶沧,马拴友:《赤字、国债与经济增长关系的实证分析——兼评积极财政政策是否有挤出效应》,《经济研究》2001 年第 2 期。

周佰成,刘艳武,丁志国:《国债的现行状况及最优规模分析》,《金融研究》2002 年第 1 期。

Aiyagari, S. Rao, 1994, "Uninsured Idiosyncratic Risk and Aggregate Saving", *Quarterly Journal of Economics*, 109:659—684.

Aiyagari, S. Rao, 1995, "Optimal Capital Income Taxation with Incomplete Markets, Borrowing Constraints, and Constant Discounting", *Journal of Political Economy*, 103:1158—1175.

Aiyagari, S. Rao and E. R. McGrattan, 1998, "The Optimum Quantity of Debt", *Journal of Monetary Economics*, 42:447—469.

Barro, Robert J., 1974, "Are Government Bonds Net Wealth?",

Journal of Political Economy, 82:1095—1117.

Barro, Robert J., 1990, "Government Spending in a Simple Model of Endogenous Growth", *Journal of Political Economy*, 98:103—125.

Chamley, Christophe, 1981, "The Welfare Cost of Capital Income Taxation in a Growing Economy", *Journal of Political Economy*, 89: 468—496.

Chamley, Christophe, 1986, "Optimal Taxation of Capital Income in General Equilibrium with Infinite Lives", *Econometrica*, 54:607—622.

Floden, M., 2001, "The Effectiveness of Government Debt and Transfers as Insurance", *Journal of Monetary Economics*, 48:81—108.

Lucas, R. E., Jr., 1990, "Supply-Side Economics: An Analytical Review", *Oxford Economic Papers*, 42:293—316.

Ramey, Garey and Valerie Ramey, 1995, "Cross-Country Evidence on the Link between Volatility and Growth", *American Economic Review*, 85:1138—1151.

Tauchen, G., 1986, "Finite State Markov Chain Approximations to Univariate and Vector Autoregressions", *Economic Letters*, 20:177—181.

Turnovsky, Stephen J., 1996, "Optimal Tax, Debt, and Expenditure Policies in a Growing Economy", *Journal of Public Economics*, 60: 21—44.

Woodford, M., 1990, "Public Debt as Private Liquidity", *American Economic Review Papers and Proceeding*, 80:382—388.

(原载《管理世界》2007 年第 8 期)

国内贸易与区际边界效应——保护与偏好

徐　勇

（中山大学）

赵永亮

（中山大学岭南学院）

一、问题的提出

1978 年经济改革以前，我国国内一直实施地区性自给自足战略，各省份长期被认为是结构雷同的经济独立体，相对封闭的不同省份在缺乏彼此贸易往来的情况下，难以从省际分工中获得收益。自斯密开始，理论上一直推崇自由贸易，强调分工和专业化程度给人们带来益处，相应的理论如李嘉图的比较优势理论、赫克歇尔和俄林的资源禀赋理论、马歇尔的外在规模经济理论（石磊，2005），被各国学者和政策指定者所推崇。然而诸多西方经济理论并未成为我国经济发展的实践指引。处于对国际政治形势的考虑，我国一直保持对内对外的内向型发展策略。

直到 20 世纪 80 年代后，深刻的变革全面开始，政府逐步从商品的分配、流通和价格设定中退出；中国对外开放步伐也呈现加速态势，各省份的努力也有目共睹，如中国各省份的平均贸易开放度从 1987 年的 14%增至 1997 年的 37%(Poncet，2003)。但是，关于国内地区一体化的绩效则褒贬不一，众多学者认为，随着改革开放的深入，尤其在 1983 年的“利改税”和 1994 年的“分税制”期间，财政为“分灶吃饭”的大包干制，地方利益得到强化，国内地区间市场封锁加剧；20 世纪 90 年代末期，相关研究显示，国内区际贸易强度呈下降趋势①。国内地区间商品贸易在各省商品吸收构成中比重的降低为国外商品和当地生产商品相应比重的增加所补偿(Poncet，2003)。因此，省际间贸易强度不断降低的原因不仅仅在于国际经济一体化的发展，更在于我国省份内部贸易的加强(即各省自给自足重度额的增强)，这似乎验证了我国市场分割的程度不断提高(而市场分割与地方保护是密切联系的，长期以来，中国地方保护的手段与形式多样，令人眼花缭乱，并且从显性走向更为隐蔽的保护壁垒②)。

尽管近年来中央政府采取了一系列措施，消除改革开放

① 通过省际之间的贸易数据，Poncet(2003)得出与 Naughton(1999)相似的结论，那就是省际间的地区性贸易在 GDP 和总贸易额中都占了较大的比重。中国省际间的平均贸易量在 1987 年、1992 年和 1997 年分别占 GDP 总量的 54%、50%和 38%。这些数据要比西欧、北美自由贸易区(NAFTA)以及东南亚国家联盟(ASEAN)等国家或地区间的相应贸易数额大得多；但是中国省际间的平均贸易量在 1987 年、1992 年和 1997 年分别占各省总贸易量的 88%、80%和 66%，显示出内贸强度的下降。

② 2001 年 4 月国务院《关于禁止在市场经济活动中实行地区封锁的规定》共列举了地方保护和地区封锁的 8 种类型，包括各种价格歧视、边界设卡，等等。国务院发展研究中心的调研显示，地方保护的措施包括限制或禁止企业进入本地，干扰司法体系、偏袒本地企业，凭借行政力量影响银行系统为本地企业融资，等等。在他们的调查问卷中，共列举了两方面 8 大类共 42 种保护手段和形式，结果显示这 42 种保护形式和手段都不同程度的存在，其中较为严重的集中在对劳动力流动的限制、对外地产品进入的诸多无形限制以及技术要素流动的限制最为严重[转引自踪家峰(2006)]。

以来出现的地区市场分割和地区保护主义的问题，努力建立符合社会主义市场经济需要的统一市场，但是相关学者认为国内统一市场的发展状况不尽如人意，地区间市场壁垒仍然在相当程度上存在。依据 Alwyn Young 在美国《经济学季刊》上的一篇大作，张军(2000)给出这位芝加哥大学经济学家的判断："中国过去 20 年里的所谓'转型'和'自由化'实际都有一些倒退。中国从只有一个中央计划到有许许多多相互竞争的计划。"Alwyn Young 认为，中国省际间的地区性贸易仅处于次优状态，实际上自从改革以来，国内地区分割的局面渐趋加剧。他在文中强调："完全可能出现这样的情况：中国经济虽然在国际层次上开放，在地方层次上却是支离破碎的。"Young(2000)的研究注意到在分权体制下，中国实际上为地方政府主导型市场经济，并认为各项改革推行过程中所遇到的一些问题成为 20 世纪 80 年代后期国内地区保护主义重新抬头的重要诱因。例如，从 1980 年开始推行的重要分权进程的政策(Poncet, 2003)；受 Tiebout(1956)经典论文《地方支出的纯粹理论》的思想影响，国内众多学者接受了 Tiebout 的"用脚投票"公共选择模式，认为分权体制是地方竞争的必要条件，可以促进地方政府的效率提升，有利于经济发展。实际上由于中央政策对沿海的倾斜，导致内地区域为了缩小因沿海地区享受优惠政策和"剪刀差"导致价格扭曲等因素所带来巨大的地区差别，而大力发展进口替代产业化政策等。在扩张冲动和激励机制下的中国地方政府利用手中的行政权力集中调配，甚至决定资源的配置，降低交易成本从而推动经济增长，但同时导致了国内市场的分割。

建立统一的全国大市场，是从计划经济体系向市场经济体系转型所要达成的最重要目标之一，历来受到中央和国家的重视①；依据"十一五"规划的思想，我国社会当前切实需要缩小区域经济发展差距，实现区域经济一体化，以此实现和谐社会的构建。

二、文献回顾：贸易的边界效应与市场分割

边界效应最早的经验实证出现在 McCallum(1995)的研究，其对美国各州和加拿大各省之间的贸易进行影响因素考察，并估计了两国之间贸易的边界效应，得出结论为加拿大各省之间的贸易量平均是各省与(相同规模和距离)美国各州贸易量的22倍，边界效应相当显著。此后学者从不同的分析角度不断证实边界效应的显著存在，如 Helliwell 在 1997 年的文献中对1989 年和 1990 年类似的边界效应值作了估计，鉴于边界效应的广泛存在性，Obstfeld 和 Rogoff(2000)认为边界效应已经成为"国际贸易之谜"(六谜之一)。在世界经济越来越一体化，全球贸易壁垒不断减弱的假定下，人们可以预期国家间的边界效应将呈减弱趋势，为了发现和验证边界效应，理论方法和实证检验不断涌现。

但是对 McCallum(1995)的后继研究显得维步艰难，主要原因是地区内部贸易数据很难获得。鉴于此，Wei(1996)用一

① 早在 1993 年中共十四届三中全会《中共中央关于建立社会主义市场经济体制若干问题的决定》中，就指出要"建立全国统一开放的市场体系，实现城乡市场紧密结合，国内市场与国际市场相互衔接，促进资源的优化配置"，该决定还对商品市场体系、要素市场体系、价格形成机制等方面的改革，进行了系统的规划。时隔十年，在十六届三中全会《中共中央关于完善社会主义市场经济体制若干问题的决定》中，再一次指出要"完善市场体系，规范市场秩序"，"加快建设全国统一市场"[转引自石磊(2006)]。

国的总产量减去其总出口量(到其贸易伙伴国)来计算各国与自己发生的贸易,该方法由于不记录地区贸易流仍可以获得边界效应的估计,而得到了广泛使用,如后期研究者(如 Chen, 2004)分别得出结论认为,OECD 国家之间以及欧盟(EU)国家之间均存在边界效应。Head 和 Mayer(2002)认为,利用 Wei (1996)的方法估计边界效应依赖于区域内部距离的测量,显然采取不同的距离测量方法直接影响边界效应的估计结果①,并且双边贸易不仅受制于彼此间的绝对距离,而且还依赖于他们同其他国家的地理位置,如西班牙和瑞典的距离基本等同于澳大利亚与新西兰的距离,但是后者之间的双边贸易更高,主要由于他们共同远离其他市场(Anderson and van Wincoop, 2003)。该情形加上内部贸易流数据的缺省,导致引力模型很难准确估计边界效应,因此,Matthias Helble(2006)利用德国与法国区域内部的物流运输数据(非货币价值数据),并借鉴了 Anderson 和 van Wincoop(2003)的思路,通过在引力模型中设置固定效应去除了各国价格指数差异的影响,并设定了国家间共同的边界、共同货币、语言、文化等虚拟变量加以控制,判定边界效应的存在以及检验其稳定性。

关于边界效应方法的应用有两类。第一类关心的是一个国家与另一个国家之间的贸易流,以此观察国家层面的市场一体化;第二类是衡量某一国家内部的市场分割,后者依赖国土内部的各个经济单位之间的贸易流量,以此作为参照水平,可以衡量

① Nitsch(2000)利用丹麦与德国的例子来阐述 Wei(1996)的方法存在问题,认为所有的国家内部距离相同是不合理的;在内部距离测量上,文献中存在两种基本方法来加以修正:第一种方法,Leamer(1997)以区域面积作为基础为矫正,其中内部距离可表示为 $\sqrt{area/\pi}$;第二种方法,Wolf(1997)利用最大城市间的公路实际距离来替代(Matthias Helble, 2006)。

边界对两个经济单位之间的贸易阻碍作用。

目前相应的国内研究甚是罕见，其中研究市场分割与壁垒的多数文献也均采用间接分析法来对待省际间的贸易变化，如叶裕民(2000)收集了1997年各省通过省级国家铁路货物运输流向的数据，分析了各省与其他省份的经济联系程度，只是从一个侧面来论证区际壁垒的存在及严重程度，因此能在多大程度上反映问题是值得商榷的，无法对区际壁垒程度进行有效量化研究，当前文献极少从实证上给出省际市场分割的壁垒程度。并且边界效应通常需要引力模型来完成估计，但国内现有研究忽视了其背后的理论基础，如黄赜琳(2006)直接利用引力模型来衡量部分行业层面的市场壁垒，未能给出市场分割的微观机制。鉴于此，本文将通过贸易流利用边界效应模型从多角度衡量我国省际的贸易壁垒程度，并构建适合我国区域内部贸易的"两地区的边界效应模型"，以弥补先前研究的不足，具体阐述如下。

三、两地区边界效应模型

在Dixit-Stiglitz(1977)和Krugman(1980)垄断竞争框架下，众多研究者以CES效用函数为基础，由消费者偏好的不对称性推导出一个类似引力模型的函数，从而易于估计出贸易的边界效应，例如Anderson(1979)，Head和Mayer(2000)、Poncet(2003)和Daria TAGLIONI(2004)。在Head和Mayer(2000)模型基础上，本文根据消费的异质性设定相对消费者偏好，以此分析地区间贸易流变动，并给出贸易边界效应的简单推导和方法实现。首先，假定经济体内只有两个地区，本省与"省外地区"或称为ROC地区(Rest of China的简称，包括所有其他省份)，消费者具有相同的 CES 效用函数，即代表性省内消费效用函数为：

$$U = (C_H^{\frac{\theta-1}{\theta}} + aC_F^{\frac{\theta-1}{\theta}})^{\frac{\theta}{\theta-1}} \tag{1}$$

θ 为产品的替代弹性($\theta < 1$)，C_H 为省内产品的消费，C_F 为本省对 ROC 地区产品的消费，a 为本省消费者的相对偏好，或者被看成消费者对 ROC 地区产品的一种厌恶程度($a = 1$ 表示消费无差异)，引入该偏好参数主要目的在于从贸易成本影响双边贸易流的过程中，分离出消费者偏好效应，尽管 Helpman (1999)认为只要控制了收入变量，还没有发现消费本土偏向(home bias)的经验证据，但是 Maurice Obstfeld(2000)认为通过相关贸易摩擦来分析本土偏向仍具有启发性。

此外，也假定 ROC 地区在相同效用函数下的消费分别为 C_H^* 和 C_F^*。本省代表性消费者具有收入 Y_H(而 ROC 地区代表性消费者具有收入为 Y_F)，以及省内外产品价格 P_H 和 P_F 时，本省代表性消费者的收入预算为 $P_HC_H + P_FC_F = Y$。依据 Wei (1996)的设定，我们也同样假定运输存在“冰山”运输成本 τ，则 ROC 地区产品输入本省的部分为 $(1-\tau)$，而本省与 ROC 地区贸易的其他壁垒统一确定为壁垒税(或称为“等价关税”)，以 t 表示；由于各省处于同一国家，因而无需考虑国际贸易的汇率换算问题，因而我们设定 ROC 地区产品到达本省的价格为：

$$P_F^* = P_F/(1-\tau)(1-t) \tag{2}$$

$$P_H^* = P_H(1-\tau)(1-t) \tag{3}$$

如果 $p \equiv P_F/P_H$ 以及 $p^* \equiv P_F^*/P_H^*$ (其中，P_H^* 和 P_F^* 分别为 ROC 地区本省产品的价格与外省产品的价格)，则

$$P \equiv p^*(1-\tau)^2(1-t)^2 \tag{4}$$

通过(1)式，对本省和 ROC 地区代表性消费者分别求解最大化效用函数，可得：

$$\frac{C_H}{C_F}=(p/a)^{\theta},\ \frac{C_H^*}{C_F^*}=(p^*/a^*)^{\theta} \tag{5}$$

结合(4)式和(5)式，我们可得：

$$\frac{C_H}{C_F}=\frac{C_H^*}{C_F^*}(a/a^*)^{-\theta}(1-\tau)^{2\theta}(1-t)^{2\theta} \tag{6}$$

此外，ROC 地区对本省产品的消费，同样受到两个地区收入对比的影响，我们认为$\frac{C_H^*}{C_F^*}$可由本省收入与 ROC 地区收入的比率决定，即满足函数关系 $\frac{C_H^*}{C_F^*}=f\left(\frac{Y_H}{Y_F}\right)$，则(6)式两边取对数，可得：

$$\ln\frac{C_H}{C_F}=\ln f\left(\frac{Y_H}{Y_F}\right)-\theta\ln(a/a^*)+2\theta\ln(1-\tau)+2\theta\ln(1-t) \tag{7}$$

(一) 贸易本土偏向(home bias)、消费偏好与边界效应分析

如果不考虑本省与 ROC 地区的规模因素，假定双方的收入是均等的；为了分析简单，我们也认为本省消费者的相对偏好 a 在地区间是无差异的，即 $a/a^*=1$，同时 $f(Y_H/Y_F)$ 为 C_H/C_F 简单的线形函数，由简单对称原则，可得关系式 $C_H/C_F=C_F^*/C_H^*$，结合(6)式我们可以得到：

$$C_H/C_F=C_F^*/C_H^*=(1-\tau)^{\theta}(1-t)^{\theta}=(p/a)^{\theta} \tag{8}$$

则可得代表性消费者对本土产品消费占对外省产品消费的比率为：

$$C_H/pC_F = p^* C_F^*/C_H^* = a^{-1}(1-\tau)^{\theta-1}(1-t)^{\theta-1} \tag{9}$$

以上 C_H/pC_F 代表贸易的本土偏向，如果不考虑其他壁垒，当 $\tau = 0.25$，$t = 0$，即贸易品在区际间存在一个较高的运输成本，Maurice Obstfeld(2000)认为在国际贸易实证研究中 0.25 并不高，在 $a = 1/3$，$\theta = 0.37$ 时 $C_H/pC_F = 4.2$，该比率基本等价于 Maurice Obstfeld 对 OECD 国家的观察值（当然若只考虑其他壁垒时令 $t = 0.25$，$\tau = 0$ 我们可以得到同样的结果）。

本土偏向的消费偏好弹性与边界效应弹性。首先，本土偏向的消费偏好弹性为固定值 $d\log(C_H/pC_F)/d\log a = -1$，即随着单位 a 的增加，本土偏向 C_H/pC_F 以同等单位的速度减小；而贸易边界壁垒程度越高，单位边界效应 t 减少对本土偏向的影响就越大还是越小？需要通过以下弹性关系式来体现，即：

$$\frac{d\log(C_H/pC_F)}{d\log t} = \frac{t}{1-t}(1-\theta) \tag{10}$$

当 $\theta = 0.37$，$t = 0.25$ 时，我们可以得到本土偏向的边界效应弹性 $t/(1-t)(1-\theta) = 0.21$，通过简单的参数代入，我们得到了一个小于 1 的弹性系数，该结论似乎与 Maurice Obstfeld (2000)的分析相悖，主要原因在于对 θ 理解的差异（不作累述）。以下我们分别从消费的相对偏好和边界效应来分析。

1. 消费的相对偏好

在无摩擦情形下，假定在一个完美世界里，贸易是无摩擦的（不存在运输成本，即 $\tau = 0$；也不存在其他的边界效应（壁垒障碍），即 $t = 0$），则贸易本土偏向的倒数直接等于本省消费者的相对偏好 a，也就是满足 $C_H/pC_F = 1/a$（如图 1），随着 a 的增加，我们可以观察到本土偏向递减的趋势；当 $a = 1$（即消费无差异时），$C_H/pC_F = 1$，该类特殊情形下，区际间不存在贸易的本土偏向（如图点 A）。

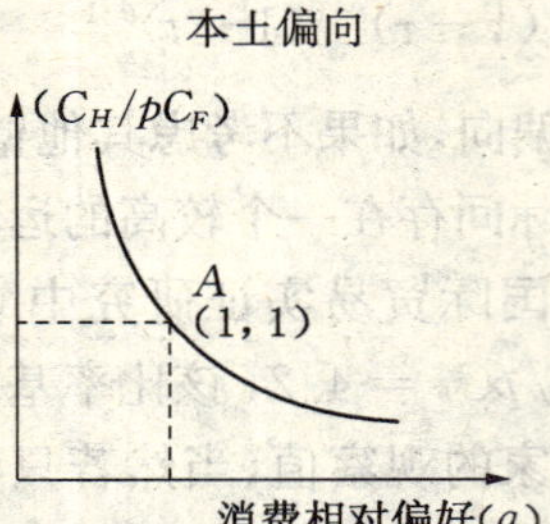

图 1　无摩擦情形

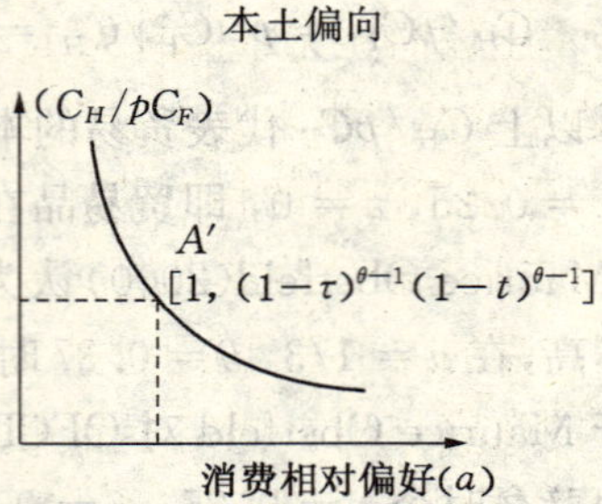

图 2　有摩擦情形

当贸易世界存在摩擦时，该情形下本土偏向曲线要高于无摩擦情形，即 A' 要高于 A，说明高额的壁垒或运输成本构建了贸易阻力的边界效应，使得区域内的消费倾向于本省产品(如图 2)。

2. *贸易的边界效应*

区际间的边界壁垒越高，$1-\tau$ 和 $1-t$ 相应越低，则本土偏向 C_H/pC_F 就越高，当区际完全分割时，贸易不再发生，于是 C_H/pC_F 倾向于无穷大(各省份完全消费各自生产的本省产品)；相应边界效应的本土偏向曲线见以下图 3 和图 4，假定不存在消费的相对偏好(如图 3)，无摩擦时，均衡本土偏向为 1(无偏向点，即点[(1, 1), 1]所示)；如果存在消费的相对偏好，则

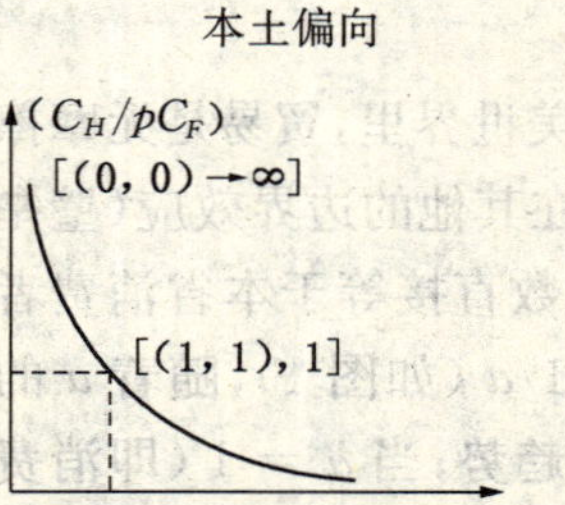

图 3　无偏好情形

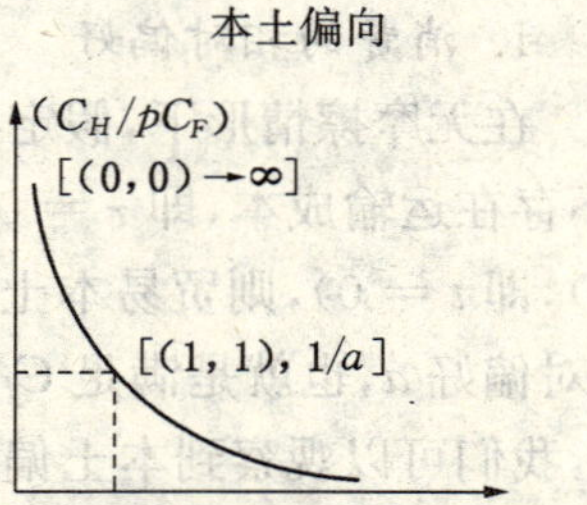

图 4　有偏好情形

均衡本土偏向在无摩擦时为 $1/a$（即点$[(1,\ 1),\ 1/a]$所示），显然，边界壁垒对本土偏向的作用大小（边界效应对 C_H/pC_F 作用程度）受制于消费的相对偏好。

（二）考虑公共支出的消费偏好

产品的保护程度）通过其支出占本省消费的比率来反映（高比率的政府支出被假定本省更具保护市场的能力）。结合(7)式，我们给出政府部门与私人部门分别对本省产品相对偏好的权重，即：

$$\ln(a/a^*) = \eta \cdot \ln(a/a^*)_{pub} + (1-\eta) \cdot \ln(a/a^*)_{priv} \quad (11)$$

其中，η 为公共消费占本省消费的比率，$(1-\eta)$ 为私人消费占本省消费的比率；$\ln(a/a^*)_{pub}$ 和 $\ln(a/a^*)_{priv}$ 分别为公共部门与私人部门的相对本土（本省）消费偏好，于是(7)式变为：

$$\ln\frac{C_H}{C_F} = \ln f\left(\frac{Y_H}{Y_F}\right) - \theta\eta \cdot \ln(a/a^*)_{pub} -$$
$$\theta(1-\eta) \cdot \ln(a/a^*)_{priv} + 2\theta\ln(1-\tau) + 2\theta\ln(1-t) \quad (12)$$

当消费偏好变量引入后，理论上将部分抵消相应的边界壁垒，通过(12)式与(7)式的比较，我们期望边界效应的系数应该有所下降①，以及政府支出变量的系数较为显著，这将反映本省公共消费相对私人消费存在较大的本土偏好。

（三）边界效应的实证模型

本文构建的两地区模型与先前的研究尽管存在设计差异，但终究需要通过省际贸易流来验证我国市场一体化程度，这就需要回到估计方程，并通过引力模型来实现回归检验，原因在于

---

① 主要鉴于新考虑的“重要变量”在引入模型后，可以部分抵消进入残差的固定效应（即边界效应）。

引力模型的灵活性，如 Engel、Charles 和 John，H. Rogers (1996)以及 McCallum(1995)等人在模型设计方面均考虑了实证方法的便捷性。

鉴于此，通过(7)式本文选取 McCallum 引力模型，以省份层面不同年份的总贸易量为基础①，构造适用于面板数据的简单回归模型，如下：

$$\ln(C_H^{it}/C_F^{it^*}) = \beta_1 \ln(Y_{it}/Y_{i^*t}) + \beta_2 \ln d_{ii^*} + \beta_4 \ln g_{pub,i} + \beta_3 East + bor_{prov} + bor_{year} + \varepsilon_{ii^*t} \quad (13)$$

(13)式左边 $C_H^{it}/C_F^{it^*}$ 是本省消费比率(即本省产品消费与 ROC 地区产品消费的比率)，主要通过贸易流比率来计算；Y_{it}/Y_{i^*t} 为本省与 ROC 地区的收入比率；d_{ii^*t} 为本省与 ROC 地区的距离。此外，其决定“冰山”运输成本 τ 的大小(依据本省与我国其他省份距离的均值，并以产出为权重计算所得，具体测算方法见 Poncet(2003))，同时我们考虑东部地区更易接近外部市场，和内陆省份存在区位差异，鉴于回归可能存在异方差，故加入东部省份的虚拟变量来控制(是东部省份为 1，否则为 0)；(12)式的 t 项需要固定效应来反映，即(13)式最后的两项 bor_{prov}

① 此外，如果选取了不同省份产业层面的数据，为了更好反映边界效应在不同产业的差异性，我们再次设定相关的模型，如下：

$$\ln(C_H^{ik}/C_F^{i^*k}) = \beta_1 \ln(Y_i/Y_{i^*}) + \beta_2 \ln d_{ii^*} + \beta_3 East + bor_{prov} + bor_{ind} + \varepsilon_{ii^*k} \quad (14)$$

$$\ln(C_H^{ik}/C_F^{i^*k}) = \beta_1 \ln(Y_i/Y_{i^*}) + \beta_2 \ln d_{ii^*} + \beta_3 \ln g_{pub,i} + \beta_4 East + bor_{prov} + bor_{ind} + \varepsilon_{ii^*k} \quad (15)$$

$C_H^{ik}/C_F^{i^*k}$ 为本省的消费比率(即对本省 k 产业产品消费与对 ROC 地区 k 产业产品消费的比率)，固定效应 bor_{prov} 和 bor_{ind} 分别表示省份固定效应与产业固定效应。

和 bor_{year}，分别表示省份固定效应和年份固定效应，用以反映不同省份的边界效应和时期边界效应的变化。(13)式中，g 为省份总消费中公共支出的比率，加入 g 反映消费的偏好效应。

此外，本文仅构建两地区(省份)模型，将所有其他地区归类为 ROC 地区。如此的构思主要在于数据的可得性，因为我国统计年鉴只有简单的省份投入产出表，并很笼统地记录每个省份对所有外部省份的零售(或批发)贸易输入数据和输入数据，因而省份之间的贸易数据难以获取，于是 ROC 地区的特征(如产量、消费支出以及与贸易对象的距离等)需要通过其他组成省份的总和(或平均值)来代替。(12)式的贸易流比率没有考虑国际贸易，但不受其影响，因为投入产出表可以直接扣除国际贸易部分。在实际估计中，模型采取贸易的相对比率，控制了国际一体化的贸易效应，两地区模型就可以完全排除第三方的干扰，主要鉴于 Sandra Poncet(2005)的思路，即使国际市场存在贸易波动演进，消费者在对待外贸需求整体缩小(或扩大)时，将按比率调整本省消费和 ROC 地区消费以便达到弥补的目的。

四、数据、回归描述与变量设置

以上省份贸易流数据主要来自我国各省份相关年份统计年鉴，各省产业部门的详细数据来自不同省份统计年鉴的国内贸易(或商业)相关数据表以及相应的投入产出表；一方面鉴于数据可得性，另一方面为了观察 1994 年我国财税改革和 1998 年国有企业改革的影响，本文选取 1997 年、2002 年与 2005 年为样本年；此外，我们一共选取了 28 个省份的三次产业数据。

边界效应通过(13)式的常数项来加以体现，在年份与产业基础上，我们能观察我国国内市场分割总体水平和演进；总体上，实证选取了1997年、2002年与2005年三个时间通过省份的面板数据，估计了跨省份贸易壁垒的年份差异与产业区别。在样本期内，如果我们发现省际间的边界效应在不断增加，这意味着国内市场仍难以走向一体化，期间的贸易障碍不容忽视。

实证结果见表1，在控制产业的差异之后，年份虚拟变量year02和year05的引入可以很好地反映期间1997—2002年及2002—2005年的平均边界效应变化，系数的大小间接反映边界效应变化程度，符号决定跨省份贸易壁垒的平均变化方向，负号表示随着时间跨省份贸易具有壁垒减少情况下的增加趋势。年份虚拟变量的回归系数需要从子样本来验证，其中回归3、回归4与回归5分别为1997年、2002年和2005年的样本，通过子样本回归的边界效应系数，我们可以考察边界效应的演进方向是否稳定，从而最终排除模型中其他干扰因素的决定影响。

区域差异与稳健性检验。我国省份贸易是否会表现出区际差异？简单地说，东西部地区由于经济结构与发展程度处于不同层次，是否表现出差异的市场分割？在东部虚拟变量忽略下，是否会出现区际的组间异方差，从而影响回归结果的稳健性，于是本文引入回归6和回归7来加以检验。

最后，最值得关注的是政府的支出偏好，我们引入回归8和回归9来考察其显著性，同时我们也注意到政府购买在工业品与农业品之间可能存在差异，在兼顾政府支出比例时，我们有理由认为工业品和农业品的省际贸易可能存在差异，也同样影响总体的回归结果(回归8、回归9引入了产业虚拟变量)。

此外，我们有理由认为公共部门与国有企业(SOEs)在传统上更具有地方色彩，一个地方国有企业的市场力量越大，我们认为该地区更具有干预市场的能力，也更具有地方保护意识；另一个原因，我们认为政企不分同样导致地方保护，而地方国营企业和集体企业的主管人员通常来自地方政府的调动，（由于同政府部门存在互调关系和交往的频繁性）他们更可能是地方政府官员的社会网络，由于这些企业属于地方政府，地方政府就要既当裁判员，又当运动员。在这种情况下，地方保护就成为地方政府的理性行为，地方政府作为地方官员的集合体，是约束条件下的最大化者，尤其是在规范地方保护的规则尚不健全，实施机制和力度十分薄弱的情况下，更是如此。

为了获取对政府公共支出比率变量的替代检验，我们引入国有企业对本省的产出份额作为工具变量，进一步检验地方政府的偏好是否造成了边界效应的相应影响。

五、边界效应的估计与检验分析

一个省与ROC地区之间的边界效应可以被看成该省份与其他地区整体的贸易壁垒，依据McCallum（1995）的测算方法，固定常数项可以通过指数形式来表示，值得注意的是，无论采取哪种单位形式来衡量边界效应，本身并不具有差异性，因为孤立的个体省份很难从边界效应绝对值来得出有价值的信息，我们需要的是通过单一指标，从时间演进和省份差异比较的动态角度来考察贸易的边界效应。

（一）边界效应的获取

正是由于以上考虑，本文作了一组（一系列）回归，从不同角度动态观察贸易的边界效应。总体来看，回归方程表现良好，反映壁垒效应的系数几乎都为预期的符号（也较为显著）。此外，我们可以通过年份虚拟变量来判断我国总体的贸易壁垒演进

表 1　贸易流的回归表

变　量	回归 1	回归 2	回归 3 1997 年样本	回归 4 2002 年样本	回归 5 2005 年样本	回归 6 西部	回归 7	东部	回归 8	回归 9 Ⅳ
边界效应	3.35***	3.12***	2.37***	3.38***	(0.48)	3.40***	3.67***	2.72***	4.67***	−2.52***
bor_{prov}	(0.46)	(0.54)	(0.35)			(0.47)	(0.56)	(0.05)	(0.23)	(0.40)
相对产量	−0.82***	−0.24	0.52	−0.59	−0.62***	0.12	−0.62*	−0.32	0.48	
$\ln(Y_i/Y_{i^*})$	(0.12)	(0.32)	(0.45)	(0.64)	(0.29)	(0.60)	(0.42)	(0.57)	(0.69)	
公共支出		0.17						0.06	0.12	
比率 $\ln g_{pub,i}$		(0.54)						(0.42)	(0.54)	
Year05	0.02**	0.04				0.27***	−0.12***	0.27	0.02	
	(0.01)	(0.03)				(0.14)	(0.06)	(0.27)	(0.94)	
Year02	0.17**	0.07**				−0.11***	0.36***	0.52	−0.04	
	(0.15)	(0.04)				(0.04)	(0.16)	(0.34)	(0.04)	
相对距离		0.72	0.62	0.59	0.52**	1.04 *	−0.23	1.66***	0.46	0.83**
$\ln d_{ii^*}$		(0.74)	(0.58)	(0.83)	(0.34)	(0.74)	(0.95)	(0.43)	(0.48)	(0.43)
东部变量		−0.07**	−0.12	0.05**	−0.16**	−0.09*			0.12**	−0.15**
East		(0.04)	(0.14)	(0.03)	(0.08)	(0.06)			(0.07)	(0.09)

（续表）

变　量	回归 1	回归 2	回归 3 1997 年样本	回归 4 2002 年样本	回归 5 2005 年样本	回归 6 西部	回归 7	东部	回归 8	回归 9 Ⅳ
工业品									0.11** (0.04)	0.02** (0.01)
Num	168	168	56	56	56	42	66	168	168	
$\overline{R}$	0.42	0.60	0.47	0.45	0.58	0.33	0.63	0.53	0.62	
Ramsey reset 检验	0.62	0.65	0.45	0.68	0.69	0.56	0.85	0.55	0.45	

注：括号内为标准误；***，**，*号分别表示 1%，5%和 10%的显著性水平；“工业品”变量：是取 0，否则取 1。

过程，回归 1 中 Year05 和 Year02 两变量显著为正，表示平均的边界效应在 1997—2002 年，2002—2005 年之间有上升的趋势。为了进一步观察我们的结论是否稳健，本文也做了相关年份(1997 年、2002 年和 2005 年)的子样本回归，结果也部分证明了 1，2，6，7 等回归的估计[①]。就回归 1 来看，平均边界效应分别从 1997 年的 28.5[exp(3.35)]增加到 2002 年的 33.8[exp(3.35+0.17)]，从 2002 年的 33.8[exp(3.35+0.17)]增加到 2005 年的 34.5[exp(3.35+0.17+0.02)]。在去除运输成本，相对产出和价格因素外，1997 年中国省份实际上消费了当地的产品要多于外省产品的 28.5 倍，2002 年更高达 33.8 倍(而 2005 年又略高于 2002 年)。

(二) 边界效应的实证结果与国际比较

以上的实证类似于(McCallum(1995)，Helliwell(1997)以及 Kyoji Fukao 2004)的分析，边界效应的估计值也接近于以上学者的研究(如 McCallum(1995)对美国与加拿大的实证，发现边界效应为 22 左右)，但能否就此进行国际比较？笔者认为直接比较未免太草率，尽管 Helliwell(1997)和 Wolf(2000)等人研究认为，我国省份间边界壁垒接近于众多主权国家之间的国界壁垒，同时又大于相应国家内部区域的边界壁垒；而 Sandra Poncet(2005)等人的研究认为，在 1992—1997 年我国国内边界效应与其他贸易区相比是升高的，但是我们需要区别的是，国际间的贸易壁垒与国内情形不同，我们所计算的诸指标与其他国家或地区(如欧盟、OECD 国家、加拿大与美国等)的市场一体化研究的相应结果仍然不具有不可比性，本文的观点不同于

---

① 年份虚拟变量的引入也说明了组间异方差的可能存在，在 F 检验下，相应年份的边界效应在 5%显著性水平下是有差异的，于是拒绝了三个子样本回归系数相等的假定。

Sandra Poncet(2003，2005)的分析，一方面在于我国省份处于一国行政管辖内，且本文没有纳入国际贸易，而国外跨区域的分析通常同时考虑国家边界和省份边界，但是我们认为影响我国省份边界效应的因素相对单一，因为我国国内省份在制度规范、立法、语言、文化以及种族等方面差异不像西方各国、OECD或北美贸易国之间的差异，前者的差异要小于后者的差异，这样的思考应该可以得到证实。此外，就人口因素来说，笔者赞同Sandra Poncet(2005)的观点，因为客观来说，我国人口规模要高于任何欧洲国家，其内部省份的人口密度也同等层次高于加拿大以及美国的各州(或省)，而基于人口的经济体可能存在规模效益，从而使得我国贸易更少依赖省份以外的地区。

(三) 我国的市场分割是否具有地域性

本文的回归也正从该角度对东西部样本进行区别分析，尽管系数在两个组之间差异较大，我们依旧发现两组区域在样本期存在增加的国内贸易壁垒，回归6和回归7的比较意味着中部省份可能比其他区域更具有封闭性(或市场分割性)，这点也可以从其他回归的区域变量“东部变量”得出(该变量几乎均为负，显示东部省份更倾向于购买外地产品)；鉴于回归6和回归7两组之间存在明显的差异，一个可能的原因是个别地区的异常性，如果从样本中去除，我们可以预期两组样本回归将可能具有收敛性，尽管存在部分收敛，但是决定性因素还是某种壁垒因素导致样本期我国普遍存在的市场分割逐渐加剧。

就引力模型的基本变量(产出和距离)，我们的结果是稳健的。从产出变量的系数可以看出，除回归3、回归6和回归8外，其他均为负号，说明随着产量的增加，地方购买本土产品的倾向是下降的；相应的子样本也基本与总体样本一致，距离变量多数显著为正，说明随着距离增加，各省份对本省产品的消费比率趋于提高。

在考察回归 8 和回归 9 时，我们也部分得到预期的结果（政府公共支出比率变量有着预期的符号，并且在 10% 水平下显著），由于该比率越大，说明省份的地方保护主义越盛行，意味着政府对本地区产品的购买偏好较大，从回归 9 来看，引入了工具变量后，其他相关变量发生了较为明显的变化，但是我们依然可以从"国有企业对本省的产出份额"变量的系数得出回归 8 类似的结果；此外，农业和工业的产业分组情况下，我们发现政府支出比率似乎更加显著为正，同时回归 8 和回归 9 系数均有所降低，取代的是产业虚拟变量"工业品"系数为正，也正意味着工农业产品在贸易壁垒方面的差异。也就是说，地方政府可能对农业更具保护意识，由于地方政府在谋求经济发展的战略思考时，可能更多地考虑对当地低价格原料的控制，以便满足当地制造业生产，相关的农产品如木材、丝绸、棉花、谷物和烟草①。当然，为了突破地方经济发展的瓶颈，地方政府的保护偏好不仅仅在于重视农业品材料，也同样在于对工业原材料（如电力、煤炭和水资源等工业品）进行保护和控制管理②；处于数据的可得性，本文未能获取完整的行业数据，以便进行观察地方保护主义的行业偏好。

为了获取省份边界效应的演进过程，我们需要对方程 1 按不同样本重新进行回归，也就是说，工业品和农业品分开得到两个面板数据，分别对各省 3 个年份的面板数据进行回归，并通过省份固定效应来获取不同省份边界效应的年份均值，然后在已有的回归（见表 1）基础上，利用边界效应的年份增量对均值进

---

① 转引自 Chinese Economic Studies(1993)；Watson 等(1996)。

② Lu(2002)，Naughton(2003)以及 Sandra Poncet(2005)均对工业品的地方保护偏好进行了阐述。

行调整得到不同年份的省份边界效应，如表 2。

表 2　边界效应的指数值

省　份	边界效应(农业品)			边界效应(工业品)		
	均值	1997 年	2005 年	均值	1997 年	2005 年
东　部						
北　京	22	25	30	27	30	37
天　津	11	12	15	12	13	16
辽　宁	122	134	164	4	4	5
河　北	25	27	33	33	37	45
上　海	10	11	13	13	15	18
江　苏	30	33	40	25	27	33
浙　江	13	15	18	18	20	25
山　东	6	7	8	20	22	27
福　建	49	55	67	60	67	81
广　东	1	2	2	4	5	6
海　南	33	37	45	10	11	13
中　部						
山　西	20	22	27	9	10	12
内蒙古	90	99	122	60	67	81
吉　林	30	33	40	25	27	33
黑龙江	4	5	6	15	16	7
安　徽	27	30	37	37	40	49
江　西	134	148	181	3	4	4
河　南	27	30	37	12	13	16
湖　北	15	16	20	6	7	8
湖　南	16	18	22	3	3	4
广　西	55	60	74	8	9	11
西　部						
贵　州	55	60	74	22	25	30
云　南	40	45	55	25	27	33

（续表）

省份	边界效应（农业品）			边界效应（工业品）		
	均值	1997年	2005年	均值	1997年	2005年
四川	18	20	25	12	13	16
陕西	7	7	9	9	10	12
甘肃	110	122	148	55	60	74
宁夏	45	49	60	45	49	60
新疆	245	270	330	60	67	81

注：边界效应为指数值，1997年和2005年的边界效应为调整值（按照年均增量调整）。

均值系数显然与表1的结论基本一致（工业品和农业品的边界效应系数对照，表面两组系数也是显著差异的；就农业品来说，地方的保护力度从西到东呈现阶梯形），但是东部与中西部省份总体来看，仍然具有相近的均值，值得关注的是，不同省份的边界效应具有很高的均值偏差，最低边界效应值为广东省仅为0.4（指数值为1），而最高的边界效应值为5.5（指数值为245），相差10倍多（指数值差异则更大[①]）。此外，就东部省份来看，广东、山东、浙江和上海均表现出较低的系数值（这也与大多数相关研究相近），说明沿海地区可能拥有更为发达的交通基础设施，具有更高的开放度，不仅对海外市场具有较高的外贸依存度，并且也易于接受内陆省份的双边贸易，显示了开放经济体的低壁垒战略。而西部省份和部分中部省份则显示了极大的边界效应，一方面可能在于计量回归的误差（实际难免的），另一方面应该归因于中西部欠发达的交通条件、不够通畅的信息以及

① 表2中的边界效应系数按指数进行了归类，结果可能导致均值偏差较大，但仍然可以从动态和省份角度来观察边界效应的演进和分布。

自然地理的障碍(普遍与东部省份保持一定的空间距离),自然条件的因素影响也从表1回归的"东部变量"看得出,封闭的自然条件导致省际间的贸易量大大减少。

六、边界效应的影响因素分析

以上实证显示边界效应在1997—2002年,2002—2005年之间有上升的趋势。于是存在两个问题:①壁垒的增加为什么持续了两个样本时期,边界贸易壁垒到底存在什么形式?②我国市场一体化的缺失到底存在什么影响因素?前个问题可以通过对众多学者的政策研究而得知①,如踪家峰(2006)根据陈甬军(1993)和银温泉、才婉茹(2001)的研究将贸易的地方保护和地区分割分成两种形式或阶段:一是硬性的强制手段,二是掩蔽的保护措施。时期上虽然不能完全与我们的实证相吻合,但是可以认为1997—2002年的国内市场更接近于前个阶段,而2002—2005年地方保护主义下的国内市场更接近于后个阶段,因为2001年后,中央开始采取措施干预硬性的地方保护主义,使得贸易保护主义隐蔽化,如雷明(2005)等人的研究也反映出国内各地区间的贸易壁垒的形式趋于隐蔽化,这些隐蔽形式主

① 2001年4月国务院《关于禁止在市场经济活动中实行地区封锁的规定》列举了地方保护和地区封锁的8种类型,后经过踪家峰(2006)归纳,将贸易的地方保护分为两大类:一是硬性,也是显性的保护和分割形式,主要有资源原材料争夺型的分割,最著名的是为此进行的各种大战,如"煤炭大战"、"棉花大战"、"苎麻大战"、"蚕茧大战"等,要素流动的阻碍型分割,如各地对人口流动的限制,对跨区作业的农机进行的阻挠;破坏市场型分割,如设卡收费、限制外来商品等;二是软硬兼施型,随着中央的各种限制措施的出台,各地的地方保护形式也逐渐随之而变,由硬的显性的分割形式过渡到软硬兼施型,并且以软的隐性形式为主,包括各种隐蔽的技术壁垒和行政性措施如多头检验、重复检验,超严执法,甚至是百般刁难(踪家峰,2006)。

要由地方政府和地方司法部门进行实施，想方设法设置不同程度的市场准入限制或歧视。

从表 2 我们已经部分得知省际间的贸易壁垒存在较大差异，因此有必要利用已估计的系数作为因变量，并寻求可能的潜在解释变量来对此进行再估计。除了公共支出比率 $\ln g_{pub,i}$，回归考虑了国有（或地方集体）企业比重，我们认为该比重高，意味着地方政府干预经济能力更强，同时也更具有地方保护欲望①。

“林氏命题”的检验。此外，我们给出林毅夫与刘培林（2005）的两个市场分割命题以待检验②。他们在其经济发展论坛工作论文《地方保护和市场分割：从发展战略的角度考察》中提到，国有企业的政策性负担和软预算约束问题以及中国不同省份的赶超战略对市场结构的影响，尤其对市场分割的影响，也就是说，分权式改革以及地方政府主导的新的赶超均可能导致地方保护和市场分割。笔者的实证可以就两个命题做部分检验，思路等同于前段的分析。

回归也引入了“财政自主变量”（财政收入占 GDP 的比率），

① 由于国有企业通常肩负着地方政府的“使命”，同时政府对国有企业通常也更具地方认同感（如一些大型国有企业的所属地政府主要依靠国有企业作为支柱产业，一方面可以带来高额的利税，另一方面可以提供大量的本地就业）；在行政（和人事调动）上，国有企业与政府部门的互动性很强，显示了政企的利益高度相关性。

② “林氏命题”（林毅夫、刘培林，2005）：命题 2：就国民经济而言，随着非国有经济的发展，经济发展战略逐渐转向比较优势战略，传统的三位一体经济体制的各个环节的改革都在深入，这必然伴随着市场一体化程度的提高。

命题 3：凡是地方政府继续执行赶超战略（具体执行赶超任务的企业可能是国有企业，也有些可能是非国有企业），且地方政府拥有一定的经济和行政力量的情形下，则地方保护和市场分割就不可避免。如果地方政府是在分权式改革中获得了更多的经济和行政力量，那么，分权式改革后的地方保护和市场分割要比之前严重。

我们认为地方政府如果拥有高额的财政收入，意味着其对经济的支配地位也较强（在 20 世纪 90 年中期财税改革以后，地方政府具有更高的财政自主权），在地方经济绩效最大化的刺激下，地方政府可能更具地方保护主义；源于财政收入缺乏导致的财政支出压力也是导致许多财力薄弱地区加强地方封锁和地方保护的动因之一。冯兴元（2002）认为，改革开放以来，中央政府向地方政府不断转移支出责任，使得地方政府的许多事务以及事业开支都必须由自身来解决，相应的义务必须依据法定条件来履行，如教育支出 2000 年达到 GDP 的 4%，医疗卫生支出增长不低于总收入的增长等等。这种支出责任一直从中央经过省级和地市级，最后转移到县乡级政府身上，从而导致县乡级支出任务最重，于是"财政自主变量"系数符号难以预期。

此外，进口率也是一个可能影响省份对内贸易的关键变量；而就业率作为政府干预的指标也被引入，以便对方程进行控制，因为我们同样有理由认为地方封锁和地方保护的动因之一就是促进本地经济增长，维持和扩大就业，减少失业以便稳定经济。

相关的变量和回归结果见表 3（解释变量的样本来自各省份 1997 年、2002 年和 2005 年相关统计数据，并做均值处理）。

从回归 a 来看，公共支出比率系数出乎意料显示为负值，但也是相对的不显著，因而也没有很高的可信度。较为显著的变量有国有企业比重和财政自主，且都显著为正，这说明一个省份如果拥有高份额的国有企业产值（即非国有企业在经济中的比重较低），则地方政府在实施地方保护策略上具有很大的干预能力和偏好，从侧面部分支持了"林氏命题"。林（2005）通过经验证据（抽样调查）只是推断其命题 2 和命题 3 的成立，结论认为非国有企业的成长有利于我国的市场一体化程度的提高。20 世纪 90 年代中后期，大量的非国有企业在没有享受国家保护和扶持的前提下成长起来，尤其1998年后国企改革完善了企业的市场机制，增强了民营资本在市场资源配置中的基础性作用，本研究鉴于数据的可得性，没有考察改革进程的影响，需后期深入分析。

表3　边界效应的影响因素

变　量	回归 a	回归 b	回归 c	回归 d	回归 e	回归 f
常　数	−8.12 (15.76)	8.67 (9.90)	−13.81 (13.7)	11.10 (14.02)	−11.46*** (5.11)	−10.93* (7.19)
公共支出比率 $\ln g_{pub,i}$	−2.50 (12.43)	−7.86 (10.18)	2.71 (10.64)	−8.82 (12.96)		
国有企业比重	7.79** (4.62)	1.22 (3.81)	6.90* (4.39)			7.97** (4.44)
财政自主	5.36** (2.32)		4.64** (2.12)		3.07** (1.86)	5.45*** (2.22)
进口率	−1.39 (1.62)			−0.10 (1.63)	−0.33 (1.36)	−1.23 (1.40)
就业率	0.32 (1.45)			0.13 (1.55)	0.26 (1.49)	0.31 (1.42)
R-squared	0.22	0.12	0.20	0.19	0.20	0.22

注：括号内系数为标准误。***，**，*号分别表示1%，5%和10%的显著性水平。

同样林(2005)也认为，分权式改革后的地方政府更具干预经济的行政力量，这又加剧了市场分割的程度。为了给予验证，模型引入财政自主变量，回归从另一个角度显示地方政府保护能力与边界效应的正相关性，回归表现良好，这也显示1994年财税制度改革后地方保护壁垒并未减弱。尽管如此，我们仍然忽略了市场分割与地方政府行为之间可能的因果关系（相关学者认为，政府的地方保护行为与购买偏好更可能来自市场分割的本身，具体分析政府行为自身的规律和行为机制，对于解决国内市场分割问题具有现实意义）。

进口率与边界效应成反向关系（但不显著），这似乎意味着进口的国际市场并非替代国内市场，反而促进了进口省份与外省的贸易联系，减少了边界效应；就业率系数为正，也并未出乎我们的意料，这反映了一个省份的市场分割程度与就业率成正向关系，但就业率在多大程度上解释了边界效应，回归 a 的结论需要再进一步来检验。

为了对回归 a 进行稳健性检验，我们以公共支出比率 $\ln g_{pub,i}$ 为基础变量又分别作了三个回归 b、回归 c 和回归 d，分别对不甚显著的就业率和进口率进行排除后再检验以及单独对此检验，总的来看，回归似乎没有太大意外，常数项和公共支出比率的标准差极高，仍不显著。为了谨慎起见，我们对解释变量的相关性提出了疑问，公共支出比率 $\ln g_{pub,i}$，财政自主与国有企业比重三个变量是否具有高度相关性，而造成回归的多重共线？通过观察三个变量的相关系数矩阵，我们发现前者与后两个变量的确存在较高的相关性（相关系数均处于 0.8 以上），因而我们认为模型可能存在多重共线的嫌疑，为此，我们在去除国有企业比重与财政自主两个变量后，继续对方程进行回归（见回归 d），结果显示公共支出比率依旧不显著，鉴于回归仍然表现不良好，我们用国有企业比重和财政自主代替公共支出比率来继续回归，结果见回归 e 和回归 f。总的来说，财政自主与国有企业比重两变量始终很稳健，因而从边界效应差异的不同因素来看，地方政府的财税自主和国有企业比重更具有解释力。一直以来，财税体制不合理、国有企业的地方所有制及政企不分等体制性因素构成了地方市场分割。

七、结论与政策含义

基于 McCallum 引力模型，本文构建了我国国内省际双边贸易的两地区模型以检验我国市场分割的程度，在考虑了引力模型的基本变量（经济规模和距离），将政府支出偏好纳入模型，实证结果得出，我国平均的边界效应在 1997—2002 年，2002—2005 年之间有上升的趋势，在去除运输成本，相对产出和价格因素外，1997 年中国省份实际上消费了当地的产品要多于外省产品的 28.5 倍，2002 年更高达 33.8 倍（而 2005 年又略高于 2002 年）；尽管结论类似于众多国外经验值，但笔者认为，由于在制度规范、立法、语言、文化以及种族等方面差异，我国边界效应的实证结果不具有国际比较性。为此，众多因素需被纳入本文的后期研究进行更深入的分析，目标在于探讨我国总体的边界效应，以此观察我国国际市场一体化程度，此处不再赘叙。

从实证结果来看，我们认为我国东中西部存在贸易边界效应的差异性（中西部壁垒高于东部），一方面由于地理条件或信息不通畅所至，另一方面在于地域基础设施建设的差异以及其他经济开放性决定；此外，我们发现工业品贸易壁垒要低于农业品贸易壁垒，也部分验证我国地方政府对原料品具有地方保护偏好。最后，本文实证检验了边界效应的不同影响因素，尽管就业率和进口率显示了预期的符号，但回归不显著；然而财政自主与国有企业比重两变量始终很稳健，具有解释力，这就坚定了我们的信念：在地方保护偏好下，地方政府对财税自主权的增强以及对经济控制力的加强都是导致省际间贸易壁垒（或市场分割）的因素。结论检验也从反面部分支持了林毅夫、刘培林（2005）的一个简要命题，即大量的非国有企业在没有享受国家保护和扶持的前提下成长起来，改善了市场机制的基础，从而促进了市场一体化程度。

依据“十一五”规划的思想，我国切实需要加强区域一体化的进程，建立统一的全国大市场，这只能得益于市场微观机制的建立和良性运作。一贯“强势”的政府不应继续通过累积权利范围干预经济组织活动，除了部分市场失灵因素外，政府所要做的并不全是替代市场，更多的则是增进市场（market-enhancing）的作用。打破地方市场分割，更需通过深层次的体制改革，完善地方政府的激励机制（如财税制度和政绩考核制度的突破）；加强法制体系建设，加大执法力度，严格执法程序等消除行政壁垒的一系列法律措施，也是促进我国区域和谐发展的必然选择。

参考文献

石磊、马士国：《市场分割的形成机制与中国统一市场建设的制度安排》，《中国人民大学学报》2006 年第 3 期。

踪家峰：《中国地方保护的研究进展》，《上海经济研究》2006 年第 6 期。

叶裕民：《中国区际贸易冲突的形成机制与对策思路》，《经济地理》2000 年第 6 期。

黄赜琳、王敬云：《地方保护与市场分割：来自中国的经验数据》，《中国工业经济》2006 年第 2 期。

陈甬军：《农产品与工业品市场封锁的生成机制比较》，《经济研究》1993 年第 7 期。

银温泉、才婉茹：《我国地方市场分割的成因和治理》，《经济研究》2001 年第 6 期。

雷明：《地方保护主义和地区间贸易壁垒的检验性分析》，《北京大学学报（哲学社会科学版）》2005 年第 1 期。

林毅夫、刘培林：《地方保护和市场分割：从发展战略的角度考察》，经济发展论坛工作论文 FED Working Papers Series No. FC20050015。

庞塞特(Poncet):《中国市场正在走向“非一体化”?——中国国内和国际市场一体化程度的比较分析》,《世界经济文汇》2002 年第 1 期。

Anderson, J. E. and E. van Wincoop, 2003, "Gravity with Gravitas: ASolution to the Border Puzzle", *American Economic Review*, 20(1): 170—192.

Alwyn, Young, 2000, "The Razor's Edge: Distortions and Incremental Reform in the People's Republie of China", *Quarterly Journal of Economics*, Vol. 115, No. 4.

Engel, Charles and John H. Rogers, 1996, "How Wide is the Border?", *American Economic Review*, 86:1112—1125.

Helliwell, John F., 1997, "National Borders, Trade and Migration", *Pacific Economic Review*, 2:165—185.

Head, Keith and Mayer, Thierry, 2002, "Illusory Border Effects: Distance Mismeasurement Inflates Estimates of Home Bias in Trade", Manuscript, CEPII, January.

Kyoji Fukao, 2004, "Why Has the Border Effect in the Japanese Market Declined? The Role of Business Networks in East Asia", RIETI Discussion Paper Series 04-E-016.

McCallum, John, 1995, "National borders matter: Canada-U. S. regional trade patterns", *American Economic Review*, 85:615—623.

Matthias Helble, 2006, "Border Effect Estimates for France and Germany Combining International Trade and Intra-national Transport Flows", HEI Working Paper.

Obstfeld, Maurice and Rogoff, Kenneth, 2000, "The Six Major Puzzles in International Macroeconomics: Is There a Common Cause?", *NBER Macroeconomics Annual*:339—389.

Wolf H. C., 2000, "Intranational home bias in trade", *The Review of Economics and Statistics*, 82(4):555—556.

Wei, Shang-Jin, 1996, "Intra-national versus inter-national trade: how stubborn are nations in global integration", National Bureau of Economic Research Working Paper No. 5531246 C. L.

Sandra Poncet, 2005, "A Fragmented China: Measure and Determinants of Chinese Domestic Market Disintegration", *Review of International Economics*, 13(3):409—430.

（原载《管理世界》2007 年第 9 期）

“先征后返”、公司税负与税收政策的有效性*

吴联生

（北京大学光华管理学院）

李　辰

（美国卡耐基-梅隆大学）

一、引　　言

在由计划经济体制向社会主义市场经济体制转轨的过程中，地方政府的角色发生了重大变化。在计划经济体制下，地方政府没有独立的经济利益，一切重大决策均由中央政府做出，地方政府只是按照中央政府赋予的权力去实现国家整体利益。但在向社会主义市场经济体制转轨的过程中，中央政府赋予了地方政府一定的相对独立的利益和经济管理的自主权，特别是放权让利改革和“分灶吃饭”财政体制等项措施相继出台之后，地方政府独立利益主体的地位日益突出，使地方政府担当了推动地区经济增长的重任。也就是说，虽然地方政府没有合法的市场主体地位，但在相当程度上已经成为事实上的一个经济主体。由于中央政府的目标是实现社会经济福利最大化，而地方政府

* 本文系国家自然科学基金项目“公司实际税负与盈余管理”（项目批准号：70572020）的研究成果。感谢匿名审稿人提出的建设性建议。

的目标是实现本行政区域内的经济增长、社会稳定和充分就业等,所以两者并不完全一致,这可能会导致中央政府的政策并不能得到地方政府的有效执行。

税收政策是中央政府进行宏观调控的重要手段。根据1993年12月31日颁布并于1994年1月1日起正式实施的《中华人民共和国企业所得税暂行条例》的规定,企业所得税实行33%的比例税率,小规模企业执行18%和27%两档优惠税率。另外,我国对经济特区(深圳、珠海、汕头、厦门和海南省)、沿海开放城市(14个城市)、沿海经济开放地区(10个省市)、经济技术开发区(32个城市)、专为台湾省设立的投资区(4个区)、上海浦东开发区和保税区(13个城市和地区)、高新技术开发区(52个区)、边境开放城市(13个)及苏州工业园区等等实行税收优惠政策。然而,一些地方政府为了争夺资本市场上的流动性资金,展开了税收竞争①,自行制定并实施了企业所得税“先征后返”优惠政策。所谓企业所得税“先征后返”优惠政策是指,各地税务部门对企业先按33%的法定税率征收所得税,然后再由地方财政部门将一定比例(通常返还18%,企业最终承担的税率为15%)的所得税额返还给企业。地方政府之所以给这些公司“先征后返”的所得税优惠政策,是因为这些公司无法像其他公司那样可以获得中央政府认可的优惠税率,而有了“先征后返”所得税优惠政策,这些公司的税率大抵可以与其他公司相当。

随后,国务院国发〔2000〕2号文件颁发了《关于纠正地方自行制定税收先征后返政策的通知》②,通知指出,地方政府自行

---

① 陈晓、肖星、王永胜:《税收竞争及其在我国资本市场中的表现》,《税务研究》2003年第6期。

② 转引自国务院国发〔2000〕2号文件《关于纠正地方自行制定税收先征后返政策的通知》。

制定和实施的"先征后返"企业所得税优惠政策不仅扰乱了税收秩序，违背了统一税政、集中税权的原则，而且违背了公共财政的要求，削弱了财政调控能力，甚至形成了潜在的财政风险，因此，要求自2000年1月1日起，各地区自行制定的"先征后返"所得税优惠政策一律停止执行。财政部进而印发的〔2000〕99号文件《关于进一步认真贯彻落实国务院〈关于纠正地方自行制定税收先征后返政策的通知〉的通知》规定，上市公司"先征后返"所得税优惠政策保留至2001年12月31日，即自2002年1月1日起，以前享受"先征后返"所得税优惠的上市公司将按照33%的税率全额缴纳企业所得税。这样，中央政府明确要求2002年1月1日起取消上市公司的"先征后返"所得税优惠政策。

地方政府和中央政府的这一系列举动引起了学界的关注。姚君的研究表明，取消"先征后返"所得税优惠政策之前，在我国深沪两市的上市公司中，有700多家公司涉及"先征后返"所得税优惠政策。① 这表明"先征后返"优惠政策对上市公司的纳税行为已经产生了重大影响，但姚君并没有对地方政府实施"先征后返"优惠政策以及中央政府取消该优惠政策给上市公司纳税行为所带来的影响进行深入研究。王延明利用1994年至2000年的186家上市公司的数据研究发现，法定税率变动对公司税负变动的影响只有50%，这在一定程度上表明，中央政府的税收政策并没有得到完全有效的执行，其重要原因之一就在于地方政府实行的"先征后返"所得税优惠政策对中央政府税收政策的影响。②但是，王延明也没有具体研究地方政府实行"先征后返"所得税优惠政策以及中央政府取消该政策对企业纳税行为产生的影响。

---

① 姚君：《"先征后返"与上市公司税负研究》，《税务研究》2003年第2期。

② 王延明：《上市公司所得税率变化的敏感性分析》，《经济研究》2002年第9期。

那么，地方政府实行的企业所得税“先征后返”政策，是否影响了中央政府税收政策的有效性？中央政府取消“先征后返”所得税优惠政策的决定，是否得到了地方政府的有效执行？中央政府取消“先征后返”所得税优惠政策，对企业所得税负担到底产生了怎样的影响？本文拟对其进行系统研究，从不同的角度来分析我国税收政策的有效性。

本文将北京、天津、河北、山东、江苏、浙江、福建、广东、上海、海南等 10 个省市的上市公司作为研究样本，对享受与不享受所得税“先征后返”优惠政策的公司在取消该政策的前后两个年度(2001 年和 2002 年)的所得税负担进行比较；而后在控制所得税负担的年度变化以及其他因素影响的基础上，对地方政府实行“先征后返”所得税优惠政策与中央政府取消该项政策对企业所得税负担的影响进行回归分析，并根据回归结果分析中国税收政策的有效性。

二、假设与检验模型

地方政府自行制定并实施企业所得税“先征后返”优惠政策，主要目的在于降低没有享受其他税收优惠政策的公司的所得税负担，提高公司业绩，为公司上市及再融资提供保障。2002 年，企业所得税归属政策发生了变化，即 2002 年以前，企业所得税由上市公司注册地政府收缴和支配，不上缴中央政府，但是自 2002 年起，变为由中央和地方平均分享，地方政府只能保留对该部分财政收入 50%的支配权。这一政策的变化增加了地方政府的财政压力，迫使其难以维持原来的所得税“先征后返”优惠政策。可见，按照中央政府的规定，取消地方政府的“先征后返”优惠政策，将会提高原来享受该优惠政策的公司的税负。据此，提出假设1。

假设1：取消“先征后返”所得税优惠政策之前，享受与不享受该政策的公司的所得税负担没有显著差异；取消“先征后返”所得税优惠政策，提高了原来享受该项政策的公司的所得税负担。

地方政府对部分公司实行“先征后返”所得税优惠政策的前提是，这些公司没有享受其他的所得税优惠政策，其所得税负担高于享受了其他所得税优惠政策的公司，因此在竞争中处于不利地位。地方政府实行“先征后返”所得税优惠政策，可以降低这些公司的所得税负担，改善其竞争的不利地位。但是取消“先征后返”优惠政策，将会使其重新回到高税负的状态。据此，提出假设2。

假设2：取消“先征后返”所得税优惠政策后，原来享受该项优惠政策的公司的所得税负担将高于没有享受该项优惠政策的公司的所得税负担。

为了检验假设1，本文运用所有样本公司取消“先征后返”所得税优惠政策前后两个年度（2001年和2002年）的数据，采用如下模型进行检验。

$$ETR = \beta_0 + \beta_1 Year + \beta_2 Rt + \beta_3 Year * Rt + \beta_c ConVars + \varepsilon_1 \tag{1}$$

其中，ETR是公司的实际税率（effective tax rate）[1]，用来

① 公司实际税率是已有研究中普遍采用的用以衡量公司所得税负担的指标。参见T. M. Porcano，1986，“Corporate Tax Rates：Progressive，Proportional，or Regressive”，*The Journal of the American Taxation Association*，vol. 7，no. 2：17—31；T. Shevlin，S. Porter，1992，“The Corporate Tax Comeback in 1987：Some Further Evidence”，*The Journal of the American Taxation Association*，vol. 14，no. 1：58—79；S. Gupta，K. Newberry，1997，“Determinants of the Variability in Corporate Effective Tax Rates：Evidence from Longitudinal Data”，*Journal of Accounting and Public Policy*，vol. 16，no. 1：1—39。

衡量公司的所得税负担，其具体计算方法为：实际税率 =（所得税费用一递延所得税费用）/ 息税前利润①；Year 代表样本数据所属年度，如果观测值是 2002 年的数据，则 Year = 1，否则，Year = 0；Rt 表示公司在 2001 年是否享受了“先征后返”所得税优惠政策，如果享受了，则 Rt = 1，否则，Rt = 0；系数 β_1 表示没有享受“先征后返”所得税优惠政策的公司，2002 年的实际税率相对于 2001 年的变化，如果 β_1 显著为正，则表明 2002 年公司实际税率显著高于 2001 年；系数 β_2 表示 2001 年享受“先征后返”所得税优惠政策公司的实际税率与不享受该政策的公司的实际税率的差异，如果 β_2 显著为正，则表明 2001 年享受“先征后返”所得税优惠政策的公司的实际税率显著高于不享受该政策的公司的实际税率；系数 β_3 表示相对于不享受“先征后返”所得税优惠政策的公司来说，取消“先征后返”所得税优惠政策是否影响了享受“先征后返”所得税优惠政策公司的实际税率，如果 β_3 显著为正，则表明剔除公司实际税率在 2002 年与 2001 年之间的变化以及取消该政策之前 2001 年两类公司实际税率的差异，取消“先征后返”所得税优惠政策显著提高了享受该项优惠政策的公司的实际税率；β_0 为截距项；ε_1 为残差项。

ConVars 表示控制变量，用来控制其他相关因素对公司实际税率的影响。根据已有研究，控制变量主要包括公司规模、财务杠杆、资产结构、投资机会、获利能力以及国有股比例。

(1) 公司规模。关于公司规模与实际税率之间的关系，目前主要有两种不同的观点。一种观点认为大公司受到公众更广

① 这是多种公司实际税率的计算方法中的一种，下文中用这种方法计算的实际税率用 ETR_1 表示。T. M. Porcano，1986，“Corporate Tax Rates: Progressive, Proportional, or Regressive”，*The Journal of the American Taxation Association*，vol. 7，no. 2：17—31。

泛的关注，这个“政治成本”将导致其实际税率较高；①另一种观点认为，大公司的实际税率较低，因为它们可以运用更多的资源进行税收筹划与政治游说。②已有研究在实际税率与公司规模的关系问题上，尚未得到比较一致的结论。Zimmerman(1983)的研究、Gupta 和 Newberry(1997)的研究、Kern 和 Morris(1992)的研究以及 Wilkie 和 Limberg(1990)的研究都发现，实际税率与公司规模之间存在显著的正相关关系；③ Porcano(1986)的研究、Holland(1998)的研究以及 Kim 和 Limpaphayom(1998)的研究则发现它们之间存在显著的负相关关系；④而 Stickney 和 McGee(1982)的研究和 Shevlin 和 Porter(1992)的

① J. L. Zimmerman, 1983, "Taxes and Firm Size", *Journal of Accounting and Economics*, vol. 5, no. 1: 119—149.

② J. J. Siegfried, 1972, *The Relationship between Economic Structure and the Effect of Political Influence: Empirical Evidence from the Federal Corporation Income Tax Program*, Ph. D. dissertation, University of Wilconsin.

③ J. L. Zimmerman, 1983, "Taxes and Firm Size", *Journal of Accounting and Economics*, vol. 5, no. 1: 119—149; S. Gupta, K. Newberry, 1997, "Determinants of the Variability in Corporate Effective Tax Rates: Evidence from Longitudinal Data", *Journal of Accounting and Public Policy*, vol. 16, no. 1: 1—39; B. B. Kern, M. H. Morris, 1992, "Taxes and Firm Size: The Effect of Tax Legislation during the 1980s", *The Journal of the American Taxation Association*, vol. 14, no. 1: 80—96; P. J. Wilkie, S. T. Limberg, 1990, "The Relationship between Firm Size and Effective Tax Rate: A Reconciliation of Zimmerman (1983) and Porcano(1986)", *The Journal of the American Taxation Association*, vol. 11, no. 2: 76—91.

④ T. M. Porcano, 1986, "Corporate Tax Rates: Progressive, Proportional, or Regressive", *The Journal of the American Taxation Association*, vol. 7, no. 2: 17—31; K. Holland, 1998, "Accounting Policy Choice: The Relationship between Corporate Tax Burden and Company Size", *Journal of Business Finance and Accounting*, vol. 25, no. 3/4: 265—288; K. A. Kim, P. Limpaphayom, 1998, "Taxes and Firm Size in Pacific-Basin Emerging Economies", *Journal of International Accounting, Auditing and Taxation*, vol. 7, no. 1: 47—63.

研究则没有发现它们之间存在显著的相关关系。①

(2) 财务杠杆。在计算企业所得税时,利息作为费用在税前利润中扣除,因此,利息具有抵税功能。财务杠杆高的公司,其利息费用以及由此而抵扣的企业所得税相应也较高,因而其实际税率相对较低。这样,财务杠杆与公司实际税率之间存在负相关关系。反过来看,财务杠杆高的公司,其更有动力通过增加举债而利用利息的抵税功能来降低企业所得税负担,这则表明财务杠杆与公司实际税率之间可能存在正相关关系。Stickney 和 McGee(1982)的研究发现,公司的财务杠杆与实际税率负相关;②Gupta 和 Newberry(1997)的研究发现,计算公司实际税率的方法不同,财务杠杆与公司实际税率之间的关系也会不同,既可能显著负相关,也可能不存在显著的相关关系;③Kim 和 Limpaphayom(1998)运用不同的方法计算实际税率,对不同国家不同阶段的财务杠杆与公司实际税率的关系进行研究,结果也有所不同;④Derashid 和 Zhang(2003)的研究则没有

---

① C. P. Stickney, V. E. McGee, 1982, "Effective Corporate Tax Rates: The Effect of Size, Capital Intensity, Leverage and Other Factors", *Journal of Accounting and Public Policy*, vol. 1, no. 2:125—152; T. Shevlin, S. Porter, 1992, "The Corporate Tax Comeback in 1987: Some Further Evidence", *The Journal of the American Taxation Association*, vol. 14, no. 1:58—79.

② C. P. Stickney, V. E. McGee, 1982, "Effective Corporate Tax Rates: The Effect of Size, Capital Intensity, Leverage and Other Factors", *Journal of Accounting and Public Policy*, vol. 1, no. 2:125—152.

③ S. Gupta, K. Newberry, 1997, "Determinants of the Variability in Corporate Effective Tax Rates: Evidence from Longitudinal Data", *Journal of Accounting and Public Policy*, vol. 16, no. 1:1—39.

④ K. A. Kim, P. Limpaphayom, 1998, "Taxes and Firm Size in Pacific-Basin Emerging Economies", *Journal of International Accounting, Auditing and Taxation*, vol. 7, no. 1:47—63.

发现财务杠杆与实际税率之间存在显著的相关关系。①

（3）资产结构。资产结构包括资本密集度和存货密集度两方面。②由于固定资产的加速折旧可以降低税负，因此资本密集度与实际税率负相关；资本密集度高，往往意味着存货密集度低，因此，存货密集度与公司实际税率正相关。Gupta 和 Newberry（1997）的研究发现，资本密集度和存货密集度与实际税率之间的确分别存在负相关和正相关的关系；③Derashid 和 Zhang（2003）的研究也发现资本密集度与实际税率之间存在负相关关系，但没有发现存货密集度与实际税率之间存在正相关关系。④

（4）投资机会和获利能力。Spooner（1986）综合前人研究成果认为，企业投资模式和获利能力是不同年度和不同行业的公司实际税率存在较大差异的重要原因。⑤Gupta 和 Newberry（1997）的研究、Kim 和 Limpaphayom（1998）的研究以及 Derashid 和 Zhang（2003）的研究都发现，运用不同方法计算实际税率来分析不同国家

---

① C. Derashid, H. Zhang, 2003, "Effective Tax Rates and the 'Industrial Policy' Hypothesis: Evidence from Malaysia", *Journal of International Accounting, Auditing and Taxation*, vol. 12, no. 1: 45—62.

② C. P. Stickney, V. E. McGee, 1982, "Effective Corporate Tax Rates: The Effect of Size, Capital Intensity, Leverage and Other Factors", *Journal of Accounting and Public Policy*, vol. 1, no. 2: 125—152; S. Gupta, K. Newberry, 1997, "Determinants of the Variability in Corporate Effective Tax Rates: Evidence from Longitudinal Data", *Journal of Accounting and Public Policy*, vol. 16, no. 1: 1—39.

③ S. Gupta, K. Newberry, 1997, "Determinants of the Variability in Corporate Effective Tax Rates: Evidence from Longitudinal Data", *Journal of Accounting and Public Policy*, vol. 16, no. 1: 1—39.

④ C. Derashid, H. Zhang, 2003, "Effective Tax Rates and the 'Industrial Policy' Hypothesis: Evidence from Malaysia", *Journal of International Accounting, Auditing and Taxation*, vol. 12, no. 1: 45—62.

⑤ G. M. Spooner, 1986, "Effective Tax Rates from Financial Statements", *National Tax Journal*, vol. 39, no. 3: 293—306.

不同阶段的投资机会和获利能力与实际税率的关系，结论是它们之间可能存在负相关关系，也可能并不存在显著的相关性。①

（5）国有股比例。Derashid 和 Zhang（2003）的研究认为，国有股比例越高，意味着公司的游说能力越强，其实际税率也就越低。②不过，Derashid 和 Zhang 在经验证据方面没有发现它们之间存在正相关关系。

综上，本文所选择的控制变量所包含的具体指标及其定义如表 1 所示。

表 1　本文所选控制变量

变量类型	指　标	定　义
公司规模	Lnasset	年末资产总额的自然对数
财务杠杆	Leverage	年末负债总额除以年末总资产
资本密集度	Cap-int	年末固定资产净值除以年末总资产
存货密集度	Inv-int	年末存货净额除以年末总资产
获利能力	ROA	税前利润除以年末总资产
投资机会	MktBook	年末股票市场收盘价乘以流通在外普通股股数，再除以年末所有者权益
国有股比例	Gequity	国有股股数除以总股数

① S. Gupta, K. Newberry, 1997, "Determinants of the Variability in Corporate Effective Tax Rates: Evidence from Longitudinal Data", *Journal of Accounting and Public Policy*, vol. 16, no. 1: 1—39; K. A. Kim, P. Limpaphayom, 1998, "Taxes and Firm Size in Pacific-Basin Emerging Economies", *Journal of International Accounting, Auditing and Taxation*, vol. 7, no. 1: 47—63; C. Derashid, H. Zhang, 2003, "Effective Tax Rates and the 'Industrial Policy' Hypothesis: Evidence from Malaysia", *Journal of International Accounting, Auditing and Taxation*, vol. 12, no. 1: 45—62.

② C. Derashid, H. Zhang, 2003, "Effective Tax Rates and the 'Industrial Policy' Hypothesis: Evidence from Malaysia", *Journal of International Accounting, Auditing and Taxation*, vol. 12, no. 1: 45—62.

为了检验假设 2，本文运用所有样本公司取消“先征后返”所得税优惠政策后（2002 年）的数据，采用如下模型进行检验。

$$ETR = \gamma_0 + \gamma_1 Rt + \gamma_c ConVars + \varepsilon_2 \quad (2)$$

其中，Rt 与控制变量（ConVars）的定义同模型（1）；γ_1 表示 2002 年享受“先征后返”所得税优惠政策的公司的实际税率与不享受该政策的公司实际税率的差异，如果 γ_1 显著为正，则表明 2002 年享受该政策的公司的实际税率显著高于不享受该政策的公司；γ_0 为截距项；ε_2 为残差项。

三、样本选择

中央政府取消上市公司享受“先征后返”所得税优惠政策的时间为 2002 年 1 月 1 日，为了比较取消该政策前后年度的企业所得税负担的差异，本文选取的样本数据的年份为 2001 年（取消该政策的前一年度）和 2002 年（取消该政策的后一年度）。由于 2001 年出台的《关于西部大开发若干政策措施的实施意见》也涉及相关的所得税优惠政策，并在《关于西部大开发税收优惠问题的通知》中规定了所得税优惠的适用范围和具体内容，为了避免“西部大开发”税收优惠政策的影响，本文所选取的样本不包括西部地区的上市公司。由于允许中部地区比照西部大开发的优惠政策执行，所以本文的样本也不包括中部地区的上市公司。此外，2002 年中央政府提出发展东北地区等老工业基地的战略，所得税优惠政策也是该战略的重要组成部分，因此东北地区的上市公司也予以剔除。这样，本文所选取的样本包括北京、天津、河北、山东、江苏、浙江、福建、广东、上海、海南等 10 个省市的上市公司。

此外，我们对样本还作了如下处理：（1）由于上市公司的股票名称发生变化，往往表明公司已经发生重大变更，公司不同年度的实际税率的比较也就失去了合理的基础，因此剔除 2001 年或 2002 年股票名称发生变更的公司；(2)剔除样本期内计算公司实际税率公式分母为负的公司，因为这部分公司通过公式计算得到的实际税率与正常公司的实际税率含义不同，不能反映企业经营业绩与企业实际税负的关系；(3)参照已有研究的处理方法，实际税率大于 1 或者小于 0 的公司作为异常值剔除；①(4)由于计算递延所得税费用需要 2000 年的财务数据，而 2001 年和 2002 年的新上市公司没有披露 2000 年的年报，因此剔除 2001 年和 2002 年新上市的公司；(5)由于比较政策变化对同一总体的影响，样本公司应有两年的完整数据，因此剔除 2001 年或 2002 年退市的公司；(6)遵从研究惯例，剔除金融行业的公司，因为这类公司业务特殊，适用的会计准则与其他行业不同。

国外对公司实际税率已经进行了多方面的探讨。Siegfried 在 1974 年的研究中定义了公司实际税率并计算了美国 1963 年的公司实际税率；②Spooner(1986)的研究、Omer，Molloy 和

---

① 已有研究如 S. Gupta，K. Newberry，1997，“Determinants of the Variability in Corporate Effective Tax Rates: Evidence from Longitudinal Data”，*Journal of Accounting and Public Policy*，vol. 16，no. 1: 1—39；K. A. Kim，P. Limpaphayom，1998，“Taxes and Firm Size in Pacific-Basin Emerging Economies”，*Journal of International Accounting, Auditing and Taxation*，vol. 7，no. 1: 47—63；D. Singh，R. P. Wilder，K. P. Chan，1987，“Tax Rates in Small and Large Firms”，*Ameircan Journal of Small Business*，vol. 27，no. 2:245—259；C. P. Stickney，V. E. McGee，1982，“Effective Corporate Tax Rates: The Effect of Size, Capital Intensity, Leverage and Other Factors”，*Journal of Accounting and Public Policy*，vol. 1，no. 2:125—152；J. L. Zimmerman，1983，“Taxes and Firm Size”，*Journal of Accounting and Economics*，vol. 5，no. 1: 119—149。

② J. J. Siegfried，1974，“Effective Average U. S. Corporation Income Tax Rates”，*National Tax Journal*，vol. 27，no. 2:245—259.

Ziebart(1991)的研究以及 Hanlon(2003)的研究则探讨了如何运用财务报表数据计算公司实际税率的问题。①在研究公司实际税率的其他问题中,也都需要首先着手解决公司实际税率的计算问题。目前,已有研究已经形成了五种不同的计算公司实际税率的方法,它们分别是:(1)实际税率 =(所得税费用-递延所得税费用)/息税前利润;②(2)实际税率 = 所得税费用/息税前利润;③(3)实际税率 = 所得税费用/(税前利润-递延所得税费用/法定税率);④(4)实际税率 =(所得税费用-递延所得税费用)/(税前利润-递延所得税费用/法定税率);⑤(5)实际税率 =(所得税费用-递延所得税费用)/经营活动现金净流 量。⑥本文首先采用第一种方法计算公司实际税率,在对实证研究结果的稳定性进行检查时,再运用其他方法来计算实

---

① G. M. Spooner, 1986, "Effective Tax Rates from Financial Statements", *National Tax Journal*, vol. 39, no. 3:293—306; T. C. Omer, K. H. Molloy, D. A. Ziebart, 1991, "Measurement of Effective Corporate Tax Rates Using Financial Statement Information", *The Journal of the American Taxation Association*, vol. 13, no. 1:57—72; K. Hollan, 1998, "Accounting Policy Choice: The Relationship between Corporate Tax Burden and Company Size", *Journal of Business Finance and Accounting*, vol. 25, no. 3/4:265—288.

②③ T. M. Porcano, 1986, "Corporate Tax Rates: Progressive, Proportional, or Regressive", *The Journal of the American Taxation Association*, vol. 7, no. 2:17—31.

④ C. P. Stickney, V. E. McGee, 1982, "Effective Corporate Tax Rates: The Effect of Size, Capital Intensity, Leverage and Other Factors", *Journal of Accounting and Public Policy*, vol. 1, no. 2:125—152.

⑤ T. Shevlin, 1987, "Taxes and Off-Balance-Sheet Financing: Research and Development Limited Partnerships", *The Accounting Review*, vol. 62, no. 3:480—509.

⑥ J. L. Zimmerman, 1983, "Taxes and Firm Size", *Journal of Accounting and Economics*, vol. 5, no. 1:119—149.

际税率。①

根据本文所选研究样本的条件以及所使用的公司实际税率的计算方法，最后得到 417 家上市公司作为研究样本（表 2），其中，2001 年享受“先征后返”所得税优惠政策的公司有 176 家，占研究样本的 42.2%。

表 2　样本构成

2000 年及以前上市且披露了年报的北京、天津、河北、山东、江苏、浙江、福建、广东、上海、海南等 10 个省市的非金融类公司	553 家
减：无法确定是否享受“先征后返”优惠政策的公司	2 家
小计	551 家
减：息税前利润小于 0 的公司	112 家
减：实际税率小于 0 或大于 1 的公司	22 家
入选样本	417 家
其中：享受“先征后返”优惠政策的公司	176 家
不享受“先征后返”优惠政策的公司	241 家

① 征税由税务部门负责，返税由财政部门负责，返税在第二年上半年的所得税汇算清缴之后进行，反映在第二年公司的财务报表中。这的确会对公司实际税率（ETR）的精确性产生一定的影响，因为在 2001 年的“所得税”项目中，包括的是 2001 年发生的企业所得税费用减去 2000 年的退税，因而有些不匹配。但是，由于以下两方面的原因，用 ETR 来衡量“先征后返”公司实际税率仍然是可接受的。第一，由于企业的利润具有持续性，而在同样的所得税政策下，公司的所得税费用也具有持续性，这样，将上年的退税与本年的利润进行匹配是有理论基础的；第二，本文采用研究中通用的方法，将 ETR 大于 1 或者小于 0 的样本予以剔除，这样，实际上就将上年返还税款与本年利润不匹配程度高的样本进行了剔除，留下来的样本则属于上年返还税款与本年利润匹配程度不错的、能够予以接受的样本。

四、检验结果

表3报告了2001年和2002年全部样本、不享受“先征后返”所得税优惠政策的样本和享受“先征后返”所得税优惠政策的样本的基本情况。从表3可以看出，无论是全部样本，还是享受和不享受“先征后返”所得税优惠政策的公司，2002年公司实际税率的平均值和中位数都高于2001年。这可能意味着2002年的公司实际税率相对于2001年来说有所上升。无论是2001年还是2002年，不享受所得税“先征后返”优惠政策的公司的实际税率均低于享受该政策的公司。其中，不享受该政策的公司2001年实际税率平均为12.53%，2002年虽然有所上升，平均值也仅为14.50%，上升幅度仅为1.90%。这说明不享受该政策的公司在很大程度上仍然在享受着其他的所得税优惠政策。不过，享受该政策的公司2001年的实际税率平均值为14.27%，而2002年上升为19.84%，上升幅度高达5.57%，远远高于不享受该政策的公司实际税率上升的幅度。这可能预示着取消所得税“先征后返”优惠政策，提高了享受该政策的公司的实际税率。

表4报告了全部样本、不享受和享受“先征后返”所得税优惠政策的样本2002年相对2001年的公司实际税率的增长情况。结果表明，三组样本2002年与2001年的实际税率之差，无论是在t检验下，还是在符号秩检验下，它们都在1%水平上显著大于零。这说明无论是全部样本、不享受该政策的样本，还是享受该政策的样本，2002年的公司实际税率都显著高于2001年。表5报告了不享受与享受该政策的公司2001年和2002年的实际税率以及这两年实际税率增长幅度的比较结果。从表5可以发现，所有的平均值之差和中位数之差都显著地小于零。

表 3　描述统计

	ETR_1	Lnasset	Leverage	Cap-int	Inv-int	ROA	MktBook	Gequity
Panel A：2001 年								
(1) 全部样本								
平均值	0.132 7	21.181 6	0.437 5	0.285 6	0.152 7	0.054 4	5.528 5	0.311 9
中位数	0.117 9	21.130 0	0.438 7	0.253 5	0.112 3	0.047 9	3.773 9	0.313 7
标准差	0.095 6	0.845 1	0.177 6	0.185 2	0.141 7	0.036 9	13.345 2	0.277 0
最小值	0.000 0	18.939 8	0.011 7	0.001 7	0.000 0	−0.029 7	1.449 1	0.000 0
最大值	0.613 7	24.032 2	0.966 6	0.861 2	0.762 7	0.207 5	257.519 4	0.885 8
(2) 不享受"先征后返"所得税优惠政策的样本								
平均值	0.125 3	21.230 6	0.451 0	0.252 4	0.156 3	0.054 9	6.505 8	0.304 3
中位数	0.111 8	21.215 7	0.463 7	0.222 6	0.105 4	0.046 7	4.015 8	0.295 0
标准差	0.097 7	0.936 7	0.189 4	0.180 2	0.152 7	0.041 0	17.351 4	0.280 4
最小值	0.000 0	18.939 8	0.011 7	0.001 7	0.000 2	−0.029 7	1.449 1	0.000 0
最大值	0.559 4	24.032 2	0.966 6	0.817 4	0.762 7	0.207 5	257.519 4	0.849 8
(3) 享受"先征后返"所得税优惠政策的样本								
平均值	0.142 7	21.114 6	0.419 1	0.331 1	0.147 7	0.053 7	4.190 4	0.322 2
中位数	0.125 2	21.008 7	0.424 0	0.317 0	0.114 9	0.050 2	3.549 9	0.348 8

（续表）

	ETR_1	Lnasset	Leverage	Cap-int	Inv-int	ROA	MktBook	Gequity
标准差	0.091 9	0.697 5	0.158 9	0.182 9	0.125 2	0.030 4	2.708 9	0.272 9
最小值	0.000 0	19.435 5	0.062 0	0.015 6	0.000 0	−0.010 8	1.453 5	0.000 0
最大值	0.613 7	23.126 2	0.866 7	0.861 2	0.742 3	0.157 2	29.893 1	0.885 8
Panel B：2002 年								
(1) 全部样本								
平均值	0.167 5	21.293 3	0.450 7	0.296 8	0.148 7	0.052 1	3.894 2	0.305 6
中位数	0.151 2	21.222 1	0.450 1	0.268 7	0.111 9	0.045 4	2.803 3	0.306 0
标准差	0.112 8	0.845 9	0.172 1	0.189 6	0.140 2	0.042 2	8.074 2	0.275 5
最小值	0.000 0	19.092 6	0.012 6	0.001 6	0.000 0	−0.028 1	1.122 8	0.000 0
最大值	0.614 2	24.170 9	0.938 1	0.862 0	0.799 3	0.336 1	161.216 5	0.885 8
(2) 不享受“先征后返”所得税优惠政策的样本								
平均值	0.145 0	21.349 9	0.463 0	0.262 9	0.154 2	0.052 4	4.463 8	0.297 3
中位数	0.127 9	21.369 7	0.454 5	0.233 4	0.113 2	0.045 4	3.003 5	0.284 9
标准差	0.102 8	0.933 2	0.183 2	0.186 5	0.151 4	0.045 0	10.441 4	0.277 8
最小值	0.000 0	19.092 6	0.012 6	0.001 6	0.000 5	−0.028 1	1.146 3	0.000 0
最大值	0.535 0	24.170 9	0.938 1	0.841 8	0.799 3	0.317 3	161.216 5	0.849 8

(续表)

	ETR_1	Lnasset	Leverage	Cap-int	Inv-int	ROA	MktBook	Gequity
(3) 享受“先征后返”所得税优惠政策的样本								
平均值	0.198 4	21.215 9	0.433 8	0.343 2	0.141 2	0.051 8	3.114 1	0.316 9
中位数	0.195 7	21.157 2	0.443 0	0.335 5	0.111 9	0.045 4	2.602 4	0.328 8
标准差	0.118 7	0.704 5	0.154 6	0.184 5	0.123 1	0.038 3	2.096 8	0.272 7
最小值	0.000 0	19.639 3	0.065 7	0.016 8	0.000 0	0.001 7	1.122 8	0.000 0
最大值	0.614 2	23.215 6	0.861 3	0.862 0	0.696 3	0.336 1	22.026 4	0.885 8

表 4 “先征后返”所得税优惠政策取消前后公司实际税率的比较

ΔETR_1	平均值之差	t 检验(t)	中位数之差	符号秩检验(S)
(1) 全部样本	0.034 9	7.04***	0.022 9	17 021***
(2) 不享受“先征后返”所得税优惠样本	0.019 7	3.37***	0.012 3	3 879***
(3) 享受“先征后返”所得税优惠样本	0.055 7	6.68***	0.051 6	4 234***

注:ΔETR_1 为 2002 年公司实际税率($ETR_{1,2002}$)与 2001 年公司实际税率($ETR_{1,2001}$)之差,即 $\Delta ETR_1 = ETR_{1,2002} - ETR_{1,2001}$;平均值之差的检验方法是 t 检验,中位数之差的检验方法是符号秩检验;*** 表示 1%水平上显著。

这说明无论是 2001 年还是 2002 年，享受该政策的公司的实际税率显著高于不享受该政策的公司的实际税率；同时，享受该政策的公司的实际税率增长幅度显著高于不享受该政策的公司的增长幅度。表 4 和表 5 的检验结果与表 3 的统计结果一致。

表 6 报告了所有样本公司所有观测值（包括 2001 年和 2002 年）的主要变量之间的相关系数。结果显示，Year 与 ETR_1 在 1%水平上显著正相关，表明 2002 年公司实际税率显著高于 2001 年公司实际税率；Rt 与 ETR_1 在 1%水平上显著正相关，表明享受"先征后返"所得税优惠政策的公司的实际税率显著高于不享受该政策的公司；Year 与 Rt 的交叉项与 ETR_1 显著正相关，表明享受该政策的公司 2002 年的实际税率显著高于其 2001 年的实际税率，并且高于不享受该政策的公司 2001 年和 2002 年的实际税率。其他变量之间没有显著的高度相关关系。表 7 报告了所有样本公司 2002 年主要变量之间的相关系数。结果显示，Rt 与 ETR_1 在 1%水平上显著正相关，表明享受"先征后返"所得税优惠政策的公司 2002 年的实际税率显著高于不享受该政策的公司的实际税率，其他变量之间也没有显著的高度相关关系。

表 8 报告了取消地方政府"先征后返"所得税优惠政策的经济后果。模型 1(1)的样本为所有研究样本 2002 年和 2001 年的观测值，模型 2(1)的样本为所有研究样本 2002 年的观测值，均采用普通最小二乘法进行回归，被解释变量均为 ETR_1。

根据表 8 模型 1(1)的多元回归结果，Year 的估计系数显著为正，表明没有享受"先征后返"所得税优惠政策的公司 2002 年的实际税率应该显著高于其 2001 年的实际税率。Rt 的估计系数不显著，表明 2001 年享受该政策的公司与不享受该政策的公司的实际税率之间没有显著差异。交叉变量 Year * Rt 的估计

表 5　不同公司的实际税率及其变化的比较

ETR_1	平均值之差	t 检验(t)	中位数之差	秩和检验(Z)
(1) $ETR_{1,2001}$	-0.0174	-1.85^{*}	-0.0134	2.31^{**}
(2) $ETR_{1,2002}$	-0.0534	-4.80^{***}	-0.0678	4.98^{***}
(3) ΔETR_1	-0.0360	-3.53^{***}	-0.0393	3.92^{***}

注：平均值之差 = 不享受“先征后返”所得税优惠政策样本平均值 − 享受“先征后返”所得税优惠政策样本平均值；中位数之差 = 不享受“先征后返”所得税优惠政策样本中位数 − 享受“先征后返”所得税优惠政策样本中位数；平均值之差的检验方法是 t 检验，中位数之差的检验方法是秩和检验；*** 表示 1%水平上显著，** 表示 5%水平上显著，* 表示 10%水平上显著。

表 6　全部样本的相关系数

	ETR_1	Year	Rt	Year * Rt	Lnasset	Leverage	Cap-int	Inv-int	ROA	MktBook	Gequity
ETR_1		0.165***	0.165***	0.236***	0.025	−0.177***	0.051	0.083**	0.068**	−0.124***	0.014
Year	0.165***		0.000	0.517***	0.066*	0.038	0.030	−0.014	−0.029	−0.074**	−0.011
Rt	0.172***	0.000		0.605***	−0.073**	−0.086**	0.210***	−0.038	−0.011	−0.082**	0.033
Year * Rt	0.232***	0.517***	0.605***		−0.013	−0.030	0.144***	−0.035	−0.019	−0.075**	0.015
Lnasset	0.022	0.068*	−0.079**	−0.013		0.145***	0.119***	0.036	0.042	−0.253***	0.195***
Leverage	−0.187***	0.041	−0.081**	−0.023	0.162***		−0.210***	0.305***	−0.312***	0.207***	0.011
Cap-int	0.051	0.029	0.225***	0.153***	0.078**	−0.234***		−0.438***	0.094***	0.011	0.078**
Inv-int	0.063*	−0.015	−0.005	−0.022	−0.014	0.346***	−0.413***		−0.139***	−0.031	−0.017
ROA	0.121***	−0.057*	0.034	−0.014	0.043	−0.350***	0.111***	−0.163***		−0.047	0.013

（续表）

	ETR$_1$	Year	Rt	Year * Rt	Lnasset	Leverage	Cap-int	Inv-int	ROA	MktBook	Gequity
MktBook	−0.188***	−0.297***	−0.145***	−0.253***	−0.620***	0.129***	−0.176***	0.051	0.039		−.008
Gequity	0.009	−0.009	0.037	0.019	0.165***	0.018	0.082**	−0.029	−0.015	−0.043	

注：上半部分为 Pearson 相关系数，下半部分为 Spearman 相关系数；*** 表示 1%水平上显著，** 表示 5%水平上显著，* 表示 10%水平上显著。

表 7　2002 年样本的相关系数

	ETR$_1$	Rt	Lnasset	Leverage	Cap-int	Inv-int	ROA	MktBook	Gequity
ETR$_1$		0.234***	0.005	−0.155***	0.096*	0.081	0.076	−0.121**	0.007
Rt	0.244***		−0.078	−0.084*	0.209***	−0.046	−0.007	−0.083*	0.035
Lnasset	0.016	−0.084*		0.167***	0.113**	0.054	0.048	−0.271***	0.201***
Leverage	−0.154***	−0.077	0.183***		−0.219***	0.302***	−0.271***	0.192***	0.017
Cap-int	0.117**	0.228***	0.081	−0.248***		−0.459***	0.126**	0.011	0.083*
Inv-int	0.088*	−0.023	0.011	0.355***	−0.438***		−0.141***	−0.041	−0.007
ROA	0.135***	0.032	0.075	−0.312***	0.169***	−0.149***		−0.028	0.000
MktBook	−0.166***	−0.159***	−0.602***	0.123**	−0.155***	0.032	0.016		−0.018
Gequity	−0.019	0.039	0.169***	0.027	0.088*	−0.019	−0.013	−0.028	

注：上半部分为 Pearson 相关系数，下半部分为 Spearman 相关系数；*** 表示 1%水平上显著，** 表示 5%水平上显著，* 表示 10%水平上显著。

表 8　取消地方政府“先征后返”所得税优惠政策的经济后果：ETR_1

	模型 1(1)		模型 2(1)	
	参　数	t 值	参　数	t 值
截距	0.077 9	0.83	0.134 0	0.93
Year	0.020 1	2.19**		
Rt	0.012 2	1.20	0.046 7	4.21***
Year * Rt	0.037 3	2.66***		
Lnasset	0.003 5	0.77	0.000 7	0.10
Leverage	−0.121 7	−5.27***	−0.095 9	−2.71***
Cap-int	0.024 3	1.12	0.059 6	1.81*
Inv-int	0.129 8	4.57***	0.148 1	3.37***
ROA	0.073 9	0.80	0.130 2	0.99
MktBook	−0.000 5	−1.32	−0.000 9	−1.30
Gequity	0.002 7	0.21	−0.002 8	−0.14
F 值	11.17***		6.10***	
Adj R^2	0.109		0.089	

注：*** 表示 1%水平上显著，** 表示 5%水平上显著，* 表示 10%水平上显著。

系数显著为正，表明在剔除公司实际税率2002年与2001年之间的变化以及取消“先征后返”所得税优惠政策之前2001年两类公司实际税率差异的条件下，取消“先征后返”所得税优惠政策显著提高了享受该政策的公司的实际税率。根据模型2(1)的多元回归结果，Rt的估计系数显著为正，表明享受该政策的公司2002年的实际税率显著高于不享受该政策的公司的实际税率。

以上结论表明，2001年在地方政府实行“先征后返”所得税优惠政策的情况下，享受该优惠政策的公司与不享受该优惠政策的公司的实际税率之间没有显著差异。这说明如果没有这项优惠政策，享受了该政策的公司的实际税率显著高于不享受该优惠政策但享受其他所得税优惠政策的公司的实际税率，“先征后返”政策使这些公司的实际税率与享受其他所得税优惠政策的公司没有显著差别。这表明，地方政府实施的“先征后返”所得税优惠政策对中央政府税收政策的宏观调控作用产生了一定程度的干扰。取消地方政府实行的“先征后返”所得税优惠政策，显著地提高了原来享受该政策的公司的实际税率；且取消地方政府“先征后返”所得税优惠政策后(2002年)，原来享受该政策的公司的实际税率显著高于原来不享受该政策的公司的实际税率。也就是说，取消地方政府的“先征后返”所得税优惠政策，不仅显著提高了原来享受该政策的公司的实际税率，并且使其实际税率由与不享受该政策的公司的实际税率没有显著差异，变为显著高于不享受该政策的公司的实际税率。这表明中央政府取消“先征后返”所得税优惠政策，不仅在一定程度上得到了地方政府的执行，并且有效地减弱了地方政府“先征后返”所得税优惠政策所带来的负面影响。

五、稳定性检查

公司实际税率的计算方法主要有五种，以上研究结论均基于第一种计算方法，即 ETR_1 =（所得税费用－递延所得税费用）/ 息税前利润。由于第五种公司实际税率的计算①依据在于经营活动现金净流量，而根据中国所得税法律规定，所得税税负的计算基础并不是现金流量，而是建立在以权责发生制为基础的利润之上，只不过纳税所运用的利润与会计利润存在微小的差别，因此，本文不采用该方法。下文运用其他三种方法计算公司实际税率，对上文研究结论的稳定性进行检查。三种计算公司实际税率的方法分别为：ETR_2 = 所得税费用/息税前利润；ETR_3 = 所得税费用/（税前利润－递延所得税费用/法定税率）；ETR_4 =（所得税费用－递延所得税费用）/（税前利润－递延所得税费用 / 法定税率）。运用同样的样本选择标准，分别得到满足运用 ETR_2、ETR_3 和 ETR_4 来计算公司实际税率所需要的样本，其样本数分别为 421 家、410 家以及 408 家，其规模以及享受与不享受“先征后返”所得税优惠政策公司的比例，与上文所运用的样本均没有很大的差别。

表 9　取消地方政府“先征后返”所得税优惠政策的经济后果：ETR_2、ETR_3 和 ETR_4

	模型 1(2)		模型 1(3)		模型 1(4)	
	参数	t 值	参数	t 值	参数	t 值
截距	0.079 9	0.86	0.234 1	1.93*	0.228 5	1.90*
Year	0.020 0	2.20**	0.035 0	2.93***	0.035 0	2.94***

① 实际税率 =（所得税费用－递延所得税费用）/ 经营活动现金流量。

（续表）

	模型 1(2)		模型 1(3)		模型 1(4)	
	参数	t 值	参数	t 值	参数	t 值
Rt	0.012 0	1.20	0.011 4	0.86	0.011 6	0.89
Year * Rt	0.036 1	2.60***	0.038 2	2.09**	0.037 8	2.08**
Lnasset	0.003 4	0.76	−0.003 6	−0.62	−0.003 3	−0.56
Leverage	−0.124 2	−5.43***	−0.036 7	−1.22	−0.038 0	−1.28
Cap-int	0.018 0	0.84	0.042 1	1.48	0.049 7	1.75*
Inv-int	0.135 4	4.80***	0.209 7	5.69***	0.197 5	5.41***
ROA	0.082 6	0.90	−0.426 9	−3.48***	−0.453 6	−3.74***
MktBook	−0.000 5	−1.26	−0.000 9	−2.07**	−0.000 9	−2.15**
Gequity	0.003 5	0.27	0.006 3	0.38	0.005 1	0.31
F 值	11.29***		10.75***		10.70***	
Adj R^2	0.109		0.106		0.106	
	模型 2(2)		模型 2(3)		模型 2(4)	
	参数	t 值	参数	t 值	参数	t 值
截距	0.140 1	0.98	0.346 3	1.76*	0.327 7	1.70*
Year						
Rt	0.045 9	4.17***	0.046 8	3.09***	0.045 8	3.09***
Year * Rt						
Lnasset	0.000 6	0.09	−0.008 6	−0.90	−0.007 6	−0.81
Leverage	−0.100 8	−2.87***	0.000 1	0.00	−0.002 3	−0.05
Cap-int	0.044 7	1.37	0.082 2	1.79*	0.098 4	2.19**
Inv-int	0.152 3	3.49***	0.264 3	4.43***	0.248 8	4.27***
ROA	0.136 7	1.05	−0.438 1	−2.42**	−0.468 4	−2.65***
MktBook	−0.000 9	−1.22	−0.001 6	−1.70*	−0.001 7	−1.80*
Gequity	0.000 6	0.03	−0.004 8	−0.18	−0.008 0	−0.30
F 值	5.98***		5.75***		5.79***	
Adj R^2	0.087		0.085		0.086	

注：* * * 表示 1%水平上显著，* * 表示 5%水平上显著，* 表示 10%水平上显著。

表 9 报告了运用 ETR_2、ETR_3 和 ETR_4 计算公司实际税率得到的取消地方政府“先征后返”所得税优惠政策的经济后果。模型 1(2)、模型 1(3)和模型 1(4)的样本为所有研究样本 2002 年和 2001 年的观测值;模型 2(2)、模型 2(3)和模型 2(4)的样本为所有研究样本 2002 年的观测值。模型 1(2)和模型 2(2)的被解释变量为 ETR_2,模型 1(3)和模型 2(3)的被解释变量均为 ETR_3,模型 1(4)和模型 2(4)的被解释变量均为 ETR_4。以上回归均采用普通最小二乘法。

表 9 的研究结论表明,无论是运用 ETR_2、ETR_3 还是 ETR_4 计算公司实际税率,模型 1(2)、模型 1(3)以及模型 1(4)中的 Year 的估计系数都显著为正,Rt 估计系数均不显著,交叉变量 Year * Rt 的估计系数都显著为正;而模型 2(2)、模型 2(3)以及模型 2(4)中 Rt 估计系数都显著为正。以上回归结果分别与表 8 中模型 1(1)和模型 2(1)的结果一致,表明上文的研究结论均没有发生改变。

六、结 论 与 启 示

本文基于地方政府自行制定并实施的企业所得税“先征后返”优惠政策,以及中央政府取消该优惠政策的事例,运用上市公司的数据,从企业所得税负担的角度研究了中央政府税收政策的有效性。研究结果表明,地方政府的“先征后返”所得税优惠政策,降低了不享受中央政府认可的所得税优惠政策的公司的所得税负担,从而使它们与享受中央政府所得税优惠政策的公司的所得税负担没有显著差异。这表明地方政府的“先征后返”所得税优惠政策,影响了中央政府税收政策宏观调控作用的发挥,损害了中央政府税收政策的有效性;中央政府取消“先征后返”所得税优惠政策的规定，显著提高了原来享受该优惠政策的公司的所得税负担，并最终使它们的所得税负担显著高于享受中央政府认可的所得税优惠政策的公司。这表明中央政府取消“先征后返”优惠政策的规定，虽然会影响地方政府的利益，但是的确在一定程度上得到地方政府的执行，并最终使中央政府税收政策的有效性得到了恢复。

以上研究结论，可以带给我们如下几方面的启示。

第一，中央政府与地方政府的目标差异以及由此导致的利益冲突，是我国经济转轨过程中客观存在的问题。而如何处理这一问题，不仅会影响地方的经济发展速度，也会影响全国经济发展的协调程度与中央政府宏观调控目标的实现进程。因而，恰当处理中央政府与地方政府之间的关系，已经成为我国经济发展过程中必须予以重视的重大问题。

第二，企业所得税是地方政府财政收入的重要来源，改变企业所得税归属，可以改变地方政府的行为。中央政府取消企业所得税“先征后返”优惠政策的规定，之所以能够在一定程度上得到地方政府的执行，关键在于中央政府改变了企业所得税的归属政策，即将原来由地方政府独享变为由中央和地方平均分享。正是这一政策的变化增加了地方政府的财政压力，使得地方政府不得不遵守中央政府取消“先征后返”所得税优惠政策的规定。可见，企业所得税归属安排是中央政府引导地方政府行为的重要途径之一。

第三，企业所得税负担的公平性问题，是营造公平竞争的企业经营环境过程中必须予以重视的关键性问题之一。中央政府为了配合开放政策的实施，为了发展区域经济以及鼓励某些产业的发展，曾经对外商投资企业和外国企业、相关经济区域以及相关行业实行所得税优惠政策。但是，从没有享受中央政府所得税优惠政策的企业的角度来看，它们必定会处于不利的竞争地位，从而给它们的发展带来重大的影响。因此，中央政府在实行企业所得税优惠政策时，还需要着重考虑如何恰当处理地区经济发展与整体经营环境的公平性之间的关系问题。①

（原载《中国社会科学》2007 年第 4 期）

① 目前，内资企业与外资企业的所得税负担的不公平问题，已经在 2007 年 3 月 16 日第十届全国人民代表大会第五次会议通过的《中华人民共和国企业所得税法》中得到解决。根据企业所得税法，外资企业和内资企业的所得税合并，两税合并后，内外资企业的所得税税率统一为 25%。

外国直接投资对中国企业的溢出效应分析：

来自中国第一次全国经济普查数据的报告*

平新乔等

（北京大学中国经济研究中心）

在中国过去 28 年的改革开放过程中，外国直接投资（FDI）一直在中国的资本形成、就业、出口、市场发育与发展等方面起着十分重要的作用。直到 2006 年，中国仍保持着 FDI 的最大发展中东道国的地位。然而，对于外国直接投资是否对中国企业产生了技术溢出效果，在理论学术界、政策决策部门与企业界存在不同看法。Huang（2003）认为外国直接投资在中国 20 世纪 80 年代至 90 年代的迅速增长中与技术溢出毫无关系，跨国公司与港澳台资企业主要利用中国内地体制对民营企业的歧视与地方分割，才保持了对中国民族企业的竞争优势，从而使 FDI 在过去的 20 年内在中国获得迅速扩张。但是，吴延兵（2006）、王红岭等（2006）、仝月婷与胡又欣（2005）则利用企业数据进行

---

* 本文为“市场换技术效应分析”课题组研究成果。课题组成员：平新乔、关晓静、邓永旭、李胤、梁爽、陈工文、章椹元、周艺艺。本文为国家统计局与国务院第一次全国经济普查领导小组委托课题的研究报告。作者感谢国家统计局的支持，感谢北京市教育共建项目“西方经济学”（项目编号：XK100010501）对本研究的资助。

经验研究，发现 FDI 对中国制造业有显著的正溢出效应。

人们通常粗略地把引进外资的战略归纳为“以市场换技术”，即以中国国内市场的潜在价值来吸引外资企业投资，从而使中国企业学到世界先进技术。问题在于，中国市场对外资的开放是否换来了技术溢出？这里涉及一系列相关的问题：如何度量技术？如何估算技术溢出效果？毫无疑问，中国的技术水平与世界技术的前沿之间至今仍存在相当大的差距，也毫无疑问，中国应当学习国外先进技术。然而，学习国外先进技术可以通过多种渠道：如通过进出口贸易、来料加工契约方式、引进设备、引进人才、购买专利以及共建研发基地等，当然也可以通过 FDI。为什么我们要如此强调以 FDI 的方式来学习国外先进技术？从理论上说(Kinoshita，2001)，引进外国直接投资企业的方式，会通过四种渠道对 FDI 的东道国企业产生正的技术溢出效应：(1)示范—模仿效应；(2)竞争效应；(3)对外联系效应；(4)培训效应，即通过劳动力从跨国公司到本国企业的流动，将外国直接投资企业的先进管理、先进技术转移给本国企业。在中国的 FDI 是否通过上述渠道对我们传输或溢出了技术呢？

本文利用中国第一次全国经济普查数据估算 FDI 对中国制造业的技术溢出效应。中国第一次全国经济普查是将原计划在 2005 年开展的第四次全国工业普查与 2006 年开展的第三次全国基本单位普查合并，在 2005 年完成的对中国境内从事第二产业和第三产业的全部法人单位、产业活动单位和个体工商业户的普查。普查的标准时间是 2004 年 12 月 31 日，时期资料为 2004 年度。由于资料的可得性限制，我们只获得加总后按地区(共 410 个市级单位)与按 3 位数分类的制造业产业(共 190 个 3 位数产业)数据的子样本。该样本只加总规模以上的内资企业、港澳台资企业与外资企业的财务数据与科技活动数据。这里所谓的“规模以上”是指产品销售收入在500万元以上的企业。样本中的中国“内资企业”包括国有企业、集体企业、股份合作企业、国有联营企业、集体联营企业、国有与集体联营企业、其他联营企业、国有独资公司、其他有限责任公司、股份有限公司、私营独资企业、私营合伙企业、私营有限责任公司、私营股份有限公司、其他内资企业等15类企业;“港澳台企业”包括与港澳台合资经营企业、与港澳台合作经营企业、港澳台商独资经营企业、港澳台商投资股份有限公司等4类企业;“外资企业”包括中外合资经营企业、中外合作经营企业、外资企业、外商投资股份有限公司等4类企业。因此,这里的“内资企业”、“港澳台资企业”与“外资企业”的划分是粗略的,无论是港澳台资企业类中,还是外资企业类中都含有内资的成分。由于数据是时点数据,我们只能做横截面数据分析。不过,由于该数据包含了迄今最新、最全面的中国境内企业R&D的活动信息,这为我们分析FDI的技术溢出效应提供了最新的第一手资料。

在以下的三节里,第一节讨论研究方法,并给出我们的三个估算模型。第二节通过横截面数据的回归分析,检验FDI对中国制造业的技术溢出效应,我们分地区(410个地级市)与分行业(190个3位数制造业产业)作了OLS分析,以便分析FDI在地区内的技术溢出与在行业内的技术溢出。第三节给出了研究的结论。

一、方法与度量

在研究FDI对其东道国经济的技术溢出的文献里,最为常用的方法是在生产函数的估算中将FDI列入解释变量集,考察

FDI 变量对东道国 GDP 的影响是否显著为正。我们在这里不打算综述关于 FDI 技术溢出的全部经验研究文献,只就近年来与我们的研究直接有关的三种方法作简单回顾。

一是 Aitken 与 Harrison(1999)的生产函数估算法。Aitken 与 Harrison 运用委内瑞拉 1976—1989 年企业普查数据,估算了 FDI 对其经济的技术溢出效应。Aitken 与 Harrison(1997)指出,FDI 对东道国企业的生产率可能会带来两种效果:一是由于 FDI 进入后挤占了东道国企业的市场份额,称为"偷窃市场效应"(steal market effect),这会使内资企业减少产量,内资企业的固定成本分摊到比原来更小的产出规模上,从而最终降低内资企业的生产率;二是由于 FDI 的技术溢出(通过人员在外资企业到内资企业的流动;通过新产品的示范;通过 FDI 企业在下游产业对上游的内资企业的订货,会对内资企业提供技术支持;通过 FDI 的出口导向,内资企业可以学到生产技术和营销技术,等等)会使内资企业的平均成本曲线下移从而提高内资企业的生产率。至于这两种效应哪一种占上风?不同的国家可能会有不同的结果,甚至同一个接受 FDI 的国家在不同的发展时期也会呈现不同的结果。Aitken 和 Harrison 的论文特别指出,通常关于 FDI 技术溢出的效果估算存在"识别"问题:FDI 往往会投资于东道国内生产率较高的区域与产业,因此,即使在计量上发现 FDI 与东道国的生产率之间存在正相关关系,也难以说明因果关系。为此,借助于面板数据的优势,他们控制了地区、时间与产业哑变量,分别考察了 FDI 在区域内和在产业内的溢出效应。他们的回归模型中的被解释变量是取对数的企业产出($\ln y$),解释变量除了生产函数中常见的资本(K)与劳动(L)之外,加进了企业 i 所在的行业 t 中的 FDI 份额,与企业 i 所在的区域 j 中的 FDI 份额,FDI 份额的变量是用 FDI 企业就业占全部就业的比重来定义的。这个回归方法对于企业数据的计量分析是十分贴切的，其好处是可以区分出 FDI 在产业内的技术溢出与地区内的技术溢出。

二是 Sabirianova-Svejnar-Terrell（简称 SST 模型）（2005）对捷克与俄罗斯内 FDI 溢出效应的比较研究。SST 模型在四个方面对我们的启发是：(1)定义了引进 FDI 的东道国与世界先进水平之间的“技术差距”。这就是假定 FDI 企业的全要素生产率（TFP_f）代表国际先进水平，从而用内资企业的全要素生产率（TFP_d）与 TFP_f 之间的比率（TFP_f/TFP_d）来度量东道国与世界先进水平的差距。(2)SST 模型在估算 FDI 的溢出效应时区分了 FDI 份额对内资企业生产率的溢出效应与 FDI 份额对外资企业本身的溢出效应。(3)关于溢出效应的度量仍然是用 FDI 的份额对取对数后的产出（t）的回归系数来度量。(4)SST 模型引进了 FDI 随时间变化的效应分析，它用 FDI 存在的时间长度（t）与 FDI 份额的交叉项系数来度量这一效应。SST 模型的经验结果是，无论是在捷克，还是在俄罗斯，FDI 对东道主企业的生产率都产生显著的负面效应：从 1992—1994 年这一阶段到 1995—1997 年这一阶段，FDI 的进入反而使捷克与俄罗斯离世界先进水平更远了；在 1995—1997 年这一阶段到 1998—2000 年这一阶段，FDI 也没有使这两国缩小与世界先进技术水平之间的差距。

三是 Kinoshita（2001）关于 FDI 与东道国 R&D 交互作用而产生技术溢出效应的计量分析模型。SST 模型（2005）已经指出，FDI 之所以对东道国会发生负面效应，可能是由于东道国的 R&D 没能发挥吸收作用。而关于这一点，Kinoshita 早在 2001 年就已经在计量模型中加以考虑。Kinoshita 认为，东道国的研发活动具有两方面的作用：一是研发本身会对企业生产率发生正向作用，这是 R&D 的“创新”效应；另一方面是 R&D 对 FDI 的吸收效应，引进 FDI 的东道国应该具有与 FDI 相匹配的技术水平，才能吸收 FDI 带来的先进技术，而这种吸收 FDI 技术的技术水平是由 R&D 活动产生的。于是，在 Kinoshita 的计量模型里，引入了 $\left(\frac{R\&D}{Y}\right)$ 这一变量（为研发支出占增加值的比重），以及 $\left(\frac{R\&D}{Y}\times FDI\right)$ 这一交叉项（这里，“FDI”是用 FDI 企业就业占全部就业比重定义的）。Kinoshita 尽管也用 FDI 企业的全要素生产率 TFP_f 与内资企业的全要素生产率 TFP_d 之间的差来定义东道国与 FDI 企业母国之间的技术差距，并且在文中列出了 15 个主要产业中（TFP_f-TFP_d）的平均值的差，但在估算 FDI 对东道国的溢出效应时，仍将 $\frac{\Delta Y}{Y}$（即东道国增加值的增长率）作为因变量。Kinoshita 运用捷克制造业（1995—1998 年）1 217 家企业的面板数据作回归，结果发现 FDI 对东道国的 $\frac{\Delta Y}{Y}$ 并不具有显著的作用（且系数为负），但 $\left(\frac{R\&D}{Y}\times FDI\right)$ 这一交叉项的回归系数显著为正，说明尽管 FDI 没有对捷克发生直接的技术溢出作用，但东道国企业通过 R&D 与技术创新仍吸收了 FDI 的技术。

我们的经验分析借鉴了以上三个计量模型的方法。依次对以下三个估算模型作了 OLS 回归：

$$\ln(TY)_i=\alpha_0+\beta_1\ln TK_i+\beta_2\ln TL_i+\beta_3 FDI_i+\varepsilon_i \quad (1)$$

$$\ln(DY)_i=\alpha_0+\beta_1\ln DK_i+\beta_2\ln DL_i+\beta_3 FDI_i+\varepsilon_i \quad (2)$$

$$(TFPDIF)_i=\alpha_0+\alpha_1 FDI_i+\alpha_2(R\&D)_{d_i}+\alpha_3(FDI_i\times(R\&D)_{d_i})+\varepsilon_i \quad (3)$$

在上述三个估算模型中，工业总产值记为 Y，TY 表示总的工业总产值（普查涵盖的2004年底的制造业内全部内资与FDI企业的工业总产值）；DY 表示内资企业的工业总产值。K 与 L 分别表示企业固定资本量与就业量，同样，TK 与 TL 中的“T”都表示“总”（内资加FDI企业）；而 DK 与 DL 分别表示内资企业的固定资本量与就业量。“FDI”是用FDI企业就业占全部就业的比重度量的。“TFP”是指全要素生产率，定义如下：

$$TFP_{ji} = \ln Y_{ji} - \hat{\beta}_1 \ln K_{ji} - \hat{\beta}_2 \ln L_{ji}$$

j 代表外资企业、港澳台资企业和内资企业三类企业，从而，“TFPDIF”（内资企业生产技术水平与外资企业生产技术水平的差距）便定义为：

$$(TFPDIF)_i = TFP_{ji} - TFP_{di}$$

下标 d 表示内资，下标 f 表示FDI，f 又分“港澳台”与外资。

我们之所以将“TFPDIF”作为中国与世界先进技术水平之间的差距，是基于以下两点理由：（1）一般认为，“TFP”即“索洛余项”实际上代表一国的技术水平或制度因素对生产率的效应；（2）在SST模型、Kinoshita模型中，已经用其来定义东道国与FDI母国之间的技术差距，我们只是在这一定义基础上，把“TFPDIF”作为估算模型的因变量，旨为发现FDI，内资企业的R&D（我们用内资企业的R&D支出/就业量来定义 $(R\&D)_d$）、$(FDI)_i$ 与 $(R\&D)_{d_i}$ 的交叉项对于中国缩小与世界技术水平之间差距的作用，从而以数字来回答：市场是否换来了技术？

具体的估算过程如下：

在对方程(1)的回归中,我们把 FDI 分为两类,一类是港澳台资企业,另一类是其他的 FDI,我们称为“外资”企业。所以,对方程(1)的回归由于变量 FDI 分为两类,我们实质上作了两个回归。又由于我们的数据分地区(观察规模为 410 个地级市)与分行业(观察规模为 190 个 3 位数制造产业),从而我们对方程(1)的回归便有 4 个结果。

关于方程(1)的回归结果可能带来 Aitken 与 Harrison 指出过的“识别问题”:FDI 与 ln(TY)之间的正相关系数可能会高估 FDI 对东道国的溢出作用,因 FDI 一般会流向经济发达地区。因此,我们在方程(2)专门考察 FDI 对内资企业生产率 ln(TY)的作用,结果也分 4 种:分地区的港澳台资溢出效应,分行业的港澳台资溢出效应,分地区的外资溢出效应,分行业的外资溢出效应。

对方程(3)的回归基于对内资、港澳台资、外资三类企业的生产函数中的全要素生产率的分别估算,由此我们得到内资与港澳台企业之间全要素生产率之差的数列,以及内资与外资企业之间的全要素生产率之差的数列。因此,对方程(3)的回归又可分为两类:港澳台资(FDI_K)对 TFPDIF 的效应;外资(FDI_f)对 TFPDIF 的效应。由于对每一类“TFPDIF”估算又可分地区与行业,我们同样得到 4 个结果。

二、FDI 对中国制造业的溢出作用

(一) FDI 对中国制造业总体的溢出作用

我们将 FDI 分为两类:除港澳台资以外的“外资”与“港澳台资”。然后分别考察它们对 ln TY 的效应。

表 1　外资份额对所有企业总产出的影响

	分地区总产出回归结果		分行业总产出回归结果	
	(1) 外资份额＝外资企业就业人口/总的就业人口	(2) 外资份额＝外资企业的资本总额/总资本额	(3) 外资份额＝外资企业就业人口/总的就业人口	(4) 外资份额＝外资企业的资本总额/总资本额
总资本量	0.735***	0.745***	0.680***	0.657***
(ln *TK*)	(0.031)	(0.031)	(0.050)	(0.050)
总就业人数	0.327***	0.317***	0.315***	0.334***
(ln *TL*)	(0.033)	(0.034)	(0.058)	(0.058)
外资份额	1.115***	0.841***	0.899***	0.871***
(FDI)	(0.172)	(0.137)	(0.248)	(0.226)
截距项	−0.014	−0.048	0.918***	1.029***
(cons)	(0.158)	(0.158)	(0.229)	(0.221)
R^2	0.96	0.96	0.96	0.96

说明：$\ln TY_i = \alpha + \beta_1 \ln TK_i + \beta_2 \ln TL_i + \beta_3 FDI_i + \varepsilon_i$，上标 *** 表示在 1%水平上显著，括号内的数字为标准差。

表 1 给出了“外资”对于中国制造业总体生产率的效应。可以看出，“外资”的直接投资(FDI)在地区内与 ln(*TY*)的系数，在行业内与 ln(*TY*)的系数均在 1%水平上显著为正；以就业比率定义的 FDI 份额，在地区内与 ln(*TY*)的系数(1.115)要大于其在行业内与 ln(*TY*)的系数(0.899)；但以资本比率定义的 FDI 份额在行业内与 ln(*TY*)的系数值(0.871)则高于其在地区内与 ln(*TY*)的系数值(0.841)。无论是分地区回归，还是按行业数据进行回归，我们都发现，按就业比率定义的 FDI 份额对 ln(*TY*)的系数都要高于按资本比重定义的 FDI 份额对 ln(*TY*)的系数。这意味着，如果正相关系数代表 FDI 对中国经济的溢出作用，则在地区内通过就业而传导的溢出作用要远大于在行业内通过就业而传递的溢出作用；在外资行业内通过资本形成而传递的溢出作用要稍大于地区内通过资本形成而传递的溢出

作用；外资通过就业（人力资本）传递的溢出作用要大于通过资本形成而传递的溢出作用。

表 2 给出了港澳台资企业的 FDI 对中国制造业总生产率的效应分析。与表 1 相比较，我们发现，无论是分地区看，还是分行业看，港澳台资都与外资一样，在 1%的水平上与中国制造业总生产率显著正相关。如果把“正相关系数”看成是溢出的一种度量，则可以从表 2 看出，按就业比重定义的 FDI 份额，在地区内对 ln(*TY*)的溢出效应(1.04)要大于在行业内的溢出效应(0.911)；但若按资本比重来定义 FDI 份额，则其在行业内对 ln(*TY*)的溢出效应(1.04)要大于其在地区内的溢出效应(0.886)。表 2 与表 1 的不同之处在于，港澳台资通过就业而传递的溢出效应不再对通过资本形成而传递的溢出效应占优。

表 2　港澳台资企业份额对所有企业总产出的影响

	分地区总产出回归结果		分行业总产出回归结果	
	(1) 港澳台企业份额＝港澳台企业就业人口/总的就业人口	(2) 港澳台企业份额＝港澳台企业的资本总额/总资本额	(3) 港澳台企业份额＝港澳台企业就业人口/总的就业人口	(4) 港澳台企业份额＝港澳台企业的资本总额/总资本额
总资本量	0.771***	0.765***	0.711***	0.710***
(ln *TK*)	(0.031)	(0.031)	(0.053)	(0.052)
总就业人数	0.292***	0.300***	0.277***	0.279***
(ln *TL*)	(0.034)	(0.034)	(0.061)	(0.060)
港澳台企业	1.04***	0.886***	0.911***	1.040***
份额(HFDI)	(0.178)	(0.170)	(0.278)	(0.291)
截距项	−0.137	−0.137	0.884***	0.876***
(cons)	(0.158)	(0.159)	(0.235)	(0.232)
R^2	0.96	0.96	0.96	0.96

说明：$\ln TY_i = \alpha + \beta_1 \ln TK_i + \beta_2 \ln TL_i + \beta_3 HFDI_i + \varepsilon_i$，*HFDI* 表示港澳台资，上标 *** 表示在 1%水平上显著，括号内的数字是标准差。

(二) FDI 对中国制造业内资企业的溢出作用

上一分节所显示的结果难以说明“因果性”,显著正相关的系数可能远远高估 FDI 对中国经济的溢出效应。这一分节我们只观察 FDI 对内资企业的总生产率的效应。结果如表 3 与表 4 所示。

表 3 给出“外资”对内资的溢出效果估算。由于在产出、资本与劳动变量中都减去了 FDI 企业的对应值,只考察外资的 FDI 份额对内资企业总生产率 ln(DY)的效应,我们将表 3 与表 1 相比,便可以发现有以下不同:(1)外资的 FDI 份额对 ln(DY)的作用系数$\hat{\beta}_3$ 值在 4 列中都显著变小了。(2)只有在分地区回归的结果中,外资份额才与内资企业的总生产率 ln(DY)显著正相关,但其显著性已下降(从 99%下降为 95%)。(3)若从分行业的回

表 3 外资份额对内资企业总产出的影响

	分地区总产出回归结果		分行业总产出回归结果	
	(1) 外资企业份额=外资企业就业人口/总的就业人口	(2) 外资企业份额=外资企业的资本总额/总资本额	(3) 外资企业份额=外资企业就业人口/总的就业人口	(4) 外资企业份额=外资企业的资本总额/总资本额
内资企业资本量(ln DTK)	0.726***	0.735***	0.610***	0.609***
	(0.030)	(0.030)	(0.055)	(0.055)
内资企业就业人数(ln DTL)	0.337***	0.327***	0.372***	0.370***
	(0.034)	(0.034)	(0.062)	(0.062)
外资企业份额(FDI)	0.419***	0.328**	0.315	0.207
	(0.170)	(0.137)	(0.266)	(0.241)
截距项(cons)	0.013	−0.01	1.293***	1.339***
	(0.157)	(0.157)	(0.243)	(0.236)
R^2	0.96	0.96	0.96	0.96

说明:$\ln DY_i = \alpha + \beta_1 \ln DK_i + \beta_2 \ln DL_i + \beta_3 FDI_i + \varepsilon_i$,上标 *** 表示在 1%水平上显著,** 表示在 5%水平上显著,括号内的数字是标准差。

归结果看，外资份额与内资企业的总生产率之间已没有显著的相关性。这说明，即使把正相关系数读成“正溢出效应”，这种溢出效应在行业内部也是不存在的。(4)外资在地区内通过就业对内资企业的正溢出效应(0.419)仍大于通过资本形成的渠道对内资企业发生的正溢出效应(0.328)。

再看港澳台资对制造业内资企业总生产率的效应(见表4)则可以发现：(1)与表2比较，港澳台资份额对 ln(DY)的效应在对应的4列中都大大下降了，这说明无论从地区溢出看，还是从行业溢出看，港澳台资对内资企业的净溢出作用都要比上一分节中显示的效应低许多。(2)表4与表3相比可以发现，港澳台资对内资企业总生产率的净溢出作用要大出2—3倍。(3)外资企业在分行业的回归里对内资企业不再具有显著的正相关关系，而港澳台资企业在分行业的回归中与内资企业的总生产率仍然显著正相关。这说明港澳台资企业对内资企业的正溢出作用要比外资企业对内资企业的正溢出作用强劲。(4)在地区内的溢出中，港澳台资通过就业渠道对内资企业的溢出效应大于其通过资本形成的渠道对内资企业的效应，但在行业内溢出中，港澳台资企业通过资本形成发生的溢出效应要大于其通过就业渠道而发生的溢出效应。

(三) FDI 对于中国内资企业缩小与外资企业之间技术差距的作用

这一分节，我们考察内资企业与外资企业在全要素生产率上的差距，然后检验 FDI 份额是否对于中国企业缩小与国际先进技术水平之间的差距发生了有益的作用？中国内资企业的 R&D 活动是否具有“创新作用”或“增进吸收能力”的作用？

表 4　港澳台资企业份额对内资企业总产出的影响

	分地区总产出回归结果		分行业总产出回归结果	
	(1) 港澳台企业份额＝港澳台企业就业人口/总的就业人口	(2) 港澳台企业份额＝港澳台企业的资本总额/总资本额	(3) 港澳台企业份额＝港澳台企业就业人口/总的就业人口	(4) 港澳台企业份额＝港澳台企业的资本总额/总资本额
内资企业资本量(ln *TK*)	0.737*** (0.030)	0.740*** (0.030)	0.637*** (0.055)	0.659*** (0.057)
内资企业就业人数(ln *TL*)	0.327*** (0.033)	0.323*** (0.033)	0.346*** (0.062)	0.321*** (0.063)
港澳台企业份额(HFDI)	0.694*** (0.175)	0.547*** (0.167)	0.714** (0.286)	0.880*** (0.309)
截距项(cons)	−0.042 (0.155)	−0.048 (0.157)	1.157*** (0.244)	1.09*** (0.248)
R^2	0.96	0.96	0.95	0.95

说明：$\ln DY_i=\alpha+\beta_1\ln DK_i+\beta_2\ln DL_i+\beta_3 HFDI_i+\varepsilon_i$，上标 *** 表示在 1%水平上显著，** 表示在 5%水平上显著，括号内的数字是标准差。

我们以公式(3)为基础进行分析。为了按公式(3)进行回归，我们首先按地区(410 个地区)与按产业(190 个 3 位数制造产业)对内资企业与外资企业、内资企业与港澳台资企业对应作了 4 次生产函数的估算，由于外资企业与港澳台资企业并未全部进入这 410 个地区与 190 个产业，并且中国政府对外资与港澳台资在产业准入上是有区别的，因此，当我们在地区观察值中删去外资为零的观察单位所剩下的观察单位数与删去港资为零的单位后剩下的样本规模是不一样的；同样地，在分产业的回归中，删去外资为零的观察值后的样本规模会不同于删掉港澳资为零的观察值后的样本规模。因此，事实上，我们要对“外资”与“港澳台资”企业各作分地区、分行业的生产函数估算，共获得 4 个数列的“全要素生产率”。同时，按上面这 4 个数列，我们再对应构造内资企业的子样本，估算出对应的 4 个关于内资企业的全要素生产率的数列。

结果与 Kinoshita(2001)的发现类似。当我们将按地区、按行业的外资企业的 TFP 数列、港澳台资企业的 TFP 数列与对应的内资企业 TFP 数列比较时，发现：(1)这 6 个数列（分地区的外资、港澳台资、内资企业的 TFP 序列、分行业的外资、港澳台资、内资企业的 TFP 序列）中的每个数列中都各有正、负数；(2)由上述 6 个数列构成的关于 FDI 企业与内资企业之间在全要素生产率上面之差的 4 个序列 $[TFP_{ij}$(外资) $- TFP_{ij}$(内资)$_{i=1}^{410(地区)}$，$_{j=1}^{190(行业)}$；TFP_{ij}(港澳台资) $- TFP_{ij}$(内资)$_{i=1}^{410(地区)}$，$_{j=1}^{190(行业)}]$ 中的每一个差序列也各由正负数组成；(3)但令我们惊讶的是，无论是简单算术平均数，还是加权平均数，外资企业 TFP 平均数与内资企业 TFP 平均数之差都是负的；(4)在两个港澳台资企业 TFP 与内资企业 TFP 之差的序列中，按地区求出港澳台资 TFP 算术平均数和加权平均数与对应的内资企业 TFP 均值之差都为正；而按行业算出的 TFP 之差的序列中，按算术平均与加权平均后求得的港澳台资 TFP 均值和内资企业的 TFP 均值之差都为负。4 个 TFP 均值之差的平均数的信息如表 5 所示。

在表 5 中，所谓加权平均数中的权数 W_{ih} 为 h 类资本（h 等于外资、港澳台资、内资三类）中在地区（或行业）i 中投入的比率，即 $W_{ij} = \frac{K_{ih}}{K_h}$。

我们对 TFP 估算值所基于的生产函数估算采取了不含截距的方法，以此获得关于外资、港澳台资与内资分地区、分行业的 6 个 TFP 序列，按表 5 的方法重新计算 FDI 类企业的 TFP 与内资企业的 TFP 之差，结果如表 6 所示。

表 5 TFP 的平均数之差(TFP 按含截距的生产函数估算)

A:外资 TFP 与内资 TFP 比较	
分 地 区	分 行 业
内资企业 TFP 加权平均值=0.014 737	内资企业 TFP 加权平均值=1.518 172
外资企业 TFP 加权平均值=−0.029 55	外资企业 TFP 加权平均值=0.610 152
TFPD IFF(TFP 差值)=($\overline{TFP}_{外资}-\overline{TFP}_{内资}$)=−0.044 29	TFPD IFF(TFP 差值)=($\overline{TFP}_{外资}-\overline{TFP}_{内资}$)=−0.908 02
内资企业 TFP 算术平均值=−0.001 29	内资企业 TFP 算术平均值=1.370 562
外资企业 TFP 算术平均值=−0.087 04	外资企业 TFP 算术平均值=0.466 489
TFPD IFF(TFP 差值)=($\overline{TFP}_{外资}-\overline{TFP}_{内资}$)=−0.085 75	TFPD IFF(TFP 差值)=($\overline{TFP}_{外资}-\overline{TFP}_{内资}$)=−0.904 07
B:港澳台资 TFP 与内资 TFP 比较	
分 地 区	分 行 业
内资企业 TFP 加权平均值=0.129 921	内资企业 TFP 加权平均值=1.183 785
港澳台资企业 TFP 加权平均值=0.438 732	港澳台资企业 TFP 加权平均值=0.660 1
TFPD IFF(TFP 差值)=($\overline{TFP}_{港澳台资}-\overline{TFP}_{内资}$)=0.308 811	TFPD IFF(TFP 差值)=($\overline{TFP}_{港澳台资}-\overline{TFP}_{内资}$)=−0.523 69
内资企业 TFP 算术平均值=0.193 243	内资企业 TFP 算术平均值=1.059 542
港澳台资企业 TFP 算术平均值=0.356 43	港澳台资企业 TFP 算术平均值=0.552 322
TFPD IFF(TFP 差值)=($\overline{TFP}_{港澳台资}-\overline{TFP}_{内资}$)=0.163 187	TFPD IFF(TFP 差值)=($\overline{TFP}_{港澳台资}-\overline{TFP}_{内资}$)=−0.507 22

表 6　TFP 的平均数之差(TFP 按无截距的生产函数估算)

A:外资 TFP 与内资 TFP 比较	
分　地　区	分　行　业
内资企业 TFP 加权平均值=0.016 172 291	内资企业 TFP 加权平均值=−0.046 27
外资企业 TFP 加权平均值=0.076 742 827	外资企业 TFP 加权平均值=0.043 466
TFPD IFF(TFP 差值)=($\overline{TFP}_{外资}-\overline{TFP}_{内资}$)=0.060 570 536	TFPD IFF(TFP 差值)=($\overline{TFP}_{外资}-\overline{TFP}_{内资}$)=0.089 737
内资企业 TFP 算术平均值=−2.620 54E-05	内资企业 TFP 算术平均值=0.020 35
外资企业 TFP 算术平均值=−0.002 449 619	外资企业 TFP 算术平均值=0.011 051
TFPD IFF(TFP 差值)=($\overline{TFP}_{外资}-\overline{TFP}_{内资}$)=−0.002 423 414	TFPD IFF(TFP 差值)=($\overline{TFP}_{外资}-\overline{TFP}_{内资}$)=−0.009 299
B:港澳台资 TFP 与内资 TFP 比较	
分　地　区	分　行　业
内资企业 TFP 加权平均值=−0.081 26	内资企业 TFP 加权平均值=−0.034 11
港澳台资企业 TFP 加权平均值=0.003 33	港澳台资企业 TFP 加权平均值=0.017 627
TFPD IFF(TFP 差值)=($\overline{TFP}_{港澳台资}-\overline{TFP}_{内资}$)=0.084 586	TFPD IFF(TFP 差值)=($\overline{TFP}_{港澳台资}-\overline{TFP}_{内资}$)=0.051 738
内资企业 TFP 算术平均值=0.001 824	内资企业 TFP 算术平均值=0.015 837
港澳台资企业 TFP 算术平均值=0.010 441	港澳台资企业 TFP 算术平均值=0.011 77
TFPD IFF(TFP 差值)=($\overline{TFP}_{港澳台资}-\overline{TFP}_{内资}$)=0.008 618	TFPD IFF(TFP 差值)=($\overline{TFP}_{港澳台资}-\overline{TFP}_{内资}$)=0.004 07

我们可以看到，由于对生产函数采取无截距估算，使TFP序列发生一些变化，结果使外资企业的TFP加权平均数与内资企业的TFP加权平均数之差，无论是从地区的角度看，还是按行业的角度看都为正；然而，若取算术平均数，则内资的TFP仍要高于外资的TFP(见表6板块A)。港澳台资的TFP，若按地区平均(无论是加权平均，还是算术平均)，高于内资的TFP均值；而按行业看，则加权后港澳台资TFP均值会高于内资TFP的加权平均数，从算术平均数意义上的TFP来说，港澳台资并不胜于内资企业。

所以，若以无截距的生产函数作为估算基础，若对加权平均后的TFP值进行比较，则内资与FDI企业之间是存在一定的技术差距的。

那么，FDI的进入是否有助于内资企业缩小与外资企业或港澳台资企业的技术差距呢？我们按公式(3)对此作了OLS回归，回归结果如表7与表8。

表7　外资份额对缩小中国企业与外资企业之间技术差距的效应

	分地区总产出回归结果		分行业总产出回归结果	
	(1)有截距项	(2)无截距项	(3)有截距项	(4)无截距项
用就业衡量的外资份额	−0.158	−0.108	0.399	−0.051
(FDI份额)	(0.418)	(0.417)	(0.309)	(0.322)
人均研发投资	−0.149***	−0.145***	−0.076***	0.002
(RDPER)	(0.056)	(0.056)	(0.059)	(0.061)
FDI份额与人均R&D	0.454*	0.452*	0.058	−0.046
的乘积(FDI*RDPER)	(0.262)	(0.261)	(0.094)	(0.098)
截距项	0.024	0.097	−0.883***	0.006
(cons)	(0.069)	(0.069)	(0.075)	(0.078)
R^2	0.033	0.034	0.027	0.011

说明：$TFPDIF_i=\alpha+\beta_1 FDI_i+\beta_2 RDPER_i+\beta_3 FDI*RDPER_i+\varepsilon_i$，$RDPER$是用内资企业R&D的值除以内资企业总就业人数。“有截距项”与“无截距项”各指估算TFP的生产函数有无截距项。上标***表示在1%水平上显著，*表示在10%水平上显著，括号内的数值是标准差。

从表 7 中我们可以看到:(1)外资的 FDI 对 TFPDIF 的作用大都为负($\hat{\beta}_1$ 的 4 个估算值中有 3 个为负)说明外资份额提高后对于内资企业缩小与外资技术差距是有正面作用的,但作用并不显著,并且,无论是按有截距项的生产函数估算 TFP,还是按无截距项的生产函数估算 TFP,外资份额对 TFPDIF 的作用都不显著。

(2) 中国内资企业本身的研发(人均 R&D 支出)则对缩小内资企业与国际先进技术水平之间的差距有正面作用($\hat{\beta}_1$ 的估算值在按地区估算的模型中显著为负,且显著水平为 1%);在按行业估算的模型中,人均研发支出对缩小内资企业与国外技术水平之间差距的作用不显著。

(3) 外资的直接投资与内资研发的交叉项系数的估算值在分地区回归模型中为正,且在 10% 水平上显著,说明外资进入与内资研发之间的交互作用不利于内资企业缩小与国际先进技术水平的差距,意味着外资进入后可能由于"市场偷窃"效应而使内资企业降低了对研发投入的动力。也说明国内研发在增加"吸收能力"方面尚有差距。

(4) 尽管估算 TFP 的值与生产函数中含不含截距项有关系,但表 7 显示,在估算 FDI 份额、研发以及 FDI 与研发交叉项对 TFPDIF 的效应时,生产函数中含不含截距项基本上是无影响的。因此,我们可以得出结论:外资进入的份额对于内资企业缩小与国际先进水平之间的距离方面,即使存在正面效应,效应也不显著,倒是内资企业的研发即自主创新会显著地缩小中国企业与国际先进技术水平之间的距离。

表 8　港澳台资份额对缩小国内企业与港澳台资企业之间技术差距的效应

	分地区总产出回归结果		分行业总产出回归结果	
	(1)有截距项	(2)无截距项	(3)有截距项	(4)无截距项
用就业衡量的港澳台资份额	0.155	−0.023	−1.179*	−1.666**
(FDI 份额)	(0.368)	(0.372)	(0.651)	(0.677)
人均研发投资	−0.033	−0.046	−0.147	−0.112
(RDPER)	(0.066)	(0.067)	(0.103)	(0.107)
FDI 份额与人均 R&D 的乘积	−0.179	−0.185	0.714	0.681
(HFDI * RDPER)	(0.202)	(0.204)	(0.562)	(0.584)
截距项	0.207	0.083	−0.307***	0.221*
(cons)	(0.081)	(0.082)	(0.114)	(0.119)
R^2	0.014	0.023	0.025	0.058

说明：$TFPDIF_i = \alpha + \beta_1 HFDI_i + \beta_2 RDPER_i + \beta_3 HFDI * RDPER_i + \varepsilon_i$，HFDI 是用就业衡量的港澳台资比重。RDPER 是用内资企业 R&D 除以内资企业就业人数。上标 *** 表示在 1%水平上显著，上标 ** 表示在 5%水平上显著，上标 * 表示在 1%水平上显著，括号内的数值为标准差。

我们再看港澳台资（HFDI）份额对 TFPDIF 的作用。表 8 显示：(1)在分行业回归的模型中，$\hat{\beta}_1$ 在 10%或 5%水平上显著为负，说明港澳台资的进入倒是会显著地缩小内资企业与港澳台资企业在技术上的差距，即内资企业在学习技术上可能更易于与港澳台资企业融合；(2)人均研发支出对于内资企业缩小与港澳台资企业的技术差距并无显著作用，尽管人均 R&D 投资的作用方向正确。这说明内资企业的研发可能更侧重于对付外资企业的竞争压力，而不太重视将 R&D 投向缩小与港澳台企业之间的技术差距。(3)港澳台资份额与内资企业 R&D 的交互项作用在分地区、分行业的 4 个估算模型中都不显著，不过在按地区回归的模型中 $\hat{\beta}_3$ 的作用方向正确，说明港澳台资进入对内资企业的 R&D 不存在像外资企业那种对内资企业 R&D 的不利作用。

因此，与表 7 相比，我们发现，第一，港澳台资进入会使内资企业在技术上显著缩小与港澳台资企业的距离，而外资企业进入没有这方面的显著作用；第二，外资进入会不利于内资企业通过研发而缩小与国际先进技术水平之间的距离，但港澳台资进入则没有这种显著的负面作用。

三、结　论

中国对 FDI 出让了市场份额，是否换到了技术？我们的研究从三个层次上回答了这个问题：第一，从最粗浅的 FDI 份额与中国制造业（各类企业其中包括 FDI 企业）的总生产率相关系数来说，FDI 显著与中国制造业的总生产率正相关。但这种正相关系数显然会过高地估算 FDI 对中国的技术溢出程度；第二，从 FDI 与剔除了 FDI 的内资企业的总生产率之间的相关系数看，我们已经发现在第一层次上的“技术溢出”大为减弱了，在产业内外资份额已与内资企业的总生产率不显著相关了，只有港澳台资份额仍与内资企业的总生产率显著正相关；第三，从 FDI 份额对中国企业缩小与国际先进技术水平之间距离的效果看，则我们更是看到，外资进入在这一方面并无显著作用，且外资进入会妨碍内资企业通过研发自主创新而缩小与国际先进水平之间距离的努力；倒是港澳台资进入会显著地缩小内资企业与港澳台资企业在技术上的差距，也没有发现由于港澳台资进入而不利于内资企业通过 R&D 缩小差距的努力投入的证据。因此，如果层层深入分析，我们只能得到这样的结论：除港澳台资以外的外资，在技术净溢出方面并无多少显著的证据，倒是让我们发现了外资进入会不利于中国企业通过 R&D 而缩小与世界先进技术水平之间差距的证据;然而,在上述三个层次上,港澳台资进入对于内资企业都存在正技术溢出的证据。

由于我们的数据只是一个时点上的横截面数据,且不是企业数据,只是一个经加总后的区域与行业数据,因此,我们的估算会忽略区域内与行业内 FDI 对不同企业的不同作用,而只能呈现 FDI 在一个区域与一个行业内经过相互抵消后的溢出作用。横截面数据也估算不出 FDI 对中国经济历史的、动态的作用,因为即使对 2004 年底的横截面数据分析看不出 FDI 正的溢出作用,也不能由此否认中国内资企业的生产率现状是由 FDI 引入后才得以形成的可能性。基于以上两点考虑,对估算结果的解释应持谨慎态度。

参考文献

仝月婷、胡又欣:《外商直接投资的生产率溢出效应:对中国制造业的实证研究》,《经济学报》2005 年第 1 卷。

王红岭、李稻葵、冯俊新:《FDI 与自主研发:基于行业数据的经验研究》,《经济研究》2006 年第 2 期。

吴延兵:《R&D 与生产率——基于中国制造业的实证研究》,《经济研究》2006 年第 11 期。

Aitken, Brian J. and Harrison, Ann E., 1997, "Do Domestic Firms Benefit from Foreign Direct Investment? Evidence from Panel Data", Mimeo, Columbia University.

——, 1999, "Do Domestic Firms Benefit from Direct Foreign Investment? Evidence from Venezuela", *American Econom ic Review*.

Huang, Yesheng, 2003, *Selling China: Foreign Direct Investment during the Reform Era*, New York: Cambridge University Press.

Kinoshita, Yuko, 2001, "R&D and Technology Spillovers via FDI: Innovation and Absorptive Capacity", *CEPR Working Paper*, 349a, Number, University of Michigan.

Sabiranova, Klara, Svejnar, Jan and Terrell, Katherine, 2005, "Distance to The Efficiency Frontier And Foreign Direct Investment Spillovers", *Journal of the European Econom ic Association*, April-May.

(原载《世界经济》2007 年第 8 期)

作为信号发送和可置信承诺的国企改革*

朱林可　王　争

（浙江大学经济学院）

一、引　　言

在现有的研究文献中，已有不少对国企改革①的原因做过探索（如 Guo and Yao，2005；王红领等，2001；朱恒鹏，2004等），其中地区竞争是被强调的因素之一（Jin et al.，2001；Li et al.，1998）。但这些关于地区竞争对国企改革的影响的研究，强调的主要是产品市场上的地区竞争（Li 等，1998），而作为地区竞争的重要内容之一（尤其是对于沿海地区），地区之间对 FDI 的竞争对国企改革的影响却很少得到关注。少数涉及这一问题的文献，又未能在理论上和实证上有效地说明 FDI 影响国企改革的机制是什么。本文的目的就是在理论上说明 FDI 对国企改革的影响机制，并在实证上加以检验。

罗小朋（1995）认为，地区之间对外资的竞争，迫使地方政府打破国有企业铁板一块的格局，允许外资与国有企业合营，这推

* 作者感谢张旭昆教授和汪淼军对文章初稿提出的宝贵意见。感谢朱希伟、宋华盛、曹正汉，以及第六届中国青年经济学者论坛上陆铭和几位评论人提出的评论意见。

① 本文所指的国企改革主要是指国有企业的民营改制。

动了国有企业的改革。Cao 等(1999)在研究地区竞争对国企改革的影响时,也指出了 FDI 的作用。他们认为,FDI 影响国企改革的路径主要有三种:外资的进入,使国有企业在产品市场上受到更多的竞争压力,从而推动了国企改革的发生;FDI 为国企的改革提供了资金支持;为了吸引 FDI,地方政府需要获得资金建设基础设施,而出售国有企业为地方政府提供了一个收入来源。Tong(2005)也认为,那些处于对外资开放的行业中的国有企业更容易发生改革,因为它们面对着更多的来自 FDI 的竞争。Girma 和 Gong(2005)发现,FDI 对一个地区的国有企业的全要素生产率(TFP)有显著的负的影响,他们认为这是由于外资企业以更高的工资吸引走了国企的高技术人才。这一发现说明,FDI 的增加确实加剧了国有企业的生存压力,在这个意义上,他们的发现支持了 FDI 通过竞争压力推动国企改革的假说。不过他们强调的竞争压力,主要来自劳动力市场,与以往文献强调产品市场上的竞争有所不同。Fung 等(2005)发现,一个地区制造业总产出中,国有企业所占的比重与该地区能吸引到的 FDI 负相关。但是他们并没有深入研究这其中的影响机制,也没有说明这是否意味着,为了吸引更多的 FDI,地方政府会更有动力进行国企改革。Li 等(2006)在研究 FDI 的区位决定因素时发现,一个地区的私有化程度对吸引 FDI 有正的影响,他们认为,这是因为私有化程度越高,意味着更高的市场开放程度、更公平的竞争和更具活力的劳动力市场。这反过来意味着,地区之间对外资的竞争可能会推动私有化进程。但这其中的作用机制,作者并没有加以深入研究。

综上所述,目前文献中关于 FDI 影响国企改革的路径的假说主要可以概括为以下三种:“竞争压力假说”,外资的进入,使国有企业在产品市场以及劳动力市场上受到更多的竞争压力,这推动了国企改革的发生;"资金支持假说",FDI 为国企的民营改制提供了资金支持;"收入来源假说",国企改革为地方政府提供了一个获取基础设施建设资金的收入来源。其中,"竞争压力假说"是文献中强调比较多的。

但是,上述假说的缺陷是,它们都没有考虑地方政府之间以及地方政府与外资之间的互动。本文尝试提出另外两种替代性(也可能是补充性)的假说:"信号发送假说"。在信息不对称下,外资可能选择国企改革规模作为一个地方政府开明程度的信号,而为了发送信号吸引外资,地方政府将更多地推动国企改革。这一假说的合理性体现在:首先,在中国,由于经济和政治上的地方分权,不同的地方政府的行为存在着很大差异,这种行为的差异化导致外资在到中国来投资选址时,面对很大的信息不对称问题;其次,国企改革作为一个敏感的政治和经济问题(尤其是在 90 年代中期以前),是一个能够反映政府类型(开明与否)的较好的信号。

本文提出的另一个假说是:"可置信承诺假说"。大规模的国企改革,减少了地方政府干预市场的动机,从而使得维护公平竞争的承诺变得可信,因此能吸引更多的外资,而预期到这一点使得地方政府更有动力去推动国企改革。[①]这一假说的合理性体现在:首先,政府能否维护公平竞争,减少市场干预,是外资所关心的一个问题;其次,国有企业缺乏自生能力是政府干预市场的一个重要动机(林毅夫,2004),而国企改革减少了这种动机,

① 需要说明的是,本文提出的这两个假说不仅对解释外资对国企改革的影响有帮助,而且也有助于理解地区之间对内资的竞争对国企改革的影响。同时,这两个假说也可以推广到地区之间竞争外资(或内资)对政府改革的影响,例如广东顺德的政府改革和国企改革就是同时发生的,而改革背后的动力主要在于吸引外资(和内资)。

因此能增加地方政府维护公平竞争的承诺的可置信程度。

对上述五种假说进行检验,以确定其适用性是本文的主要目的所在。本文接下来的内容安排如下:第二部分建立理论模型,以说明本文提出的"信号发送假说"和"可置信承诺假说"。第三部分提出与各假说相对应的可检验的含义。第四部分是对数据和变量的说明。第五部分是计量模型和检验。最后是结论。

二、模型:作为信号发送和可置信承诺的国企改革

(一)作为信号发送的国企改革

我们在这里把地方政府分为开明的和保守的两种类型,分别用O型和C型表示。其中前者的概率是P,后者的概率是$1-P$。这里的政府类型是指所有那些外资关心但是却无法直接知道的地方政府的私人信息,包括地方政府对市场经济的态度、是否愿意维护公平竞争乃至政府官员的意识形态倾向,等等,简言之,即地方政府的开明程度。国企改革的成本函数是$\frac{(q-a_i)^2}{2}$,这里q表示国企改革的规模,$i=\mathrm{O}$或C。a_i是外生决定的最优的国企改革规模(在不考虑外资的情况下),并且有$a_o>a_c$,即开明的地方政府比保守的地方政府愿意进行更多的国企改革(在不考虑外资的情况下)。显然,当$q=a_i$时,国企改革的成本最小。为简单起见,这里假设地方政府的目标函数为:$U_i=FDI-\frac{(q-a_i)^2}{2}$,即地方政府希望得到更多的FDI,并承担更少的国企改革成本。

为了简单起见,这里把外资看成一个单一的行为主体。外资根据地方政府的类型决定FDI的规模。如果它认为地方政府的类型是O,则选择高的FDI,H;反之,则选择低的FDI,L。

1. 完全信息

在完全信息下，外资根据地方政府的类型选择 FDI 的规模。O 型地方政府得到 H，C 型地方政府得到 L。由于 FDI 的规模与国企改革无关，因此地方政府根据自己的类型选择最优的国企改革规模，即 O 型政府选择，C 型政府选择。在完全信息下，FDI 与国企改革不会相互影响。①

2. 不完全信息

在不完全信息下，外资不能直接判断地方政府的类型。但由于不同类型的地方政府会选择不同规模的国企改革，因此外资可以根据国企改革规模来判断地方政府的类型。但同时，由于意识到这一点，C 型地方政府就有动机去模仿 O 型地方政府，进行一样多的国企改革，以吸引更多的 FDI；而 O 型政府为了与 C 型政府区分开来，②就有动机进行比原来更多的国企改革，使得 C 型政府无法模仿。这一信号发送的竞争的结果，可能出现分离均衡，也可能出现混同均衡。下面给出更详细的分析。

(1) 分离均衡。

若 $q_o = q^*$，$q_c = a_c$ 构成分离均衡，则 q^* 必须满足下述不等式组：

$$\begin{cases} H-\dfrac{(q^*-a_o)^2}{2}\geqslant L \\ H-\dfrac{(q^*-a_c)^2}{2}\leqslant L \end{cases}$$

① 但是在不控制政府类型的情况下，国企改革与 FDI 会表现出一种“伪相关”，因为开明的地方政府得到的 FDI 更多，进行的国企改革也更多，反之则反之。在本文的实证部分，由于采用固定效应和一阶差分模型，已经控制了政府类型，因此不会存在“伪相关”的问题。

② 这里假设，地方政府是 O 型的概率足够小，使得在出现混同均衡时，外资只愿意选择低的 FDI，L。

解上述不等式组得：$a_c + \sqrt{2(H-L)} \leqslant q^* \leqslant a_o + \sqrt{2(H-L)}$，这里设 $a_o - a_c < \sqrt{2(H-L)}$。①这里给出了所有可能的分离均衡的范围。但是由于这一范围内的 q^* 对于 C 型政府来说是相对于 $q_c = a_c$ 的劣战略（由上面第二个不等式可知），因此根据剔除劣战略标准，对于外资来说，当观察到这一范围内的 q 时，不应以任何正的概率认为该地方政府是 C 型的。因此，O 型的地方政府只要选择 $q^* = a_c + \sqrt{2(H-L)}$，就可以将自己与 C 型政府区分开来，而这一选择对它来说是成本最低的。因此，唯一合理的分离均衡是：

$$q_o^* = a_c + \sqrt{2(H-L)} > a_o$$

$$q_c^* = a_c$$

$$t^*(FDI) = \begin{cases} H & if\ q \geqslant q_o^* \\ L & otherwise \end{cases}$$

其中，$t^*(FDI)$是外资的最优策略。与完全信息下（即 FDI 不影响国企改革时）的情况相比，O 型地方政府选择的国企改革规模增加了。因此，地区之间对 FDI 的竞争推动了国企改革。此外，其他情况则与完全信息下的一致：C 型地方政府仍然选择 $q_c^* = a_c$，得到低的 FDI；而 O 型地方政府则得到高的 FDI。此时，即使在控制政府类型之后，我们仍可以观察到国企改革与

---

① 如果这一条件不满足，则唯一合理的分离均衡是 $q_o = a_o$，$q_c = a_c$，与完全信息下的结果一样。这一条件的直觉含义是：a_o 和 a_c 的差距不能如此之大，以至于开明的政府在不考虑外资的情况下，已经进行了比保守的政府多得多的国企改革，使得保守的政府如果去模仿的话就会得不偿失。在这种情况下，即使考虑到吸引 FDI 的问题，开明的政府也没必要进行更多的国企改革，因为在原来的水平上，保守的政府就已经无法模仿了。但是考虑到中国的地方政府数量较多，相邻的两种类型的地方政府差异一般不会如此之大，因此这一条件在现实中应该是可以满足的。

FDI 的正相关关系。因为 O 型的地方政府如果选择低的国企改革(不管是出于什么原因),它就只能得到低的 FDI;而 C 型的地方政府如果选择高的国企改革(不管是出于什么原因),也能得到高的 FDI。这是因为。在不完全信息下,(在本模型中)外资只能根据国企改革规模来判断政府类型。

(2) 混同均衡。

当 O 型政府的概率 P 足够小时,若出现混同均衡,则外资会选择 L,无论政府的类型可能是什么。但此时,C 型政府的最优选择是 $q_c = a_c$,同样 O 型政府的最优选择是 $q_o = a_o$。因此,当 P 足够小时,混同均衡不存在。

当 P 足够大时,混同均衡存在。此时,混同均衡的范围是下述不等式组的解:

$$\begin{cases} H-\dfrac{(q^* - a_o)^2}{2} \geqslant L \\ H-\dfrac{(q^* - a_c)^2}{2} \geqslant L \end{cases}$$

解得:$a_o-\sqrt{2(H-L)} \leqslant q^* \leqslant a_c+\sqrt{2(H-L)}$,这里仍然设 $a_o - a_c < \sqrt{2(H-L)}$。其中,$[a_o-\sqrt{2(H-L)},\ a_o]$ 范围内的混同均衡可以用直观标准剔除,得到合理的混同均衡的范围:

$$q_o^* = q_c^* = q^* \in [a_o,\ a_c+\sqrt{2(H-L)}]$$

$$t^*(FDI) = \begin{cases} H & if\ q \geqslant q^* \\ L & otherwise \end{cases}$$

可见,在混同均衡时,C 型政府的国企改革规模比完全信息下提高了(由原来的 a_c,提高到 a_o 以上),而 O 型政府的国企改革规模在绝大多数情况下也提高了(除了 $q_o^* = q_c^* = a_o$ 的情况)。因此在这里,地区之间对 FDI 的竞争也促进了国企改革。

同时，从上述结果可以看出，无论在分离均衡还是在混同均衡中，$(H-L)$ 越大，FDI 对国企改革的促进作用也越大。这里的含义是：外资越看重国企改革这一信号所反映出来的政府类型，则 FDI 对国企改革的影响也越大。

现将上述结果总结如下：

命题一：在信息不对称下，无论是在分离均衡还是在混同均衡中，地区之间对 FDI 的竞争都促进了国企改革。在分离均衡下，只促进 O 型政府的国企改革；在混同均衡下，则至少促进 C 型政府的改革，并且在绝大多数情况下也促进 O 型政府的改革。

命题二：$(H-L)$ 越大，则 FDI 对国企改革的促进也越大。而 $(H-L)$ 的大小由外资对政府类型的关心程度决定。

命题三：在分离均衡时，FDI 的规模与国企改革正相关，即更多的国企改革会导致更多的 FDI。

（二）作为可置信承诺的国企改革

地方政府能否减少对市场的干预、维护公平竞争，是外资所关心的问题。而在国有企业占据重要地位的经济中，地方政府有强烈的干预市场竞争以保护国有企业的动机，因此，政府关于维护公平竞争的承诺是不可信的（即使在引进外资的时候，地方政府给出了这样的承诺）。通过推进国企改革，减少国有经济比重，地方政府会减少干预市场的动机，从而提高政府维护公平竞争的承诺的可信性，因此，可以吸引到更多外商投资（FDI）。预期到这一点，地方政府便有更多的动力去推进国企改革。地方政府与外资之间的博弈如图 1 所示。

地方政府首先行动，选择国企改革的水平（H 表示高，L 表示低）；然后外资决定 FDI 的规模（H 表示高，L 表示低）；最后地方政府决定是否干预市场（T 表示干预，N 表示不干预）。若地方政府第一阶段选择 L，则接下来无论外资选择 H 还是 L，地方政府在第三阶段的最优选择都是 T；若第一阶段地方政府选择 H，则地方政府第三阶段的最优选择是 N，这是因为国企改革减少了干预市场的收益，但是干预市场的成本（如造成的声誉损失）是不变的。给定地方政府的上述策略，外资在第二阶段的最优策略是：若地方政府选择 H，则也选择 H；反之，选择 L。因为当地方政府选择 H 时，意味着外资进入之后不会受到干预，此时选择 H 最优；反之，则选择 L 最优。

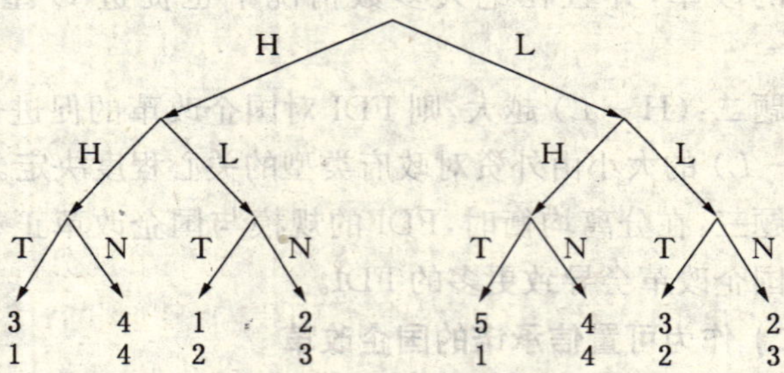

图 1　地方政府与外资之间的博弈

根据以上分析，博弈的均衡要么是（H，H，N），要么是（L，L，T）。具体哪一个均衡会出现，取决于地方政府在增加国企改革的成本和获得更多 FDI 的收益之间的权衡。在图 1 所给出的例子里，最后的均衡是（H，H，N）。对于那些增加国企改革的边际成本非常高的地方政府来说，最后的均衡结果就是（L，L，T）。这意味着，在现实中我们会观察到国企改革的规模与 FDI 正相关。

对于地方政府来说，由于增加国企改革是有成本的，因此最希望出现的结果是（L，H，T）。但是要使外资在第二阶段选择 H，则必须让它相信地方政府在第三阶段会选择 N。地方政府可以给出这样的承诺，但是这种承诺是不可信的，因为在第一阶段选择 L 的情况下，对地方政府最优的是在第三阶段选择 T。为了使第三阶段选择 N 的承诺可信，则地方政府必须在第一阶段选择 H，因为在这种情况下，第三阶段选择 N 就成了它的最优选择。因此，为了作出可置信的承诺以吸引到更多的外资，地方政府就必须在第一阶段选择高的国企改革。

由于增加国企改革会增加成本，因此在不考虑外资的情况下，大多数地方政府都会选择 L。但是，当吸引 FDI 的目标进入到地方政府的考虑中后，那些增加国企改革的边际成本比较低的地方政府就会选择高的国企改革，以获得高的 FDI。这样，吸引 FDI 的考虑就促进了国企改革。

上述理论假说的经验含义是：高的国企改革（H）会导致高的 FDI（H），而低的国企改革（L）会导致低的 FDI（L），即国企改革与 FDI 正相关。这一点与信号发送模型中出现分离均衡时的情况是一样的。但在这里，根据常识我们可以判断，能够使承诺变得可信的国企改革规模必须是足够大的，因为否则就难以影响到政府干预市场的动机。而在信号发送假说中，这一要求是不需要的，因为反映地方政府类型的是国企改革的相对规模。在本文的实证部分，我们正是利用这一特征，来区分两个假说的。

现将上述结果总结如下：

命题四：为了作出可置信的承诺以吸引 FDI，那些改革国有企业的边际成本比较低的地方政府会增加国有企业的改革。

命题五：在上述模型中，国企改革的规模与 FDI 的规模正相关。不过所要求的国企改革规模必须足够大。

三、待验证的含义

本文要检验的五个假说可以分为两类。“竞争压力假说”和“资金支持假说”属于第一类。它们的特点是：认为先有 FDI，后有国企改革，在计量上表现为 FDI 对国企改革的影响。这两个假说的区别是，前者所强调的竞争压力对国企改革产生的影响是渐进的，在计量上应该表现为 FDI 对国企改革的滞后几年的影响；后者的影响发生作用的时间间隔则可以短一些。

后三个假说（“收入来源假说”、“信号发送假说”和“可置信承诺假说”）属于第二类，它们的特点是：认为先有国企改革，后有 FDI 的增加，在计量上表现为国企改革对 FDI 的影响。不过先前的国企改革的目的正是为了推动后来的 FDI 的增加，在这个意义上吸引 FDI 的考虑推动了国企改革。“收入来源假说”与“信号发送假说”和“可置信承诺假说”的区别是，前者所强调的机制（国企改革通过为基础设施建设提供资金而促进外资的增加）起作用的时间间隔比较长，因此，在计量上应该表现为国企改革对 FDI 的滞后几年的影响。而后两个假说（也即本文提出的假说）所强调的机制起作用的时间则可以比较短，因为它们起作用的时间也就是信息传递的时间，因此，在计量上应该可以得到滞后时间比较短，甚至是当年的影响。而“信号发送假说”和“可置信承诺假说”的区别在于，“可置信承诺假说”要求能对 FDI 产生影响的国企改革规模必须足够大，因为小规模的国企改革不足以影响政府干预市场的动机，从而也不足以影响政府关于维护公平竞争的承诺的可置信程度。而“信号发送假说”则没有这种要求，它强调的是国企改革相对于其他地区的规模，而不是绝对规模。

此外，根据“信号发送假说”，我们还可以推论：由于在 90 年代上半期，国企改革的推动者主要是地方政府，而且这段时间内国企改革在政治上和经济上的敏感性，使得它可以成为反映政府类型的较好的信号；而在 1997 年以后，中央政府成了国企改革的有力推动者，全国上下都在进行大规模的国企改革，因此，它也就丧失了作为反映地方政府类型的信号功能。同时，随着外资对中国的投资环境的了解加深，信息不对称的问题也会逐渐减弱。根据以上理由，我们可以预期“信号发送假说”更适用于 90 年代早期的国企改革，而不是 90 年代中期以后的国企改革。

最后，由于 FDI 主要分布在东部，中西部的 FDI 在经济中的角色往往并不重要(见表 1)。因此可以预期我们要寻找的 FDI 对国企改革的影响，主要出现在东部地区。

四、数据和变量说明

我们使用了一个从 1991 年到 2002 年的 28 个省市(不包括海南、西藏和重庆)的面板数据。数据主要来自历年的《中国统计年鉴》、《中国工商行政管理年鉴》和《新中国 50 年财政资料汇编》等。表 1 给出了主要变量的统计描述。

表 1　相关变量的描述性统计

变量名	地区	样本数	均值	标准差	最小值	最大值
国企改革	东部	132	0.038	0.0618	−0.05	0.2996
	中西部	204	0.026	0.0692	−0.408	0.3107
FDI 增长率	东部	132	0.4095	0.8595	−0.518	5.59
	中西部	204	0.838	3.328	−0.81	43.97
FDI 占总投资比重	东部	132	0.1696	0.1196	0.0169	0.6155
	中西部	204	0.0345	0.0279	0.0002	0.1228
基础设施	全国	336	0.0679	0.0167	0.0261	0.113

（续表）

变 量 名	地 区	样本数	均值	标准差	最小值	最大值
非国有经济占工业总产值比重	全 国	336	0.48	0.211 2	0.101	0.936
外资企业占 GDP 比重	全 国	252	7.004	6.425	0.243	34.5
国企职工占总人口比重	全 国	336	0.099	0.058	0.027 8	0.33
人均 GDP	全 国	336	2 232.6	2 096	443	15 329

注：人均 GDP 以 1978 年价格计算。国企改革以国有单位就业职工变化率度量，减少取正值。外资企业占 GDP 比重缺少 1991、1993 和 2002 年的数据。

选择国有经济单位职工人数变化率（下称 SOE 改革）作为国企改革的度量（如果人数减少，变化率取正值，反之，取负值），主要是出于以下考虑。首先，一般采用的民营经济比重或国有经济比重的度量（朱恒鹏，2004；Li et al.，1998）存在很大问题。因为 90 年代以来既是国有企业改革的推进期，也是民营经济飞速发展的时期，因此经济比重的变化可能更多的是民营经济发展的结果，而不是国企改革的结果。此外，国企改革的主要内容都会反映在就业的变化上，这比采用国有企业数量的变化率要好，因为后者只能反映民营改制这一方面的改革。当然，国企改革的另一些内容，如公司治理结构的改革就难以反映到就业上来，这是这一衡量指标的缺陷。

采用 FDI 的增长率（下称 FDIgrate）作为解释变量，是出于以下考虑：

设时间 t 时的全国 FDI 总额为 Q_t，有 n 个地区，第 i 个地区 t 时获得的 FDI 的份额为 λ_{it}，满足 $\sum_{i=1}^{n}\lambda_{it}=1$。因此，第 i 个地区 t 时获得的 FDI 总额 $FDI_{it}=\lambda_{it}Q_t$。因此有 $\ln FDI_{it}=\ln\lambda_{it}+$

$\ln Q_t$，从而 $\frac{\dot{FDI}_{it}}{FDI_{it}}=\frac{\dot{\lambda}_{it}}{\lambda_{it}}+\frac{\dot{Q}_t}{Q_t}$。由于 $\frac{\dot{Q}_t}{Q_t}$ 对所有的地区都相同，因此地区之间 FDI 的增长率的差异取决于各地区所占 FDI 份额的增长率的差异。根据“信号发送假说”和“可置信承诺假说”可以推断，国企改革更多的地区可以吸引更多的 FDI，在总量不变的情况下，这会增加该地区的 FDI 份额，即 $\frac{\dot{\lambda}_{it}}{\lambda_{it}}$ 为正，同时减少其他地区的 FDI 份额，即 $\frac{\dot{\lambda}_{it}}{\lambda_{it}}$ 为负。因此，这两个假说预言，国企改革更多的地方，其 FDI 增长率也更高。

其他一些变量的度量方法说明如下。基础设施由交通运输、仓储及通讯业产出占 GDP 比重度量。外资企业占 GDP 比重由三资企业数除以 GDP 得到，这一变量用以度量 FDI 的聚集效应。国企职工占总人口比重用以度量国有企业在经济中的重要性。人均 GDP 是为了度量经济发展水平的影响。这些变量在回归时用来作为控制变量。

五、计量模型和检验

本文的主题是研究 FDI 对国企改革的影响，但在待检验的五个假说中，有三个(收入来源假说、信号发送假说和可置信承诺假说)既包含了 FDI 对国企改革的影响，也包含了国企改革对 FDI 的影响。而且在时间先后上，后三个假说都预测先有国企改革的增加，后有 FDI 的增长。但是在计量上，对于后三个假说的含义，我们只能捕捉到国企改革对 FDI 的影响，而相反的影响我们只能从间接的推断得到——既然国企改革的增加确实能吸引到更多的 FDI，而 FDI 的增加又是地方政府追求的目标，因此,理性的地方政府自然会采用国企改革这一手段来达到增加FDI的目的,在这一意义上我们可以说,FDI促进了国企改革。

出于上述考虑,本文的这一节内容分为两部分。第一部分检验FDI对国企改革的影响,第二部分检验国企改革对FDI的影响。由于在理论上没有理由认为当年的FDI会影响到国企改革①(回归的结果也支持这一判断),因此,我们认为在这里不存在FDI与国企改革的共时决定问题,因此没有采用联立方程模型进行估计,而是分别单独估计了两个方程。

(一) FDI对国企改革的影响

这一部分对"竞争压力假说"和"资金支持假说"进行检验。计量模型的设定为:

$$Y_{it} = \alpha_i + \gamma_t + \delta Z_{i(t-k)} + \sigma W_{it} + \mu_{it}$$

其中,Y_{it}表示第i省第t年的国企改革,以国企职工的变化率来衡量。α_i是固定效应,采用固定效应模型是为了排除不随时间变化的地区特征对国企改革的影响。γ_t是年份虚拟变量。$Z_{i(t-k)}$是FDI的增长率及其滞后变量,以及这些变量与地区虚拟变量的交叉项。W_{it}是控制变量,包括人均GDP,非国有经济比重,国企职工占总人口比重。μ_{it}是随机误差项。作为对比,我们同时用一阶差分法进行了估计。表2给出了回归结果。

从表2中可以看到,只有滞后1年的FDI的增长率对国企改革有显著的正影响,当年的FDI增长率和滞后一年、两年的影响都不显著。这一结果不支持"竞争压力假说",而更接近"资金支持假说"的预测。在固定效应模型中,滞后1年的交叉项显著为负,这说明FDI对国企改革的影响在中西部没有像在东部

① 从文献中可以找到的关于FDI对国企改革的影响的两个假说("竞争压力假说"和"资金支持假说")都不认为当年的FDI会影响到当年的国企改革。

那么大，这一结果也与预期的一致。

表 2　FDI 对国企改革的影响

SOE 改革	固定效应		一阶差分	
	系数	*P* 值	系数	*P* 值
FDIgrate				
—	.014 038 7	0.125	.013 394 7	0.241
L1	.016 942 3**	0.011	.016 559 6*	0.057
L2	.001 320 4	0.721	.006 212 6	0.292
L3	−.000 511 3	0.881	.003 123 6	0.475
DF				
—	−.009 570 8	0.293	−.008 667 2	0.434
L1	−0.117 904*	0.073	−.008 802 6	0.298
L2	−.000 652 8	0.858	−.005 882	0.308
L3	.000 746 7	0.824	−.003 111	0.469
nonstate	.008 930 4	0.757	−.009 947 2	0.816
Rgdppc78	2.70e−06	0.678	.000 016 7	0.166
stateworkpts				
—	−3.318 634***	0.000	−4.122 442***	0.000
L1	2.423 164***	0.000	2.696 297***	0.000
L2	.967 604 1***	0.004	1.175 8***	0.003
Year1998	.588 329***	0.000	.089 379 2***	0.000
Obs.	251		223	
Prob > F	0.000 0		0.000 0	
R^2 within		0.863 7		
between		0.539 6	0.824 4	
overall		0.777 7	0.807 0(adjusted)	

注：(1) FDIgrate 是 FDI 增长率。DF 是地区虚拟变量与 FDI 增长率的交叉项，地区虚拟变量对非东部取 1。nonstate 是非国有经济在工业总产值中的比重，Rgdppc78 是以 1978 年价格计算的人均 GDP，stateworkpts 是国企职工占总人口的比重。回归方程中包括全部年份虚拟变量，这里只报告 1998 年。

(2) *、** 和 *** 分别表示 10%、5% 和 1% 的显著性水平。

(3) —、L1、L2 和 L3 分别表示当年、滞后 1 年、2 年和 3 年的变量。

此外，上述结果还表明，非国有经济比重和人均 GDP 对国企改革没有影响，而国企职工占总人口的比重及其两个滞后变量都对国企改革有显著影响，而且这种影响在当年是负的，而滞后 1 年和 2 年是正的。这里的原因可能是，一方面国企职工越多，改革受到的阻力越大，因此，当年的改革比较少；另一方面，国企职工越多，说明国有经济的存量越大，因此，要求改革的压力也越大，而且这种压力最终超过了阻力，推动了国企改革。1998 年的时间虚拟变量的影响显著为正，因为这一年正是全国的国企改革高潮。

上述结果在固定效应和一阶差分模型中都相同，说明比较稳健。

(二) 国企改革对 FDI 的影响

这一部分检验“收入来源假说”、“信号发送假说”和“可置信承诺假说”。计量模型的设置为：

$$Y_{it} = \alpha_i + \gamma_t + \delta Z_{i(t-k)} + \sigma W_{it} + \mu_{it}$$

其中，Y_{it} 表示第 i 省第 t 年的 FDI 增长率，α_i 是固定效应，γ_t 是年份虚拟变量。$Z_{i(t-k)}$ 是国企改革及其滞后变量。W_{it} 是控制变量，包括基础设施，外商投资企业聚集程度，人均 GDP，国企职工占总人口比重。μ_{it} 是随机误差项。

首先对全国的样本进行回归，没有发现国企改革对 FDI 的影响（见附表 1 第 1 列结果）。分别对东部和中西部的样本进行回归，发现只有在对东部的回归中，国企改革对 FDI 增长率有滞后 3 年的影响（见附表 2），而在中西部这种影响不存在（见附表 1 第 2 列结果）。然后再将东部的样本分成 1991—1996 年和 1997—2002 年两部分分别进行回归①（见表 4 和表 5），发现在

① 之所以以 1997 年为界划分两个阶段，是因为从东部国企改革的平均水平来看，1997 年前后有一个明显的变化。而且，从中央政策来看 1997 年前后也有明显的变化。1997 年后是“抓大放小”政策开始在全国范围内正式实施的时间，并在 1998 年达到高潮。

1997年以前，回归的结果与本文提出的模型的预期非常一致。而对中西部的样本也进行这样的分时间段的回归，仍然没有发现国企改革对FDI的影响。下面对回归结果进行详细的解释。

由于我们的回归结果只发现了1997年以前东部地区的国企改革对FDI的影响，而在这段时期内东部地区的国企改革规模普遍不大(见表3)，这样小规模的国企改革不大会影响到政府维护公平竞争的承诺的可置信程度，因此这里得到的回归结果不能用“可置信承诺假说”解释。因此，下面的分析主要论证“信号发送假说”对回归结果的解释能力。

首先，需要解释回归结果的地区差异，为什么在中西部国企改革对FDI没有影响呢，国企改革要成为一个反映政府类型的有效的信号，必须满足两个条件：一是有相当数量的地区进行了国企改革；二是不同类型的政府选择的国企改革水平有显著的差异。但是在1991—1996年这段时间内，如表3所示，在中西部所有102个样本点内，只有19个样本点的国企改革是正的，而且在这19个样本点中，除了5个例外，其他14个样本点的国企改革都在1%以下(见附表3)。由于进行国企改革的地区如此之少，而且改革的规模也非常小，因此，外资就难以根据国企改革来判断地方政府的类型，在中西部就观察不到国企改革对FDI的影响。而在东部，所有66个样本点中，有28个样本点的国企改革是正的，而且平均的改革规模比中西部要大得多。从标准差来看，东部的变化幅度也要大一些。从这些数据可以看出，在1991—1996年间，东部各地区之间，在国企改革发生与否和发生的规模大小上，都存在比较大的差异性，因此，国企改革就具备了成为反映政府类型的信号的基本条件。而在这一期间的中西部地区，国企改革则不具备这一条件。

表 3　1991—1996 年 SOE 改革＞0

地　区	样本数	均值	标准差
中西部	19	.008 655 6	.010 837 9
东　部	28	.023 001 3	.020 214 7

从表 4 可以看到，在 1991—1996 年这段时期内的东部地区，除了滞后 2 年的变量之外，国企改革的所有其他变量对 FDI 的影响都显著为正，而且显著程度无论在统计意义上还是在经济意义上都非常高(如当年的国企改革增加 1 个百分点，FDI 增长率将增加 24 个百分点左右)。[①]这一结果无论在固定效应模型中，还是在一阶差分模型中都保持不变。国企改革对 FDI 有当年的和滞后一年的显著为正的影响，这一结果无法用“收入来源假说”加以解释，因为这一假说预测的影响出现的时间滞后比较长。而且当年的影响也不大可能是因为 FDI 对国企改革的共时影响造成的，因为在理论上，无法说明当年的 FDI 的增加为什么会对国企改革产生如此迅速的显著影响。而用本文提出的“信号发送假说”就能较好的解释这一结果，因为这个假说预测国企改革会在短期内对 FDI 产生显著影响。

① 表 4 报告的结果，由于样本规模较小而变量数较多，因此自由度较小。为了验证结果的可靠性，我们去掉了一些不显著的变量，发现结果基本不变。同时我们加进了 1997 年的样本，发现当年的国企改革对 FDI 的显著影响消失了，而滞后 1 年的显著影响仍然存在。如果我们接受本文后面的推测，即 1997 年以前的国企改革具有信号作用，而 1997 年以后的国企改革不具有信号作用。那么 1996 年的国企改革就对 1997 年的 FDI 有显著影响，而 1997 年的国企改革对当年的 FDI 则没有显著影响。因此，加入 1997 年的样本之后，会影响到当年的国企改革对 FDI 影响的显著性，而不影响滞后 1 年影响的显著性。

表 4　东部(1991—1996 年)

SOE 改革	固定效应		一阶差分	
	系数	P 值	系数	P 值
soe 改革				
—	24.38***	0.007	24.38***	0.003
L1	28.597***	0.000	27.524 73***	0.000
L2	3.727	0.210	2.729 052	0.383
L3	17.51***	0.001	14.000 7***	0.004
infra	−4.284 971	0.139	−5.686**	0.026
ffcluster	.068 970 3	0.164	.89*	0.084
rgdppc78	−0.001 02***	0.009	−.000 8**	0.038
stateworker				
—	201.84***	0.001	204.585***	0.000
L1	−23.862 5	0.541	−35.693 79	0.270
L2	−120.02***	0.001	−112.44***	0.002
Obs.	33		22	
Pro ＞ F	0.000 0		0.000 0	
R^2	within	0.979 5		
	between	0.327 3		0.972 0
	overall	0.120 1		0.9411(adjusted)

注：infra 是基础设施，ffcluster 是外商投资企业聚集程度。回归过程中，包括了全部年份虚拟变量。

表 5　东部(1997—2002 年)

FDIgrate	固定效应		一阶差分	
	系数	P 值	系数	P 值
soe 改革				
—	.403 7	0.814	−1.035	0.574
L1	−2.323	0.271	−3.331 819	0.147
L2		0.055	2.54	0.168
L3		0.014		0.014

（续表）

FDIgrate	固定效应		一阶差分	
	系数	P值	系数	P值
infra		0.079		0.070
ffcluster	.018 8	0.124	.034 876 8	0.117
rgdppc78	.000 046	0.729	−.000 053 6	0.717
stateworkepts				
—	4.940 835	0.438	3.367 314	0.599
L1	−9.637	0.283	−8.605	0.258
L2	7.458	0.340	7.542	0.351
Obs.	66		66	
Pro > F	0.013 4		0.017 2	
within		0.475	0.401 4	
between		0.005 4	0.221 9(adjusted)	
overall		0.048 2		

注：回归过程中，包括了全部年份虚拟变量。

滞后3年的国企改革对FDI有显著为正的影响，而且不随时间变化，这一结果与“收入来源假说”的预测相一致，即国企改革通过为基础设施建设提供资金而促进了FDI的增加。

从表5我们可以看到，在1997年以后，国企改革对FDI只有滞后3年的影响（在固定效应模型中有滞后两年的影响），当期和滞后1年都没有显著影响。这一结果与1997年以前的情况形成鲜明对比。怎样解释这一影响机制的跨时间变化呢？

我们知道，国企改革要成为一个反映地方政府类型的有效的信号，必须要求不同类型的政府选择的国企改革水平有显著的差异，而这又要求不同类型的政府在推进改革的成本上有很大的不同。在20世纪90年代前半期，国企改革的发生主要是自下而上，由地方政府推动的，国企改革还是一个在政治上很敏感的问题，因此一般的地方政府不敢推动国企改革，而只有那些决心走市场经济道路的、比较开明的地方政府才敢于进行国企改革。因此，在这段时间内，国企改革的水平就成为比较好的反映政府类型的信号，从而能够对 FDI 产生显著的影响。而在 20 世纪 90 年代中期以后，国企改革的方针已经得到中央的认可，而且是由中央自上而下大力推进的，全国上下都在进行大规模的国企改革。在这种情况下，由于无论政府类型如何，都在进行国企改革。因此，国企改革就难以成为反映政府类型的很好的信号，所以我们就无法观察到它对 FDI 的显著影响。此外，到 90 年代中后期，外资也已经开始比较了解中国的投资环境，信息不对称的问题减弱了，因此国企改革的信息揭示功能也便下降了。

表 6　国企改革情况的跨时间变化

地区	时间	样本数	SOE 改革＞0	均值	标准差	变异系数
东部	1991—1996 年	66	28	－.002 4	.027	11.42
	1997—2002 年	66	64	.078 5	.06	0.76
中西部	1991—1996 年	102	19	－.017 2	.042 35	2.46
	1997—2002 年	102	99	.069 7	.063 37	0.91

从表 6 我们可以看到，1997 年以前，在东部的 66 个样本点(11 个省市，6 年的数据)中，只有 28 个样本点的国企改革指标是正的。也就是说，很多省市在这段时间内，不仅没有发生国企改革，甚至国企的规模还在膨胀。而在 1997 年以后，有 64 个样本点的国企改革指标是正的。也就是说，在这段时间内，几乎所有的省市都在进行国企改革。这说明，在 1997 年以前，是否发生国企改革在地区之间存在着较大差异；而在 1997 年以后，国企改革则成了一件全国普遍发生的事情。此外，从变异系数我们也可以看出，在 1997 年以前，国企改革的规模在不同的样本点之间存在着很大的差异，而在 1997 年之后，这种差异变小了。

这些数据都说明，在 1997 年以前，国企改革可以成为一个比较好的信号，而在 1997 年以后，由于国企改革的地区差异性变小，因此不能成为有效的信号。表中给出的中西部的情况与东部基本一致。这解释了国企改革对 FDI 增长率的影响方式在 1997 年前后的变化。

六、结　论

本文提出了两个关于 FDI 如何促进国企改革的假说：信号发送假说和可置信承诺假说。在信息不对称下，国企改革可以成为一个地方政府开明程度的信号，为了发送信号吸引 FDI，地方政府有动力进行更多的国企改革。同时，国企改革减少了地方政府干预市场的动机，从而使得维护公平竞争的承诺变得可信，因此能吸引更多的 FDI。为了作出可置信的承诺以吸引 FDI，地方政府也会更有积极性推动国企改革。本文对这两个假说进行了检验，结果显示，信号发送假说较好地吻合了 90 年代中前期东部地区的情况。同时，我们发现国企改革与 FDI 的相互影响机制存在跨地区和跨时间的差异，本文的实证部分也对此进行了解释。

其次，本文也对文献中出现过的，与 FDI 对国企改革的影响有关的另外三个假说进行了检验。发现文献中强调较多的 FDI 通过竞争压力而促进国企改革的假说，并没有得到实证结果的支持；而 FDI 通过提供资金支持而促进国企改革的假说，则与实证结果一致。此外，国企改革通过为基础设施建设提供收入来源而促进 FDI 增加的假说，也与实证结果不矛盾。①

本文的价值在于，对 FDI 与国企改革的相互影响机制提出

① 不过对于这几个假说，本文的检验还是很不充分的。要得出更确定的结论，必须做进一步的实证研究。

了两个具有解释力的假说，补充了文献中已有的假说。同时，本文对这些假说在实证上进行了较全面的检验，而缺乏详细的实证检验正是这一方面文献的一大缺陷。

当然，本文的研究还存在很多不足之处。尤其是在国企改革和 FDI 可能存在共时决定的情况下，没有采用联立方程估计方法。这可能造成估计结果的偏误，进一步的研究应该致力于寻找国企改革的恰当的工具变量。此外，由于对样本进行分地区分时间段的回归，造成模型的自由度太小，这也可能影响回归结果的可信程度。虽然本文对这一问题进行了一些补救，但还不能认为完全解决了问题。

最后，需要指出的是，本文提出的这两个假说不仅对解释外资对国企改革的影响有帮助，而且也有助于理解地区之间对内资的竞争对国企改革的影响。同时，这两个假说也可以推广到地区之间竞争外资（或内资）对政府改革的影响，例如广东顺德的政府改革和国企改革就是同时发生的，而改革背后的动力主要在于吸引外资。

附录

附表 1　国企改革对 FDI 的影响（全国和中西部 1991—2002 年）

FDIgrate	全国		中西部	
	系数	P 值	系数	P 值
soe 改革				
—	.043 125	0.978	.635 644 5	0.810
L1	−.047 655	0.976	−.155 749 8	0.952
L2	.063 937 2	0.962	−.590 264 3	0.801
L3	−.068 798 8	0.950	−.923 919 6	0.591
infra	.024 362 9	0.991	1.888 24	0.564
ffcluster	.013 567 5	0.651	−.063 309 9	0.662
rgdppc78	−.000 087	0.706	−.000 523	0.701

(续表)

FDIgrate	全国		中西部	
	系数	P值	系数	P值
stateworker				
—	2.272 707	0.812	—.302 996	0.990
L1	.179 225 9	0.986	.801 995 8	0.974
L2	—1.651 107	0.866	—2.572 318	0.905
Obs.	224		136	
Pro > F	0.005 4		0.647 1	
R^2	0.153 2		0.107 7	
	0.083 3(adjusted)		—0.029 9(adjusted)	

附表 2　国企改革对 FDI 的影响(东部 1991—2002 年)

FDIgrate	全国	
	系数	P值
soe 改革		
—	—1.853 782	0.305
L1	—.997 107 8	0.647
L2	1.298 417	0.447
L3	2.997 432	0.042
infra	—2.580 487	0.156
ffcluster	.034 773 4	0.107
rgdppc78	—.000 111 2	0.427
stateworker		
—	3.320 955	0.610
L1	—3.719 745	0.620
L2	3.195 464	0.686
Obs.	88	
Pro > F	0.000 0	
R^2	0.599 6	
	0.502 4(adjusted)	

注:附表 1 和附表 2 的回归中都包含了全部年份虚拟变量。上面报告的都是一阶差分模型的结果。

附表 3　中西部 1991—1996 年国企改革为正的省份

省　份	年份	SOE 改革
内蒙古	1993	.003 310 2
	1996	.000 661 6
吉　林	1996	.002 327 4
黑龙江	1995	.018 547 1
	1996	.026 141 7
安　徽	1994	.010 320 8
湖　北	1996	.005 271 5
四　川	1994	.015 660 9
	1996	.000 408 3
贵　州	1993	.043 388 4
	1995	.006 676 9
云　南	1995	.001 139 8
陕　西	1993	.001 227
甘　肃	1994	.001 908 4
	1996	.004 743 8
青　海	1993	.007 017 5
	1994	.001 766 8
宁　夏	1994	.004 942 3
新　疆	1993	.008 996

参考文献

林毅夫:《自生能力、经济发展与转型:理论与实证》,北京大学出版社 2004 年版。

罗小朋:《地区竞争与产权——中国改革的经济逻辑》,《当代中国研究》1995 年第 1、2 期合刊。

钱颖一、许成钢:《中国的经济改革为什么与众不同》,《经济社会体制比较》1993 年第 11 期。

钱颖一:《现代经济学与中国经济改革》,中国人民大学出版社 2003 年版。

王红领、李稻葵、雷鼎鸣:《政府为什么会放弃国有企业的产权》,《经济研究》2001 年第 8 期。

张维迎、栗树和:《地区竞争与中国国有企业的民营化》,《经济研究》1998 年第 12 期。

朱恒鹏:《地区间竞争、财政自给率和公有制企业民营化》,《经济研究》2004 年第 10 期。

Cao, Y., Y. Qian and B. R. Weingast., 1999, "From Federalism, Chinese Style to Privatization, Chinese style", *Economics of Transition*, 7, 1:103—131.

Girma Sourafel and Yundan Gong, 2005, FDI, Linkages and the Efficiency of State-owned Enterprises in China, University of Nottingham Research Paper, No. 2005/34.

Guo Kai and Yang Yao, 2005, "Causes of Privatization in China: Testing Several Hypotheses", *Economics of Transition*, 13 (2): 211—238.

Jin Hehui, Yingyi Qian and Barry Weingast, 2005, "Regional Decentralization and Fiscal Incentive", *Journal of Public Economics*, 89(9—10):1719—1742.

K. C. Fung, Alicia Garcia-Herrero, Hitomi Iizaka and Alan Siu, 2005, "Hard or Soft? Instituional Reforms and Infrastructure Spending as Determinants of Foreign Investment in China", *The Japanese Economic Review*, 56(4):408—416.

Li Shaomin, Shuhe Li and Weiying Zhang, 2000, "The Road to Capitalism: Competition and Institutional Change in China", *Journal of Comparative Economics*, 28(2):269—292.

Li Shaomin and Seung Ho Park, 2006, "Determinants of Locations of Foreign Direct Investment in China", *Management and Organization Review*: 95—119.

Tong Sarah Y., 2005, FDI and SOEs in China: Friends or Enemies, 2005 年中国经济学年会论文。

(原载《南方经济》2007 年第 8 期)

中国农村劳动力迁移过程中的部门选择与性别差异*

易君健　耿龙波

（香港中文大学经济系）

一、引　言

在计划经济时期，中国劳动力市场被人为地分成两个相互隔离的部分：城镇劳动力市场与农村劳动力市场。通过户口以及与户口配套的制度安排，政府严格地限制了城乡之间、区域之间和部门之间的劳动力流动，从而在根本上分离了城镇劳动力市场与农村劳动力市场，并导致了城镇居民与农村居民在收入水平上的巨大差距。其中，Knight 和 Song（1999，2005），Meng（2000），Meng 和 Zhang（2001），蔡昉、都阳和王美艳（2003，2005）等对中国劳动力市场分割的历史原因和社会经济后果均做了系统的研究。然而，自 1978 年开始的改革开放以及随后 20 余年快速的经济增长，导致了城镇劳动力市场对农村劳动力需求的快速扩张。随着户籍管制的逐步放松，越来越多的农村

---

* 本研究受教育部重大攻关课题“建立城乡统一的劳动力市场，实现城乡劳动力平等就业研究”（06JZD0014）的资助。作者感谢香港中文大学 Myoung-jae Lee 教授的悉心指导以及匿名审稿人所提出的建设性意见。

劳动力开始迁移至城镇，并在城镇开始工作。图 1 描述了农业部统计的 1983 年至 2003 年农村劳动力的流动情况。虽然在整个 20 世纪的 60 至 70 年代，中国农村劳动力的迁移几乎可以忽略不计(Knight and Song，1999，256—257)，但是 1989 年中国跨省的农村劳动力流动总量已经达到了 700 万，而这一数字在 2000 年时已经上升到了 3 000 万。同样，这一趋势也可以从改革开放以来农村就业量占全部就业总量比例的变化趋势中看出。虽然在改革开放之前，农村就业量占总就业量的比例超过了 70%，这一指标在改革开放之后开始稳步下降，至 2003 年时已经不到 50%了(《中国统计年鉴》，2004)。因此就迁移劳动力总量和规模而言，以上数据均表明中国目前正在经历着人类历史上史无前例的劳动力迁移。

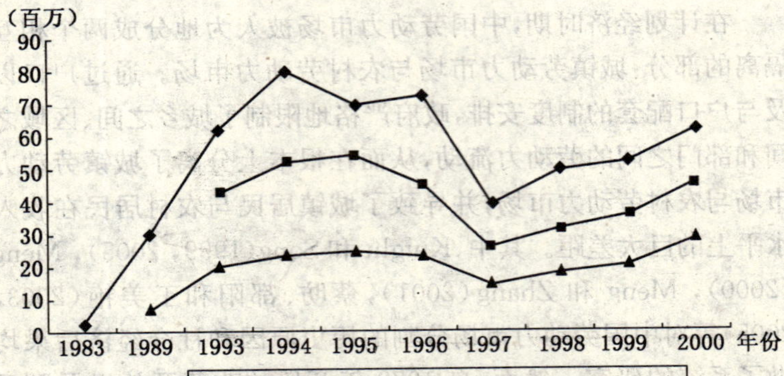

资料来源：蔡昉、都阳、王美艳：《劳动力流动的政治经济学》，上海三联书店、上海人民出版社 2003 年版，第 268 页。

图 1　中国农村劳动力的迁移规模：1983—2000 年(百万)

同时，作为一个转型经济，中国的经济改革导致了中国企业的所有制结构发生了巨大的改革。在经济改革之前，全民所有制企业占据了国民经济的主导，辅之以部分集体所有制企业。然而至 2003 年时，国内生产总值（GDP）中国有部门、民营部门与国外部门的比例已成三足鼎立之势。图 2 描述了 2003 年国有部门、民营部门与国外部门的生产总值占 GDP 的比例①。从中可以清楚看出，虽然国有部门仍然占据了最大比例的份额，但是其比例仅为 38%，略微超过民营部门和国外部门的 31%。因此，随着经济改革的进一步深化，民营部门与国外部门已经在扮演着越来越重要的角色。

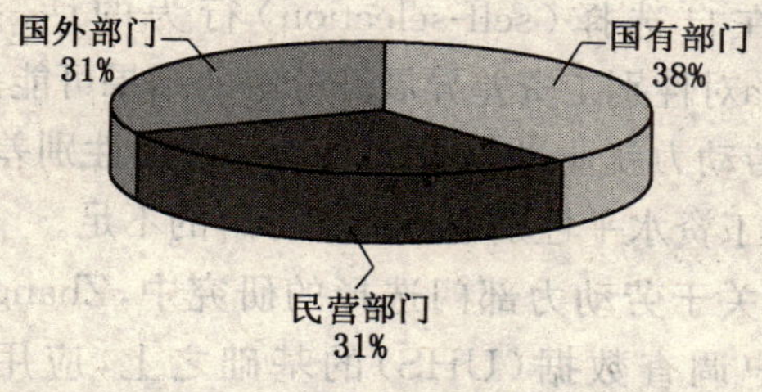

资料来源：国家统计局，《中国统计年鉴》(2004)，中国统计出版社。

图 2　中国各所有制部门所占 GDP 份额

那么，农村劳动力在迁移的时候是如何在这三个部门之间进行选择的呢？迁移过程中的女性劳动力在哪些部门拥有比较优势（或劣势）呢？这是本文研究的中心问题。对这些问题的分析将有助于加深对农村劳动力迁移过程的理解，并对中国经济转型过程中的就业问题具有重要的政策含义。虽然目前已有大量的文献对中国农村劳动力迁移的决定因素展开了理论和经验方面的探讨（Zhao，1999，2002；Knight and Song，1999；易君

① 本文对企业所有制划分的标准为：国有部门包括全民所有制企业和集体所有制企业；民营部门包括个体企业和私营企业；国外部门包括中外合作、合资企业以及外商独资企业。

健，2006），但是对农村劳动力迁移过程中的部门选择行为的分析却相对缺乏。同时，虽然王美艳（2003）、Liu，Meng和Zhang（2000），姚先国和赖普清（2004），姚先国和谭岚（2005）等对中国劳动力市场中的户籍歧视与性别歧视行为进行了计量分析，但是几乎所有的文献均集中于工资水平上的歧视研究，缺乏对农村劳动力在城镇不同所有制企业选择行为上的性别差异的系统研究。如果转型期间不同所有制企业存在不同的工资结构（Blau and Kahn，1995），同时不同性别的劳动者在不同部门就业决策上存在自选择（self-selection）行为的话，那么应用Blinder-Oaxaca对性别工资差异展开分解的结果可能是有偏的。因此，对农村劳动力就业过程中部门选择行为性别差异的分析将弥补直接对工资水平性别差异展开分解的不足。

在已有的关于劳动力部门选择的研究中，Zhang（2004）在基于城镇住户调查数据（UHS）的基础之上，应用了Multi-Logit-OLS-Corrected技术对城镇住户在国有企业、集体企业、政府部门与民营企业之间的部门选择以及在不同的部门之间的工资差异进行了计量分析[①]。其结果表明，年龄较大的劳动者一般选择国有企业，而女性或已婚劳动力更倾向于民营企业。Zhang同时发现，就业渠道和教育程度对部门选择存在显著的影响。其中，通过个人工作搜寻方式的劳动者一般就业于民营企业，而教育程度对民营企业的选择行为存在显著的负面效应。本文同样应用Multi-nominal Logit（MNL）模型对劳动者的部门选择行为展开分析，但是与Zhang（2004）的不同之处在于本

① Liu，Meng和Zhang（2000）将整个经济分为三个部门：国有部门、集体部门和民营部门。在Liu等（2000）与Zhang（2004）中均将中外合作、合资和外商独资企业划分到民营部门，而本文认为将国外部门和民营部门分开是必须的，因为这是完全不同的两种类型的所有制企业，并且面对不同的税收制度。

文是基于农村劳动力的抽样调查数据，从而集中于对农村劳动力迁移过程中部门选择的行为进行研究。同时，由于农村迁移劳动力很少进入政府部门，而正如图2所示，国外部门已经成为中国经济中的一个重要组成部分，所以我们将整个经济分为三个部门——国有部门、民营部门与国外部门。与已有文献相比，由于本文所应用的农村劳动力抽样调查数据拥有非常丰富的个人特征、家庭特征、迁出地特征、迁入地特征、工作寻访特征与目前的职业特征变量，等等，因此，本文可以对农村劳动力流动过程中的部门选择行为展开非常系统的研究。同时，在基于MNL模型回归结果的基础之上，本文将对农村女性迁移劳动力在不同部门之间的性别差异展开比较分析。由于数据的限制，目前有关劳动力市场中性别歧视的文献主要集中于城镇居民（姚先国、谭岚，2005），而本文对劳动力市场中的性别歧视行为拓展到农村迁移劳动力，将加深对中国整个劳动力市场中性别歧视状况的了解。

本文的结构安排如下：第二节为数据的描述性统计分析；第三节设定了本文应用的计量模型并报告了经验分析结果；第四节讨论了农村女性迁移劳动力在不同部门之间的性别差异；第五节提出了研究的政策含义。

二、数据描述

本文所采用的数据来自国家自然科学基金重点项目"中国人力资本投资与劳动力市场管理研究"课题组于2004年1—3月间以农村迁移劳动力为对象所作的抽样调查（课题号：70233003）。调查范围涉及安徽、河南、湖南、江苏、江西、四川和浙江共7个省份，包括家庭住户399户，劳动力713人，其中外出务工劳动力420人，占58.09%。调查内容既包括了个人、家庭和职业特征变量，同时也包括了迁入地和迁出地的特征变量。其中个人特征变量包括：性别、年龄、婚姻、教育、收入、支出及健康，等等；家庭特征变量包括：家庭的人口总数、抚养儿童或老人数量、家庭其他人员的收入、支出、承包土地数量，等等；目前职业特征变量包括：就业企业的所有制性质、企业规模、行业，是否提供保险、是否签订工作合同，等等；同时也包括个人寻找工作的渠道或方式。同时，我们的调查问卷中也包括了农村劳动力的户籍特征变量。虽然农村迁移劳动力中的大部分仍然是农村户口，但是仍然有部分劳动力在迁移之前或者之后，随着中国户籍制度的逐步放松，已经转变成为了城市户口。本调查样本中总计包括拥有城市户口的农村迁移劳动力 58 人，占 13.81%。由于中国的户籍以及与户籍相关的制度安排仍然在劳动力市场中扮演着一个重要的角色，为了更为全面地分析农村劳动力的迁移过程，我们把这一部分劳动者也包括在全部的分析样本中。

根据农村迁移劳动力目前就职企业的所有制性质，我们将部门选择分成三类：国有部门，占 16%；民营部门，占 23%；国外部门，占 61%。令人惊讶的是，我们样本中约 2/3 的农村迁移劳动力就业于国外部门。从某种程度上说，农村劳动力的就业部门分布比例显示了改革开放以来的中国正在融入经济全球化的过程。随着劳动成本的上升，发达国家逐渐的将其制造业部门转移到劳动成本较低的中国。因此，中国在成为“世界工厂”的同时，大幅增加了对非技术性劳动力的需求，消化了其数量庞大的农村剩余劳动力。

表 1 为变量定义及其统计性描述。通过对各变量的平均值在不同部门之间展开比较，我们可以得到许多有趣的发现。首先，在选择国有部门的劳动力当中有 39%拥有城市户籍，而这一指标在选择国外部门的劳动力当中仅占 5%。这表明国外部

门的企业对劳动者的户籍特征更少的关注，而仍然处于政府管制下的国有部门，特别是全民所有制企业仍然倾向于招聘具有城镇户口的劳动力。其次，国有部门中59%的劳动者是通过正规的工作搜寻渠道（劳动力市场）而就职于目前的工作岗位。与此形成鲜明对照的是，国外部门中的大部分（74%）是通过个人渠道（朋友、亲戚或老乡）而找到工作的。这一点与 Knight 和 Song(1999, 2005)的研究结论保持一致，表明中国的劳动力市场还远未达到成熟的阶段。由于在劳动力市场中广泛存在的信息不对称和逆向选择行为，国外部门的企业在改革开放的早期很难在劳动力市场中招募到素质合格的职工，因此这些企业在很大程度上依赖于目前已有员工的推荐或介绍。而国有部门由于在当地劳动力市场中拥有相对信息优势，所以主要通过本地劳动力市场招募职工。最后，在农村迁移劳动力对待签署合同的态度和部门选择之间的分布可以看出，几乎所有就业于民营部门的劳动力（91%）均认为合同在保护其合法利益方面起着重要的作用，而这一比例在国外部门仅为59%，其原因部分来自民营企业或个体企业普遍存在的相对恶劣的工作环境、超过国家法定的工作时间以及拖欠职工工资的现象。而国外部门虽然存在同样的问题，但是其情况相对较为缓和，提供了相对较好的工作环境，并在遵守劳动法律方面较民营企业更为严格。

另外，表1表明农村女性迁移劳动力更加倾向于选择民营部门的企业。其中，32%的女性迁移劳动力选择了民营部门，然而这一指标在国有部门仅为14%。根据 Zhang(2004)和 Liu 等(2000)，在所有的部门，特别是民营部门，女性工资系统性的低于男性劳动力。因此，私有部门更多地利用了女性劳动力劳动成本较低的优势，从而女性劳动力的工资水平可能在民营部门可能存在系统的歧视。教育水平在本文中被分为四个层次：小学，占 7%；中学，占 50%；高中，占 31%；专科及以上，占 12%。其中，拥有较高学历的农村迁移劳动力倾向于选择国有部门，而国外部门一般雇佣较低学历的农村迁移劳动力。这说明国外发达国家主要向中国转移的是其劳动力密集型的，以降低其劳动成本为主要目的的制造业。另外，Dong 和 Bowles(2002)发现在政府部门和国外部门的就业行为上存在着选择性偏差，而本文的调查数据表明这种选择性偏差可能来自于教育水平效应。

表 1　变量定义与统计性描述

		全部样本	国有部门	民营部门	国外部门
sector	1:国有部门； 2:私有部门；3:国外部门	2.46 (0.75)	16%	23%	61%
age	年龄	28.78 (7.38)	28.84 (7.28)	27.83 (6.33)	29.11 (7.76)
no. member	家庭成员数量	4.57 (1.31)	4.38 (1.07)	4.64 (1.44)	4.60 (1.31)
avgland	家庭人均土地拥有量(亩)	0.90 (0.67)	0.98 (0.72)	0.91 (0.70)	0.88 (0.64)
hukou	1:城镇户口；0:农村户口	0.14 (0.46)	0.39 (0.49)	0.18 (0.47)	0.05 (0.44)
marriage	1:已婚；0:未婚	0.56 (0.50)	0.50 (0.50)	0.54 (0.50)	0.59 (0.49)
female	1:女性；0:男性	0.22 (0.42)	0.14 (0.35)	0.32 (0.47)	0.21 (0.41)
recruit-ment	1:通过亲戚、朋友、老乡或同学找到目前工作；0:其他	0.62 (0.49)	0.41 (0.50)	0.40 (0.49)	0.76 (0.43)
contract	1:认为劳动合同很重要 0:其他	0.69 (0.46)	0.77 (0.43)	0.91 (0.28)	0.59 (0.49)
avgincome	家庭中除被调查者之外其他劳动成员平均年收入	2.84 (1.72)	2.27 (1.89)	3.10 (1.79)	2.89 (1.62)

（续表）

		全部样本	国有部门	民营部门	国外部门
craft	1:在农村学习过手艺	0.57	0.66	0.48	0.58
	0:其他	(0.50)	(0.48)	(0.50)	(0.49)
training	1:就业于目前职业之前接受过培训;0:其他	0.44	0.57	0.43	0.41
		(0.50)	(0.50)	(0.50)	(0.49)
secondary	1:初中毕业	0.50	0.41	0.36	0.57
	0:其他	(0.50)	(0.50)	(0.48)	(0.50)
high	1:高中毕业	0.31	0.27	0.46	0.27
	0:其他	(0.46)	(0.45)	(0.50)	(0.45)
college	1:大专、本科或以上	0.12	0.20	0.16	0.09
	0:其他	(0.33)	(0.40)	(0.37)	(0.28)

注:(1)数据来源:浙江大学经济学院 2004 年 1—3 月针对农村迁移劳动力的抽样调查;(2)括号中为标准差;(3)avgincome 为取值 1—5 的离散变量,其中 1 代表收入在 1 000 元以下,2 代表 1 000—2 000, 3 代表 2 000—10 000; 4 代表 10 000—20 000, 5 代表 20 000 以上,单位为元。

三、农村劳动力转移过程中部门选择的决定因素分析

(一) Multinomial Logit 模型

根据经济学的理性选择假设,我们假定农村迁移劳动力能够在三个相互排斥(exclusive)的部门选择行为所带来的效用进行排序,并且在给定其偏好和预算约束时,选择给其带来最大效用的部门就业。然后根据 McFadden(1973),我们设定迁移劳动力效用方程的随机表达式如下:

$$U_{ij} = V_{ij} + \varepsilon_{ij} + z'_i\gamma_j + \varepsilon_{ij} \tag{1}$$

其中, $i = 1, \cdots, N$、$j = 1, 2, 3$; U_{ij} 表示第 i 个农村迁移劳动力选择第 j 个部门所带来的效用; z'_i 表示影响第 i 个农村迁移劳

动力部门选择行为的外生变量向量；而 ε_{ij} 为误差项。那么，当且仅当 $U_{ij} \geqslant \max U_{ik}$ 时，第 i 个农村迁移劳动力才选择第 j 个部门，其中 $j \neq k$, $k = 1, 2, 3$。如果 ε_{ij} 为 $i.i.d$ 并服从 *Type I Gumbel* 分布，即 $F(\varepsilon_{ij}) = \exp[\exp(-\varepsilon_{ij})]$；那么第 i 个劳动者选择第 m 个部门就业的概率为：

$$\Pr(Y_i = m)\frac{\exp(z'_i\gamma_m)}{\sum_{j=1}^{3}\exp(z'_i\gamma_j)}, m = 1, 2, 3 \tag{2}$$

其中，Y_i 为一随机变量，表明第 i 个农村迁移劳动力选择了第 m 个部门就业。由于任何劳动者选择三个部门的概率之和为 1（即（$\sum_{m=1}^{3}\Pr(Y_i = m) = 1$）），通过将第一个部门的选择概率进行标准化（即 $\gamma_{m-1} = 0$），那么得到如下标准化后的选择概率为：

$$\Pr(Y_i = 1) = \frac{1}{1 + \sum_{j=2}^{3}\exp(z'_i\gamma_j)} \tag{3}$$

$$\Pr(Y_i = m) = \frac{\exp(z'_i\gamma_m)}{1 + \sum_{j=2}^{3}\exp(z'_i\gamma_j)}, m = 2, 3 \tag{4}$$

MNL 模型的一个重要的性质是选择任何两种部门的概率之比与第三种选择无关（independence of irrelevant alternatives, IIA），这是应用 MNL 模型的一个很强的假设。根据方程(3)和(4)中，我们可以清楚的推导出 MNL 模型的 IIA 性质：

$$\ln\left(\frac{\Pr(Y_i = m)}{\Pr(Y_i = k)}\right) = z'_i(\gamma_m - \gamma_k) \tag{5}$$

从方程(5)中可以看出，劳动者 i 选择第 m 个部门的概率与选择第 k 个部门的概率之比独立于第三个部门。如果令 $m = 2, 3$,

$k=1$，我们就推导出 MNL 模型最后需要估计的两个方程（虽然有三种可能的选择，但是由于选择三个部门的概率之和为 1，所以最后仅需要识别两个方程）的随机表达式为（$\gamma_{k=1}=0$）：

$$\ln\left(\frac{\Pr(Y_i=m)}{\Pr(Y_i=1)}\right)=z'_i\gamma_m+\varepsilon_m,\ m=2,\ 3 \tag{6}$$

由于我们最后估计出来的方程是选择两个部门的概率之比，因此对回归系数的解释非常复杂。通过回归系数中的 $\gamma_{m,r}$（r 表示影响个体选择决策的第 r 个变量）的符号，我们可以得知相对于选择第一个部门，$z_{i,r}$影响个体 i 选择第 m 个部门的概率的方向，但是我们并不能推导出 $z_{i,r}$影响个体 i 选择第 m 个部门的概率总的方向，即：

$$\frac{\partial}{\partial z_{i,r}}\ln\left(\frac{\Pr(Y_i=m)}{\Pr(Y_i=1)}\right)=\gamma_{m,r}\neq\frac{\partial\Pr(Y_i=m)}{\partial z_{i,r}} \tag{7}$$

另外，我们也不能根据回归出来的系数比较变量 $z_{i,r}$对选择 $m=2$ 和 $m=3$ 之间进行比较，因为当 $z_{i,r}$变化时，它同时影响三种选择的概率，即“其他条件不变（ceteris paribus）”的假设不再成立。因此，为了计算出我们可以直接解释的 $\partial\Pr(Y_i=m)/\partial z_{i,r}$（即 $z_{i,r}$影响个体 i 选择第 m 个部门的边际效应），我们必须把估计出来的$\hat{\gamma}_j$ 代回到方程（3）和（4）。举一个例子，如果变量 $z_{i,r}$为 0—1 虚拟变量，那么 $z_{i,r}$影响个体i 选择第 1 个部门的边际效应为：

$$\Delta p_1=\hat{p}_1^1-\hat{p}_1^0=\frac{1}{1+\sum_{j=2}^{3}\exp(z'_i\hat{\gamma}_j)}-\frac{1}{1+\sum_{j=2}^{3}\exp(x'_i\hat{\gamma}_j)} \tag{8}$$

其中，z'_i与 x'_i的区别是在前者中第 r 个变量 $z_{i,r}$为 1，而在后者中为 0。这样，通过计算出每个变量对三种选择的边际效应，我们就可以直接对 MNL 模型展开解释。因此，本文对经验分析结论的解释主要集中于边际效应。值得注意的是任何变量对三个部门选择概率的边际效应之和为零，即：

$$\sum_{m=1}^{3} \frac{\partial \Pr(Y_i = m)}{\partial z_{i,\, r}} = 0 \tag{9}$$

这是因为 $\sum_{m=1}^{3} \Pr(Y_i = m) = 1$①。

（二）经验分析结论

MNL 模型中的变量包括：年龄、年龄平方、家庭成员数量、家庭人均田地拥有量、家庭中除被调查者外其他成员的人均收入，以及性别、婚姻状况、寻找到目前工作的渠道、是否认为合同重要、是否学过手艺、是否接受过培训、教育水平等虚拟变量。因此，回归方程中的基准个体为一个单身男性并拥有农村户口的，仅接受过小学教育，并未参加过手艺或培训的，而且通过劳动力市场寻找到目前工作、认为合同并不重要的农村迁移劳动力。MNL 模型的回归结果及其边际效应（marginal effect）报告在表 2 中，其中国有部门作为基准选择项。边际效应的计算取值于年龄、年龄平方、家庭成员数量、家庭人均替代拥有量、家庭其他成员人均收入变量的均值，和所有虚拟变量为零。根据边际效应的定义，任一特定变量对三种部门选择的边际效应之和应为零。如上一小节中方程（7）所示，虽然 MNL 模型的回归系数可以表明相对于选择国有部门，该系数对应变量影响选择私有部门或国外部门的方向（符号），但是却不能在国外部门与私

① 关于 MNL 模型的数学推导过程与统计特征请参阅 Lee（1996）与 Borooah（2001）。

有部门之间展开直接比较。同时，也无法得知该变量影响选择三个部门的绝对大小。所以，通过将回归系数转换成为边际效应，我们可以直接通过边际效应系数对影响三个部门选择行为的变量展开比较(Lee, 1996)。

另外，Hausman 和 McFadden(1995)的研究结论表明，MNL 模型的大样本一致性估计性质强烈的依赖于可供选择项目的不相关性(independence of irrelevant alternatives, IIA)的假设。IIA 的原假设认为是否存在第三种选择并不影响原有的两种选择的概率之比。因此，我们应用了 Hausman 检验对 IIA 展开检验。然而，我们在应用 Hausman 检验对回归结果中展开检验，其未受约束和受约束的方差-协方差矩阵之差为非正定，因此 Hausman 检验失效。我们进而应用广义 Hausman 展开检验，其卡方统计量 $\chi^2_{(15)} = 12.61$，p 值为 0.632。因此，我们并不能拒绝 IIA 假设，而表明应用 MNL 模型对农村流动劳动力的部门选择行为展开分析是合适的。

表 2 报告了农村迁移劳动力部门选择 MNL 模型(方程(6))的估计结果，括号中为经过了异方差调整的稳健性标准差(heteroskedasticity adjusted standard error)。从表 2 中可以看出，年龄对农村迁移劳动力部门选择的影响较小，但是年龄较大的迁移劳动力一般选择在民营部门，而选择国有部门或者国外部门的概率较小。其中的原因可能是由于就业于国外部门一般需要跨省迁移，而就业于民营企业或者个体企业在通常情况下仅限于省内迁移，而年龄较大的迁移劳动力一般倾向就业于离家庭较近的地区。另外，家庭成员的数量和家庭人均土地拥有量对迁移劳动力几乎不存在任何影响。与上一节中的统计描述保持一致的是，城市户口使得迁移劳动力选择国有部门的概率提高 5%，而使得选择民营部门的概率降低了 7%，同时使得选

择国外部门的概率提高了 2%。但是,估计出来的户籍变量前面的系数对所有选择部门的影响均不显著。考虑到本次抽样调查是举行在 2004 年的春季,已经距离 1978 年开始改革开放之时已经整整 26 年了,因此户口因素对现代农村迁移劳动力的部门选择已经不再像过去那么重要了。

表 2　农村迁移劳动力部门选择 Multinomial Logit Model 估计

	估计参数		边际效应		
	民营部门	国外部门	国有部门	民营部门	国外部门
age	0.13	0.00	−0.01	0.02	−0.01
	(0.24)	(0.16)	(0.03)	(0.03)	(0.03)
agesq/100	−0.21	0.02	0.01	−0.03	0.02
	(0.35)	(0.21)	(0.02)	(0.04)	(0.03)
no. member	0.09	0.07	−0.01	0.01	0.00
	(0.15)	(0.14)	(0.01)	(0.02)	(0.02)
avgland	−0.01	−0.09	0.01	0.01	−0.02
	(0.26)	(0.26)	(0.02)	(0.03)	(0.04)
hukou	−0.77	−0.31	0.05	−0.08	0.03
	(0.60)	(0.55)	(0.05)	(0.06)	(0.07)
marriage	0.67	0.44	−0.04	0.05	0.01
	(0.64)	(0.51)	(0.05)	(0.07)	(0.08)
female	1.11	0.29	−0.06	0.12	−0.06
	(0.55)	(0.53)	(0.03)	(0.06)	(0.07)
recruitment	−0.04	1.39	−0.12	−0.12	0.24
	(0.42)	(0.36)	(0.04)	(0.05)	(0.04)
contract	1.22	−0.81	0.02	0.24	−0.26
	(0.52)	(0.39)	(0.03)	(0.06)	(0.05)
avgincome	0.33	0.28	−0.01	0.02	0.02
	(0.12)	(0.10)	(0.01)	(0.01)	(0.01)
craft	−0.42	−0.40	0.05	−0.02	−0.03

（续表）

	估计参数		边际效应		
	民营部门	国外部门	国有部门	民营部门	国外部门
	(0.47)	(0.43)	(0.03)	(0.05)	(0.06)
training	−0.65	−0.61	0.07	−0.04	−0.04
	(0.44)	(0.36)	(0.03)	(0.05)	(0.05)
secondary	1.81	1.43	−0.18	0.10	0.08
	(1.06)	(0.60)	(0.11)	(0.12)	(0.09)
high	2.65	1.43	−0.18	0.23	−0.05
	(1.12)	(0.67)	(0.09)	(0.13)	(0.10)
college	2.18	0.76	−0.11	0.25	−0.14
	(1.32)	(0.85)	(0.07)	(0.06)	(0.13)
截距项	−6.52	−1.17			
	(3.93)	(2.96)			
观察值	355				
Pseudo R^2	0.19				
IIA 检验	$\chi^2_{(15)} = 12.61$ $p = 0.632$				
Log-likelihood	−267.59				

注：(1)变量定义与数据的统计性描述见表 1；(2)括号中为异方差-稳健性标准差；(3)在 Multinomial Logit Estimation 中国有部门为基准项；(4)边际效应是基于样本中 age，agesq，avgland，No. member，avgincome 为均值，其他变量为 0 时计算所得。

值得注意的是，女性劳动力显著地偏好于选择民营部门。其中，性别为女性使得选择民营部门概率显著地提高了 14%，而使得选择国有部门和国外部门的概率分别降低了 6%和 8%。Zhang(2004)对城镇居民就业的部门选择展开分析时得到了相似的结论，性别为女性使得城镇劳动力选择国有部门的概率降低了 6.8%，而使得选择民营部门的概率提高了 5.8%。因此，我们认为农村女性迁移劳动力在不同的部门可能拥有不同的优势或劣势，并在下一节中将对部门选择的性别差异进行分解。而已婚的农村迁移劳动力同样倾向于选择民营部门，其选择民营部门的概率提高了 5%，而其选择国有部门的概率降低了 6%，这一点同样与 Zhang(2004)的研究结论保持一致。我们对农村迁移劳动力部门选择的研究与 Zhang(2004)对城镇居民就业的部门选择的分析相似说明：中国的农村劳动力市场与城镇劳动力市场正在逐渐的融合，从微观上来看城镇居民与农村迁移劳动力的就业行为特征开始呈现出一定程度的一致性。

正如上一节的描述性统计分析所示，寻找工作的渠道对部门选择行为的影响高度显著，并且从统计意义上看其影响程度非常之高。其中，通过个人渠道(即朋友、同学、亲戚或老乡的介绍)寻找工作的迁移劳动力选择国外部门的概率显著地提高了 29%，而选择国有部门和民营部门的概率分别降低了 12%和 17%。其次，在“认为劳动合同是否重要”的问题上，不同的对待态度对农村迁移劳动力的部门选择存在显著地影响。这说明不同部门的企业在遵守国家劳动合同方面存在显著的差别，而且其“口碑”显著地影响了农村劳动力就业过程中的部门选择。另外，家庭其他成员的平均收入对农村迁移劳动力的部门选择同样存在显著的影响，其提高了选择民营部门和国有部门的概率，而降低了选择国有部门的概率。最后，接受过手艺或者其他正规培训提高了农村迁移劳动力选择国有部门的概率而降低了选择民营部门和国外部门的概率。这部分的原因来自民营部门或国外部门企业对农村劳动力的需求仍然停留在低技术性水平。

同样是在人力资本方面，教育水平却呈现出与培训对农村迁移劳动力部门选择行为不同的影响。图 3 描述了不同教育水平对部门选择的边际效应。从中可以看出，在任一教育水平，其对选择民营部门概率的影响程度都超过了对国有部门和国外部门的选择概率。教育对选择民营部门存在显著的正面效应，并且其影响程度呈现出单调递增的特征，具有大学学历的农村迁移劳动力层次上选择民营部门的概率提高幅度甚至超过了25%。反过来，教育对选择国有部门的影响呈现出拐点变化。虽然仅接受初中教育水平降低了选择国有部门的影响，但是从高中教育水平到大学教育水平，其对国有部门选择的负面影响程度逐渐递减，并且变得不显著。然而，教育水平对选择国外部门的影响正好与选择民营部门相反，呈现出单调递减的趋势。这一研究结论与 Zhang(2004)对城镇居民就业部门选择的研究结论相反，该文的计量分析结论表明教育水平对选择国有和政府部门的影响呈现出单调递增的趋势。我们对城镇居民和农村迁移劳动力在不同教育水平对国有部门不同选择的行为特征来自这两个群体在国有部门就业职位的差异，农村迁移劳动力在国有部门一般就职于那些非正规的临时岗位，其对教育水平的要求一般较低；而城镇劳动力一般就职于那些正规的、具有福利保障的职位，因此其对教育水平要求较高。另外，农村迁移劳动力接受教育水平高低对选择国外部门的边际效应呈现出的单调递减特征部分的可以归因于国外部门职工招聘“二分”的特点。国外部门对劳动力的需求一般处于两个较为极端的角度：一方面是接受过很好教育的管理层白领员工；另一方面是低技术素质的蓝领员工。而农村迁移劳动力一般处于低技术素质的一段。而教育水平对选择民营部门的边际效应存在单调递增的特征可能说明在私有部门，农村迁移劳动力具有一定的职位晋升空间，而不像国外部门和国有部门一样呈现出明显的职位或等级的二分特征。

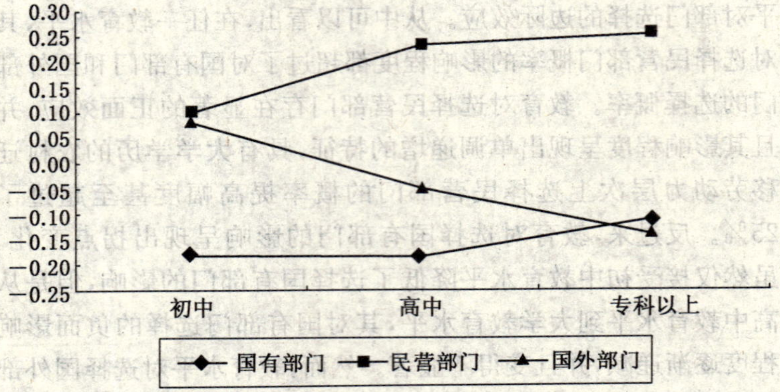

资料来源：同表 2。

图 3　教育水平对农村迁移劳动力部门选择的边际效应

四、农村迁移劳动力部门选择过程中的性别差异

从上一节的分析中我们发现，农村迁移劳动力在部门选择过程中存在显著的差异，因此本节将集中于分析这种差异到底在多大程度上是由于女性与男性不同的个体、家庭或其他行为特征的差异所导致的（即方程（1）中的 z_i 的差异），而在多大程度上是由于纯粹的性别歧视所导致的？表 3 的第一栏报告了根据特征变量均值计算出来的总的，以及男性与女性部门选择的概率分布。而表 3 的第二栏则报告了样本中不同性别在不同部门就业的概率分布。通过比较表 3 的前面两栏，我们发现根据回归结果计算出来的概率分布与样本中的概率分布存在显著的差异。这是由于选择不同部门就业的农村迁移劳动力全体的特征变量均值存在的差异所导致。因此，为了回答本节首先提出的两个问题，我们需要对全部的性别差异展开分解。接着，我们对不同性别的农村迁移劳动力在不同部门的分布概率进行“模

拟”。首先，我们假设样本中所有的农村迁移劳动力都是女性，然后根据特征变量均值计算出全部迁移劳动力进行部门选择的概率分布；其次，我们假设样本中所有的迁移劳动力都是男性，同样根据特征变量均值计算出部门选择的概率。这两次性别模拟计算出来的结果报告在表3的最后一栏。通过比较表3的上中下三栏，我们发现其概率分布存在着显著的差异。

表3　农村迁移劳动力男性与女性预测的部门分布概率

	国有部门	民营部门	国外部门
根据解释变量均值计算出来的男性与女性部门分布概率			
全部迁移者	0.11	0.19	0.70
女性	0.03	0.27	0.69
男性	0.15	0.16	0.69
调查样本中男性与女性的部门分布概率			
全部迁移者	0.16	0.23	0.62
女性(s_j^F)	0.10	0.32	0.58
男性(s_j^M)	0.17	0.20	0.63
全部劳动力模拟为男性与女性的部门分布概率			
女性($\bar{p}_j^F$)	0.19	0.32	0.60
男性($\bar{p}_j^M$)	0.17	0.20	0.69

那么，对农村迁移劳动力部门选择过程中的性别差异可以根据如下三个方程展开分解(Borooah, 2000)。其中全部性别差异的计算方程为：

$$\mu_j^F = \frac{s_j^F}{s_j^M} \tag{10}$$

纯粹的性别歧视的计算方程为：

$$\lambda_j^F = \frac{\bar{p}_j^F}{\bar{p}_j^M} \tag{11}$$

特征变量之间的性别差异为：

$$\delta_j^F = \frac{\lambda_j^F}{\mu_j^F} \tag{12}$$

其中，s_j^F 和 s_j^M 表示样本中的男性和女性在第 j 个部门的概率；$\bar{p}_j^F$ 和 $\bar{p}_j^M$ 表示将样本中全部的迁移劳动力模拟为女性和男性在第 j 个部门的概率；而 λ_j^F 表示相对于男性而言，女性在 j 个部门的纯粹性别优势/劣势。以上的比率如果大于 1，那么说明农村女性迁移劳动力在第 j 个部门拥有相对优势；反之则为劣势。分解的结果报告在表 5 中。

从表 5 中可以看出，在不同的部门存在不同程度的性别差异。首先，女性虽然在国有部门处于非常明显的性别劣势，但是这种劣势主要是由于女性的个人或家庭特征所导致的，比如说，个人的人力资本状况，而从纯粹的性别歧视角度来看，女性在国有部门处于优势地位。其次，女性在民营部门不管从纯粹性别差异，还是从个人特征而言，均处于优势地位。而女性在民营部门所拥有的纯粹优势，可能部分的来自民营部门所集中的行业特征。因为中国民营部门的发展主要集中于轻纺工业、餐饮业和其他娱乐行业，在这些行业中女性相对于男性而言具有天然的比较优势。同时，这些行业对技术的要求较低，所以女性在民营部门并不拥有其他特征方面的优势地位。令人感到的惊奇的是，我们最后发现的纯粹性别歧视仅仅发生在国外部门。在缺乏更多数据的前提下，我们无法对这种纯粹性别歧视的源泉展开进一步的分解。一种可能的解释来自国外部门企业技能偏态型的歧视，即国外部门主要集中于电子、机械和其他制造行业的生产，而在这些生产性行业中对体能的要求较高，因此男性可能具有比较优势①。总而言之，虽然农村迁移劳动力在部门选择过程中虽然存在较为显著的性别差异，但是其纯粹的性别歧视并不明显。本文对部门选择性别歧视的研究结论与 Liu 等(2000)对部门工资性别歧视的分析结果保持一致，其中可能的解释来自改革开放以来的市场竞争促使企业对低成本的追求纠正了其性别的偏好。

表 4　农村迁移劳动力部门选择性别差异的分解

	全部差异	个体特征差异	纯粹性别歧视
女性 vs. 男性			
国有部门	0.59	0.53	1.12
民营部门	1.60	1.00	1.60
国外部门	0.92	1.07	0.86

五、结　　论

改革开放以来，中国所经历的农村劳动力迁移为人类历史上规模最大的人口迁移。同时，经济转型时期的中国企业正呈现出所有制多样化的特征。在最近农村迁移劳动力抽样调查数据的基础之上，本文对农村劳动力迁移过程中的部门选择行为和性别差异展开了经验分析。经验分析的主要结论为：

(1) 首先，在年龄、性别和婚姻状况等个人特征变量对农村

---

① 本文仅限于对农村迁移劳动力部门选择过程中的性别差异展开分析，而对部门之间的性别差异展开系统的分析需要同时对其工资或收入水平的性别差异展开研究。由于本文的主题集中于农村劳动力迁移过程中的部门选择行为，所以对该部分的性别歧视不包括在本文中。

迁移劳动力的部门选择行为上与已有针对城镇居民就业的部门选择行为的经验研究结论保持一致，这说明中国的城镇劳动力市场与农村劳动力市场可能开始出现一定程度的融合。但是，就农村迁移劳动力的人力资本状况（特别是教育水平）对其部门选择的影响而言，却与城镇居民就业的部门选择相反。教育水平对农村迁移劳动力选择民营部门的影响呈现出单调递增的趋势，部分可能的原因是仅在民营部门的企业中农村迁移劳动力才存在职位晋升的空间，而在国有部门企业和国外部门企业中呈现出明显的职位或等级的二分特点。因此，农村迁移劳动力仍然在这两个部门的企业中集中于低层。

(2) 其次，家庭和迁出地等特征变量对农村迁移劳动力的部门选择行为几乎不存在任何影响。这一点与 Zhao(1998)对农村劳动力迁移的决定因素分析结论保持一致，说明决定农村劳动力迁移，同时决定农村迁移劳动力部门选择的影响因素以城镇劳动力市场中的拉力为主，而迁出地的社会经济状况对其迁移行为的推力并不显著。

(3) 另外，农村迁移劳动力工作搜寻渠道对其就业部门选择行为存在显著的影响，特别是其通过私人工作搜寻渠道（朋友、亲戚、老乡或同学的介绍）对选择国外部门企业存在高度显著的正面影响。而对这种单一、非市场化工作搜寻渠道的依赖，可能导致农村迁移劳动力出现一定程度上的职业和部门隔离。这说明劳动力市场中的信息不对称仍然非常严重，特别是在农村迁移劳动力与国外部门企业之间的匹配方面，中国劳动力市场中介机构仍待进一步发展。

(4) 最后，虽然农村迁移劳动力在进行部门选择时呈现明显的性别差异，但是这种差异主要来自其自身特征变量之间的差异，纯粹的性别歧视并不特别明显。我们认为在民营部门和国外部门的纯粹的性别差异可能主要来自这两个部门所集中行业的技术需求特征。

总而言之，基于本文的经验分析结论，我们认为农村迁移劳动力在城镇就业时仍然存在显著的部门差异，特别是在国有部门与国外部门的企业中农村迁移劳动力仍然在一定程度上经历着职业隔离；同时，针对农村迁移劳动力就业的市场中介仍然有待进一步的发展和完善。由于中国经济的成功转型有赖于农村剩余劳动力向城镇的成功转移、安置和就业，本文对农村迁移劳动力就业部门选择微观行为的分析有助于加深中国二元经济向一元经济转型机制的理解。加强农村迁移劳动力的人力资本投资与建立和完善现代化的劳动力市场中介组织是推动经济快速转型、和谐发展的关键所在。当然，考虑到本文调查样本较小，因此，本文的研究结论对整个中国经济转型过程中的政策含义的解释应该保持谨慎态度。我们期望有覆盖面更为广泛、样本量更大的数据来支持着对中国二元劳动力市场融合过程中微观机制的进一步研究。

参考文献

Blau, F. and L. Kahn, 1995, "The Gender Earnings Gap: Some International Evidence", in Freeman R., and L. Katz, (eds.) *Differences and Changes in Wage Structures*, University of Chicago Press.

Boudarbat, B., 2004, "Employment Sector Choice in a Developing Labor Market", Working paper.

Borooah, V. K., 2001, *Logit and Probit*, Sage Publications, Inc.

DeBrauw, A., J. Huang, S. Rozelle, L. Zhang and Y. Zhang, 2002, "The Evolution of China's Rural Labor Markets during the Reforms", *Journal of Comparative Economics*, 30:329—353.

Dong, X. and P. Bowles, 2002, "Segmentation and Discrimination in

China's Emerging Industrial Labor Market", *China Economic Review*, 13: 170—196.

Hausman and McFadden, D., 1984, "Specification Tests for the Multinomial Logit Model", *Econometrica*, 52:1219—1240.

Knight, J. and Song, L., 1999, *The Rural-Urban Divide: Economic Disparities and Interactions in China*, Oxford University Press.

Knight, J. and Song, L., 2005, *Towards a Labor Market in China*, Oxford University Press.

Lee, M., 1996, *Methods of Moments and Semparametric Econometrics for Limited Dependent Variable Model*, Springer-Verlag.

Liu, P., X. Meng and J. Zhang, 2000, "Sectoral Gender Wage Differentials and Discrimination in the Transitional Chinese Economy", *Journal of Population Economics*, 13:331—352.

McFadden, D., 1973, "Conditional Logit Analysis of Quantitative Choice Behavior", in Zarambka P., Ed., *Frontiers in Econometrics*, New York: Academic Press.

Meng, X. and J. Zhang, 2001, "The Two-tier Labor Market in Urban China: Occupational Segregation and Wage Differentials between Urban Residents and Rural Migrants in Shanghai", *Journal of Comparative Economics*, 29:485—504.

Meng, X., 2000, *Labor Market Reforms in China*, Cambridge University Press.

Rozelle, S., T. Edward, A. DeBrauw, 1999, "Migration, Remittances, and Agricultural Productivity in China", *American Economic Review*, 89:289—291.

Shu, X. and Y. Bian, 2003, "Market Transition and Gender Gap in Earnings in Urban China", *Social Forces*, 81:1107—1145.

Zhang, H., 2004, "Self-Selection and Wage Differentials in Urban China: A Polychotomous Model with Selectivity", MIT working paper.

Zhao, Y., 1999, "Leaving the Countryside: Rural to Urban Migration Decisions in China", *American Economic Review*, 89:281—286.

Zhao, Y., 2002, "Causes and Consequences of Return Migration: Recent Evidence from China", *Journal of Comparative Economics*, 30: 376—394.

蔡昉、都阳、王美艳:《中国劳动力市场转型与发育》,商务印书馆 2005 年版。

蔡昉、都阳、王美艳:《劳动力流动的政治经济学》,上海三联书店、上海人民出版社 2003 年版。

王美艳:《转轨时期的工资差异:歧视的计量分析》,《数量经济与技术经济研究》2003 年第 5 期。

姚先国、赖普清:《中国劳资关系的城乡户籍差异》,《经济研究》2004 年第 7 期。

姚先国、谭岚:《家庭收入与中国城镇已婚妇女劳动参与决策分析》,《经济研究》2005 年第 7 期。

易君健:《中国农村劳动力的流动与就业》,《新政治经济学评论》2006 年第 5 期。

(原载《世界经济文汇》2007 年第 4 期)

图书在版编目(CIP)数据

中国经济学.2007/北京天则经济研究所编.—上海:
格致出版社:上海人民出版社,2009.1
ISBN 978-7-5432-1558-0

Ⅰ.中…　Ⅱ.北…　Ⅲ.经济学-中国-2007-文集
Ⅳ.F120.2-53

中国版本图书馆CIP数据核字(2008)第197315号

责任编辑　钱　敏
封面装帧　王晓阳

中国经济学——2007
北京天则经济研究所 编

出　版　世纪出版集团　www.ewen.cc　格致出版社　www.hibooks.cn　上海人民出版社
(200001　上海福建中路193号24层)

编辑部热线 021-63914988
市场部热线 021-63914081

发　行　世纪出版集团发行中心
印　刷　上海市印刷七厂
开　本　850×1168毫米　1/32
印　张　15.25
插　页　2
字　数　348,000
版　次　2009年2月第1版
印　次　2009年2月第1次印刷
ISBN 978-7-5432-1558-0/F·139
定　价　38.00元